# 10

# People Who Shaped the World

## History's Most Influential Figures

Author: Simon Mayer

© Simon Mayer 2025

A&S Culture and Art Publishing

The work, including all its parts, is protected by copyright. Any use outside the narrow limits of copyright law, without the consent of the author, is prohibited and punishable. This applies in particular to electronic or other reproduction, translation, distribution and making available to the public.

# Contents

**Preface** .................................................................................. 8
**About the Author** ................................................................. 10

**Cyrus the Great** – Founder of the Persian Empire and advocate of human rights ........................................................ 11
**Buddha** – Spiritual teacher and founder of Buddhism ........ 15
**Confucius** – Chinese philosopher who spread ethical and social teachings ......................................................................... 19
**Socrates** – The Father of Western Philosophy ..................... 23
**Plato** – Greek philosopher, founder of the Academy in Athens ... 27

**Aristotle** – Greek philosopher and scientist .......................... 31
**Alexander the Great** – Macedonian conqueror who built a vast empire ................................................................................ 35
**Euclid** – The Father of Geometry ......................................... 39
**Ashoka** – Indian emperor who promoted Buddhism .......... 43
**Archimedes** – Greek mathematician and engineer .............. 47

**Qin Shihuangdi** – First emperor of China and builder of the Great Wall ............................................................................ 51
**Julius Caesar** – The Architect of Rome's Imperial Era ........ 55
**Augustus Caesar** – First Roman emperor and founder of the Principate ............................................................................. 59
**Jesus Christ** – Religious leader and central figure of Christianity ............................................................................... 63
**Paul of Tarsus** – Missionary and theologian of early Christianity ............................................................................... 67

**Cai Lun** – Chinese inventor of paper .................................... 71
**Constantine the Great** – Roman emperor who legitimized Christianity ............................................................................... 75

**Attila the Hun** – Ruler of the Huns and conqueror of Europe ... 79

**Muhammad** – Founder and prophet of Islam .............................. 83

**Umar ibn al-Khattab** – Second caliph and architect of the Islamic empire ............................................................................. 87

**Charlemagne** – King of the Franks and father of Europe .......... 91

**William the Conqueror** – Norman duke and king of England ... 95

**Pope Urban II** – Initiator of the Crusades ................................... 99

**Genghis Khan** – Founder and leader of the Mongol Empire .... 103

**Johannes Gutenberg** – The Inventor of the Printing Press ....... 107

**Christopher Columbus** – Explorer of the "New World" .......... 111

**Leonardo da Vinci** – Renaissance polymath and genius ............ 115

**Vasco da Gama** – Portuguese explorer who discovered the sea route to India ............................................................................ 119

**Nicolaus Copernicus** – Astronomer and founder of the heliocentric model ........................................................................ 123

**Michelangelo** – Italian artist and sculptor of the Renaissance ... 127

**Ferdinand Magellan** – The navigator who led the first circumnavigation of the world .................................................... 131

**Martin Luther** – Leader of the Protestant Reformation ............. 135

**Elizabeth I** – Queen of England and symbol of the "Golden Age" .................................................................................. 139

**Francis Bacon** – Philosopher and founder of the scientific method ........................................................................................... 143

**Galileo Galilei** – Father of modern science and astronomy ....... 147

**William Shakespeare** – The greatest playwright in English literature ........................................................................................ 151

**Johannes Kepler** – Mathematician and pioneer of planetary motion theory ................................................................................ 155

**William Harvey** – Discoverer of blood circulation .................... 159

**René Descartes** – French philosopher and mathematician ........ 163

**Oliver Cromwell** – English statesman and Lord Protector..........167

**John Locke** – The architect of modern liberalism........................171

**Antoni van Leeuwenhoek** – The father of microbiology............175

**Isaac Newton** – Founder of classical mechanics............................179

**Peter the Great** – The Tsar who transformed Russia....................183

**Johann Sebastian Bach** – The Master of Baroque Music............187

**Voltaire** – Enlightenment philosopher who advocated for freedom of speech and religion..........................................................191

**Benjamin Franklin** – Scientist, politician, and Founding Father of the USA....................................................................................195

**Jean-Jacques Rousseau** – The philosopher of freedom and democracy..................................................................................................199

**Adam Smith** – The father of modern economics..........................203

**Immanuel Kant** – Enlightenment Philosopher known for his work on ethics and metaphysics..........................................................207

**George Washington** – First U.S. president and leader of the American Revolution................................................................................211

**James Watt** – Developer of the steam engine.................................215

**Thomas Jefferson** – Third U.S. president and author of the Declaration of Independence.................................................................219

**Antoine Laurent de Lavoisier** – The Father of Modern Chemistry..................................................................................................223

**Mayer Amschel Rothschild** – Founder of an influential financial dynasty......................................................................................227

**Edward Jenner** – The Pioneer of Vaccination................................232

**Wolfgang Amadeus Mozart** – Composer and child prodigy of music......................................................................................................236

**John Dalton** – Chemist and founder of atomic theory.................240

**Napoleon Bonaparte** – French emperor and reformer of Europe.......................................................................................................244

**Ludwig van Beethoven** – Composer and pioneer of Romantic music .................................................................................. 248

**Simón Bolívar** – The Liberator of South America ....................... 252
**Louis Daguerre** – Pioneer of photography .................................. 256
**Michael Faraday** – Discoverer of electromagnetic induction .... 260
**Charles Babbage** – The Father of the Computer ........................ 264
**Abraham Lincoln** – U.S. president who led the country during the Civil War and abolished slavery ....................................... 269

**Charles Darwin** – The Father of Evolutionary Theory ............... 273
**Otto von Bismarck** – Founder of the German Empire ............... 277
**Karl Marx** – Founder of Marxism and critic of capitalism .......... 281
**William Thomas Green Morton** – The Pioneer of Anesthesia ................................................................................................. 285
**Gregor Mendel** – The Father of Genetics .................................... 289

**Louis Pasteur** – Pioneer of microbiology and immunology ....... 293
**James Clerk Maxwell** – Founder of modern electrodynamics .............................................................................. 297
**Nikolaus August Otto** – The Inventor of the Internal Combustion Engine ............................................................................. 301
**Dmitry Mendeleev** – The Architect of the Periodic Table ........ 305
**Wilhelm Conrad Röntgen** – The Discoverer of X-Rays ............ 309

**Thomas Alva Edison** – Inventor of the light bulb and innovator ............................................................................................... 313
**Alexander Graham Bell** – Inventor of the Telephone ............... 317
**Vincent van Gogh** – Dutch painter of Post-Impressionism ...... 322
**Sigmund Freud** – The Father of Psychoanalysis ......................... 326
**Nikola Tesla** – Visionary of modern electricity ............................ 330

**Max Planck** – Founder of quantum physics ................................... 334

**Henry Ford** – Revolutionary of the automotive industry ............ 338
**The Wright Brothers** – Inventors of the first airplane ................ 342
**Marie Curie** – Discoverer of radioactivity ........................................ 347
**Mahatma Gandhi** – Leader of India's nonviolent independence movement ........................................................................ 351

**Vladimir Lenin** – Leader of the Russian Revolution and founder of the Soviet Union ................................................................. 355
**Guglielmo Marconi** – Pioneer of wireless communication ........ 359
**Winston Churchill** – British prime minister during World War II. ............................................................................................................. 363
**Joseph Stalin** – Dictator of the Soviet Union ................................. 367
**Albert Einstein** – Physicist known for the theory of relativity ... 371

**Alexander Fleming** – Discoverer of penicillin ............................... 375
**Adolf Hitler** – Leader of Nazi Germany ........................................... 379
**Mao Zedong** – Leader of the Chinese Revolution ......................... 384
**Georges Lemaître** – Father of the Big Bang Theory .................... 388
**Werner Heisenberg** – Founder of quantum mechanics ............... 392

**Nelson Mandela** – Leader of the fight against apartheid in South Africa .............................................................................................. 396
**Jack Kilby** – Inventor of the integrated circuit ............................... 400
**Martin Luther King Jr.** – U.S. civil rights leader ......................... 404
**Mikhail Gorbachev** – Leader of the Soviet Union who initiated Perestroika ............................................................................... 408
**Tim Berners-Lee** – Inventor of the World Wide Web ................. 412

**Epilogue** ..................................................................................................... 416
**Further Works of the Author** ............................................................. 418
**Imprint** ...................................................................................................... 427

# Preface

The history of humanity is a vast and intricate tapestry woven with events, innovations, and ideas that have shaped our lives. But behind every major transformation stand individuals – visionaries, leaders, thinkers, and inventors – whose actions, ideas, and convictions have profoundly influenced the course of world history.

This book is a tribute to 100 remarkable personalities who, in various ways, shaped the world. It takes you on a journey through millennia of human development, from the dawn of civilization to the modern era. Along the way, we encounter rulers and revolutionaries, scientists and artists, philosophers and explorers – people who, through their courage, intelligence, ambition, or vision, have left an indelible mark on history.

## Why This Book?

The world we live in today is the result of countless generations' achievements. Yet, some individuals have had a particularly lasting impact on the course of history through their actions and ideas. This book aims not only to inform but to inspire. It introduces personalities who dared to think differently, challenge boundaries, and reshape society.

Each of these 100 influential figures has made a significant contribution – whether in politics, science, art, philosophy, or technology. Their achievements range from laying the foundations of mathematics to pioneering medical breakthroughs and leading social movements for justice and freedom.

## The Selection Process

Compiling such a list is always a challenge. Who decides who belongs among history's most influential people? This selection is based on extensive historical research and analysis. Criteria such as societal impact, scientific or artistic contributions, political power, moral and ethical values, and long-term influence on future generations were all considered.

Of course, history is subjective. While some names, like Julius Caesar, Albert Einstein, or Mahatma Gandhi, are undisputedly included, others may be less well-known but are no less significant in shaping the course of history.

## A Journey Through the Ages

This book invites you on a time-traveling expedition, from the earliest civilizations to the present day. You will explore the teachings of Socrates, the ancient philosopher, delve into the genius of Leonardo da Vinci, the Renaissance polymath, and discover the groundbreaking visions of Nikola Tesla.

You will learn how Martin Luther shook the Christian world, how Marie Curie revolutionized science, and how Nelson Mandela fought against apartheid. Each chapter not only provides an overview of the individual's life but also examines their lasting influence on humanity.

## A Book for Every History Enthusiast

Whether you are a dedicated history buff or simply curious about the people who have shaped our world, this book is for you. It aims not just to impart knowledge but also to spark reflection. What can we learn from history? What lessons can we draw from past successes and failures?

May the stories of these 100 remarkable personalities inspire you to reflect on the course of history – and perhaps even to leave your own mark on the world.

# About the Author

Simon Mayer is an author and dedicated literary researcher with a deep passion for knowledge and cultural heritage. After completing his academic studies in history, philosophy and law, he committed himself wholeheartedly to making complex ideas accessible and engaging for a wide audience. His work is driven by the belief that history, literature, and philosophy are not only disciplines to be studied but living sources of inspiration and insight for our everyday lives.

Through his books and research, Simon Mayer aims to illuminate the timeless relevance of great thinkers, the richness of the past, and the power of human ideas. With a clear and captivating writing style, he invites readers to rediscover the world through the lens of wisdom, curiosity, and critical reflection.

# Cyrus the Great
Founder of the Persian Empire and advocate of human rights

Cyrus the Great, also known as Cyrus II of Persia, established the Achaemenid Empire, marking the beginning of the first Persian Empire He reigned from approximately 559 BCE until his death in 530 BCE and is widely regarded as one of history's most remarkable rulers. Cyrus was a visionary leader who united various tribes and nations under his rule, creating one of the largest empires the world had ever seen. His military conquests, administrative innovations, and policies of tolerance and respect for the cultures of his subjects set a precedent for future rulers. His legacy remains influential in governance, human rights, and empire-building to this day.

## Origin

Cyrus the Great was born around 600 BCE in Anshan, a region in present-day southwestern Iran. He belonged to the Achaemenid dynasty, a noble Persian family that ruled over Anshan under the dominion of the Median Empire. His father, Cambyses I, was a minor king under the Medes, while his mother, Mandane, was a princess of Media and the daughter of Astyages, the king of the Median Empire.

His mixed heritage granted him a unique position, as he was connected to both the Persian and Median elite. This lineage would later serve him well in his quest for power, as he was able to unite the Persian and Median factions under his leadership. Despite being a subject of the Medes, the Persians maintained their cultural identity, and Cyrus would later use their growing discontent with Median rule to his advantage.

## Childhood and Youth

Legends and historical accounts about Cyrus's childhood vary, but one of the most famous stories comes from the Greek historian Herodotus. According to Herodotus, King Astyages of Media had a prophetic dream that his grandson, Cyrus, would overthrow him. To prevent this, Astyages ordered that the infant Cyrus be killed. However, the servant tasked with the job could not bring himself to do it and instead gave the baby to a shepherd named Mithradates, who raised him as his own.

Cyrus grew up among common people, unaware of his royal heritage. As a young man, his noble qualities and leadership abilities became apparent, and his true identity was eventually discovered. When he was brought before Astyages, the king decided to spare him but kept a close watch on him. This story, though legendary, highlights the idea that Cyrus was destined for greatness from an early age.

## Adulthood

By the time Cyrus reached adulthood, he had gained considerable support among the Persian tribes. Around 559 BCE, he ascended to the throne of Anshan following the death of his father, Cambyses I. At this time, Persia was still a vassal state under Median rule. However, Cyrus sought to change this and began rallying his people to revolt against the Medes.

In 550 BCE, he launched a rebellion against his grandfather, Astyages. With the support of disaffected Median nobles and his own Persian army, he successfully defeated Astyages and took control of the Median Empire. Instead of destroying the Median elite, Cyrus incorporated them into his administration, ensuring a smooth transition of power.

Following his victory over the Medes, Cyrus continued his conquests. In 547 BCE, he defeated King Croesus of Lydia, bringing much of Anatolia under Persian rule. He then turned his attention to Babylon, which he conquered in 539 BCE. His conquest of Babylon was notably peaceful, and he was welcomed as a liberator. The famous Cyrus Cylinder, often considered the world's first declaration of human rights, details his policies of tolerance and respect for local traditions.

As a ruler, he spent much of his time traveling between different parts of his empire, ensuring that his administrative system functioned efficiently. He established a system of satrapies, or provinces, each governed by a satrap who was responsible for collecting taxes and maintaining order.

Cyrus was also known for his deep respect for different cultures and religions. Unlike many conquerors of his time, he allowed the peoples he ruled to maintain their traditions and customs. His famous decree allowing the Jewish exiles in Babylon to return to Jerusalem and rebuild their temple is an example of his progressive policies. This act earned him a lasting place of honor in Jewish history.

## Private Life

Cyrus's private life remains somewhat obscure, as ancient sources primarily focus on his military and administrative achievements. However, it is known that he had several wives, with Cassandane, a noblewoman of Persian lineage, being the most prominent. She bore him several children, including his successor, Cambyses II.

## Death

Cyrus the Great died in 530 BCE while campaigning against the Massagetae, a nomadic tribe in Central Asia. According to Herodotus, he was killed in battle by Queen Tomyris, the leader of the Massagetae, who sought vengeance for the death of her son. Other sources suggest that he may have died from wounds sustained in battle or due to natural causes.

His body was taken to Pasargadae, where he was buried in a grand tomb that still stands today. The tomb of Cyrus remains one of the most significant monuments from the Achaemenid era and serves as a testament to his enduring legacy.

## Character

Cyrus was known for his wisdom, benevolence, and strategic acumen. Unlike many conquerors, he preferred diplomacy and integration over destruction and oppression. His ability to unite diverse peoples under his rule without forcing them to abandon their customs made him a unique and effective ruler.

He was also deeply religious and believed that his rule was sanctioned by the gods. However, he did not impose Persian beliefs on his subjects, instead allowing religious freedom throughout his empire. His respect for different cultures and traditions set him apart from many rulers of his time and contributed to the long-lasting stability of the Achaemenid Empire.

## Influence on Humanity

Cyrus the Great's impact on history is profound. His policies of tolerance and governance influenced countless future rulers, from Alexander the Great to the Roman emperors. His model of administration, which divided the empire into satrapies, became a blueprint for future empires.

The Cyrus Cylinder, discovered in the 19th century, is often cited as one of the earliest declarations of human rights. In it, Cyrus proclaims his respect for the traditions, languages, and religions of the people he conquered. This document has been recognized by organizations such as the United Nations as a symbol of justice and human rights.

Cyrus's legacy also extends to modern political thought. His idea that rulers should govern with justice and fairness rather than oppression continues to inspire leaders and historians alike. In Iran, he remains a national hero, celebrated as the father of the Persian nation.

His influence can also be seen in religious texts. The Hebrew Bible refers to him as a divinely appointed ruler who helped the Jewish people return to their homeland. His policies of tolerance and fair governance are still studied today as an example of enlightened leadership.

In conclusion, Cyrus the Great was not only a formidable conqueror but also a visionary leader whose ideas on governance, religious freedom, and human rights continue to resonate. His achievements laid the foundation for one of history's greatest empires, and his legacy endures as a symbol of justice, wisdom, and leadership.

# Buddha
## Spiritual teacher and founder of Buddhism

Buddha, also known as Siddhartha Gautama, was a spiritual leader and the founder of Buddhism, one of the world's major religions. His teachings on suffering, enlightenment, and the path to liberation have influenced millions over the centuries. Born into a royal family, he renounced his privileged life to seek spiritual truth and ultimately attained enlightenment. His teachings have shaped the spiritual and philosophical traditions of many cultures and continue to guide individuals seeking inner peace and wisdom.

## Origin

Siddhartha Gautama was born in the 6th or 5th century BCE in Lumbini, a region in present-day Nepal. He belonged to the Shakya clan, a powerful ruling family of the time. His father, King Suddhodana, was the ruler of Kapilavastu, and his mother, Queen Maya, was a woman of great piety and virtue. According to legend, before his birth, Queen Maya had a prophetic dream in which a white elephant entered her womb, signifying the birth of an extraordinary child destined for greatness.

Shortly after his birth, a sage named Asita visited the royal palace and prophesied that the newborn prince would either become a great king or renounce worldly life to attain spiritual enlightenment. This prophecy greatly influenced how Siddhartha was raised, as his father sought to shield him from any experience of suffering to ensure he would follow the path of kingship rather than renunciation.

## Childhood and Youth

Siddhartha was raised in opulence and luxury within the palace walls. His father provided him with the best education, ensuring he was well-versed in governance, martial arts, and philosophy. He was surrounded by beauty and pleasure, never allowed to witness pain, suffering, or death. To keep him engaged in worldly matters, King Suddhodana ensured that Siddhartha was provided with every possible comfort and indulgence.

Despite these efforts, Siddhartha was naturally inquisitive and contemplative. At the age of 16, he was married to Princess Yasodhara, and together they had a son named Rahula. However, the comforts of palace life failed to satisfy him, and he grew increasingly curious about the realities of the world beyond the palace walls.

At the age of 29, he ventured outside the palace and encountered what would later be known as the Four Sights: an old man, a sick man, a corpse, and a wandering ascetic. These experiences profoundly affected him, making him aware of the impermanence of life and the inevitability of suffering. He realized that worldly pleasures were fleeting and that a deeper truth lay beyond the material world.

## Adulthood

Determined to find a solution to human suffering, Siddhartha made a life-altering decision. He left behind his family, his luxurious life, and his royal title to embark on a spiritual quest. This event is known as the Great Renunciation. He wandered as an ascetic, seeking wisdom from renowned spiritual teachers and practicing extreme forms of self-discipline, including prolonged fasting and meditation.

For six years, he endured severe austerities, hoping that self-mortification would lead him to enlightenment. However, he eventually realized that such extreme practices were not the path to true awakening. Instead, he embraced the Middle Way – a balanced approach between indulgence and self-denial.

One night, while meditating under a Bodhi tree in Bodh Gaya, he attained enlightenment. At the age of 35, he became the Buddha, or the "Awakened One." He understood the nature of suffering (dukkha), its causes, and the path to liberation, which he articulated in the Four Noble Truths and the Eightfold Path.

## Private Life

Buddha's renunciation of worldly life meant that he had little personal attachment after enlightenment. However, he remained deeply compassionate toward all beings. He returned to his homeland and taught his family, including his father, wife, and son, about his newfound wisdom. Many of his relatives and former companions became his disciples

While he had abandoned the conventional life of a householder, he maintained a strong spiritual family – his monastic order, the Sangha. His followers, monks and laypeople alike, were considered his true family, bound together by the pursuit of enlightenment. His personal life was dedicated entirely to teaching, traveling, and spreading the Dharma.

## Death

At the age of 80, after decades of teaching and guiding disciples, Buddha entered Parinirvana, the final passing beyond suffering. He passed away in Kushinagar, India, after consuming a meal that caused illness. Despite his frail health, he continued to teach until his last moments, instructing his followers to rely on the Dharma as their guiding light.

According to Buddhist scriptures, his final words emphasized the impermanence of life: "All conditioned things are subject to decay. Strive on with diligence." With this, he peacefully departed from the world, leaving behind a legacy that would continue to inspire generations.

## Character

Buddha was known for his profound wisdom, boundless compassion, and unwavering patience. He treated all beings with kindness, regardless of caste, status, or background. His teachings were inclusive, emphasizing that enlightenment was accessible to all, irrespective of societal distinctions.

His humility was another defining trait. Despite being revered as an enlightened being, he never claimed divinity but instead presented himself as a teacher and guide. He encouraged self-inquiry, urging his followers to test his teachings through personal experience rather than blind faith.

Buddha's approach to spirituality was pragmatic, avoiding dogma and rigid doctrines. He advocated for ethical conduct, mindfulness, and wisdom as the means to achieve liberation from suffering. His ability to communicate complex spiritual truths in simple terms made his teachings accessible to people from all walks of life.

## Influence on Humanity

Buddha's impact on humanity is immense and enduring. His teachings laid the foundation for Buddhism, a tradition that has influenced millions across the world. His philosophy has shaped not only religious thought but also psychology, ethics, and mindfulness practices.

One of his most significant contributions is the emphasis on compassion and nonviolence (ahimsa). His teachings inspired movements for peace and social harmony in many cultures. Buddhist principles have influenced leaders such as Mahatma Gandhi and the Dalai Lama in their advocacy for nonviolent resistance and human rights.

Mindfulness, a concept deeply rooted in Buddhism, has gained widespread acceptance in modern psychology and wellness practices. Meditation techniques derived from Buddhist traditions are now widely used for stress reduction, mental clarity, and emotional well-being.

Moreover, Buddha's teachings on impermanence, suffering, and detachment have provided countless individuals with a means to navigate life's challenges with greater wisdom and resilience. His message of self-transformation and the pursuit of inner peace remains as relevant today as it was over two millennia ago.

In conclusion, Buddha's life and teachings continue to guide those seeking meaning, wisdom, and liberation from suffering. His legacy endures in the form of Buddhism, influencing countless lives through its message of compassion, mindfulness, and enlightenment.

# Confucius
Chinese philosopher who spread
ethical and social teachings

Confucius, known in Chinese as Kong Fuzi or Kong Qiu, was a philosopher, teacher, and political thinker whose ideas have profoundly influenced Chinese civilization and many other societies worldwide. Born in the 6th century BCE, he developed a moral and ethical system that emphasized virtues such as respect, loyalty, righteousness, and proper conduct in social relationships. His teachings, recorded in the "Analects", became the foundation of Confucianism, a philosophical and ethical tradition that has guided Chinese governance, education, and personal behavior for over two millennia.

## Origin

Confucius was born in 551 BCE in the state of Lu, located in what is now Shandong Province, China. He was born into the noble but impoverished Kong family, which traced its lineage to the Shang Dynasty, an ancient ruling house of China. His father, Kong He (also known as Shuliang He), was a military officer of considerable reputation, though he was already elderly when Confucius was born. His mother, Yan Zhengzai, was much younger and played a crucial role in raising and educating her son after his father passed away when Confucius was only three years old.

Despite his aristocratic background, Confucius grew up in modest circumstances. His family lacked wealth and status, which exposed him to the struggles of ordinary people. This early experience of hardship influenced his later thinking, particularly his emphasis on the importance of education, moral integrity, and societal harmony.

## Childhood and Youth

As a child, Confucius exhibited a keen interest in learning. He was naturally inquisitive and showed an exceptional ability to grasp philosophical and ethical concepts. Although he did not have access to formal schooling, he pursued knowledge independently, studying ancient texts and absorbing wisdom from older scholars.

According to legend, Confucius was fascinated by rituals and etiquette from a young age. He was known to arrange sacrificial offerings as a child, mimicking the ceremonies of state officials. This passion for order and tradition became a defining feature of his philosophy.

During his teenage years, he worked in minor government positions, such as managing livestock and overseeing grain supplies. These roles provided him with practical administrative experience and a deeper understanding of governance and societal structure. He married at the age of 19 and had a son, Kong Li, as well as a daughter, though little is known about her.

## Adulthood

Confucius spent much of his early adulthood as a teacher and scholar. He believed that education should be available to all, not just the aristocracy, and began accepting students from different social backgrounds. His teaching style was based on dialogue and critical thinking, encouraging students to reflect on moral and ethical dilemmas rather than merely memorize texts.

His growing reputation as a scholar led to his appointment as a government official in Lu. He held various administrative positions and was eventually promoted to Minister of Justice. During his tenure, he implemented policies that emphasized meritocracy, honesty, and adherence to moral principles. He believed that rulers should lead by example and that a just society could be built on the foundation of virtue rather than coercion.

Despite his efforts, Confucius eventually fell out of favor due to political rivalries. He resigned from his post and embarked on a long period of travel, visiting various Chinese states in search of a ruler who would embrace his teachings. Though he was often met with resistance, he continued to promote his vision of a harmonious society based on ethical governance and personal virtue.

## Private Life

Confucius was deeply committed to his studies and teachings, and little is recorded about his private life beyond his immediate family. His marriage was reportedly not a close one, and he eventually separated from his wife. However, he remained devoted to his son and took great care in his education.

As a teacher, Confucius surrounded himself with a group of loyal disciples who recorded his sayings and teachings. These students played a crucial role in preserving and spreading his ideas after his death. He was known for his humility and simplicity, preferring to live modestly rather than seek wealth or power.

Confucius valued human relationships and believed that family was the foundation of a stable society. He taught that filial piety – respect for one's parents and ancestors – was one of the highest virtues. This belief became a cornerstone of Confucian thought and influenced Chinese social structures for centuries.

## Death

Confucius returned to Lu in his later years and spent his final days compiling and editing classical texts, including the "Book of Documents", "Book of Poetry", and "Spring and Autumn Annals". He continued teaching until his death in 479 BCE at the age of 72 or 73.

He died a disappointed man, believing that his efforts to reform society had largely failed. However, his disciples carried on his legacy, ensuring that his teachings would influence future generations. Over time, Confucianism became the dominant ideology in China, shaping its culture, government, and ethical values for over two thousand years.

## Character

Confucius was known for his wisdom, integrity, and devotion to moral principles. He embodied the values he taught, emphasizing humility, respect, and continuous self-improvement. His deep concern for social harmony and ethical governance set him apart from other thinkers of his time.

He was a pragmatist who believed that individuals could cultivate virtue through education and self-discipline. Unlike many religious figures, he did not focus on supernatural beliefs but instead sought practical solutions to societal issues through ethical conduct and good governance.

Confucius also emphasized the importance of relationships, believing that human interactions should be guided by mutual respect and responsibility. His teachings on the "Five Relationships" (ruler-subject, father-son, husband-wife, elder brother-younger brother, and friend-friend) became fundamental to Chinese social philosophy.

## Influence on Humanity

The impact of Confucius on humanity cannot be overstated. His ideas laid the foundation for Confucianism, which became the guiding philosophy of Chinese civilization for over two millennia. His teachings influenced not only China but also Korea, Japan, Vietnam, and other parts of East Asia.

Confucianism shaped the structure of Chinese government, education, and family life. The civil service examination system, which selected government officials based on merit rather than birthright, was inspired by his emphasis on moral integrity and knowledge. This system remained in place for over a thousand years, promoting social mobility and effective governance.

Beyond governance, Confucius's emphasis on education inspired a culture of scholarship and intellectual pursuit. His teachings on ethics and interpersonal relationships continue to be studied and applied in modern psychology, leadership training, and conflict resolution.

Even today, Confucian principles influence societal values in East Asia, promoting respect for elders, loyalty, and the importance of education. His philosophy also resonates with global audiences, offering timeless wisdom on how to live a virtuous and fulfilling life.

In conclusion, Confucius was not only a philosopher but also a social reformer whose ideas transcended his time. His vision of a just, harmonious society built on moral integrity continues to inspire individuals and governments worldwide, making him one of history's most enduring figures.

# Socrates
## The Father of Western Philosophy

Socrates, one of the most influential figures in Western philosophy, lived in 5th-century BCE Athens. He is best known for his method of inquiry, his commitment to seeking truth, and his profound influence on later philosophical thought. Unlike many philosophers of his time, Socrates left behind no written works, and what we know about him comes primarily from his students, particularly Plato and Xenophon. His life was dedicated to questioning, teaching, and engaging in public discourse, ultimately leading to his trial and execution. His legacy continues to shape philosophy, ethics, and education worldwide.

## Origin

Socrates was born around 470 BCE in Athens, Greece. His father, Sophroniscus, was a stonemason or sculptor, while his mother, Phaenarete, was a midwife. His family was relatively modest, and Socrates did not come from nobility or great wealth. Despite this, he had access to education and was exposed to the vibrant intellectual culture of Athens.

Ancient Athens was a flourishing city-state known for its democracy, philosophy, and the arts. Socrates grew up in the period following the Persian Wars when Athens reached its peak in terms of power and cultural development. This environment played a crucial role in shaping his intellectual pursuits and his dedication to critical thought and ethical reasoning.

## Childhood and Youth

Little is recorded about Socrates' early years, but he likely received a traditional Athenian education. As a young man, he would have studied subjects such as poetry, gymnastics, music, and philosophy. He may also have been trained in his father's trade as a stonemason, though some sources suggest he did not practice this craft extensively.

During his youth, Socrates developed a deep interest in philosophical inquiry. He was particularly drawn to questions about morality, virtue, and the nature of knowledge. Unlike the Sophists of his time, who taught rhetoric and persuasion for practical purposes, Socrates sought to uncover fundamental truths through rigorous questioning.

Socrates also served as a hoplite (a heavily armed soldier) in the Athenian military. He participated in several campaigns during the Peloponnesian War, including battles at Potidaea, Delium, and Amphipolis. His bravery and endurance were noted by his peers, and he was said to have displayed remarkable self-discipline even in the harshest conditions.

## Adulthood

As he grew older, Socrates became a well-known figure in Athens, frequently engaging in philosophical discussions in the marketplace (agora). He did not charge fees for his teachings, unlike the Sophists, believing that the pursuit of wisdom should be free and accessible to all.

Socrates developed his distinctive method of inquiry, known as the Socratic Method. This approach involved asking a series of probing questions to expose contradictions in his interlocutors' beliefs and encourage critical thinking. He believed that knowledge begins with recognizing one's own ignorance, a principle summed up in his famous statement: "I know that I know nothing."

His discussions often challenged conventional Athenian values, particularly in matters of politics, religion, and ethics. Many Athenians found his relentless questioning unsettling, as it undermined traditional beliefs and authority. However, he also gained a devoted following, including prominent figures such as Plato, Alcibiades, and Xenophon.

## Private Life

Socrates married Xanthippe, a woman known for her sharp tongue and reputedly difficult temperament. They had three sons together. Some historical accounts portray Xanthippe as argumentative and impatient with Socrates' lack of concern for material wealth. However, these depictions may have been exaggerated or influenced by later writers who sought to contrast her with Socrates' philosophical ideals. Despite his family responsibilities, Socrates led a simple and frugal life. He disdained material possessions, choosing instead to focus on intellectual and ethical pursuits.

He often wandered barefoot through Athens, engaging in philosophical debates and seeking wisdom wherever he could find it.

Though he had many admirers, Socrates also made powerful enemies. His criticisms of Athenian politics, his disregard for traditional piety, and his association with controversial figures like Alcibiades and Critias contributed to his eventual downfall.

## Death

In 399 BCE, Socrates was put on trial for allegedly corrupting the youth of Athens and impiety (not believing in the gods of the city). His trial was highly political, as Athens had recently suffered a humiliating defeat in the Peloponnesian War and was in a state of social and political turmoil. Many Athenians saw Socrates as a destabilizing influence.

Despite being given the opportunity to propose an alternative punishment, Socrates refused to renounce his teachings or go into exile. Instead, he maintained his innocence and argued that he had only sought to encourage virtue and wisdom among the Athenian people. The jury found him guilty, and he was sentenced to death by drinking hemlock, a potent poison.

His final moments were recorded in Plato's "Phaedo", which describes how he met his death with calmness and dignity, engaging in philosophical discourse until the very end. His execution marked the end of his life but the beginning of his profound legacy.

## Character

Socrates was known for his intellectual humility, resilience, and unwavering commitment to truth. He was deeply moral and believed that a good life was one spent in pursuit of virtue and wisdom. His willingness to die for his beliefs demonstrated his integrity and his dedication to philosophical inquiry.

Despite his reputation as a gadfly – someone who persistently challenges and provokes others – Socrates was also deeply compassionate. He cared deeply about his students and sought to help others discover the path to ethical living.

His method of questioning remains a powerful tool in philosophy, education, and law, emphasizing the importance of critical thinking and self-examination.

## Influence on Humanity

Socrates' impact on philosophy and humanity is immeasurable. Though he left no writings of his own, his ideas were preserved through the works of his students, particularly Plato, who established the foundations of Western philosophy in the "Republic", "Apology", and "Phaedo". Aristotle, in turn, was influenced by Plato, creating a philosophical lineage that has shaped intellectual thought for centuries.

His emphasis on ethical inquiry influenced subsequent philosophical traditions, including Stoicism, Existentialism, and modern ethical theories. The Socratic Method is still widely used in legal education, scientific investigation, and critical thinking exercises.

Socrates also laid the groundwork for discussions on democracy, individual rights, and moral responsibility. His belief in questioning authority and seeking truth remains relevant in contemporary debates about justice, governance, and education.

In conclusion, Socrates was more than just a philosopher – he was a revolutionary thinker who challenged the status quo and sought to illuminate the path to wisdom. His legacy endures, reminding humanity of the importance of intellectual courage, ethical integrity, and the relentless pursuit of truth.

# Plato
Greek philosopher, founder of the Academy in Athens

Plato, one of the most influential philosophers in history, was a student of Socrates and the teacher of Aristotle. His contributions to philosophy, politics, ethics, and epistemology have had a profound impact on Western thought. His dialogues, particularly "The Republic", "The Symposium", and "The Apology", continue to be studied and debated today. Plato founded the Academy in Athens, one of the earliest institutions of higher learning, which played a significant role in the development of philosophy and science. His work has shaped countless intellectual traditions and remains a cornerstone of philosophical inquiry.

## Origin

Plato was born around 427 BCE in Athens, Greece, during the Peloponnesian War between Athens and Sparta. His birth name was Aristocles, but he later adopted the name Plato, which some believe was derived from the Greek word for "broad," possibly referencing his broad shoulders or wide-ranging intellect. He came from an aristocratic family with strong political connections; his father, Ariston, was believed to be descended from the legendary King Codrus of Athens, while his mother, Perictione, was related to the famous Athenian lawmaker Solon.

Plato's noble lineage exposed him to the political affairs of Athens from an early age. His family's status ensured that he received an excellent education, studying poetry, music, mathematics, and gymnastics. However, it was his exposure to philosophy, particularly through his association with Socrates, that shaped his intellectual pursuits and ultimately led him to abandon political ambitions in favor of philosophical inquiry.

## Childhood and Youth

As a young boy, Plato exhibited an extraordinary intellect and curiosity. He was educated in the traditional subjects of Athenian aristocracy, including rhetoric, poetry, and mathematics. His early writings indicate a deep admiration for Homer and the poets of Greek antiquity, though he later became critical of their portrayal of gods and morality.

Plato's formative years were deeply influenced by the turbulent political climate of Athens. The city was embroiled in the Peloponnesian War, and the eventual defeat of Athens in 404 BCE led to a brief but brutal rule by the Thirty Tyrants, an oligarchic regime that included some of Plato's relatives. However, their tyranny and subsequent overthrow by democratic forces disillusioned him with politics and led him to seek a deeper understanding of justice and governance.

During his youth, Plato became a devoted follower of Socrates, whose method of questioning and dialectical reasoning left a profound impact on him. Socrates' emphasis on ethics, virtue, and the examined life resonated deeply with Plato, shaping his philosophical outlook for the rest of his life.

## Adulthood

Following the execution of Socrates in 399 BCE, Plato left Athens and traveled extensively. He visited Egypt, where he studied mathematics and philosophy, and may have traveled to Italy and the Near East, where he encountered Pythagorean thought. These experiences broadened his intellectual horizons and influenced his later works, particularly his ideas on metaphysics and the nature of reality.

Upon returning to Athens, Plato established the Academy around 387 BCE, a school dedicated to philosophy, mathematics, and science. The Academy attracted some of the greatest minds of the time, including Aristotle. It became a center for intellectual discourse and remained active for nearly 900 years, influencing generations of scholars and philosophers.

During this period, Plato wrote extensively, producing a series of dialogues in which Socrates often appeared as the main character. His works explored themes such as justice, the nature of reality, ethics, and the ideal society. "The Republic", one of his most famous works, presents his vision of a just society ruled by philosopher-kings who possess wisdom and virtue.

Plato also engaged in political philosophy, seeking to apply his theories in practical governance. He traveled to Syracuse in Sicily, where he attempted to advise the ruling tyrants, but his efforts to establish a philosopher-king were unsuccessful, and he was briefly imprisoned. This experience reinforced his skepticism toward political power and deepened his commitment to philosophical inquiry.

## Private Life

Plato never married and had no known children. His life was dedicated entirely to philosophical pursuits, teaching, and writing. Unlike his mentor Socrates, who actively engaged with the public, Plato spent much of his time within the Academy, nurturing the next generation of thinkers.

Although little is known about his personal relationships, he maintained close friendships with many of his students and fellow philosophers. He was deeply committed to the intellectual and moral development of his pupils, believing that knowledge and virtue were essential to a fulfilling life. His dialogues reflect his belief in the importance of dialogue, debate, and continuous learning.

## Death

Plato died around 347 BCE at the age of 80. Some accounts suggest he passed away peacefully in his sleep, while others claim he died while attending a wedding. Regardless of the circumstances, his influence remained strong, and his Academy continued to thrive long after his death.

His legacy was carried forward by his students, particularly Aristotle, who would go on to develop his own philosophical system. The Academy continued to be a beacon of learning until it was eventually closed by Emperor Justinian in 529 CE.

## Character

Plato was a man of deep intellectual rigor, integrity, and a relentless pursuit of truth. He was not only a philosopher but also a visionary who sought to understand the fundamental nature of reality and human existence. His idealism and belief in the power of reason set him apart from many of his contemporaries.

Unlike the Sophists, who taught rhetoric for persuasion, Plato was committed to uncovering absolute truths through rational inquiry. He was deeply concerned with ethics and the role of individuals in society, advocating for a system in which wisdom and virtue guided leadership rather than ambition and wealth.

His writings suggest that he was a passionate advocate for education and lifelong learning. He believed that the highest good was the pursuit of knowledge and that a just society could only be achieved through the cultivation of wisdom and virtue.

## Influence on Humanity

Plato's influence on Western thought is immeasurable. His works laid the foundation for much of Western philosophy, particularly in metaphysics, epistemology, ethics, and political theory. His concept of the "Forms", which posits that abstract ideals such as justice and beauty exist beyond the material world, has shaped philosophical discourse for centuries.

His writings on governance and the ideal state influenced political philosophy, inspiring thinkers such as Augustine, Aquinas, Machiavelli, and Karl Marx. His ideas on education and the role of philosophy in society have left a lasting impact on academic institutions and pedagogical methods.

The Socratic dialogues, which form the basis of his work, continue to be studied in philosophy courses worldwide. His influence extended to Christian and Islamic philosophy, with scholars such as Augustine and Avicenna integrating Platonic thought into theological discussions.

Even in contemporary times, Plato's insights into justice, democracy, and the human condition remain relevant. His belief in reason, dialogue, and the pursuit of truth serves as a guiding principle for philosophical inquiry and ethical reflection.

In conclusion, Plato was not only one of the greatest philosophers of antiquity but also a towering figure whose ideas continue to shape the way humanity understands knowledge, governance, and the purpose of life. His legacy endures, making him a true intellectual giant whose influence spans centuries and civilizations.

# Aristotle
Greek philosopher and scientist

Aristotle, one of the most influential philosophers in history, made lasting contributions to multiple fields, including logic, metaphysics, ethics, politics, biology, and physics. A student of Plato and the teacher of Alexander the Great, Aristotle's works have profoundly shaped Western thought. His systematic approach to knowledge and inquiry laid the foundation for modern scientific and philosophical traditions. His influence continues to be felt today, demonstrating the enduring power of his intellectual legacy.

## Origin

Aristotle was born in 384 BCE in the city of Stagira, located in the Macedonian region of northern Greece. His father, Nicomachus, was a physician to King Amyntas III of Macedon, which provided Aristotle with exposure to the Macedonian court and its intellectual and political environment. His mother, Phaestis, was also of noble lineage. Aristotle's early years in Stagira were shaped by his family's medical background, which likely influenced his later studies in biology and natural sciences. The environment in which he grew up emphasized practical knowledge and empirical observation, both of which would become central to his philosophical methodology.

## Childhood and Youth

When Aristotle was still a young boy, his father passed away, and he was placed under the care of a guardian. This loss likely contributed to his strong inclination toward intellectual pursuits rather than following his father's medical profession. Recognizing his potential, his guardian arranged for him to study at Plato's Academy in Athens, the most prestigious learning institution of its time.

At the age of 17, Aristotle moved to Athens and became a student at Plato's Academy. He remained there for nearly 20 years, studying philosophy, logic, and mathematics. Although he was deeply influenced by Plato, he gradually began to develop his own ideas, often diverging from his mentor's teachings. While Plato emphasized the realm of ideal forms, Aristotle focused on empirical observation and the material world.

During his time at the Academy, Aristotle distinguished himself as a brilliant thinker and an eloquent speaker. However, despite his long association with Plato, he was not chosen as his successor when Plato died. Instead, Plato's nephew, Speusippus, took over the Academy, prompting Aristotle to leave Athens.

## Adulthood

Following his departure from Athens, Aristotle traveled extensively, spending time in Asia Minor and the island of Lesbos, where he conducted extensive research in biology and natural sciences. He studied marine life and the classification of organisms, laying the groundwork for future advancements in biology.

In 343 BCE, Aristotle was invited to the court of King Philip II of Macedon to tutor his son, Alexander. For several years, he educated the young prince, who would later become known as Alexander the Great. Under Aristotle's guidance, Alexander studied philosophy, politics, ethics, and science. Although Alexander later pursued a path of conquest and empire-building, Aristotle's teachings had a significant impact on his approach to governance and administration.

After his time in Macedon, Aristotle returned to Athens in 335 BCE and founded his own school, the Lyceum. Unlike Plato's Academy, the Lyceum emphasized empirical research and systematic observation. Aristotle and his students, known as the Peripatetics, conducted studies in various fields, including biology, physics, logic, politics, and ethics.

At the Lyceum, Aristotle wrote extensively, producing some of his most important works, including "Nicomachean Ethics", "Politics", "Metaphysics", "Poetics", and "The Organon". These texts covered a wide range of subjects and laid the foundation for many academic disciplines.

## Private Life

Despite his public role as a philosopher and teacher, Aristotle led a relatively private life. He married Pythias, the niece of Hermias, a ruler of

Atarneus. Together, they had a daughter, also named Pythias. After his wife's death, Aristotle later entered into a relationship with a woman named Herpyllis, with whom he had a son named Nicomachus.

Aristotle's writings suggest that he valued family life and believed in the importance of ethical conduct within personal relationships. His ethical philosophy emphasized moderation and balance, a principle that he likely applied to his own life.

He maintained a circle of close friends and students, many of whom became prominent scholars in their own right. His method of teaching was based on dialogue and active engagement, fostering a strong intellectual community at the Lyceum.

## Death

Aristotle's later years were marked by political unrest. Following the death of Alexander the Great in 323 BCE, anti-Macedonian sentiments grew in Athens, making it unsafe for Aristotle due to his past association with the Macedonian court. Accused of impiety, he chose to flee Athens rather than face prosecution. He reportedly remarked that he did not want Athens to "sin twice against philosophy," a reference to the execution of Socrates.

He retreated to the city of Chalcis on the island of Euboea, where he lived quietly until his death in 322 BCE at the age of 62. Some accounts suggest that he died of natural causes, possibly due to a stomach illness.

## Character

Aristotle was a meticulous thinker, deeply committed to the pursuit of knowledge and the application of reason. Unlike his teacher Plato, who leaned toward idealism, Aristotle was a pragmatist who emphasized empirical observation and logical analysis. He was known for his intellectual humility, often acknowledging gaps in knowledge and advocating for continuous learning. His emphasis on moderation, balance, and ethical behavior reflected his belief in living a virtuous life. Despite his profound influence, Aristotle did not see himself as an infallible authority, encouraging his students to question and refine ideas.

He also demonstrated a keen interest in the natural world, conducting detailed observations that contributed to the early development of the scientific method. His curiosity and dedication to systematic inquiry made him one of history's most formidable intellectuals.

## Influence on Humanity

Aristotle's contributions to philosophy, science, and education have shaped human thought for over two millennia. His works influenced medieval scholars, including Islamic and Christian philosophers such as Avicenna, Averroes, and Thomas Aquinas.

His writings on logic formed the basis of Aristotelian logic, which remained the dominant framework for logical reasoning until the development of modern formal logic. His contributions to ethics, particularly in "Nicomachean Ethics", introduced the concept of virtue ethics, which remains a significant field in moral philosophy.

In political philosophy, his ideas on governance, democracy, and the rule of law influenced the development of Western political theory. His classification of government systems, including monarchy, aristocracy, and democracy, remains relevant in contemporary discussions on political structures.

Aristotle's influence also extended to the natural sciences. His early classifications of animals and his emphasis on empirical observation laid the groundwork for later developments in biology and the scientific method.

In modern times, his legacy endures in philosophy, science, and education. Universities and academic institutions continue to study his works, and his intellectual legacy remains central to the development of critical thought and rational inquiry.

In conclusion, Aristotle was not only a philosopher but also a polymath whose ideas continue to shape our understanding of the world. His relentless pursuit of knowledge and his systematic approach to learning make him one of the greatest thinkers in human history.

# Alexander the Great
Macedonian conqueror who built a vast empire

Alexander III of Macedon, commonly known as Alexander the Great, was one of the most successful military commanders in history. Born in 356 BCE, he became king of Macedon at the age of 20 and went on to create one of the largest empires the world has ever seen. By the time of his death in 323 BCE, he had conquered much of the known world, from Greece to Egypt, Persia, and as far as India. His unparalleled military genius, visionary leadership, and influence on global culture and governance continue to shape modern civilization.

## Origin

Alexander was born in 356 BCE in Pella, the capital of Macedon, a powerful kingdom in northern Greece. His father, King Philip II of Macedon, was a formidable military leader who had transformed Macedon into a dominant power in Greece. His mother, Olympias, was a princess of Epirus and a devout follower of the cult of Dionysus, which played a significant role in Alexander's religious beliefs.

According to legend, Olympias claimed that Alexander was the son of Zeus, reinforcing his belief in his divine destiny. His royal lineage and the ambitious reforms of his father shaped his early life, instilling in him a sense of duty, ambition, and a desire for greatness.

## Childhood and Youth

Alexander's childhood was marked by a rigorous education and exposure to military and political affairs. Recognizing his son's potential, Philip II hired Aristotle, one of the greatest philosophers of the ancient world, as Alexander's tutor. Under Aristotle's guidance, Alexander studied philosophy, science, medicine, literature, and the art of governance. Aristotle's teachings had a profound impact on Alexander's intellect and shaped his approach to leadership and strategy.

Beyond academics, Alexander received military training from an early age. He displayed remarkable physical prowess and courage, demonstrating his skills in combat and horsemanship. One of the most famous stories from his youth was his taming of Bucephalus, a wild horse that no one else could ride. This act symbolized his exceptional bravery and determination.

During his teenage years, Alexander accompanied his father on military campaigns, gaining firsthand experience in warfare and statecraft. He fought at the Battle of Chaeronea in 338 BCE, where he played a crucial role in securing a decisive victory for Macedon against the Greek city-states. This victory cemented his reputation as a capable and fearless leader.

## Adulthood

In 336 BCE, Philip II was assassinated, and Alexander ascended to the throne at the age of 20. Facing internal rivalries and external threats, he swiftly consolidated power, eliminating potential rivals and securing the loyalty of the Macedonian army. Once his rule was stabilized, he turned his attention to his father's unfinished ambition – conquering the Persian Empire.

In 334 BCE, Alexander launched his legendary campaign against Persia, beginning with a decisive victory at the Battle of Granicus. Over the next few years, he defeated the Persian king Darius III at the battles of Issus (333 BCE) and Gaugamela (331 BCE), effectively bringing the vast Persian Empire under his control.

His military campaigns extended beyond Persia. He marched into Egypt, where he was welcomed as a liberator and crowned Pharaoh. There, he founded the city of Alexandria, which would become one of the most important cultural and intellectual centers of the ancient world. He continued his conquests into Central Asia and India, where he fought the fierce King Porus at the Battle of the Hydaspes in 326 BCE. Although victorious, his troops, weary from years of campaigning, refused to march further, forcing him to turn back.

## Private Life

Despite his intense military focus, Alexander had a complex personal life. He married Roxana, a noblewoman from Bactria, to solidify alliances in the region. He later took additional wives, including Stateira, the daughter of Darius III, as part of his strategy to merge Persian and Macedonian cultures. He encouraged his soldiers to marry Persian women, promoting the fusion of Greek and Eastern traditions.

Alexander's closest relationships were with his childhood friend and general, Hephaestion, whom he regarded as his most trusted companion. Their deep bond has led to speculation about the nature of their relationship, though historical records remain inconclusive.

His personal life was also marked by moments of emotional intensity and impulsive actions. He executed close advisors and friends, including Parmenion and Cleitus, in fits of rage or political necessity, reflecting the pressures and isolation of his leadership.

## Death

In 323 BCE, after years of continuous military campaigns, Alexander returned to Babylon, where he planned new conquests, including an expedition to Arabia. However, his health rapidly deteriorated, and he died on June 10 or 11, 323 BCE, at the age of 32. The exact cause of his death remains a mystery, with theories ranging from poisoning to malaria, typhoid, or complications from battle wounds.

His sudden death left his vast empire without a clear successor, leading to a period of turmoil known as the Wars of the Diadochi, during which his generals fought for control of his territories. His empire was ultimately divided among his top commanders, laying the foundation for the Hellenistic kingdoms that shaped the ancient world.

## Character

Alexander was a charismatic and visionary leader, known for his military genius, strategic brilliance, and relentless ambition. He possessed an unshakable belief in his destiny and saw himself as a bridge between East and West, promoting cultural exchange and fusion.

He was both merciful and ruthless – showing clemency to conquered peoples while executing perceived traitors and rivals. His leadership style combined inspiration with discipline, earning the loyalty of his troops, who revered him as a godlike figure.

Despite his successes, he was also deeply flawed. His increasing paranoia, impulsive decisions, and excessive drinking contributed to strained relationships with his advisors. Nevertheless, his ability to inspire, innovate, and adapt ensured his place in history as one of the greatest leaders of all time.

## Influence on Humanity

Alexander's legacy extends far beyond his military conquests. He spread Greek culture, language, and ideas across the regions he conquered, leading to the Hellenistic Era – a period of cultural flourishing that influenced art, philosophy, science, and governance.

The cities he founded, most notably Alexandria in Egypt, became centers of learning and trade, attracting scholars, merchants, and artists from diverse backgrounds. The blending of Greek and Eastern cultures led to advancements in philosophy, medicine, astronomy, and literature.

His military tactics and strategies are still studied in modern military academies, and his leadership principles continue to inspire political and business leaders. His vision of a united, multicultural empire set a precedent for later empires, including Rome and Byzantium.

In conclusion, Alexander the Great was more than just a conqueror; he was a transformative figure whose influence shaped the ancient world and continues to impact modern civilization. His ambition, leadership, and vision ensured that his name would be remembered throughout history as one of the greatest figures of all time.

# Euclid
## The Father of Geometry

Euclid, known as the "Father of Geometry," was a Greek mathematician whose work laid the foundation for modern mathematics, particularly in the field of geometry. He is best known for his monumental work, "Elements", a compilation of mathematical knowledge that remained the definitive textbook for over two millennia. Although little is known about his personal life, his contributions to mathematics have had an enduring impact on scientific thought, education, and engineering. His axiomatic approach to geometry shaped mathematical inquiry and logical reasoning, influencing not only mathematics but also philosophy and physics.

## Origin

Euclid is believed to have been born around 300 BCE, though the exact date and location of his birth remain uncertain. Historians suggest he was born in Greece, possibly in Athens or Alexandria, but no definitive records confirm this. His Greek heritage placed him within one of the most intellectually vibrant cultures of antiquity, at a time when philosophy, science, and mathematics were flourishing.

His historical presence is primarily recorded through the works of later scholars, such as Proclus, a 5th-century CE philosopher. According to Proclus, Euclid taught at the Library of Alexandria, an institution founded by Ptolemy I, the ruler of Egypt, as a center for learning and scholarship. This suggests that Euclid spent much of his professional life in Alexandria, contributing to its intellectual legacy.

## Childhood and Youth

There is little documented evidence regarding Euclid's early life, education, or family background. However, given the depth of his mathematical knowledge and the structured nature of his works, it is widely assumed that he received a thorough education in mathematics, philosophy, and the sciences. His formative years likely involved rigorous training in the teachings of earlier mathematicians such as Pythagoras, Plato, and Eudoxus.

It is also possible that Euclid studied at Plato's Academy in Athens, a leading center of mathematical and philosophical thought. Plato's emphasis on abstract reasoning and the pursuit of ideal forms may have influenced Euclid's methodical approach to mathematics. If this is the case, his early exposure to logical structures and deductive reasoning would later manifest in the axiomatic system he developed in "Elements".

## Adulthood

By the time Euclid was an established mathematician, he had likely moved to Alexandria, Egypt, where he taught and conducted research. The city, under Ptolemaic rule, was a hub of intellectual activity, attracting scholars from across the Greek world. Euclid's role in the Library of Alexandria solidified his status as a leading mathematician of his time.

His most significant contribution, "Elements", was written during this period. The work, consisting of thirteen books, systematically presents geometric principles, definitions, postulates, and proofs. It builds upon the knowledge of earlier mathematicians but introduces a rigorous axiomatic structure that would become the standard for mathematical reasoning.

Apart from "Elements", Euclid is also credited with other mathematical treatises, including:

- **Data**: A study of geometric properties and magnitudes.
- **Optics**: A work on the nature of vision and the laws of perspective.
- **Phaenomena**: A treatise on spherical astronomy.
- **On Divisions of Figures**: A study of the division of geometric shapes.

Euclid's teachings attracted many students, and his systematic method of deductive reasoning became the foundation of mathematical education for centuries. His works were used not only in the Hellenistic world but also in later Islamic and European mathematical traditions.

## Private Life

Very little is known about Euclid's personal life. Unlike other historical figures of his time, no surviving records detail his relationships, family, or personal experiences. This lack of biographical information suggests that he was primarily focused on his scholarly pursuits and teaching.

His anonymity in historical texts has led some scholars to speculate that "Euclid" may have been a collective name representing multiple mathematicians working under Ptolemaic rule. However, this theory remains speculative, as his works demonstrate a coherent and unified structure indicative of a single author.

Despite the mystery surrounding his private life, Euclid's intellectual legacy is unquestionable. His dedication to mathematics and logical reasoning ensured that his contributions would endure for generations.

## Death

The exact date and circumstances of Euclid's death are unknown. Based on historical estimates, he likely died around 270 BCE in Alexandria. There are no surviving accounts detailing his later years or burial, further contributing to the enigmatic nature of his life.

However, his death did not mark the end of his influence. His work continued to be studied and expanded upon by mathematicians and scholars across different civilizations. The absence of personal details in historical records does not diminish his intellectual legacy, which remains a cornerstone of mathematical thought.

## Character

Euclid is often portrayed as a rational, methodical, and disciplined thinker. His work exhibits a remarkable clarity and precision, emphasizing logical reasoning over intuition. His ability to present complex ideas in an accessible and systematic manner suggests a deep commitment to education and knowledge dissemination.

A famous anecdote about Euclid illustrates his character. When a student asked him what benefit he would gain from studying geometry, Euclid is said to have responded by instructing a servant to give the student a coin, remarking that learning should not be pursued for material gain. This story reflects his belief that the pursuit of knowledge should be valued for its intrinsic merit rather than its immediate practical rewards.

Euclid's intellectual humility is also notable. Unlike some of his contemporaries, he did not seek personal glory or political power. His primary concern was advancing mathematical knowledge and ensuring that it could be systematically understood and taught.

## Influence on Humanity

Euclid's impact on mathematics and science is profound. His "Elements" became the most influential mathematical textbook in history, studied by scholars for over 2,000 years. It was widely used in Greek, Roman, Islamic, and European mathematical traditions, shaping the development of geometry and logical reasoning.

During the Islamic Golden Age, Arab mathematicians translated "Elements" into Arabic, preserving and expanding upon Euclid's ideas. In medieval Europe, the work was reintroduced through Latin translations and became a standard part of mathematical education.

Euclid's influence extended beyond mathematics. His logical approach to problem-solving laid the foundation for modern scientific methods. Philosophers such as René Descartes and Isaac Newton built upon Euclidean principles to develop their own theories in physics and calculus. Even Albert Einstein acknowledged the impact of Euclidean geometry on his theory of relativity.

The legacy of Euclid's work continues to shape contemporary education. His axiomatic approach remains central to geometry curricula worldwide, and his emphasis on deductive reasoning continues to inspire mathematicians and scientists.

In conclusion, Euclid's contributions to mathematics have endured the test of time, establishing him as one of history's most influential intellectuals. His work not only defined the principles of geometry but also influenced the broader realms of logic, science, and philosophy. Though much of his personal life remains unknown, his intellectual achievements ensure that his name and legacy live on.

# Ashoka

Indian emperor who promoted Buddhism

Ashoka the Great, one of the most revered rulers in Indian history, was the third emperor of the Maurya Dynasty. He ruled nearly the entire Indian subcontinent from approximately 268 to 232 BCE. Initially known for his military conquests, Ashoka underwent a profound transformation following the brutal Kalinga War. His embrace of Buddhism and commitment to nonviolence, moral governance, and welfare policies had a lasting impact on India and beyond. His reign marked a golden era of political stability, religious tolerance, and the propagation of Buddhist philosophy, making him one of the most remarkable figures in world history.

## Origin

Ashoka was born around 304 BCE in Pataliputra (modern-day Patna, India), the capital of the Maurya Empire. He was the son of Emperor Bindusara and the grandson of Chandragupta Maurya, the founder of the Mauryan dynasty. His mother was believed to be Subhadrangi, a woman of non-royal but noble lineage, though historical sources vary on this detail.

The Mauryan Empire, established in 321 BCE by Chandragupta, was the largest empire in Indian history at the time. Under Bindusara, it expanded further, and Ashoka was born into an era of great military and political strength. However, succession politics within the royal family was complex, and Ashoka's rise to power was not without challenges.

## Childhood and Youth

Ashoka grew up in the grandeur of the Mauryan court, where he received a rigorous education in administration, warfare, philosophy, and governance. As a prince, he was trained in military tactics and statecraft, making him an exceptional warrior and strategist.

Unlike some of his brothers, Ashoka was not initially the heir apparent. His older brothers, particularly Susima, were favored for the throne.

However, Ashoka distinguished himself through his intelligence, courage, and leadership. His skills earned him the trust of many court officials and generals, making him a formidable contender for the throne.

As he matured, Ashoka was appointed as the governor of various provinces, including Ujjain and Taxila. These governorships gave him firsthand experience in administration and governance, preparing him for the responsibilities of ruling a vast empire. His time in Taxila was particularly significant, as he played a crucial role in quelling a rebellion there, proving his military prowess and political acumen.

## Adulthood

After the death of Bindusara in 273 BCE, a fierce struggle for succession ensued. Ashoka emerged victorious after a bloody power struggle, allegedly killing several of his brothers, including Susima, to secure the throne. He officially became emperor in 268 BCE.

As emperor, Ashoka initially followed in the footsteps of his predecessors, focusing on territorial expansion and military conquests. His most notable campaign was the conquest of Kalinga (modern Odisha) around 261 BCE. Although the war resulted in a decisive Mauryan victory, it came at a tremendous human cost – over 100,000 people were killed, and thousands more were displaced.

The immense suffering caused by the war deeply affected Ashoka. According to historical accounts, he was filled with remorse and sought solace in Buddhism. This moment marked a turning point in his reign, leading him to abandon aggressive military conquests in favor of a governance model based on Dharma (moral law and righteousness).

## Private Life

Ashoka had multiple wives, with Devi, Karuvaki, and Asandhimitra being the most well-known. His first wife, Devi, was instrumental in his conversion to Buddhism. She was a follower of Buddha and played a significant role in influencing his views on nonviolence and compassion.

With Devi, he had two children – Mahinda and Sanghamitta – who later became prominent Buddhist missionaries, spreading Buddhism to Sri

Lanka and Southeast Asia. His marriage to Karuvaki is also significant as she is mentioned in one of his inscriptions, a rare occurrence for royal consorts.

Despite being a powerful ruler, Ashoka chose a life of simplicity in his later years. He devoted himself to Buddhist principles and spent much of his time promoting peace, welfare, and social justice.

## Death

Ashoka ruled for approximately 37 years, passing away around 232 BCE. His death led to a decline in the Mauryan Empire, as his successors failed to maintain the stability and unity he had established. The empire eventually fragmented, and the Mauryan dynasty came to an end about 50 years after his death.

His death marked the end of an era, but his legacy endured. His influence on governance, morality, and religious tolerance left an indelible mark on Indian history and Buddhist philosophy.

## Character

Ashoka's character evolved significantly over the course of his life. Initially a ruthless warrior and ambitious ruler, he transformed into a benevolent and compassionate emperor after witnessing the horrors of war. His embrace of Buddhism was not just personal but also reflected in his policies and governance.

He promoted nonviolence, religious tolerance, and ethical conduct in both personal and administrative matters. His ability to acknowledge his past mistakes and dedicate himself to peace and justice demonstrates immense moral courage and wisdom. Unlike many rulers, Ashoka ruled with empathy, prioritizing the well-being of his people over territorial expansion.

His character was further exemplified in his numerous edicts, inscribed on pillars and rocks across the empire. These edicts emphasized kindness, justice, and respect for all religions, highlighting his commitment to creating a just society.

## Influence on Humanity

Ashoka's impact on humanity is immeasurable. His transformation from a ruthless conqueror to a peace-loving ruler set a precedent for governance based on moral values rather than brute force.

One of his greatest contributions was the spread of Buddhism. Under his patronage, Buddhism transitioned from a regional sect to a global religion. He sent missionaries to Sri Lanka, Central Asia, Southeast Asia, and beyond, establishing Buddhism as a major spiritual force. His son Mahinda and daughter Sanghamitta played pivotal roles in bringing Buddhism to Sri Lanka, where it remains a dominant faith today.

Ashoka's policies of religious tolerance and social welfare were groundbreaking. He established hospitals, built roads, and promoted education and environmental conservation. His emphasis on nonviolence and moral governance influenced later rulers, including Mahatma Gandhi, who drew inspiration from Ashoka's principles in his fight for India's independence.

Furthermore, Ashoka's edicts are among the oldest surviving written documents in Indian history, providing invaluable insights into his reign and philosophy. They continue to be studied by historians, scholars, and political leaders worldwide.

---

In conclusion, Ashoka was more than just an emperor; he was a visionary whose legacy of peace, compassion, and moral governance transcends time. His reign remains a model of ethical leadership, and his influence continues to inspire movements for social justice, religious harmony, and global peace. His journey from conquest to conscience is a testament to the transformative power of self-reflection and moral responsibility.

# Archimedes
Greek mathematician and engineer

Archimedes of Syracuse was one of the greatest mathematicians, engineers, and inventors of ancient Greece. His discoveries and innovations in geometry, calculus, physics, and engineering have had a lasting impact on science and mathematics. Known for his principle of buoyancy, the invention of war machines, and contributions to the understanding of levers and pulleys, Archimedes' work continues to influence modern science and engineering. Despite living over two millennia ago, his discoveries remain foundational in physics, mathematics, and technological innovation.

## Origin

Archimedes was born around 287 BCE in the city of Syracuse, a Greek settlement on the island of Sicily. Syracuse was a prominent center of commerce, culture, and learning, and it played a crucial role in the interactions between Greek and Roman civilizations. Archimedes' father, Phidias, was an astronomer, which likely influenced his early interest in mathematics and science.

Syracuse was an independent Greek city-state, but it often found itself in conflicts with Rome and Carthage, shaping the historical context in which Archimedes lived and worked. Given the city's strategic importance, its rulers actively supported scientific and military advancements, further fostering Archimedes' intellectual development.

## Childhood and Youth

Little is known about Archimedes' early life, but given his later intellectual prowess, he likely received an extensive education. As a young man, he traveled to Alexandria, Egypt, one of the leading centers of learning in the ancient world. There, he studied under mathematicians like Conon of Samos and Eratosthenes, both of whom were pioneers in geometry and astronomy.

During his time in Alexandria, Archimedes was exposed to the teachings of Euclid, whose work in geometry greatly influenced him. It is believed that he engaged in academic exchanges with scholars at the Great Library of Alexandria, refining his mathematical skills and laying the groundwork for his later discoveries.

Upon completing his studies, Archimedes returned to Syracuse, where he continued his work in mathematics, physics, and engineering.

## Adulthood

As an adult, Archimedes became a prominent figure in the court of King Hiero II of Syracuse. He was highly respected for his intellectual contributions and his ability to apply theoretical knowledge to practical problems.

One of his most famous contributions was his formulation of the principle of buoyancy, now known as "Archimedes' Principle". According to legend, King Hiero II suspected that a goldsmith had adulterated his gold crown with silver. Archimedes discovered a way to determine the crown's composition by observing the water displacement caused by its volume, reportedly shouting "Eureka!" upon making this realization. This principle remains fundamental in fluid mechanics today.

Archimedes also studied levers and pulleys, famously declaring, "Give me a place to stand, and I will move the Earth." His work in mechanics led to the creation of machines capable of lifting heavy objects with minimal effort, influencing later developments in engineering and physics.

## Private Life

Although Archimedes was deeply devoted to his studies and inventions, little is known about his personal life. He did not marry, and historical records provide no evidence of a family. His life was primarily dedicated to scientific pursuits, and he was known to become so absorbed in his work that he would forget to eat or bathe. Despite his intellectual pursuits, Archimedes maintained friendships with many scholars of his time. His correspondence with Eratosthenes and other mathematicians in Alexandria demonstrates his willingness to exchange ideas and expand his knowledge beyond Syracuse.

# Death

Archimedes met a tragic end in 212 BCE when Syracuse fell to the Roman Republic during the Second Punic War. The Romans, led by General Marcus Claudius Marcellus, besieged Syracuse for two years. Archimedes played a crucial role in the city's defense, designing war machines, including catapults and mirrors that allegedly set enemy ships on fire by concentrating sunlight.

Despite his contributions to Syracuse's defense, the city eventually fell to the Romans. According to historical accounts, a Roman soldier killed Archimedes despite orders from Marcellus to capture him alive. The most widely accepted version of the story states that Archimedes was deeply engaged in a mathematical problem when a soldier interrupted him Annoyed by the disruption, he reportedly said, "Do not disturb my circles," before being slain. His death marked the end of one of the greatest scientific minds of the ancient world, but his legacy lived on through his writings and inventions.

# Character

Archimedes was known for his deep intellectual curiosity and commitment to knowledge. His ability to bridge the gap between theoretical mathematics and practical engineering was unparalleled in his time He had a playful yet intense approach to problem-solving, often delighting in puzzles and challenges.

Despite his immense knowledge, Archimedes remained humble, focusing more on his discoveries than on seeking personal glory. His writings suggest a man dedicated to understanding the universe rather than pursuing wealth or power. His concentration and devotion to his work were so intense that he often ignored the world around him, leading to the famous anecdote about his death.

# Influence on Humanity

Archimedes' impact on science, mathematics, and engineering is immeasurable. His works laid the foundation for many fields that continue to shape modern knowledge.

**1. Mathematics** – Archimedes contributed significantly to geometry, calculus, and numerical analysis. His method of exhaustion foreshadowed integral calculus, and his studies on spirals, spheres, and cylinders remain foundational in modern mathematics.

**2. Physics** – His principles of buoyancy and mechanics revolutionized physics. Archimedes' work on levers and pulleys is still taught in physics and engineering courses today.

**3. Engineering** – His war machines and innovative designs influenced military tactics for centuries. Many of his principles are still applied in mechanical engineering and hydraulics.

**4. Astronomy** – Although primarily known for his mathematical and engineering contributions, Archimedes also developed models for understanding planetary motion and celestial mechanics.

**5. Scientific Thought** – His rigorous approach to problem-solving set the precedent for scientific methodology. His logical and empirical approach to mathematics inspired later thinkers, including Galileo Galilei, Isaac Newton, and Johannes Kepler.

**6. Modern Applications** – His inventions, such as the Archimedean screw (used for water lifting), are still in use today, particularly in irrigation and industrial processes.

Archimedes' legacy extends far beyond his lifetime. His works were preserved by Islamic scholars during the medieval period and later translated into Latin, inspiring the scientific revolution in Europe. Today, his contributions are recognized as fundamental in both theoretical and applied sciences.

---

In conclusion, Archimedes was more than a mathematician – he was a visionary whose ideas continue to influence the modern world. His relentless pursuit of knowledge, ingenuity, and practical applications of mathematical principles make him one of the most remarkable figures in human history. His legacy as a scientist, engineer, and thinker remains unparalleled, cementing his place as one of the greatest minds of all time.

# Qin Shihuangdi
First emperor of China and builder of the Great Wall

Qin Shihuangdi, also known as Qin Shi Huang, was the founder of the Qin Dynasty and the first emperor of a unified China. He ruled from 221 BCE to 210 BCE and is best known for his ambitious political reforms, vast construction projects, and authoritarian rule. His reign laid the foundation for modern China through centralization, standardization, and military conquest. Though his methods were often ruthless, his legacy remains unparalleled in Chinese history.

## Origin

Qin Shihuangdi was born in 259 BCE as Ying Zheng in the state of Qin, one of the warring states vying for dominance over China. His father, King Zhuangxiang of Qin, was a ruler of the Qin state, while his mother, Lady Zhao, was originally a concubine of the influential Lü Buwei, a wealthy merchant and political strategist. Lü Buwei played a crucial role in placing Ying Zheng's father on the throne, making him a key figure in the young prince's early life.

The state of Qin, located in western China, had been expanding its influence under a series of strong rulers. By the time of Ying Zheng's birth, Qin had already begun its campaign to unify the warring states. From an early age, Ying Zheng was destined for power, growing up in an environment dominated by military strategy and political maneuvering.

## Childhood and Youth

Ying Zheng's early years were marked by political intrigue. When his father died in 246 BCE, he ascended the throne at the age of 13. Due to his youth, Lü Buwei acted as regent, exerting significant influence over the administration. However, as Ying Zheng matured, he sought to consolidate his power and rid himself of political rivals.

At the age of 22, Ying Zheng successfully eliminated Lü Buwei and other powerful courtiers, asserting his direct control over the Qin state. His decisive actions demonstrated his political acumen and ambition, setting the stage for his future conquests.

During his youth, Ying Zheng was exposed to the philosophies of Legalism, a strict political doctrine that emphasized centralized rule, harsh punishments, and absolute authority. These principles would heavily influence his governance once he became emperor.

## Adulthood

Upon taking full control of Qin, Ying Zheng launched a series of aggressive military campaigns against the other warring states. Between 230 BCE and 221 BCE, he systematically conquered the six remaining states – Han, Zhao, Wei, Chu, Yan, and Qi – establishing the first unified Chinese empire. In 221 BCE, he declared himself "Qin Shihuangdi", meaning "First Emperor of Qin."

As emperor, Qin Shihuangdi implemented sweeping reforms to consolidate his rule. He standardized currency, weights, and measures, ensuring uniformity across the empire. He also unified the written script, making communication more efficient across diverse regions.

To maintain control, he centralized the administration, abolishing the feudal system and replacing hereditary aristocrats with appointed officials loyal to the emperor. He divided China into administrative units, each governed by bureaucrats who answered directly to the imperial government. These policies strengthened the state and laid the foundation for future dynasties.

Qin Shihuangdi was also responsible for several monumental construction projects. He ordered the building of a vast network of roads and canals to improve trade and military movement. His most famous project was the construction of the Great Wall of China, intended to protect the empire from northern invaders. Though it was later expanded by subsequent dynasties, the Great Wall remains a lasting symbol of his reign.

Despite his achievements, Qin Shihuangdi ruled with an iron fist. He suppressed dissent, banning and burning books that promoted Confucian thought, which he saw as a threat to his authority. Scholars who opposed his policies were executed, and strict laws ensured compliance among the population.

## Private Life

Qin Shihuangdi's personal life remains largely shrouded in mystery. He never named an empress, and his relationships with concubines were not well-documented. However, historical records suggest that he had several children, though political instability after his death led to their downfall.

A deeply superstitious man, Qin Shihuangdi was obsessed with immortality. He commissioned alchemists and scholars to find an elixir of eternal life, consuming various potions that may have contained toxic substances such as mercury. His fear of death drove him to construct an elaborate underground mausoleum, guarded by the famous Terracotta Army.

Despite his power, Qin Shihuangdi was deeply paranoid. He frequently changed locations to avoid assassination attempts and relied heavily on a network of spies to root out potential threats.

## Death

In 210 BCE, Qin Shihuangdi died during one of his inspection tours across the empire. The exact cause of his death remains uncertain, but many historians believe it was due to mercury poisoning from the elixirs he consumed in his quest for immortality.

His death triggered a power struggle among his advisors and heirs. His prime minister, Li Si, and chief eunuch, Zhao Gao, manipulated the succession process, leading to the eventual collapse of the Qin Dynasty. Within a few years of his passing, the empire he built fell into chaos, paving the way for the Han Dynasty.

## Character

Qin Shihuangdi was a complex figure, embodying both visionary leadership and ruthless authoritarianism. He was highly intelligent, ambitious, and relentless in his pursuit of power. His ability to unify China demonstrated strategic brilliance, but his harsh methods and suppression of intellectual freedom made him a feared ruler.

His belief in Legalism shaped his ruling style – he valued order, obedience, and strict enforcement of laws. While his policies strengthened the empire, they also created resentment, contributing to the Qin Dynasty's rapid downfall after his death.

Despite his harshness, he was also a pragmatic leader who sought efficiency and standardization. His administrative reforms ensured that China remained a unified state for centuries, influencing future dynasties.

## Influence on Humanity

Qin Shihuangdi's legacy is profound and far-reaching. His unification of China laid the foundation for over two millennia of imperial rule. Many of his reforms – such as standardized currency, writing, and measurement systems – continued to shape China's governance and economy long after his death.

His construction projects, including the Great Wall and his grand mausoleum, remain marvels of engineering and cultural heritage. The discovery of the Terracotta Army in 1974 provided invaluable insights into ancient Chinese art, military organization, and burial practices.

While his authoritarian rule and book burnings are often criticized, his emphasis on centralization and bureaucracy influenced the structure of future Chinese administrations. His reign set the precedent for a strong, centralized state, a concept that remains integral to China's governance today.

In conclusion, Qin Shihuangdi was both a tyrant and a visionary, a ruler whose impact shaped China's history and identity. His ruthless tactics secured his empire, but his legacy transcended his lifetime, influencing governance, culture, and historical discourse for centuries to come.

# Julius Caesar
## The Architect of Rome's Imperial Era

Julius Caesar, one of the most influential figures in Roman history, was a military general, statesman, and dictator whose actions shaped the future of the Roman Empire. His conquests, political strategies, and eventual assassination marked the transition from the Roman Republic to the Roman Empire. Known for his military brilliance, ambitious reforms, and charismatic leadership, Caesar's legacy continues to resonate through history. His influence extends beyond politics and warfare, affecting literature, governance, and the very calendar we use today.

## Origin

Gaius Julius Caesar was born on July 12 or 13, 100 BCE, into the ancient and aristocratic "gens Julia", a patrician family claiming descent from the Trojan prince Aeneas, and ultimately from the goddess Venus. His father, Gaius Julius Caesar, served as a praetor, while his mother, Aurelia, was known for her intelligence and influence over her son.

Despite his noble lineage, the Caesar family was not among the wealthiest or most powerful in Rome. They aligned themselves with the populares, a political faction that championed the rights of the common people against the optimates, the conservative senatorial elite. This early association with reformist politics played a crucial role in shaping Caesar's views and ambitions.

## Childhood and Youth

Caesar's youth was marked by political turmoil, as Rome faced internal struggles between the populares and optimates. When he was 16, his father died suddenly, making him the head of the family. Around the same time, the dictator Lucius Cornelius Sulla emerged as the dominant political force in Rome, launching purges against his enemies, including those associated with the populares.

Caesar's family was targeted due to their ties to Sulla's rival, Gaius Marius, who was also Caesar's uncle by marriage. To avoid persecution, Caesar fled Rome and joined the military in Asia Minor, serving under Marcus Minucius Thermus. During his service, he displayed exceptional bravery, earning the "civic crown", Rome's highest military honor. Sulla eventually pardoned him, but the experience reinforced Caesar's belief in self-reliance and strategic political maneuvering.

Upon returning to Rome, Caesar pursued oratory and legal studies. His persuasive public speaking and legal skills gained him recognition, setting the stage for his political career. He soon embarked on a path that combined military prowess with political ambition, seeking positions that would increase his influence in Roman affairs.

## Adulthood

Caesar quickly ascended the political ladder, beginning with minor roles before achieving major offices. In 69 BCE, he was elected quaestor, the first step in the Roman "cursus honorum" (the sequence of public offices leading to higher positions). He later served as an aedile, organizing public games and feasts to win public favor. In 63 BCE, he became Pontifex Maximus, the chief priest of Rome, demonstrating his ability to manipulate both politics and religion.

One of the defining moments in his rise was his appointment as governor of Hispania Ulterior in 61 BCE. There, he successfully led military campaigns, showcasing his strategic brilliance. His successes in Hispania earned him a triumph, but he instead pursued a consulship in 59 BCE, forming the First Triumvirate with Pompey and Crassus. This alliance allowed him to pass reforms benefiting the populares, further strengthening his power.

Caesar's military genius was most evident during the Gallic Wars (58–50 BCE), where he expanded Roman territory by conquering Gaul (modern France and Belgium). His detailed account of these campaigns, "Commentarii de Bello Gallico", not only cemented his reputation as a great general but also served as political propaganda to justify his actions.

However, tensions with the Senate and Pompey grew. In 49 BCE, defying orders, he famously crossed the Rubicon River with his army, igniting a civil war. Within a year, he defeated Pompey's forces and took control of Rome, marking the beginning of his dictatorship.

## Private Life

Caesar's personal life was as eventful as his military and political career. He married three times – first to Cornelia, then to Pompeia, and finally to Calpurnia. His first wife, Cornelia, was the mother of his only legitimate child, Julia, who later married Pompey. Her death deeply affected him.

Caesar was also known for his numerous affairs, most notably with Cleopatra VII of Egypt. Following Pompey's defeat, he traveled to Egypt, where he became involved with Cleopatra, assisting her in securing the throne. Their relationship produced a son, Ptolemy XV, commonly known as Caesarion.

Despite his marriages and affairs, his primary love was power. His ability to charm and manipulate both allies and enemies made him a dominant force in Roman politics.

## Death

As dictator, Caesar enacted numerous reforms, including the Julian calendar and economic policies aimed at reducing debt. However, his accumulation of power alarmed the Senate, particularly the optimates, who feared he sought to make himself king.

On March 15, 44 BCE – the infamous Ides of March – Julius Caesar was assassinated by a group of senators led by Brutus and Cassius. Stabbed 23 times in the Theater of Pompey, his alleged last words, "Et tu, Brute?", express his deep sense of betrayal by Brutus, whom he had trusted as a friend. His assassination plunged Rome into chaos, leading to another civil war. His adopted heir, Octavian (later Augustus), avenged his death and ultimately became Rome's first emperor, fulfilling Caesar's vision of centralized rule.

## Character

Caesar was a complex figure – charismatic, intelligent, and ruthlessly ambitious. He was a master of strategy, both on the battlefield and in politics, often using propaganda and populist measures to secure power

He was also known for his generosity, offering clemency to defeated enemies, yet he could be merciless when necessary. His ability to inspire loyalty was unmatched, as his soldiers and supporters followed him through treacherous battles and political upheavals.

While he sought absolute power, he also believed in pragmatic governance, enacting laws that benefited the lower classes and restructuring Rome's administration for efficiency.

## Influence on Humanity

Julius Caesar's impact on history is immense. His military strategies and writings continue to be studied in military academies worldwide. His reforms, particularly the Julian calendar, form the basis of our modern calendar.

His model of centralized governance influenced the development of the Roman Empire, setting a precedent for future rulers. His name, "Caesar," became synonymous with leadership, inspiring titles such as "Kaiser" in Germany and "Tsar" in Russia.

Beyond governance and military tactics, Caesar's life and assassination have been immortalized in literature, most notably in Shakespeare's "Julius Caesar", reinforcing his place in cultural history.

In conclusion, Julius Caesar was more than a general and statesman – he was a force of change whose influence shaped the course of Western civilization. His legacy endures in politics, military strategy, literature, and governance, making him one of the most pivotal figures in world history.

# Augustus Caesar
First Roman emperor and founder of the Principate

Augustus Caesar, originally known as Gaius Octavius and later Gaius Julius Caesar Octavianus, was the first emperor of Rome and one of the most consequential figures in world history. As the adopted heir of Julius Caesar, he rose from a relatively modest background to become Rome's supreme ruler, initiating the transition from the Roman Republic to the Roman Empire. His reign, which lasted from 27 BCE until his death in 14 CE, established political stability, economic prosperity, and an era of relative peace known as the Pax Romana. His influence extended far beyond his lifetime, shaping governance, military structure, and cultural developments that would define Rome for centuries.

## Origin

Gaius Octavius was born on September 23, 63 BCE, in the town of Velletri, southeast of Rome. He came from a relatively wealthy equestrian family, though not from the highest ranks of the Roman aristocracy. His father, also named Gaius Octavius, was a respected politician and governor of Macedonia. His mother, Atia Balba Caesonia, was the niece of Julius Caesar, which linked Octavius to one of the most powerful men in Rome.

Octavius' father died when he was just four years old, leaving him under the guardianship of his mother and stepfather, Lucius Marcius Philippus. Despite his non-patrician background, his familial connection to Julius Caesar would prove crucial in shaping his future. His early life was largely overshadowed by the political turbulence in Rome, as civil wars and power struggles defined the late Republic.

## Childhood and Youth

Octavius received a rigorous education in rhetoric, philosophy, and military training. He showed early signs of intelligence and ambition, qualities that would later define his leadership. His mother and grandmother ensured that he was well-prepared for a political career, and his connection to Julius Caesar provided opportunities for advancement.

In 46 BCE, Julius Caesar, who had declared himself dictator of Rome, invited the young Octavius to join him in Hispania for a military campaign. Though illness prevented Octavius from completing the journey, this invitation underscored Caesar's growing interest in him. Two years later, in 44 BCE, Julius Caesar was assassinated by a group of senators, sending Rome into chaos. In his will, Caesar unexpectedly named Octavius as his adopted son and heir, granting him not only immense wealth but also a legitimate claim to power.

At just 18 years old, Octavius returned to Rome and quickly positioned himself as Caesar's rightful successor. He adopted the name Gaius Julius Caesar Octavianus (Octavian) and began consolidating support among Caesar's allies and legions. His rise to power was far from smooth, as he faced opposition from Mark Antony, a powerful general and former ally of Julius Caesar, as well as the Roman Senate.

## Adulthood

The power struggle following Caesar's death led to the formation of the Second Triumvirate in 43 BCE, consisting of Octavian, Mark Antony, and Marcus Lepidus. Together, they waged war against Caesar's assassins, Brutus and Cassius, ultimately defeating them at the Battle of Philippi in 42 BCE. With their enemies vanquished, the three leaders divided the Roman world among themselves.

However, tensions between Octavian and Antony soon escalated. Antony allied himself with Cleopatra, the queen of Egypt, which alarmed many Romans who feared foreign influence over Roman affairs. In 31 BCE, Octavian's forces decisively defeated Antony and Cleopatra at the Battle of Actium. Both Antony and Cleopatra later committed suicide, leaving Octavian as the sole ruler of Rome.

In 27 BCE, Octavian officially ended the Republic and assumed supreme power. The Senate granted him the title "Augustus," meaning "the revered one," and he became Rome's first emperor. Although he maintained the facade of republican governance, in reality, he held absolute control, ushering in the Roman Empire.

## Private Life

Augustus' personal life was marked by strategic marriages and political alliances. His first marriage to Clodia, the stepdaughter of Mark Antony, ended quickly. His second marriage to Scribonia produced his only biological child, Julia the Elder, but the union was short-lived.

His most significant marriage was to Livia Drusilla, whom he wed in 38 BCE. Livia became a trusted advisor and partner, playing a significant role in shaping imperial policies. Though Augustus had no sons of his own, he carefully planned his succession, ultimately selecting his stepson, Tiberius, as his heir.

Augustus was known for his relatively modest lifestyle, avoiding excessive luxury and promoting traditional Roman values. He emphasized family life, moral reforms, and social stability, enforcing laws that encouraged marriage and childbearing among the elite.

## Death

After ruling Rome for over four decades, Augustus died on August 19, 14 CE, at the age of 75. He passed away in Nola, reportedly in the presence of his wife Livia. His final words, according to historical sources, were: "I found Rome a city of bricks and left it a city of marble."

His death marked the official end of the Republic and the full institutionalization of the Roman Empire. Tiberius, his stepson and adopted heir, succeeded him, continuing the dynasty Augustus had established.

## Character

Augustus was a shrewd and pragmatic leader who understood the complexities of power. Unlike Julius Caesar, who sought direct dominance, Augustus was careful to maintain the illusion of republican institutions while holding ultimate authority. He was a master of propaganda, using literature, architecture, and coinage to craft his image as Rome's benevolent leader.

He was also highly disciplined and strategic. His ability to outmaneuver political rivals, maintain stability, and implement long-term reforms demonstrated his foresight and patience. Though he could be ruthless when necessary, he preferred to govern through consensus and institutional reforms rather than through overt displays of force.

## Influence on Humanity

Augustus' impact on world history is immeasurable. His reign marked the beginning of the Pax Romana, a period of relative peace and stability that lasted for over two centuries. His administrative, legal, and economic reforms set the foundation for the Roman Empire, influencing governance in Europe and beyond for centuries.

Key contributions of Augustus include:

**1. Political System** – He created the principate, a system that balanced imperial authority with traditional Roman institutions.

**2. Military Reforms** – Augustus professionalized the Roman military, establishing a standing army and a praetorian guard.

**3. Cultural Influence** – He patronized the arts, supporting poets like Virgil, Horace, and Ovid, who shaped Roman literary traditions.

**4. Infrastructure** – He initiated vast construction projects, including roads, aqueducts, and temples, many of which still stand today.

**5. Legal Reforms** – His policies influenced Roman law, which became the basis for many modern legal systems.

Even in modern times, Augustus' legacy endures. His approach to governance, consolidation of power, and emphasis on stability continue to serve as a model for political leadership. His reign transformed Rome into a centralized empire, ensuring its dominance for centuries.

In conclusion, Augustus Caesar was a visionary leader whose rule reshaped the ancient world. His ability to navigate political turmoil, implement long-lasting reforms, and secure Rome's future earned him a place among history's greatest rulers. His legacy continues to influence political and historical thought, proving that his impact was not confined to his own era but extended to shaping the course of human civilization.

# Jesus Christ
Religious leader and central figure of Christianity

Jesus Christ, one of the most influential figures in human history, is regarded as the central figure of Christianity. His teachings, life, death, and resurrection have shaped religious, philosophical, and cultural developments for over two millennia. Whether viewed as the Son of God, a prophet, or a historical figure, Jesus' impact on humanity is unparalleled. His message of love, compassion, and salvation continues to resonate with millions of believers worldwide.

## Origin

Jesus Christ was born around 4 BCE in Bethlehem, a small town in Judea, under Roman rule. His parents, Mary and Joseph, were devout Jews. According to the Gospels, Mary conceived Jesus through the Holy Spirit, making His birth miraculous. He was born during the reign of King Herod the Great, who, fearing the prophecy of a newborn king, ordered the massacre of infants in Bethlehem. To protect their child, Mary and Joseph fled to Egypt and later returned to Nazareth, where Jesus grew up.

The name "Jesus" originates from the Hebrew "Yeshua," meaning "salvation" or "God saves." The title "Christ" comes from the Greek "Christos," meaning "the anointed one." According to Jewish prophecy, Jesus was believed to be the Messiah who would bring salvation to humanity.

## Childhood and Youth

Little is documented about Jesus' childhood, but the Gospels provide a few glimpses into His early years. He grew up in Nazareth, a modest town in Galilee, where He was raised in a Jewish household. His earthly father, Joseph, was a carpenter, and it is assumed that Jesus learned this trade as well.

One significant episode from His youth is recorded in the Gospel of Luke. At the age of 12, Jesus accompanied His parents to Jerusalem for the Passover festival. When they left the city, they realized He was missing and found Him in the temple, engaged in deep discussion with Jewish teachers. His wisdom astonished the elders, foreshadowing His future role as a teacher and spiritual leader.

Though not much is known about His adolescence, Jesus likely lived an ordinary Jewish life, adhering to religious customs and studying the Hebrew scriptures.

## Adulthood

At around 30 years old, Jesus began His public ministry. Before embarking on His mission, He was baptized by John the Baptist in the Jordan River. This event marked the beginning of His spiritual work, as the Holy Spirit descended upon Him, and a voice from heaven declared, "This is my beloved Son, in whom I am well pleased" (Matthew 3:17).

For the next three years, Jesus traveled throughout Galilee, Judea, and surrounding areas, preaching about the Kingdom of God, healing the sick, and performing miracles. His teachings emphasized love, humility, forgiveness, and faith in God. Some of His most famous teachings include:

- **The Sermon on the Mount** – A collection of moral and ethical teachings, including the Beatitudes, which outline the blessings for the humble, merciful, and peacemakers.
- **Parables** – Short, allegorical stories used to convey deep spiritual truths, such as the Parable of the Good Samaritan and the Parable of the Prodigal Son.
- **Miracles** – Acts of divine power, including healing the sick, feeding thousands, calming storms, and even raising the dead.

Jesus also gathered a group of twelve disciples, who became His closest followers and helped spread His teachings. His growing popularity, however, drew the ire of religious leaders, who saw Him as a threat to their authority and traditions.

## Private Life

Jesus led a life of humility and simplicity. Unlike many leaders of His time, He had no political aspirations or material wealth. He associated with the poor, sinners, and outcasts, demonstrating His message of inclusivity and love.

Jesus never married. Instead, He focused entirely on His divine mission.

His relationship with His family was complex. While His mother, Mary, played a significant role in His life, His siblings initially doubted His identity as the Messiah. However, after His resurrection, some of His brothers, particularly James, became influential leaders in the early Christian movement.

## Death

Jesus' increasing influence alarmed both Jewish religious authorities and the Roman rulers. The Pharisees and Sadducees saw Him as a blasphemer, while the Roman governor, Pontius Pilate, viewed Him as a potential political threat.

During the Passover festival, Jesus was arrested in the Garden of Gethsemane, following Judas Iscariot's betrayal. He was subjected to a series of trials before the Jewish Sanhedrin and Roman authorities. Despite Pilate's reluctance, the crowd demanded His crucifixion, and He was sentenced to death.

Jesus was scourged, forced to carry His cross, and crucified at Golgotha. As He suffered on the cross, He spoke words of forgiveness, compassion, and fulfillment of prophecy. After hours of agony, He died, saying, "It is finished" (John 19:30).

His body was placed in a tomb, but three days later, according to Christian belief, He rose from the dead. His resurrection became the cornerstone of Christian faith, symbolizing victory over sin and death.

## Character

Jesus' character was defined by love, compassion, humility, and unwavering faith. He embodied divine wisdom, yet He was approachable to the common people. His willingness to forgive even His enemies showcased His divine mercy. He was also a revolutionary figure, challenging societal norms and advocating for justice, truth, and righteousness. Despite being persecuted, He remained steadfast in His mission, never retaliating with violence but responding with love and grace.

His humility was evident in His choice of lifestyle, and His teachings emphasized service over power. He washed the feet of His disciples, teaching that true leadership comes from serving others.

## Influence on Humanity

Jesus Christ's influence on humanity is immeasurable. His teachings laid the foundation for Christianity, the world's largest religion, with billions of followers across the world. His message of love, forgiveness, and salvation continues to inspire people from all walks of life.

His impact extends beyond religion. His teachings on morality, justice, and compassion have shaped laws, ethics, and philosophies. Many humanitarian movements, including those led by figures like Martin Luther King Jr. and Mahatma Gandhi, were inspired by Jesus' principles.

His legacy in art, literature, and music is vast, with countless works depicting His life and message. The Christian calendar is based on His birth, dividing history into B.C. (Before Christ) and A.D. (Anno Domini).

In conclusion, Jesus Christ's life, death, and resurrection changed the course of human history. His message of unconditional love and hope continues to guide and inspire billions, proving that His influence transcends time and culture. Whether seen as the Son of God or a moral teacher, His legacy endures as a beacon of faith and truth for all humanity.

# Paul of Tarsus
Missionary and theologian of early Christianity

Paul of Tarsus, also known as Saint Paul, is one of the most influential figures in Christianity. Originally a persecutor of Christians, he underwent a dramatic conversion and became one of the most important apostles, spreading the message of Jesus Christ throughout the Roman Empire. His letters, which form a significant portion of the New Testament, have shaped Christian theology, ethics, and ecclesiastical structure. His missionary journeys and theological contributions continue to impact religious thought and practice to this day.

## Origin

Paul was born around 5 CE in Tarsus, a prominent city in the Roman province of Cilicia (modern-day Turkey). His birth name was Saul, a common Jewish name, reflecting his Jewish heritage. He was born into a devout Jewish family of the tribe of Benjamin, and his family adhered strictly to the Pharisaic tradition of Judaism. Saul was also a Roman citizen, a status that granted him privileges and protection within the empire. This dual identity – Jewish by religion and Roman by citizenship – would later play a crucial role in his ministry.

Tarsus was a significant center of Greek learning and culture, and as a result, Saul grew up exposed to both Jewish and Greco-Roman traditions. His ability to bridge these cultural worlds later enabled him to communicate effectively with diverse audiences.

## Childhood and Youth

Saul was raised in a strict Jewish household, where he was deeply immersed in Hebrew scriptures and traditions. At a young age, he was sent to Jerusalem to study under the renowned rabbi Gamaliel, one of the most respected teachers of Jewish law at the time. Under Gamaliel's tutelage, Saul became well-versed in the Torah, the Prophets, and Jewish traditions. He excelled in religious studies and became a zealous adherent of Pharisaic Judaism. During his youth, Saul developed a deep-seated opposition to the emerging Christian movement. He viewed the followers of Jesus as heretics who threatened the purity of Jewish faith. His zeal for the law led him to become an active persecutor of Christians, participating in the arrest and execution of early believers. One of the most notable events in this period of his life was his presence at the stoning of Stephen, the first Christian martyr (Acts 7:58). Saul's dedication to eradicating Christianity was unwavering, and he sought to destroy the movement by any means necessary.

## Adulthood

Saul's life took a dramatic turn while he was on his way to Damascus to arrest more Christians. According to the Book of Acts, he experienced a divine encounter with Jesus Christ. A bright light from heaven blinded him, and he heard a voice saying, "Saul, Saul, why are you persecuting me?" (Acts 9:4). This moment marked his conversion to Christianity. He was led to Damascus, where a disciple named Ananias healed his blindness and baptized him. From that point forward, he took the name Paul and dedicated his life to spreading the Gospel.

Paul began his ministry in the synagogues, preaching that Jesus was the Messiah. His message was met with resistance, and he faced persecution from both Jews and Romans. Despite this, he embarked on extensive missionary journeys, traveling throughout Asia Minor, Greece, and Rome. He established Christian communities in major cities such as Corinth, Ephesus, and Philippi, writing letters to these communities to guide and strengthen their faith.

Paul's theological contributions were profound. He emphasized that salvation was available to all people, not just Jews, through faith in Jesus Christ. His teachings on grace, justification, and Christian ethics formed the foundation of Christian doctrine. His letters, including Romans, Corinthians, Galatians, and Ephesians, addressed complex theological issues and provided practical instructions for Christian living.

## Private Life

Paul's life was primarily dedicated to his mission, and there is little evidence that he married or had children. In his letters, he expressed a preference for celibacy, arguing that it allowed him to focus entirely on his calling (1 Corinthians 7:7-8). He lived a life of hardship, often traveling long distances, facing imprisonment, beatings, and other forms of persecution.

He also formed deep friendships and mentorships with fellow believers. Figures such as Barnabas, Timothy, Luke, and Silas played significant roles in his ministry. He relied on these companions for support and collaboration as he spread the Gospel.

Paul was known for his adaptability. He worked as a tentmaker to support himself financially, refusing to rely solely on donations from churches. This self-sufficiency allowed him to maintain his integrity and credibility as a missionary.

## Death

Paul's unwavering commitment to spreading Christianity ultimately led to his arrest. He was imprisoned multiple times, and according to tradition, he was eventually taken to Rome for trial. The details of his final days are uncertain, but historical sources suggest that he was executed during the reign of Emperor Nero, around 64-67 CE.

It is believed that Paul was beheaded, a method of execution reserved for Roman citizens. His martyrdom solidified his status as one of the great figures of early Christianity. Though he died, his teachings and writings continued to spread, shaping the development of the Christian church for centuries to come.

## Character

Paul was a man of intense conviction and passion. Before his conversion, his zeal was directed toward preserving Jewish traditions by persecuting Christians. After his transformation, that same zeal was redirected toward spreading the Gospel. He was tireless in his mission, enduring immense suffering without wavering in his faith.

He was also deeply intellectual, crafting some of the most profound theological reflections in Christian history. His ability to engage both Jewish and Gentile audiences demonstrated his wisdom and adaptability.

Despite his strong personality, he remained humble, often referring to himself as the "least of the apostles" (1 Corinthians 15:9).

Paul's resilience, courage, and dedication to truth made him a formidable leader. Even in his final letters, written from prison, he encouraged fellow believers to remain steadfast in their faith.

## Influence on Humanity

Paul's influence on humanity cannot be overstated. He played a crucial role in transforming Christianity from a small Jewish sect into a global faith. His missionary efforts established Christian communities across the Roman Empire, paving the way for Christianity's expansion.

His letters form a significant portion of the New Testament and continue to be studied for their theological depth and moral guidance. Concepts such as grace, faith, and the universality of salvation are central to Christian doctrine because of Paul's writings.

Beyond theology, his ideas have shaped Western thought, ethics, and legal principles. His teachings on love, unity, and moral responsibility have influenced countless movements, from civil rights to humanitarian efforts.

Paul's legacy extends far beyond religion. His life serves as a testament to the power of transformation, showing how an individual can change and dedicate themselves to a higher purpose. His ability to articulate deep spiritual truths while remaining grounded in practical wisdom ensures that his impact will endure for generations.

In conclusion, Paul of Tarsus was more than an apostle; he was a revolutionary thinker, a tireless missionary, and a foundational figure in Christianity. His legacy lives on in the millions of believers who continue to find inspiration in his words and example.

# Cai Lun
Chinese inventor of paper

Cai Lun, a Chinese eunuch, official, and inventor of the Han Dynasty, is best known for his revolutionary invention of paper around 105 CE. His contributions to Chinese civilization and the world at large cannot be overstated. Before his innovation, writing materials were costly and cumbersome, relying on silk, bamboo, and wooden tablets. Cai Lun's ingenuity led to the creation of a lightweight and inexpensive writing medium that transformed communication, record-keeping, and literature, making knowledge more accessible. His influence continues to shape education, administration, and culture worldwide.

## Origin

Cai Lun was born around 50 CE in Guiyang (modern-day Leiyang, Hunan Province) during the Eastern Han Dynasty. Although little is known about his early ancestry, it is believed that he came from a modest background. The Han Dynasty was a period of great intellectual and technological advancement, with developments in metallurgy, medicine, and governance. The empire was flourishing, with Emperor Ming of Han and later Emperor He of Han overseeing its stability and expansion.

Cai Lun's birthplace, Hunan, was a region known for its cultural significance and natural resources, which may have played a role in his later experimentation with paper-making materials. Despite his humble beginnings, he managed to rise through the ranks of the imperial court, demonstrating both intelligence and political acumen.

## Childhood and Youth

There is little recorded about Cai Lun's early life, but given his later rise to prominence, it is assumed that he received an education suited for a government official. The Han Dynasty valued scholarship and bureaucratic service, and young men with potential were often groomed for administrative roles. His ability to navigate the political structures of the imperial court suggests that he was well-versed in Confucian philosophy, classical literature, and bureaucratic procedures.

Cai Lun entered the service of the Han court as a eunuch, a common practice in ancient China for those seeking high-ranking government positions. Eunuchs often held considerable influence in the emperor's inner circle, as they were trusted officials who had no familial ambitions that could threaten the imperial lineage. Through his diligence and intellect, he steadily ascended in the court hierarchy, eventually becoming a close advisor to Emperor He of Han.

## Adulthood

Cai Lun's career as a court official saw him taking on numerous responsibilities, including overseeing the manufacture of weapons and other administrative duties. However, his most significant contribution came in 105 CE when he presented his invention of paper to the emperor.

Before Cai Lun's time, Chinese writing was recorded on materials such as silk, bamboo, and wooden tablets. Silk was expensive and limited in supply, while bamboo and wood were cumbersome and impractical for extensive documentation. Recognizing the need for a more efficient writing material, Cai Lun experimented with various substances, including tree bark, hemp, rags, and fishnets, eventually developing a process that produced a lightweight, durable, and affordable paper.

His invention was officially recognized by Emperor He, who praised him for his ingenuity. The new paper was easier to produce and transport, and it quickly gained popularity throughout the empire. It was not long before it replaced traditional writing materials and became the standard medium for scholars, administrators, and artists.

Cai Lun's contributions earned him great favor at court, and he was promoted to higher ranks within the imperial administration. He was granted noble titles and given considerable influence over court affairs. However, his association with palace intrigues and shifting political alliances would later contribute to his downfall.

## Private Life

Despite his high standing, little is known about Cai Lun's personal life. As a eunuch, he was unable to have children or engage in conventional family life, a common sacrifice for those in his position. His life was likely centered around his duties in the imperial court, where he was deeply involved in administrative and technical developments. While there are no records of close friendships or relationships, Cai Lun's legacy suggests he was deeply dedicated to his work. His contributions to paper-making and his continued service in the government indicate a man whose life was devoted to intellectual and technological progress rather than personal indulgence.

## Death

Cai Lun's fortunes took a turn for the worse following the death of Emperor He of Han. With the ascension of Emperor An of Han, political shifts led to the downfall of many of the former emperor's close officials. Cai Lun, who had been closely associated with the powerful Empress Dowager Deng, fell out of favor. Facing accusations and potential disgrace, he chose to take his own life in 121 CE rather than endure humiliation. While his end was tragic, his contributions to history had already cemented his legacy. His invention continued to spread across China and eventually reached other parts of the world, profoundly influencing global civilization.

## Character

Cai Lun was an innovator, a dedicated servant of the Han court, and a visionary thinker. His ability to recognize the need for a better writing material and his determination to develop and perfect it demonstrate his intellectual prowess. Despite being a eunuch, a status often looked down upon in certain historical narratives, he managed to secure significant power and influence through his merit and ingenuity. His story is also one of resilience and adaptability. Rising from modest beginnings, he navigated the complexities of imperial politics, making lasting contributions despite the risks involved in court life. Though his demise was a result of political intrigue, his legacy endured far beyond his time.

## Influence on Humanity

Cai Lun's invention of paper was a turning point in human history. His method of paper-making eventually spread beyond China, reaching the Islamic world by the 8th century and Europe by the 12th century. The availability of paper revolutionized communication, education, and governance.

**1. Advancement of Literature and Education** – Paper enabled the mass production of books, allowing knowledge to be preserved and disseminated more efficiently. This had a profound impact on literacy rates and intellectual development.

**2. Government and Bureaucracy** – Paper made record-keeping more efficient, contributing to the growth of organized government structures. The Han Dynasty's administrative efficiency was significantly enhanced by the adoption of paper.

**3. Art and Culture** – Paper became an essential medium for calligraphy, painting, and documentation, shaping the artistic traditions of East Asia.

**4. Scientific and Technological Growth** – The ability to record findings and share knowledge more effectively laid the foundation for future scientific discoveries and technological advancements.

Today, paper remains one of the most widely used materials worldwide. Though digital technology has transformed communication, paper continues to play a vital role in education, publishing, and administration. Cai Lun's contribution is a testament to how one innovation can shape civilizations across millennia.

---

In conclusion, Cai Lun was more than just an inventor; he was a transformative figure whose ingenuity changed the course of history. His legacy endures in every book, document, and piece of artwork that has ever been created on paper. His impact is a reminder that innovation, no matter how simple it may seem, can have profound and lasting effects on humanity.

# Constantine the Great
Roman emperor who legitimized Christianity

Constantine the Great, also known as Constantine I, was one of the most pivotal figures in Roman and world history. As the first Roman emperor to convert to Christianity, he played a crucial role in shaping the future of both the empire and the Christian faith. His reign marked the transition from ancient pagan traditions to a new era of religious tolerance and state Christianity. His military victories, administrative reforms, and founding of Constantinople ensured his legacy as one of Rome's most transformative leaders.

## Origin

Flavius Valerius Constantinus, later known as Constantine the Great, was born around 272 CE in Naissus, a city in the Roman province of Moesia (modern-day Niš, Serbia). His father, Constantius Chlorus, was a distinguished Roman general who later became one of the Tetrarchs ruling the empire. His mother, Helena, was of humble origins but would later become Saint Helena due to her role in promoting Christianity.

The Roman Empire at the time of Constantine's birth was experiencing a period of instability, with multiple rulers governing different regions under the Tetrarchy system established by Emperor Diocletian. This political structure aimed to ensure stability but often led to power struggles and civil wars, setting the stage for Constantine's rise.

## Childhood and Youth

Constantine spent much of his early life at the imperial court of Emperor Diocletian in Nicomedia (modern-day Turkey). He received an excellent education in Latin and Greek, as well as military training. As the son of a high-ranking Roman official, he was exposed to the intricacies of governance, warfare, and diplomacy from a young age.

His youth was marked by political intrigue. When his father, Constantius Chlorus, was appointed Caesar (junior emperor) of the western Roman Empire in 293 CE, Constantine remained in the east as a hostage to ensure his father's loyalty. During this time, he observed Diocletian's rule and the workings of the empire firsthand.

In 305 CE, Diocletian and his co-emperor, Maximian, abdicated, leading to a shift in power. Constantine managed to escape the eastern court and rejoin his father in Britain, where he witnessed his father's campaigns against the Picts and other local tribes. Shortly after his father's death in 306 CE, Constantine was proclaimed emperor by his troops, beginning his rise to power.

## Adulthood

Constantine's rule was characterized by military campaigns, political maneuvering, and religious transformation. Initially, he had to contend with rival claimants to the throne, including Maxentius and Licinius. His defining moment came in 312 CE at the Battle of the Milvian Bridge, where he reportedly saw a vision of a cross in the sky with the words "In Hoc Signo Vinces" ("In this sign, you will conquer"). Taking this as a divine endorsement, he ordered his troops to paint Christian symbols on their shields and won a decisive victory against Maxentius.

Following his victory, Constantine consolidated his rule over the western empire. In 313 CE, he and Licinius issued the Edict of Milan, granting religious tolerance to Christians and marking a turning point in Christian history. However, tensions between Constantine and Licinius eventually led to a civil war, which Constantine won in 324 CE, making him the sole ruler of the Roman Empire.

As emperor, Constantine implemented sweeping reforms. He reorganized the military, strengthened the economy, and centralized administrative power. His most ambitious project was the foundation of Constantinople (modern-day Istanbul) in 330 CE, which became the new capital of the empire. The city was strategically located and symbolized the shift of power from Rome to the eastern provinces.

## Private Life

Constantine was married twice, first to Minervina, with whom he had a son, Crispus, and later to Fausta, the daughter of Emperor Maximian. His marriages were politically motivated, aimed at securing alliances within the imperial family.

Despite his public embrace of Christianity, Constantine's private life was marked by intrigue and tragedy. In 326 CE, he ordered the execution of his son Crispus and later his wife Fausta under mysterious circumstances. The reasons for these actions remain debated, with some historians suggesting court conspiracies or accusations of treason.

Constantine's relationship with Christianity was complex. While he favored the religion and supported the Church, he was only baptized on his deathbed, possibly as a strategic move to absolve him of his past sins.

## Death

Constantine fell ill in 337 CE while preparing for a military campaign against Persia. Realizing his time was short, he sought baptism and was baptized by Eusebius of Nicomedia, a prominent Christian bishop. He died on May 22, 337 CE, near Nicomedia.

Following his death, his three sons – Constantine II, Constantius II, and Constans – divided the empire among themselves, leading to further conflicts. Despite this, Constantine's legacy endured, and he was venerated as a saint in the Eastern Orthodox Church.

## Character

Constantine was a shrewd and pragmatic leader. His military prowess and political acumen allowed him to navigate Rome's turbulent political landscape successfully. He was ambitious, willing to make bold decisions, and adept at consolidating power.

While he embraced Christianity, some scholars argue that his motivations were as much political as they were spiritual. By aligning himself with Christianity, he gained the support of a growing religious movement, which helped stabilize his rule.

Despite his achievements, his rule was not without controversy. His actions against his son and wife, as well as his suppression of rival factions, paint a picture of a ruler who was as ruthless as he was visionary.

## Influence on Humanity

Constantine's influence on history is immense. His endorsement of Christianity led to its spread throughout the Roman Empire and beyond. His policies paved the way for Christianity to become the dominant religion of Europe, shaping Western civilization.

His founding of Constantinople had long-term consequences. The city became a cultural and economic hub for centuries and played a central role in both the Byzantine and Ottoman Empires. Today, Istanbul remains one of the world's most historically significant cities.

Constantine's legal and administrative reforms strengthened the Roman state, influencing governance structures in medieval and modern Europe. His establishment of a Christian empire shaped the relationship between church and state, a legacy that continues to influence politics and religion today.

---

In conclusion, Constantine the Great was more than just a ruler – he was a transformative figure whose decisions altered the course of history. His embrace of Christianity, political reforms, and military achievements ensured that his impact would be felt for millennia. Whether seen as a saint or a strategist, his legacy remains one of the most enduring in world history.

# Attila the Hun
Ruler of the Huns and conqueror of Europe

Attila the Hun, one of history's most feared and formidable leaders, was the ruler of the Huns from 434 to 453 CE. Renowned for his military prowess and ruthless leadership, he led his people in a series of campaigns that shook the foundations of the Roman Empire. His name became synonymous with destruction and terror, but he was also a skilled diplomat and strategist. His legacy endures as a symbol of power, ambition, and the changing face of Europe in the early medieval period.

## Origin

Attila was born around 406 CE into the ruling family of the Huns, a nomadic people of Central Asian origin who had migrated westward into Eastern Europe. The Huns had already established themselves as a formidable force, striking fear into the Roman Empire and other neighboring nations.

Attila belonged to the Hun royal lineage and was the nephew of the Hunnic kings Octar and Ruga (also spelled Rugila), who ruled over a vast confederation of tribes. By the time of his birth, the Huns had become a major power, threatening both the Eastern and Western Roman Empires. His early exposure to the politics and warfare of the Hunnic court would shape his ambitions and leadership style.

The origins of the Huns themselves remain debated among historians. Some scholars believe they were descendants of the Xiongnu, a nomadic confederation that had troubled China's borders centuries earlier. Others argue that they emerged from various Turkic and Mongolic tribes. Regardless of their origins, by Attila's time, the Huns had become a dominant force in European geopolitics.

## Childhood and Youth

As a child, Attila was raised among the elite of the Hunnic society, receiving an education in warfare, diplomacy, and leadership. He was likely trained in archery, horseback riding, and the martial traditions of his people, which emphasized speed, mobility, and psychological warfare.

The Huns relied on their famed cavalry tactics, using swift hit-and-run raids to devastate enemy forces. Attila would have been immersed in these strategies from an early age, learning the skills necessary to command an army and strike fear into his opponents.

During his youth, Attila may have traveled to the Roman Empire as part of diplomatic exchanges. In 418 CE, the Romans and Huns established agreements that included hostage exchanges. It is believed that Attila spent some time in the Roman court, where he observed Roman military organization, administration, and tactics. This exposure provided him with valuable insights that he would later use against the empire.

## Adulthood

Attila rose to power in 434 CE alongside his brother Bleda after the death of their uncle, King Ruga. The two ruled jointly, consolidating Hunnic control over vast territories in Central and Eastern Europe. They negotiated treaties with the Eastern Roman Empire, extracting large tributes in gold while simultaneously launching raids into Roman lands.

In 445 CE, Attila became the sole ruler after reportedly assassinating his brother Bleda. With full control over the Hunnic forces, he intensified his campaigns against both the Eastern and Western Roman Empires.

His most infamous raids occurred between 447 and 451 CE. He devastated the Balkans, forcing the Eastern Roman Empire to pay massive tributes to avoid further destruction. However, his most ambitious campaign came in 451 CE when he invaded Gaul (modern-day France). There, he faced a coalition of Roman and Visigothic forces led by General Flavius Aetius at the Battle of the Catalaunian Plains. This battle, one of the largest of the late Roman period, ended in a costly stalemate. Though Attila was forced to retreat, his reputation as an unstoppable force remained intact.

In 452 CE, Attila turned his attention to Italy, sacking several cities. However, he halted his advance after meeting with Pope Leo I, who reportedly convinced him to turn back. The reasons behind this decision remain unclear — some believe a combination of famine, disease, and logistical challenges forced Attila's withdrawal.

## Private Life

Despite his fearsome reputation, Attila was known for his simple lifestyle compared to other rulers of the time. He reportedly preferred a plain wooden cup over golden goblets and lived modestly, even as his warriors indulged in luxury.

Attila had multiple wives, as polygamy was common among the Huns. His marriages were often politically motivated, strengthening alliances with various tribal leaders. His personal life was marked by both ambition and intrigue, as he sought to expand his influence through strategic relationships.

One of the most notable events of his personal life was his engagement to Honoria, the sister of Emperor Valentinian III. Honoria, desperate to escape an unwanted marriage, sent Attila a plea for help, which he interpreted as a marriage proposal. He demanded half of the Western Roman Empire as her dowry, a claim that further soured relations with Rome and fueled his invasion of Italy.

## Death

Attila died unexpectedly in 453 CE under mysterious circumstances. According to historical accounts, he died on his wedding night after marrying a young woman named Ildico. Some sources claim that he suffered a fatal nosebleed due to excessive drinking, while others suggest he may have been poisoned.

Following his death, the Hunnic Empire began to unravel. His sons fought among themselves for control, weakening the once-mighty Hunnic confederation. Within a few decades, the Huns had lost their dominance, disappearing from history as a major power.

## Character

Attila was both feared and respected by his enemies and allies. He was a brilliant strategist, capable of uniting various nomadic tribes under his command. His ability to instill loyalty among his warriors and terror among his enemies made him one of the most formidable leaders of his time.

Despite his reputation as a ruthless conqueror, Attila was also a shrewd diplomat. He skillfully negotiated treaties, extracted massive tributes from the Romans, and manipulated political rivalries to his advantage. His leadership was marked by a blend of calculated aggression and tactical restraint.

Attila's austere lifestyle and preference for simplicity set him apart from other rulers who indulged in excess. However, his ambition knew no bounds, and his relentless pursuit of power ultimately defined his legacy.

## Influence on Humanity

Attila's impact on history was profound. His campaigns contributed to the destabilization of the Roman Empire, hastening its decline. His invasions forced Rome to divert resources, weaken its defenses, and ultimately struggle to maintain its vast territories.

His legacy endured in European folklore, where he was depicted as both a terrifying warlord and a legendary ruler. In the centuries that followed, his name became a symbol of conquest and destruction.

While his empire did not last, Attila's influence on military strategy, diplomacy, and leadership remained significant. His ability to unite disparate tribes and challenge the Roman Empire demonstrated the power of nomadic confederations in shaping world history.

In conclusion, Attila the Hun was a complex and formidable figure. His military genius, political acumen, and indomitable will left an indelible mark on the ancient world. His reign may have been brief, but his legend continues to captivate historians, scholars, and storytellers to this day.

# Muhammad

Founder and prophet of Islam

Muhammad ibn Abdullah, the founder of Islam and one of the most influential figures in world history, was born in 570 CE in Mecca. As the last prophet in Islamic tradition, he played a crucial role in shaping the religious, political, and social landscape of Arabia. His teachings, recorded in the Quran and Hadith, continue to influence over a billion followers worldwide.

## Origin

Muhammad was born into the Hashim clan of the Quraysh tribe, a powerful merchant family in Mecca. His lineage traced back to the prophet Abraham through his son Ishmael, giving him a noble ancestry. His father, Abdullah, died before his birth, and his mother, Amina, passed away when he was only six years old, leaving him an orphan at a young age.

Mecca was a thriving trade center, known for its religious significance due to the Kaaba, a sacred sanctuary that housed various idols worshipped by different tribes. The city's strategic location made it a hub of commerce, where caravans from across the Arabian Peninsula converged. However, it was also a society plagued by social inequalities, tribal rivalries, and polytheistic traditions.

## Childhood and Youth

After the death of his parents, Muhammad was cared for by his grandfather, Abdul Muttalib, and later by his uncle, Abu Talib. Despite his early hardships, he grew up with strong moral values and earned a reputation for honesty and trustworthiness. This integrity earned him the nickname "Al-Amin" (the trustworthy).

As a young man, Muhammad worked as a shepherd and later became involved in trade, accompanying his uncle on commercial expeditions to Syria and Yemen. His experiences in business exposed him to different cultures and religious traditions, deepening his understanding of the world beyond Mecca.

At the age of 25, Muhammad was employed by Khadijah, a wealthy widow and businesswoman, to manage her trade caravans. Impressed by his honesty and skills, she proposed marriage, and they wed despite their 15-year age difference. Their marriage was one of love and mutual respect, and they had several children, including Fatimah, who would later play a significant role in Islamic history.

## Adulthood

As Muhammad entered adulthood, he became increasingly reflective about the state of Meccan society. Troubled by the idol worship, social injustices, and tribal conflicts, he often retreated to the Cave of Hira in the mountains surrounding Mecca to meditate.

At the age of 40, during one of these retreats, he received his first revelation from the angel Gabriel. The words, later compiled into the Quran, declared the oneness of God and called for justice, compassion, and faith. Initially frightened, Muhammad confided in his wife Khadijah, who reassured and supported him.

For the next 23 years, Muhammad continued to receive revelations and began preaching Islam. His message was met with hostility from Mecca's ruling elite, who saw his monotheistic teachings as a threat to their political and economic power. Despite persecution, his followers grew in number, attracting people from all walks of life.

In 622 CE, facing increasing opposition, Muhammad and his followers migrated to Medina in an event known as the Hijra. This migration marked the beginning of the Islamic calendar and transformed Muhammad from a preacher into a statesman. In Medina, he established a constitution that promoted religious tolerance, social justice, and unity among diverse communities.

Over the next decade, Muhammad led his followers in defending their new community against Meccan aggression, culminating in the conquest of Mecca in 630 CE. Rather than seeking revenge, he granted amnesty to his former enemies and cleansed the Kaaba of idols, reaffirming the worship of one God.

## Private Life

Muhammad's personal life was marked by simplicity and humility. Despite his leadership role, he lived modestly, performing household chores and engaging with his community. He was known for his kindness, generosity, and patience, particularly toward the poor, orphans, and women.

After Khadijah's death, he married multiple wives, primarily for political and social reasons. His marriages helped unite different tribes and provided protection to widows in need. Among his wives, Aisha played a significant role in preserving his teachings and contributing to early Islamic scholarship.

Muhammad treated his family and companions with compassion and emphasized ethical conduct in all aspects of life. His interactions set an example for his followers, reinforcing the principles of justice, mercy, and righteousness.

## Death

In 632 CE, after delivering his farewell sermon during his final pilgrimage, Muhammad fell ill. He passed away in Medina at the age of 63 and was buried in his house, which later became part of the Prophet's Mosque. His death marked the end of prophetic revelation but the beginning of Islam's rapid expansion across the world.

Following his passing, his closest companions, led by Abu Bakr, ensured the continuity of his teachings and governance. The Rashidun Caliphate was established, laying the foundation for the Islamic Golden Age and the spread of Islamic civilization.

## Character

Muhammad's character was defined by humility, integrity, and compassion. He led by example, emphasizing the importance of truth, justice, and moral conduct. Despite facing immense challenges, he remained patient and steadfast in his mission.

He was known for his forgiveness, even toward those who had wronged him. His treatment of prisoners of war, his advocacy for women's rights, and his commitment to social justice reflected his deep concern for humanity.

As a leader, he balanced diplomacy with decisiveness. He negotiated treaties, resolved conflicts, and upheld ethical standards, earning the trust of his followers and adversaries alike. His ability to unite diverse communities under a single faith was a testament to his wisdom and vision.

## Influence on Humanity

Muhammad's influence extends far beyond religion. His teachings laid the foundation for a civilization that contributed to advancements in science, philosophy, art, and governance. The principles of justice, equality, and charity that he promoted continue to inspire millions worldwide.

Islam, the religion he preached, has grown into one of the world's major faiths, shaping the lives of over 1.8 billion people. The Quran and Hadith serve as guiding principles for personal and societal conduct, influencing legal systems, ethics, and culture across diverse regions.

His emphasis on education led to the flourishing of Islamic scholarship, which preserved and expanded upon the knowledge of ancient civilizations. The Islamic Golden Age saw significant achievements in medicine, astronomy, mathematics, and literature, all of which can be traced back to the values he instilled.

In modern times, his teachings on social justice, compassion, and the dignity of all human beings remain relevant. His message of monotheism and moral responsibility continues to resonate, making him one of the most significant figures in human history.

In conclusion, Muhammad's life was a testament to perseverance, faith, and transformative leadership. His legacy endures not only in religious devotion but also in the cultural, intellectual, and moral advancements that continue to shape humanity.

# Umar ibn al-Khattab
Second caliph and architect of the Islamic empire

Umar ibn al-Khattab, the second caliph of Islam, was one of the most influential leaders in Islamic history. Known for his strong leadership, justice, and administrative reforms, he played a crucial role in expanding the Islamic empire and strengthening its governance. His policies and military conquests laid the foundation for an Islamic civilization that thrived for centuries.

## Origin

Umar ibn al-Khattab was born in approximately 583 CE in Mecca, in the powerful Banu Adi clan of the Quraysh tribe. His family was of moderate standing, engaged in trade and herding. Despite not being from the wealthiest faction of the Quraysh, the Banu Adi held influence in Meccan politics. Umar's father, Khattab ibn Nufayl, was known for his strong personality, and his mother, Hantama bint Hisham, belonged to a notable lineage.

His upbringing took place in an environment that valued tribal honor, courage, and loyalty. He grew up in a society where wealth and social status played a critical role in determining one's standing, but he also witnessed the injustices within pre-Islamic Arabian society.

## Childhood and Youth

Umar was known for his physical strength and intelligence from a young age. He was one of the few individuals in Mecca who learned to read and write, a rare skill at the time. He developed a reputation as a fierce and skilled wrestler and horseman, which later played a role in his military leadership.

Before embracing Islam, Umar was deeply involved in Meccan tribal affairs. He was a staunch opponent of the Prophet Muhammad and actively participated in the persecution of early Muslims. His resistance to Islam was fueled by his adherence to the Quraysh's polytheistic traditions and his belief that Islam threatened the unity and power of his tribe.

However, Umar's life took a dramatic turn when he converted to Islam in 616 CE. According to Islamic tradition, he set out to kill the Prophet but was redirected upon learning that his own sister had embraced Islam. Moved by the recitation of the Quran, he had a change of heart and immediately pledged his faith. His conversion was a turning point for the Muslim community, as it emboldened them to practice their religion more openly.

## Adulthood

After his conversion, Umar became one of the closest companions of Prophet Muhammad. He played a crucial role in defending and organizing the Muslim community, particularly during their migration to Medina and subsequent battles against the Quraysh.

Following the death of the Prophet in 632 CE, Abu Bakr was elected as the first caliph, with Umar serving as his chief advisor. Umar's counsel was instrumental in stabilizing the Muslim community during this critical transition.

In 634 CE, after Abu Bakr's death, Umar was chosen as the second caliph of Islam. His leadership was marked by rapid territorial expansion and administrative reforms. Under his rule, the Islamic empire expanded significantly, incorporating regions such as Persia, Egypt, Syria, and Jerusalem. His military campaigns were not merely conquests but were followed by well-structured governance and economic policies that helped integrate the newly acquired lands into the Islamic state.

## Private Life

Despite ruling an empire, Umar lived a life of simplicity and humility. He rejected luxury, often wearing patched clothes and eating simple meals. Unlike many rulers of his time, he remained accessible to his people, ensuring that justice was upheld for all.

Umar had multiple wives and children, but his family never enjoyed privileges over others. He insisted on fairness, ensuring that his relatives did not receive special treatment in governance or wealth distribution. His leadership style was marked by a deep concern for social justice. He personally oversaw the distribution of state funds, ensuring that the poor, widows, and orphans were taken care of. His nights were often spent walking the streets of Medina to check on the welfare of his people.

## Death

Umar's reign came to an abrupt end in 644 CE when he was assassinated by a Persian slave named Abu Lu'lu'a Firuz. The attack occurred while he was leading the Fajr (dawn) prayer in Medina. Mortally wounded, he refused to appoint a successor, instead leaving the decision to a council of six prominent companions.

Umar died three days after the attack and was buried next to Prophet Muhammad and Abu Bakr in Medina. His death marked the end of an era of rapid expansion and the beginning of new political challenges for the Islamic state.

## Character

Umar was known for his strong sense of justice, discipline, and leadership. He was firm yet compassionate, ensuring that laws were followed while showing mercy to those in need. His governance was based on principles of accountability, and he demanded the same from his officials.

He was deeply religious and spent much of his time studying the Quran and seeking guidance from the teachings of the Prophet. His humility was evident in his rejection of lavish lifestyles, preferring instead to live like an ordinary citizen despite ruling a vast empire.

His fairness extended beyond Muslims; he implemented policies that protected non-Muslims and ensured their rights within the Islamic state. His governance was inclusive, allowing religious minorities to practice their faith freely under Islamic rule.

## Influence on Humanity

Umar's legacy continues to impact Islamic governance, legal systems, and military strategy. His administrative policies laid the groundwork for a well-organized Islamic state, influencing later Muslim rulers and historians.

**1. Legal and Administrative Reforms** – He introduced judicial reforms, established a formal treasury, and improved tax collection, ensuring economic stability within the empire.

**2. Expansion of the Islamic Empire** – Under his rule, the Muslim world expanded dramatically, bringing Islam to new regions and laying the foundation for later Islamic civilizations.

**3. Social Welfare Programs** – Umar pioneered social welfare policies, including stipends for the poor and disabled, orphan care, and food distribution programs.

**4. Religious Freedom and Tolerance** – He implemented policies that allowed religious minorities to practice freely, setting a precedent for coexistence under Islamic rule.

**5. Military Organization** – His military strategies, discipline, and leadership influenced Islamic military doctrines and were studied by later generations.

---

In conclusion, Umar ibn al-Khattab was a transformative leader whose impact went beyond military conquests. His vision of governance, justice, and social responsibility continues to inspire leaders and scholars. His leadership not only strengthened Islam but also contributed to the development of governance models that endured for centuries. His legacy as a just and powerful ruler remains one of the most significant in Islamic history.

# Charlemagne
King of the Franks and father of Europe

Charlemagne, also known as Charles the Great, was one of the most influential rulers of the Middle Ages. As King of the Franks, he expanded his kingdom into a vast empire that covered much of Western and Central Europe. His reign marked the Carolingian Renaissance, a revival of learning, culture, and administration that laid the foundation for modern European civilization. Crowned Emperor of the Romans by Pope Leo III in 800 CE, Charlemagne's leadership helped shape the medieval world and bridge the gap between the classical and modern eras.

## Origin

Charlemagne was born in 747 CE, though the exact date is uncertain. He was the son of Pepin the Short and Bertrada of Laon. His father, Pepin, was the first king of the Carolingian dynasty, having deposed the last Merovingian king, Childeric III. Charlemagne's lineage was one of power and ambition, rooted in the political maneuverings of the Frankish kingdom. At the time of Charlemagne's birth, the Frankish realm was a powerful yet fragmented entity, divided among noble families with shifting alliances. The Carolingians, through strategic diplomacy and military prowess, consolidated their rule. Charlemagne and his younger brother Carloman were groomed to continue their father's legacy, though fate would eventually place the weight of leadership solely on Charlemagne's shoulders.

## Childhood and Youth

Very little is definitively known about Charlemagne's early years. His upbringing was likely in the Frankish tradition, emphasizing military training, governance, and religious education. As a child of nobility, he would have been exposed to Latin, the administrative language of the Carolingians, and trained in martial skills necessary for ruling a warrior kingdom. When Pepin the Short died in 768 CE, the Frankish kingdom was divided between Charlemagne and his brother Carloman. This division followed the Frankish tradition of partitioning territories among heirs. However, their relationship was fraught with tension, and they ruled separately, often competing for influence. Carloman's sudden death in 771 CE left Charlemagne as the sole ruler of the Franks, setting the stage for his ambitious expansion of the kingdom.

## Adulthood

With Carloman's death, Charlemagne moved quickly to solidify his rule. He embarked on a series of military campaigns that would expand the Frankish kingdom into one of the most powerful empires of the medieval world. Some of his key conquests included:

- **Lombardy** (773-774 CE): Charlemagne invaded Italy and defeated the Lombards, declaring himself King of the Lombards and integrating their territory into his domain.
- **Saxon Wars** (772-804 CE): One of his longest and most brutal campaigns, the Saxon Wars involved the conquest and forced Christianization of the Saxons, who resisted Frankish rule for over three decades.
- **Spanish March** (778 CE): He led an expedition into the Iberian Peninsula, creating a buffer zone between Christian and Muslim territories.
- **Avar and Slavic Campaigns**: Charlemagne extended Frankish influence into Central Europe, subduing the Avars and influencing Slavic tribes.

Charlemagne's military conquests established the Frankish Empire as the dominant power in Western Europe. However, his greatest political triumph came in 800 CE when Pope Leo III crowned him Emperor of the Romans in St. Peter's Basilica, reviving the concept of a united Western Roman Empire.

## Private Life

Charlemagne's personal life was marked by multiple marriages and numerous children. He had at least four wives and several concubines, resulting in a large royal family. Some of his notable children included:

- **Louis the Pious**: His designated heir, who succeeded him as Emperor.
- **Pepin of Italy**: Ruler of the Lombard kingdom under his father's rule.
- **Charles the Younger**: Initially considered for succession but predeceased his father.

Despite his many relationships, Charlemagne maintained strict control over his household. He was known to be deeply involved in the education of his children, ensuring they were well-versed in Latin, governance, and military strategy. He also fostered a courtly atmosphere that emphasized learning and religious devotion.

## Death

Charlemagne ruled until his death on January 28, 814 CE, at the age of 66. He passed away in Aachen, his favored residence, after suffering from a prolonged illness, likely a fever or pleurisy. He was buried in Aachen Cathedral, and his tomb remains one of the most revered sites in European history. Before his death, Charlemagne had planned for the succession of his empire. He crowned his son, Louis the Pious, as co-emperor in 813 CE, ensuring a smooth transition. However, after Charlemagne's passing, the empire eventually fragmented due to internal strife and external pressures.

## Character

Charlemagne was a complex ruler, embodying both warrior-like ferocity and intellectual curiosity. He was a devout Christian who sought to unify his empire under the banner of the Church. His support for religious institutions led to the widespread Christianization of Europe, though his methods were sometimes ruthless, particularly in the forced conversion of the Saxons.

Despite his military dominance, Charlemagne was also a patron of learning and culture. He initiated the Carolingian Renaissance, a revival of classical learning, art, and scholarship. His court in Aachen became a center for intellectual activity, attracting scholars like Alcuin of York.

He was known for his strong work ethic, simple personal habits, and keen interest in governance. Unlike many medieval rulers, he took an active role in lawmaking, administration, and even the economy, standardizing weights, measures, and coinage to facilitate trade.

## Influence on Humanity

Charlemagne's influence on European history is profound. His reign laid the groundwork for the Holy Roman Empire, which would shape the political landscape of Europe for centuries. Some of his key contributions include:

**1. Unification of Western Europe** – By consolidating diverse territories, he fostered the idea of a united European identity.

**2. Educational Reforms** – His promotion of literacy and scholarship helped preserve classical knowledge during the Middle Ages.

**3. Legal and Administrative Reforms** – He codified laws, established administrative divisions, and reinforced justice systems that influenced European governance.

**4. Church-State Relations** – By aligning with the Papacy, he reinforced the connection between religious and political authority, a theme that would persist in European history.

**5. Military Innovations** – His strategies and use of cavalry tactics influenced medieval warfare.

Charlemagne's vision of a Christian, unified Europe echoed throughout history, inspiring later rulers and shaping medieval and modern European identities. His legacy as both a conqueror and a statesman ensures his place as one of the greatest figures in world history.

In conclusion, Charlemagne was not just a king; he was an architect of European civilization. His conquests, reforms, and intellectual pursuits helped bridge the ancient and medieval worlds, earning him the title "Father of Europe." His empire may have fractured after his death, but his influence endures in the political, cultural, and religious foundations of Europe today.

# William the Conqueror
## Norman duke and king of England

William the Conqueror, also known as William I of England, was a pivotal figure in European history. As the Duke of Normandy and later the first Norman King of England, he reshaped the political and cultural landscape of medieval Europe. His conquest of England in 1066 marked the beginning of Norman rule and brought profound changes to governance, feudal structures, and language.

## Origin

William was born in 1028 in Falaise, Normandy (modern-day France), as the illegitimate son of Robert I, Duke of Normandy, and Herleva, the daughter of a tanner. Due to his illegitimacy, he was sometimes called "William the Bastard" during his early years. His father's lineage traced back to Viking ancestors who had settled in Normandy in the early 10th century, making William a descendant of Norse warrior-kings. His father's rule was relatively short-lived, and upon his death in 1035, young William inherited the title of Duke of Normandy.

## Childhood and Youth

William's early life was fraught with danger. As an illegitimate child in a turbulent political environment, his claim to the duchy was constantly challenged by rival Norman nobles. Many Norman lords refused to recognize his legitimacy, leading to years of unrest and rebellion.

His childhood was marked by numerous assassination attempts and betrayals, forcing him to rely on loyal supporters such as his guardian Alan of Brittany. Despite the chaos, William received a military and administrative education, learning the skills necessary to command armies and govern effectively. By the time he reached his teenage years, he had already begun asserting control over his fractious duchy through strategic alliances and military action.

## Adulthood

William consolidated his power in Normandy throughout his youth and early adulthood. By the 1050s, he had established himself as a formidable ruler, successfully suppressing internal revolts and gaining recognition from the French monarchy. His marriage to Matilda of Flanders in 1051 further strengthened his position, creating alliances with powerful European rulers.

In 1066, following the death of King Edward the Confessor of England, William claimed the English throne based on a disputed promise made by Edward and a supposed oath of fealty from Harold Godwinson, the English noble who ultimately seized the throne. William amassed a large army and launched the Norman invasion of England.

The decisive Battle of Hastings took place on October 14, 1066, where William's forces defeated Harold's army. Harold was killed in battle, and William was crowned King of England on Christmas Day, 1066. This victory led to significant changes in English society, including the replacement of Anglo-Saxon nobility with Norman elites, the construction of castles, and the establishment of feudalism.

## Private Life

William married Matilda of Flanders in 1051, and they had several children, including Robert Curthose, William II (Rufus), and Henry I. Matilda played an important role in his reign, acting as regent in Normandy while William was in England. Their marriage was politically advantageous and contributed to the stability of his rule. Despite his success, William's life was marked by a relentless pursuit of control and authority. He could be harsh and ruthless, particularly when dealing with rebellions. His "Harrying of the North" campaign (1069-1070), aimed at suppressing northern English resistance, resulted in widespread devastation and suffering.

## Death

William's later years were troubled by conflicts both in England and on the continent. In 1087, while campaigning in France, he suffered severe injuries when his horse stumbled during the siege of Mantes. He was taken to Rouen, where he died on September 9, 1087.

His death was marked by chaos. His body was reportedly abandoned by his attendants, and when his remains were eventually interred in Caen, an incident occurred where the tomb was too small for his body, leading to an undignified burial.

Following his death, his lands were divided among his sons. Robert received Normandy, while William Rufus inherited the English throne. This division led to conflicts between his heirs, shaping the future of both England and Normandy.

## Character

William was a determined and ambitious leader, known for his military prowess, strategic mind, and political cunning. Though he was often ruthless, he was also an effective ruler who brought stability to both Normandy and England. His ability to balance diplomacy and warfare allowed him to maintain control over a vast and often rebellious domain.

He was deeply religious, commissioning the construction of monasteries and churches. However, his faith did not prevent him from using brutal tactics to maintain power, as seen in his treatment of English rebels.

Physically, William was said to be tall and robust, but later in life, he became overweight, which contributed to his health issues.

## Influence on Humanity

William's impact on history is immense. His conquest of England changed the course of British history, shaping its language, culture, and governance for centuries. Some of his key contributions include:

**1. The Norman Influence on England** – The introduction of Norman French into the English court led to linguistic and cultural blending, significantly influencing the development of the English language.

**2. Feudal System** – William implemented the feudal system in England, restructuring land ownership and governance.

**3. Castles and Military Innovations** – He built castles, such as the Tower of London, to fortify his rule and establish Norman dominance.

**4. Domesday Book** – In 1086, he commissioned the Domesday Book, a comprehensive survey of England's land and resources, which remains an invaluable historical document.

**5. Church Reform** – William strengthened ties with the papacy while also ensuring that the English Church remained under royal control.

William's reign marked the beginning of England's transformation into a centralized monarchy with strong administrative foundations. His conquest and subsequent rule set a precedent for later rulers and influenced the evolution of European medieval states.

---

In conclusion, William the Conqueror was more than just a warrior; he was a visionary leader who reshaped England and left an indelible mark on European history. His legacy continues to influence modern governance, language, and culture, making him one of the most significant figures of the medieval period.

# Pope Urban II
## Initiator of the Crusades

Pope Urban II was one of the most significant popes of the medieval period, best known for initiating the First Crusade in 1095. His call to arms at the Council of Clermont led to one of the most transformative events in European and Middle Eastern history, altering religious, political, and military landscapes for centuries. His papacy strengthened the power of the papacy in Europe and cemented his legacy as a pivotal figure in the medieval Catholic Church.

## Origin

Born as Odo of Châtillon or Odo of Lagery around 1035 in the region of Champagne, France, Pope Urban II came from a noble family. He was of Frankish descent, and his noble birth afforded him an excellent education and access to influential religious and political circles. His background in the aristocracy later aided him in dealing with European nobility during his papacy.

Odo's early life in the Church was influenced by the Gregorian Reforms, which sought to eliminate corruption and reinforce papal authority. His monastic training and association with the reformist movement shaped his future vision as a pope committed to ecclesiastical discipline and expansion.

## Childhood and Youth

Little is recorded about Odo's childhood, but as the son of a noble family, he would have received a formal education in Latin, theology, and classical studies. His early religious inclinations led him to join the influential Benedictine abbey of Cluny, a center of spiritual and intellectual activity in medieval Europe.

At Cluny, he studied under Abbot Hugh, one of the leading figures of the 11th-century Church reform movement. Odo's time at Cluny deeply ingrained in him the ideals of monastic purity, church independence from secular interference, and papal supremacy. This foundation would later define his policies as Pope Urban II.

## Adulthood

Odo's rise through the ecclesiastical ranks was swift. Recognized for his intellect and leadership skills, he was appointed prior at Cluny before Pope Gregory VII, an advocate of Church reform, appointed him Cardinal-Bishop of Ostia in 1080. In this role, Odo became one of the key supporters of the Gregorian Reforms, advocating for clerical celibacy and opposition to simony (the buying and selling of church offices).

Following the death of Pope Victor III in 1087, Odo was elected pope in 1088, taking the name Urban II. At the time, the papacy was embroiled in conflicts with the Holy Roman Emperor, Henry IV, who supported an antipope, Clement III, in an effort to weaken papal authority. Urban II spent much of his early papacy consolidating his position and strengthening alliances with European monarchs, particularly the Normans in Italy and France.

His greatest moment came in 1095 when he convened the Council of Clermont. It was here that he made his famous call for the First Crusade, urging Christians to reclaim the Holy Land from Muslim control. His speech inspired thousands to take up the cross, leading to a massive mobilization of European forces and the eventual capture of Jerusalem in 1099.

## Private Life

As a pope, Urban II led a celibate life dedicated to the Church, in accordance with Catholic doctrine. His monastic background influenced his austere lifestyle, and he was deeply committed to the ideals of piety, reform, and clerical discipline.

Unlike some of his predecessors, Urban II was not known for personal excess or political intrigue. Instead, he focused on strengthening the Church's influence and ensuring the implementation of religious reforms. He was highly active in diplomacy, forging alliances with European rulers and leveraging their power to support papal objectives.

Despite his high office, Urban II maintained a reputation for humility and dedication to the principles of Cluniac monasticism. His personal integrity helped garner respect among both secular and religious leaders.

## Death

Pope Urban II passed away on July 29, 1099, in Rome, just two weeks after the successful conclusion of the First Crusade with the capture of Jerusalem. Unfortunately, he did not live to see the full extent of the crusaders' achievements or the long-term consequences of his call to arms.

His remains were interred at St. Peter's Basilica, and in recognition of his contributions to the Church, he was beatified in 1881 by Pope Leo XIII. His death marked the end of an era of significant papal influence over European affairs and the beginning of centuries of conflict and interaction between Christian and Muslim civilizations.

## Character

Urban II was a skilled orator, a shrewd diplomat, and a visionary leader. His ability to inspire and mobilize people, as seen at the Council of Clermont, demonstrated his understanding of the power of rhetoric and religious fervor.

He was a pragmatic leader who balanced religious idealism with political strategy. While he was deeply committed to Church reforms and spiritual leadership, he also recognized the importance of military and political alliances in advancing Christian interests.

Unlike some of his predecessors, Urban II maintained a relatively positive reputation for integrity and dedication to the Church's mission. Though his call for the Crusades led to violence and upheaval, his intentions were rooted in a desire to protect Christian lands and unify Christendom under papal leadership.

## Influence on Humanity

Pope Urban II's impact on history is profound. His call for the First Crusade reshaped European and Middle Eastern geopolitics and set the stage for centuries of religious and military conflicts between Christians and Muslims.

**1. The Crusades** – The First Crusade initiated a series of religious wars that altered the course of medieval history. These conflicts shaped European nationalism, military strategies, and religious interactions for centuries.

**2. Expansion of Papal Power** – Urban II reinforced the papacy's authority over European rulers, positioning the pope as not only a religious leader but also a political force.

**3. Church Reforms** – His support for the Gregorian Reforms helped institutionalize clerical celibacy, the elimination of simony, and the separation of church and state in medieval Europe.

**4. Cultural and Economic Exchange** – The Crusades led to increased trade and cultural exchanges between Europe and the Middle East, introducing new ideas, technologies, and goods to Western Europe.

**5. Legacy of Religious Zeal** – His call to arms influenced the development of religious rhetoric in European politics, inspiring later movements such as the Spanish Reconquista and various Christian military orders.

---

In conclusion, Pope Urban II was more than just a religious leader; he was a catalyst for one of the most significant movements of the medieval era. His leadership strengthened the papacy, redefined Christian-Muslim relations, and left a legacy that shaped both European and Middle Eastern history. His vision of a united Christendom under papal authority remains one of the defining aspects of his reign and a key influence on the medieval world.

# Genghis Khan
Founder and leader of the Mongol Empire

Genghis Khan, originally named Temujin, was one of the most formidable and influential leaders in world history. As the founder and ruler of the Mongol Empire, he united disparate nomadic tribes and built the largest contiguous empire ever known. His military strategies, leadership, and administrative innovations transformed the political landscape of Asia and beyond. Though often remembered for his conquests, his legacy also includes significant contributions to trade, law, and culture.

## Origin

Genghis Khan was born as Temujin around 1162 in the rugged steppes of Mongolia, near the Onon River. His father, Yesügei, was a minor chieftain of the Borjigin clan, and his mother, Hoelun, was of the Olkhunut tribe. His birth occurred in a time of great instability, as Mongolian tribes were fragmented and engaged in constant warfare and rivalries.

Temujin's father named him after a Tatar chieftain he had defeated, symbolizing strength and warrior spirit. However, Yesügei was poisoned by rivals when Temujin was still a child, leaving his family vulnerable and without strong allies. This event marked the beginning of a tumultuous period in his early life, shaping his resilience and determination.

## Childhood and Youth

After Yesügei's death, Temujin, his mother, and his siblings were abandoned by their clan, forcing them to survive in the harsh Mongolian wilderness. They endured extreme hardships, relying on foraging and fishing. These formative years cultivated Temujin's resourcefulness and ability to lead under adversity.

As a teenager, he was captured and enslaved by a rival clan but managed to escape. His ability to endure hardship and outmaneuver enemies established his reputation among the Mongol people. He gradually built alliances by gaining the trust of other tribes, particularly those that had been marginalized by the ruling elites.

During this period, Temujin married Börte, his lifelong wife and most trusted advisor. However, she was soon kidnapped by the Merkit tribe. Temujin, with the help of his ally Toghrul of the Keraites and his childhood friend Jamukha, launched a successful raid to rescue her. This event reinforced his belief in loyalty and the importance of military strategy.

## Adulthood

As he entered adulthood, Temujin's military and political acumen became apparent. He began consolidating power by forming alliances with various Mongol and Turkic tribes, adopting meritocracy over traditional aristocracy. His leadership attracted talented generals and warriors, including Subotai and Jebe, who would become key figures in his campaigns.

In 1206, after a series of battles against rival Mongol factions, he successfully unified the Mongolian tribes and was proclaimed "Genghis Khan" (meaning "Universal Ruler"). With his authority solidified, he turned his focus outward, launching one of the most ambitious military expansions in history.

**Genghis Khan's conquests included:**

- **The Xi Xia Kingdom** (1209-1210): A significant step in asserting Mongol dominance in northern China.
- **The Jin Dynasty** (1211-1234): Genghis led a brutal campaign against this powerful Chinese dynasty, weakening it before its eventual fall.
- **The Khwarazmian Empire** (1219-1221): After the governor of Otrar killed Mongol merchants, Genghis unleashed a devastating invasion, annihilating cities like Samarkand and Bukhara.
- **The Russian Steppes and Eastern Europe** (1223): His forces defeated the Kievan Rus and other regional powers, demonstrating Mongol military superiority.

These campaigns established Mongol supremacy over vast territories and secured crucial trade routes across Asia.

## Private Life

Genghis Khan had multiple wives and numerous children, following the Mongol tradition of polygamy. However, his primary wife, Börte, held a special status as his chief consort. His sons, including Ögedei, Chagatai, Tolui, and Jochi, played vital roles in the governance and expansion of the Mongol Empire.

Despite his reputation as a ruthless conqueror, Genghis Khan was deeply loyal to his family and valued unity. He promoted his most capable generals and administrators based on merit rather than noble lineage. His ability to recognize and reward talent helped maintain stability within his vast empire.

His governance was pragmatic, emphasizing religious tolerance, law, and trade. He implemented the "Yassa", a legal code that promoted order and discipline among his people. He also encouraged literacy and commerce, facilitating the Silk Road's expansion and cultural exchange between East and West.

## Death

Genghis Khan died in 1227, during a campaign against the Xi Xia Kingdom. The exact cause of his death remains uncertain, with theories ranging from injuries sustained in battle to illness or even an accident. His death was kept secret for some time to maintain stability in the empire. According to legend, his burial site was concealed to prevent desecration. Reports suggest that those who buried him were killed to maintain secrecy, and his tomb remains undiscovered to this day, adding an air of mystery to his legacy. Following his death, his empire was divided among his sons, leading to the creation of four major khanates that continued Mongol expansion for generations.

## Character

Genghis Khan was a paradoxical figure – both ruthless and visionary. His military campaigns were marked by extreme brutality, with cities razed and populations massacred. However, he also demonstrated tolerance and pragmatism, incorporating conquered peoples into his administration and promoting trade and communication.

He valued loyalty and merit, rewarding those who proved themselves in battle and governance. His leadership style was disciplined and meritocratic, which set him apart from other rulers of his time. While feared by his enemies, he was respected and revered by his followers for his ability to lead and innovate.

## Influence on Humanity

Genghis Khan's impact on history is profound and multifaceted. His influence extended beyond military conquests and reshaped global civilization in various ways:

**1. Expansion of Trade and the Silk Road**: Under his rule, trade flourished as the Mongols secured and protected the Silk Road, fostering economic and cultural exchanges between Europe, the Middle East, and Asia.

**2. Legal and Administrative Reforms** – The "Yassa" legal code provided a framework for governance, emphasizing law and order.

**3. Cultural Exchange** – The Mongol Empire facilitated the movement of people, ideas, and technologies across continents, leading to advancements in science, medicine, and philosophy.

**4. Military Innovations** – His strategies, including psychological warfare, mobility, and adaptability, influenced military tactics for centuries.

**5. Religious Tolerance** – Genghis Khan allowed religious freedom within his empire, integrating diverse faiths and cultures.

Despite his brutal reputation, his contributions to global history are undeniable. His legacy is evident in the lasting impact of Mongol rule on Eurasian civilizations.

In conclusion, Genghis Khan was a leader of extraordinary ability, reshaping the world through his military campaigns, governance, and innovations. His empire's vast reach and influence endure in modern history, making him one of the most significant figures of all time.

# Johannes Gutenberg
The Inventor of the Printing Press

Johannes Gutenberg was a German inventor, printer, and publisher whose revolutionary invention of the movable-type printing press transformed the world. His innovation, developed in the mid-15th century, laid the foundation for the spread of knowledge, the Reformation, and the Renaissance. By making books more accessible and affordable, he democratized learning and enabled the mass production of printed material, forever changing the course of human history.

## Origin

Johannes Gutenberg was born around 1400 in Mainz, within the Holy Roman Empire (modern-day Germany). He was the son of Friele Gensfleisch zur Laden, a wealthy merchant and patrician of Mainz, and his wife, Else Wyrich. His family belonged to the upper class of society, affording him the privileges of education and access to skilled craftsmanship. The exact details of his early life remain sparse, but it is believed that he was exposed to metalworking and engraving, skills that would later influence his groundbreaking invention.

The 15th century was a period of great social and economic transformation in Europe. The increasing demand for books, combined with the limitations of manuscript copying, created a pressing need for a more efficient method of reproduction. Gutenberg's background in metallurgy and craftsmanship would eventually lead him to solve this challenge through his printing press.

## Childhood and Youth

Little is documented about Gutenberg's childhood, but given his family's status, he likely received a formal education. Mainz was a hub of trade and commerce, and his father's involvement in the goldsmith trade and minting provided young Gutenberg with early exposure to metalworking, engraving, and financial transactions. It is believed that he attended the University of Erfurt around 1418, where he may have studied subjects related to the arts and humanities. However, historical records do not confirm his graduation. What is known is that his technical background and innovative mind allowed him to experiment with different materials and techniques, particularly in metal casting and engraving.

During his youth, political unrest in Mainz forced many elite families, including Gutenberg's, to relocate. He moved to Strasbourg, where he spent many years refining his ideas and working with various craftspeople. His time in Strasbourg was crucial in shaping his later innovations.

## Adulthood

By the 1430s, Gutenberg had begun experimenting with movable-type printing, a concept that involved the creation of reusable individual letters that could be arranged to form words and printed multiple times. Before his invention, books were copied by hand or through woodblock printing, both of which were labor-intensive and expensive processes.

By the 1440s, he had returned to Mainz and began seeking financial backers for his printing project. In 1450, he secured funding from Johann Fust, a wealthy financier, which allowed him to develop and refine his printing press. This collaboration, however, would later lead to legal disputes that resulted in the loss of some of his assets.

In 1455, Gutenberg produced his most famous work, the "Gutenberg Bible", also known as the "42-line Bible" due to the number of lines per page. This book was the first major publication printed using movable type, and its production marked the beginning of the mass production of books.

Despite his groundbreaking work, Gutenberg struggled financially. Fust sued him over unpaid debts and won control of much of his printing operation. Nevertheless, Gutenberg's invention spread rapidly, and within decades, printing presses based on his technology appeared across Europe.

## Private Life

Gutenberg was known to be a reserved and industrious man, dedicating much of his life to perfecting his printing technology. There is little evidence of marriage or children, suggesting that he devoted himself entirely to his craft. Unlike many other inventors, he did not seek personal fame or wealth, focusing instead on refining his printing process. He lived much of his later life in relative obscurity, facing financial difficulties despite the widespread adoption of his printing technology. However, his contributions were eventually recognized, and in 1465, he was granted a pension by Archbishop Adolf of Nassau, which provided him with some financial security in his final years.

## Death

Johannes Gutenberg died in 1468 in Mainz. The exact circumstances of his death remain unclear, but he was likely in his late 60s at the time. He was buried in the Franciscan church in Mainz, though his grave has since been lost. Although he died without great wealth or recognition, his invention would go on to shape the course of human civilization. Within decades, printing presses based on his movable-type design had spread across Europe, laying the groundwork for the spread of knowledge and literacy.

## Character

Gutenberg was a visionary and a perfectionist, driven by a relentless pursuit of innovation. His ability to merge different crafts, from metalworking to calligraphy, demonstrates his interdisciplinary genius. Unlike many inventors who sought immediate financial gain, Gutenberg was dedicated to refining his printing technique, believing in its potential to change the world.

Despite facing financial hardships and legal disputes, he remained committed to his work. His resilience and determination ensured that his invention survived and proliferated, even if he did not personally reap its full rewards. His humility and focus on craftsmanship over personal recognition further set him apart from many of his contemporaries.

## Influence on Humanity

Gutenberg's printing press is widely regarded as one of the most important inventions in human history. Its impact was profound and far-reaching:

**1. The Spread of Literacy** – Before the printing press, books were scarce and expensive. Gutenberg's invention drastically reduced the cost of book production, making knowledge accessible to a broader population.

**2. The Renaissance and Scientific Revolution** – The ability to mass-produce books accelerated the spread of new ideas, fueling intellectual movements such as the Renaissance and the Scientific Revolution.

**3. The Protestant Reformation** – Gutenberg's press allowed Martin Luther's writings to spread rapidly, challenging the Catholic Church's authority and leading to religious transformations across Europe.

**4. Standardization of Knowledge** – With printed books, scholars could share information more accurately, reducing errors that were common in hand-copied manuscripts.

**5. Birth of the Modern Publishing Industry** – Gutenberg's invention laid the foundation for newspapers, books, and mass media, shaping communication for centuries to come.

His printing technology paved the way for modern education, journalism, and the information age. Today, the legacy of Gutenberg's work is evident in every printed book, newspaper, and digital publication that exists.

---

In conclusion, Johannes Gutenberg was not just an inventor but a revolutionary figure who changed the way humanity records, shares, and accesses knowledge. His contributions remain one of the most significant turning points in history, and his legacy continues to shape the world in profound ways.

# Christopher Columbus
## Explorer of the "New World"

Christopher Columbus was an Italian explorer and navigator whose voyages across the Atlantic Ocean led to the European discovery of the Americas. His expeditions, sponsored by Spain, initiated an era of European exploration, colonization, and transformation of the world. While he remains a celebrated historical figure, Columbus is also a subject of controversy due to the impact of his voyages on indigenous populations. This biography delves into his life, achievements, and the lasting influence he had on humanity.

## Origin

Christopher Columbus was born between August 25 and October 31, 1451, in the Republic of Genoa, a maritime city-state in present-day Italy. His birth name in Genoese dialect was Cristoforo Colombo, while in Spanish, he is known as Cristóbal Colón.

His father, Domenico Colombo, was a wool weaver and merchant, and his mother, Susanna Fontanarossa, came from a humble background. Columbus grew up in a modest household, but Genoa's status as a major seafaring center exposed him to trade, navigation, and maritime exploration from a young age.

## Childhood and Youth

Columbus's early years were shaped by Genoa's maritime culture. As a young boy, he received basic education in reading, writing, and mathematics, but his true passion was the sea. He studied geography, astronomy, and navigation, gaining skills that would later define his career.

At the age of 14, Columbus began working on merchant ships, sailing the Mediterranean Sea. During this time, he experienced first-hand the dangers of sea travel, including pirate attacks and violent storms. His experiences hardened him as a skilled navigator and sailor.

In 1476, Columbus survived a shipwreck off the coast of Portugal, where he swam to shore and settled in Lisbon. There, he worked with his brother Bartholomew Columbus, who was a mapmaker, and deepened his knowledge of cartography, navigation, and shipbuilding.

## Adulthood

By the late 15th century, European trade with Asia was dominated by Portuguese and Venetian merchants, who controlled routes to the spice trade in India and China. Columbus became convinced that the best way to reach Asia was by sailing west across the Atlantic, a theory based on incorrect estimates of the Earth's circumference.

For years, Columbus sought royal sponsorship for his expedition. After being rejected by Portugal, England, and France, he finally secured funding from King Ferdinand and Queen Isabella of Spain in 1492. They agreed to finance his voyage in exchange for gold, spices, and potential Christian conversions.

On August 3, 1492, Columbus set sail from Palos, Spain, with three ships: the Santa María, the Pinta, and the Niña. After more than two months at sea, he landed on October 12, 1492, in what is now the Bahamas. Believing he had reached islands near Asia, he called the inhabitants "Indians."

During this voyage, he explored parts of Cuba and Hispaniola (present-day Haiti and the Dominican Republic), establishing Spain's first settlement in the New World, La Navidad.

Columbus undertook three more voyages (1493, 1498, and 1502), exploring the Caribbean, Central America, and parts of South America. Despite his discoveries, he never realized he had encountered a new continent, believing he had reached islands near Asia.

As governor of Hispaniola, Columbus was accused of tyranny and mismanagement, leading to his arrest and removal by Spanish authorities in 1500. Although he was later released, his reputation suffered, and his authority diminished.

## Private Life

Columbus married Felipa Perestrello Moniz, a Portuguese noblewoman, in 1479. They had a son, Diego Columbus, who later became the governor of Hispaniola. After his wife's death, Columbus had a relationship with Beatriz Enríquez de Arana, with whom he had another son, Ferdinand Columbus, who later chronicled Columbus's voyages.

Despite his public persona, Columbus lived a life of financial struggles, often seeking royal pensions and rewards for his discoveries. His later years were marked by legal battles over his promised share of the wealth from the New World.

## Death

Columbus died on May 20, 1506, in Valladolid, Spain, at the age of 54. He suffered from arthritis and possibly heart disease. At the time of his death, he still believed he had discovered new routes to Asia, unaware of the significance of his explorations.

His remains were moved multiple times, first to Seville, then to Santo Domingo, and later to Havana, Cuba, before finally being returned to Seville, Spain.

## Character

Columbus was a multifaceted personality, driven by ambition, persistence, and deep faith. His vision and ability to persuade others of his ideas stand as a testament to his charisma and determination. However, he was also a man of significant flaws, including a limited understanding of the true nature of his discoveries and a frequently ruthless approach toward indigenous peoples.

Despite facing numerous setbacks, Columbus demonstrated remarkable resilience and was willing to take great personal risks to realize his ambitions. Yet, his stubbornness and unwavering adherence to certain beliefs earned him both admiration and criticism, shaping his complex legacy.

## Influence on Humanity

Columbus's voyages had a profound impact on world history.

**1. The Age of Exploration** – His journeys encouraged other European nations to explore and colonize the Americas.

**2. The Columbian Exchange** – His expeditions led to the exchange of crops, animals, and cultures between the Old and New Worlds.

**3. The Expansion of European Empires** – Spain established a vast colonial empire in the Americas, shaping global politics and economics.

**4. The Decline of Indigenous Civilizations** – His voyages triggered European colonization, leading to the decline of native populations due to warfare, slavery, and disease.

**5. Maritime Advancements** – His expeditions advanced navigation, cartography, and shipbuilding.

---

Christopher Columbus remains one of history's most significant yet controversial figures. His determination and navigational skills opened new frontiers, but his actions also led to suffering and exploitation. While he is credited with connecting Europe and the Americas, his legacy is a complex and debated one.

His name is remembered in cities, countries, and history books, serving as both a symbol of discovery and a reminder of colonial impact. His voyages forever changed the world, making him one of the most influential explorers in human history.

# Leonardo da Vinci
Renaissance polymath and genius

Leonardo da Vinci was one of the most brilliant minds in history, embodying the essence of the Renaissance through his work as a painter, scientist, engineer, and inventor. His insatiable curiosity and boundless creativity led to some of the most iconic artworks and scientific studies of all time. Though he is best known for masterpieces such as the "Mona Lisa" and "The Last Supper", his contributions to anatomy, mechanics, and aerodynamics remain influential even today.

## Origin

Leonardo di ser Piero da Vinci was born on April 15, 1452, in the town of Vinci, in the Republic of Florence (modern-day Italy). He was the illegitimate son of Piero da Vinci, a wealthy notary, and Caterina, a peasant woman. Despite his illegitimacy, Leonardo was acknowledged by his father and raised in the family household, though he was not entitled to his father's name or inheritance.

His birthplace, Vinci, was a picturesque village surrounded by rolling hills and farmland, which may have played a role in fostering his early love for nature. His family connections provided him with access to basic education, but he did not receive formal instruction in Greek or Latin, which were essential for scholarly pursuits at the time. Instead, Leonardo was largely self-taught, relying on keen observation and relentless experimentation.

## Childhood and Youth

As a child, Leonardo displayed an unusual talent for drawing and an intense curiosity about the world around him. Recognizing his potential, his father arranged for him to apprentice under Andrea del Verrocchio, a renowned artist and sculptor in Florence. This apprenticeship, which began around 1466, exposed Leonardo to various artistic techniques, including painting, metalworking, sculpting, and mechanical engineering. While working in Verrocchio's workshop, Leonardo quickly outshone his master. One legend claims that Verrocchio, upon seeing Leonardo's contribution to a collaborative painting, "The Baptism of Christ", was so impressed that he swore never to paint again. During this time, Leonardo also developed a keen interest in anatomy, dissecting animals to better understand musculature and movement.

His studies in Florence laid the foundation for his lifelong dedication to art and science, as he meticulously recorded his observations in detailed notebooks. His unique approach combined artistic precision with scientific inquiry, setting him apart from his contemporaries.

## Adulthood

By the 1480s, Leonardo had established himself as an independent artist and engineer. In 1482, he moved to Milan, seeking greater opportunities under the patronage of Ludovico Sforza, the Duke of Milan. There, he worked on various projects, ranging from designing military fortifications to painting some of his most celebrated works. During his time in Milan, he created "The Last Supper", one of the most famous religious paintings in history. This fresco, depicting Jesus and his disciples at the moment of betrayal, showcased Leonardo's mastery of perspective, emotion, and composition. Unfortunately, due to his experimental painting technique, the work began to deteriorate shortly after its completion.

Leonardo also delved deeper into scientific exploration, producing sketches of human anatomy, flying machines, and hydraulic systems. His notebooks from this period are filled with studies on flight, mechanics, and the human body, revealing a mind centuries ahead of its time. In 1499, Milan fell to the French, forcing Leonardo to leave the city. Over the next few years, he worked in various Italian courts, including those in Mantua, Venice, and Florence. In Florence, he painted the "Mona Lisa", a portrait that remains one of the most studied and celebrated artworks in history. The painting's enigmatic smile and masterful use of sfumato (a technique for softening transitions between colors) exemplify Leonardo's artistic genius.

## Private Life

Leonardo never married or had children. He maintained close relationships with his apprentices and patrons but remained a private and enigmatic figure. His two most trusted companions were Salai, a young apprentice he took under his wing, and Francesco Melzi, who later became the executor of his estate.

There has been much speculation about Leonardo's personal life, particularly regarding his sexuality. Some historians believe he may have been homosexual, based on legal records from his youth that suggest he was accused, but later acquitted, of sodomy. However, there is no definitive evidence regarding his romantic relationships.

Leonardo was known for his unconventional habits. He was a vegetarian at a time when this was uncommon, and he had a reputation for buying caged birds just to set them free. His notebooks also reveal his deep fascination with nature and the interconnectedness of all things.

## Death

In 1516, Leonardo accepted an invitation from King Francis I of France to serve as his painter, engineer, and architect. He moved to Château du Clos Lucé, near the king's residence, where he spent his final years working on various projects, including engineering plans and artistic studies.

On May 2, 1519, Leonardo da Vinci passed away at the age of 67. According to legend, King Francis I was at his bedside when he died, a testament to the high regard in which he was held. He was buried in the Church of Saint-Florentin in Amboise, France, though his remains were later lost during the destruction of the church in the French Revolution.

## Character

Leonardo was a true Renaissance polymath – an artist, scientist, engineer, and philosopher. His insatiable curiosity and boundless imagination drove him to explore multiple disciplines, from anatomy to hydrodynamics. He saw no division between art and science, believing that understanding the natural world was key to creating great works of art.

Despite his brilliance, Leonardo was often hesitant to complete projects. He was known to start ambitious works, only to abandon them in favor of new pursuits. His notebooks are filled with unfinished ideas, sketches, and studies, reflecting a mind that never rested.

He was also deeply humanistic, emphasizing observation and empirical evidence over superstition. His work demonstrated a profound appreciation for beauty, proportion, and the complexity of life.

## Influence on Humanity

Leonardo da Vinci's impact on humanity is immeasurable. His contributions spanned multiple fields, shaping the course of art, science, and engineering. Some of his most enduring influences include:

**1. Artistic Masterpieces** – Works like the "Mona Lisa" and "The Last Supper" set new standards in composition, perspective, and realism.

**2. Anatomical Studies** – His dissections of human cadavers led to some of the most accurate anatomical drawings of his time, influencing medical science.

**3. Engineering and Invention** – His sketches of flying machines, war devices, and hydraulic systems prefigured modern technology.

**4. Scientific Methodology** – Leonardo's emphasis on observation and experimentation paved the way for future scientific inquiry.

**5. Cultural Legacy** – His works continue to inspire artists, scientists, and thinkers around the world.

Leonardo da Vinci remains one of the most extraordinary figures in history. His genius, vision, and relentless curiosity defined the Renaissance and laid the foundation for countless advancements in art and science. His legacy endures, reminding us of the boundless potential of human creativity.

# Vasco da Gama
Portuguese explorer who
discovered the sea route to India

Vasco da Gama was a Portuguese explorer and one of the most significant figures of the Age of Exploration. As the first European to establish a direct sea route from Europe to India, he played a crucial role in expanding global trade and European imperial ambitions. His voyages transformed the economic and political landscape of the world, marking the beginning of European colonial dominance in Asia.

## Origin

Vasco da Gama was born around 1460 or 1469 in Sines, a coastal town in Portugal. He belonged to a noble family, with his father, Estêvão da Gama, serving as a knight and later a commander of the Order of Santiago. His mother, Isabel Sodré, also came from a distinguished family with strong ties to the maritime and military elite of Portugal. This noble lineage provided Vasco with access to the highest levels of Portuguese society, enabling him to pursue a career in navigation and exploration.

Portugal, under the rule of King John II and later King Manuel I, was at the forefront of maritime exploration. Inspired by the successes of earlier explorers such as Bartolomeu Dias, who had rounded the Cape of Good Hope in 1488, the Portuguese Crown sought to find a direct sea route to India to enhance trade and bypass the overland routes controlled by Muslim merchants.

## Childhood and Youth

Little is known about Vasco da Gama's early years, but he was likely educated in mathematics, astronomy, and navigation – essential skills for a seafarer of his time. Growing up in Sines, he would have been exposed to maritime life, learning the art of sailing and shipbuilding from an early age. His noble status also meant that he was trained in military and diplomatic affairs, preparing him for leadership roles in service to the Portuguese Crown.

By his late teens or early twenties, Vasco da Gama had joined the Order of Santiago, a military-religious order that played a key role in Portugal's maritime expansion. This affiliation further connected him to influential figures at court, ensuring that he would be considered for important naval missions.

## Adulthood

In 1497, King Manuel I appointed Vasco da Gama to lead an expedition to India, following the path charted by Bartolomeu Dias. On July 8, 1497, he set sail from Lisbon with four ships: the "São Gabriel", "São Rafael", "Berrio", and a supply ship. The expedition rounded the Cape of Good Hope in November and reached the Indian Ocean, making its way to the trading port of Calicut (modern-day Kozhikode, India) on May 20, 1498.

Upon arrival, Vasco da Gama faced challenges in securing trade agreements with the local ruler, the Zamorin of Calicut. Although he managed to establish initial contacts, tensions arose due to competition with Muslim merchants who already dominated the trade routes. Despite difficulties, the voyage was considered a success, as it confirmed the feasibility of a sea route to India and brought back valuable spices to Portugal.

Vasco da Gama returned to Portugal in 1499 to great acclaim. He was rewarded by King Manuel I with the title of "Dom" and substantial privileges. However, his later expeditions to India were marked by increasing violence and aggressive tactics. On his second voyage (1502-1503), he led a fleet of warships to enforce Portuguese dominance in the Indian Ocean, attacking rival traders and forcing local rulers into submission.

In 1524, he was appointed as the Viceroy of India to restore order to Portuguese-controlled territories. However, his tenure was short-lived as he fell ill and died later that year.

## Private Life

Vasco da Gama married Catarina de Ataíde, a noblewoman from a distinguished Portuguese family. Together, they had several children, including Estêvão da Gama, who later followed in his father's footsteps as an explorer and administrator in India.

Despite his high status, Vasco da Gama's life was not without controversy. His brutal tactics against rival traders and local populations earned him both admiration and criticism. His personal correspondence reveals a man deeply committed to serving Portugal's interests, often at the expense of diplomacy and peaceful negotiations.

## Death

Vasco da Gama died on December 24, 1524, in Cochin, India, likely due to illness. His remains were initially buried in India but were later transported back to Portugal, where he was interred in the Monastery of Jerónimos in Lisbon, a site that became a symbol of Portugal's maritime achievements. His death marked the end of an era of early Portuguese exploration, but his legacy endured through the vast commercial empire that Portugal established in Asia.

## Character

Vasco da Gama was a determined, ambitious, and often ruthless leader. His unwavering commitment to his mission, combined with his strategic acumen, made him one of the most successful explorers of his time. He was known for his resilience in the face of adversity, enduring long voyages and hostile encounters with unwavering focus. However, his methods were frequently criticized for their brutality. His use of force to establish Portuguese dominance in the Indian Ocean, including acts of violence against rival traders and local rulers, cast a shadow over his legacy. While his expeditions were undeniably effective, they also exemplified the darker side of European expansion.

## Influence on Humanity

Vasco da Gama's impact on world history was immense. His successful navigation of a sea route to India reshaped global trade and geopolitics, leading to the following significant outcomes:

**1. Expansion of Global Trade** – His voyages opened direct trade between Europe and Asia, reducing reliance on overland routes and establishing new economic networks.

**2. Portuguese Colonial Empire** – His expeditions laid the groundwork for Portugal's dominance in the Indian Ocean, leading to the establishment of trading posts and fortresses in Africa, India, and Southeast Asia.

**3. Cultural Exchange** – While primarily driven by commerce, his journeys facilitated cultural interactions between Europe and Asia, influencing art, cuisine, and technology.

**4. Naval and Navigational Advancements** – His success demonstrated the effectiveness of oceanic navigation and inspired further European exploration.

**5. Imperialism and Conflict** – His aggressive approach set a precedent for European colonial strategies, contributing to centuries of competition and conflict in Asia.

---

In conclusion, Vasco da Gama was a trailblazing navigator whose expeditions changed the course of history. While celebrated for his achievements, his legacy is also a reminder of the complexities of exploration, conquest, and global interaction. His voyages not only expanded Portuguese influence but also reshaped the world in ways that continue to be felt today.

# Nicolaus Copernicus
Astronomer and founder of the heliocentric model

Nicolaus Copernicus was a Renaissance-era mathematician and astronomer who formulated the heliocentric theory of the universe, fundamentally changing humanity's understanding of planetary motion. His work "De revolutionibus orbium coelestium" ("On the Revolutions of the Celestial Spheres") laid the foundation for modern astronomy and challenged long-held geocentric beliefs. Copernicus's contributions extended beyond astronomy, influencing mathematics, economics, and philosophy.

## Origin

Nicolaus Copernicus was born on February 19, 1473, in the city of Toruń, located in the Kingdom of Poland. He was the youngest of four children in a wealthy merchant family. His father, Nicolaus Copernicus Sr., was a successful copper trader, while his mother, Barbara Watzenrode, came from an influential family.

Copernicus's uncle, Lucas Watzenrode, was a prominent clergyman and later became the Bishop of Warmia, playing a crucial role in shaping his nephew's future. After his father's death in 1483, Copernicus's uncle took responsibility for his education and career advancement.

## Childhood and Youth

Nicolaus Copernicus received an extensive education that prepared him for both religious and academic pursuits. He attended the Cathedral School of Włocławek, where he studied Latin, classical literature, and the sciences. His early exposure to humanist ideals and scholarly disciplines helped shape his intellectual curiosity.

In 1491, he enrolled at the University of Kraków (now Jagiellonian University), one of the leading centers of scientific learning in Europe. There, he studied mathematics, astronomy, and philosophy, gaining an appreciation for the works of Greek and Arab scholars. Although he did not earn a degree at Kraków, his education exposed him to ideas that would later influence his astronomical theories.

Encouraged by his uncle, Copernicus traveled to Italy in 1496 to pursue further studies. He enrolled at the University of Bologna, where he studied law and canon law while also working under the renowned astronomer Domenico Maria Novara. This period was instrumental in developing his understanding of celestial movements, as he participated in astronomical observations and questioned the validity of the Ptolemaic geocentric model.

In 1501, he continued his studies at the University of Padua, focusing on medicine and philosophy. Two years later, he completed his doctorate in canon law at the University of Ferrara, further solidifying his credentials in both academic and ecclesiastical spheres.

## Adulthood

After completing his education, Copernicus returned to Poland, where he assumed administrative and religious duties under his uncle, who had secured him a position as a canon in the Frombork Cathedral. Despite his ecclesiastical obligations, Copernicus devoted much of his time to astronomy, mathematics, and economic reforms.

While serving as a canon, he conducted astronomical observations, refining his theories about planetary motion. Over time, he became convinced that the Earth was not the center of the universe but rather orbited the Sun along with other planets. This revolutionary idea directly contradicted the widely accepted geocentric model established by Ptolemy.

Between 1510 and 1514, Copernicus drafted his initial outline of the heliocentric theory, known as the "Commentariolus" (Little Commentary). This unpublished manuscript circulated among scholars and outlined the fundamental principles of his model, including:

- The Sun, not the Earth, is the center of the universe.
- The Earth rotates on its axis daily and orbits the Sun annually.
- The apparent retrograde motion of planets results from Earth's movement rather than planetary epicycles.

Though revolutionary, Copernicus hesitated to publish his findings widely, fearing opposition from both religious authorities and fellow scientists.

His responsibilities extended beyond astronomy. He contributed to economic thought by writing "Monetae cudendae ratio", which proposed monetary reforms in Poland, and he also participated in diplomatic missions and administrative governance in Warmia.

## Private Life

Despite being a canon in the Catholic Church, Copernicus never became an ordained priest. His ecclesiastical position provided him with financial stability and intellectual freedom, allowing him to pursue his research. He led a quiet and scholarly life, dedicating his time to scientific inquiry, economic administration, and medical practice.

He was known for his reserved nature, preferring intellectual debates and observations over public engagement. He never married or had children, focusing instead on his studies and duties within the Church. Copernicus's close relationships were mostly with fellow scholars and students who supported his theories.

## Death

Nicolaus Copernicus passed away on May 24, 1543, in Frombork, Poland. According to legend, he saw the first printed copy of "De revolutionibus orbium coelestium" on his deathbed. His health had been declining due to a stroke, and he died at the age of 70.

Initially buried in an unmarked grave in Frombork Cathedral, his remains were rediscovered in 2005, and after forensic analysis, they were officially reinterred in the same cathedral in 2010, with honors befitting his contributions to science.

## Character

Copernicus was an intellectual revolutionary who embodied the ideals of the Renaissance. He was methodical, patient, and meticulous in his studies, dedicating decades to refining his theories. Despite facing potential criticism, he remained committed to his research, prioritizing empirical observation and logical reasoning.

He was also a humble scholar, reluctant to engage in public disputes or seek personal fame. His cautious approach to publishing his work reflected his awareness of the contentious nature of his findings. Copernicus valued scientific inquiry and sought to advance human knowledge without unnecessary confrontation.

## Influence on Humanity

Nicolaus Copernicus's work profoundly transformed our understanding of the universe and influenced numerous scientific and intellectual movements. Some of his key contributions include:

**1. Heliocentric Model** – His theory fundamentally altered astronomy, paving the way for future discoveries by Galileo, Kepler, and Newton.

**2. Scientific Revolution** – His work marked the beginning of the Scientific Revolution, emphasizing observation and mathematical reasoning over traditional beliefs.

**3. Modern Astronomy** – By challenging the geocentric model, he laid the foundation for modern cosmology and space exploration.

**4. Influence on Enlightenment Thinkers** – His ideas influenced philosophers and scientists, promoting critical thinking and the questioning of established doctrines.

**5. Impact on the Catholic Church** – His work eventually led to conflicts between science and religion, particularly during Galileo's time, but also contributed to later reconciliations between faith and scientific inquiry.

Nicolaus Copernicus was much more than an astronomer; he was a thinker, a pioneer and a visionary whose work laid the foundations for modern science. His courage in questioning the existing world view makes him one of the most important figures in history. His legacy lives on in astronomy and today's understanding of the universe.

# Michelangelo
## Italian artist and sculptor of the Renaissance

Michelangelo Buonarroti was one of the most extraordinary artists of the Italian Renaissance, excelling in painting, sculpture, architecture, and poetry. His masterpieces, such as the Sistine Chapel ceiling, "David", and "The Last Judgment", stand as testaments to his unparalleled genius and enduring influence on Western art. His works not only defined the Renaissance but also set the standard for artistic excellence in subsequent centuries.

## Origin

Michelangelo di Lodovico Buonarroti Simoni was born on March 6, 1475, in Caprese, a small town in the Republic of Florence (modern-day Italy). His father, Ludovico di Leonardo Buonarroti Simoni, was a government official, and his mother, Francesca di Neri del Miniato di Siena, came from a modest but respected family. Shortly after Michelangelo's birth, his family moved back to Florence, a city that was the epicenter of the Renaissance.

Florence, under the rule of the powerful Medici family, was a flourishing cultural hub that attracted artists, philosophers, and scholars. This intellectual environment greatly influenced Michelangelo's artistic development and provided opportunities that shaped his future.

## Childhood and Youth

Michelangelo's childhood was marked by tragedy, as his mother died when he was only six years old. This loss had a profound effect on him, and he was placed in the care of a stonecutter's family in Settignano, a village known for its stone quarries. Living among sculptors and masons, he developed an early affinity for carving and working with stone.

At the age of 13, he was apprenticed to Domenico Ghirlandaio, a prominent Florentine painter. Under Ghirlandaio's guidance, Michelangelo learned the fundamentals of fresco painting and drawing. His exceptional talent was quickly recognized, and within a year, he was invited to study at the Medici family's academy, where he was exposed to the works of classical antiquity and the finest Renaissance minds.

During this time, Michelangelo formed relationships with key figures of the Renaissance, including Lorenzo de' Medici, known as Lorenzo the Magnificent. This patronage granted him access to a vast collection of ancient sculptures and allowed him to refine his skills under the mentorship of celebrated artists and scholars.

## Adulthood

Michelangelo's early adulthood was marked by the creation of some of his most famous sculptures. In 1496, he traveled to Rome, where he completed the "Pietà", a masterpiece depicting the Virgin Mary holding the body of Christ. The sculpture's delicate detailing and emotional intensity immediately established him as one of the leading artists of his time.

Returning to Florence in 1501, he began work on the colossal statue of "David", a symbol of civic pride and strength. The statue, completed in 1504, remains one of the most iconic sculptures in art history.

In 1508, Pope Julius II commissioned Michelangelo to paint the ceiling of the Sistine Chapel in Vatican City. Despite considering himself primarily a sculptor, Michelangelo accepted the challenge and spent four years (1508–1512) creating the frescoes. The ceiling, featuring biblical scenes such as "The Creation of Adam", is considered one of the greatest achievements in Western art.

Michelangelo continued to receive commissions from various popes and patrons throughout his career. His later works include "The Last Judgment" (1536–1541) on the Sistine Chapel's altar wall and the architectural design of St. Peter's Basilica in Rome, where he played a crucial role in the development of its iconic dome.

## Private Life

Michelangelo was known for his reclusive and deeply introspective nature. Unlike many of his contemporaries, he led a relatively modest life, avoiding luxury and preferring solitude. He never married or had children, dedicating himself entirely to his art.

His relationships with patrons and fellow artists were often tumultuous. He had a complicated yet respectful relationship with the Medici family, as well as a contentious dynamic with Pope Julius II, who frequently pressured him to complete projects. Michelangelo's personal writings and poetry reveal his complex emotions and deep spirituality. His letters and sonnets, some of which were addressed to close friends like Tommaso dei Cavalieri and Vittoria Colonna, offer insight into his thoughts on art, faith, and human existence.

## Death

Michelangelo continued to work until his final days, maintaining an unwavering dedication to his craft. He passed away on February 18, 1564, at the age of 88 in Rome. His body was transported to Florence, where he was buried in the Basilica of Santa Croce, fulfilling his wish to rest in his beloved homeland. His funeral was a grand affair, attended by many admirers and fellow artists. His death marked the end of an era, but his artistic legacy endured, influencing countless generations of artists and architects.

## Character

Michelangelo was a man of intense passion and determination. His relentless pursuit of artistic perfection often led to periods of frustration and isolation, yet he remained committed to his vision. He was known for his fiery temperament, his deep sense of spirituality, and his belief that art should reflect divine beauty and human struggle. Despite his sometimes difficult personality, he was admired for his immense talent and tireless work ethic. His ability to convey human emotion and form with such mastery made him a true artistic genius.

## Influence on Humanity

Michelangelo's contributions to art, architecture, and culture remain unparalleled. His impact on humanity can be seen in several key areas:

**1. Artistic Innovation** – His sculptures and paintings revolutionized the way the human form was depicted, emphasizing realism, anatomy, and emotion.

**2. Renaissance Ideals** – He embodied the Renaissance's humanist principles, blending classical knowledge with innovative artistic techniques.

**3. Architectural Masterpieces** – His work on St. Peter's Basilica set new standards in architectural design, influencing countless structures worldwide.

**4. Inspiration for Future Artists** – Artists such as Caravaggio, Bernini, and even modern sculptors continue to draw inspiration from his work.

**5. Cultural Legacy** – His art remains some of the most studied, admired, and reproduced in history, ensuring his influence endures for generations.

---

In conclusion, Michelangelo was more than an artist – he was a visionary whose work transcended time and space. His ability to capture the essence of human emotion and divine beauty cemented his status as one of history's greatest creative minds. His legacy continues to shape the worlds of art, architecture, and philosophy, making him a true giant of the Renaissance and beyond.

# Ferdinand Magellan
The navigator who led the
first circumnavigation of the world

Ferdinand Magellan was a Portuguese explorer whose expedition became the first to circumnavigate the Earth, a journey that forever changed the understanding of geography and global navigation. Although he did not survive the entire voyage, his leadership and determination paved the way for future explorations and established critical trade routes that shaped global commerce.

## Origin

Ferdinand Magellan was born in 1480 in Sabrosa, a small town in the northern region of Portugal. He belonged to a noble family, which granted him access to education and courtly life. His parents, Rodrigo de Magalhães and Alda de Mesquita, were minor nobility with ties to the Portuguese monarchy. Growing up in a country that was leading the Age of Exploration, Magellan was exposed to stories of great maritime journeys, which undoubtedly fueled his own ambitions.

Portugal was a dominant naval power at the time, exploring new sea routes to Asia, Africa, and the Americas. The Portuguese royal family sought to expand their influence by securing valuable spice trade routes, making maritime exploration a prestigious and lucrative pursuit.

## Childhood and Youth

Magellan's early life was shaped by the court of King John II of Portugal. At the age of 10, he became a page to Queen Leonor at the royal court in Lisbon. This position allowed him to receive an education in navigation, astronomy, cartography, and maritime affairs – essential skills for future explorers.

During his youth, he was influenced by the achievements of explorers like Bartolomeu Dias and Vasco da Gama, who had opened sea routes to India. By his late teens, Magellan had developed a deep interest in naval exploration and began studying the emerging theories about the geography of the world.

In 1505, at around the age of 25, Magellan joined the fleet of Francisco de Almeida, the first Portuguese viceroy of India. He participated in naval battles and expeditions along the East African coast and in India, gaining crucial experience in warfare and maritime navigation.

## Adulthood

Magellan spent several years serving the Portuguese Crown in various expeditions. He fought in battles against Arab and Indian fleets, helped establish Portuguese dominance in the Indian Ocean, and explored regions in modern-day Malaysia and Indonesia. However, his relationship with the Portuguese monarchy soured after he was accused of conducting unauthorized trade and was denied further royal patronage.

Frustrated with his treatment in Portugal, Magellan moved to Spain in 1517, seeking support for his ambitious plan to find a westward route to the Spice Islands (modern-day Indonesia). Spain, eager to compete with Portugal's dominance in the spice trade, saw an opportunity in Magellan's proposal. King Charles I of Spain (later Emperor Charles V) agreed to fund his expedition, providing him with five ships: the "Trinidad", "San Antonio", "Concepción", "Victoria", and "Santiago".

On September 20, 1519, Magellan set sail from Spain with a crew of about 270 men. His expedition faced numerous challenges, including mutinies, treacherous waters, and harsh weather conditions. After months of exploration, Magellan's fleet discovered the strait that now bears his name – the Strait of Magellan – at the southern tip of South America. This passage allowed them to enter the Pacific Ocean, which Magellan named due to its calm waters.

Crossing the Pacific proved to be one of the most arduous journeys in history. The crew suffered from starvation and scurvy, but in March 1521, they reached the Philippines. This marked a significant moment in global exploration, as they became the first Europeans to reach the archipelago.

## Private Life

Magellan was married to Beatriz Barbosa, the daughter of a wealthy Portuguese official in Seville, Spain. They had one son, Rodrigo, who tragically died at a young age. Due to his extended voyages, Magellan spent much of his life at sea, leaving his family behind in Spain.

Although he was deeply devoted to his maritime ambitions, his personal life was marked by hardship and sacrifice. His desire to serve Spain rather than his native Portugal led to political tensions, and he was often viewed as a traitor by the Portuguese Crown.

## Death

Ferdinand Magellan met his untimely death on April 27, 1521, in the Philippines. He was killed during the Battle of Mactan while attempting to convert the local population to Christianity and secure alliances for Spain. The local chieftain, Lapu-Lapu, resisted European influence, leading to a conflict in which Magellan was struck down by indigenous warriors.

Following Magellan's death, the expedition continued under the leadership of Juan Sebastián Elcano. The remaining ships sailed across the Indian Ocean, rounded the Cape of Good Hope, and finally returned to Spain in 1522. Of the original five ships, only the "Victoria" completed the journey, with just 18 of the original 270 crew members surviving. This marked the first recorded circumnavigation of the world, proving that vast oceanic routes connected different continents.

## Character

Magellan was known for his resilience, determination, and leadership. Despite facing mutinies, difficult weather conditions, and political opposition, he remained steadfast in his mission to find a western route to the Spice Islands.

He was also a man of ambition and faith, believing strongly in the religious mission of his voyages. His efforts to convert indigenous people to Christianity, however, led to conflicts that ultimately contributed to his death.

While his leadership was often harsh, his ability to navigate uncharted waters and manage a multinational crew demonstrated exceptional skill and endurance. His vision and commitment to exploration changed the world forever.

## Influence on Humanity

Magellan's impact on global history is profound, with several key contributions:

**1. First Circumnavigation of the Earth** – Although he did not complete the journey himself, his expedition provided irrefutable proof that distant oceans were interconnected.

**2. Global Trade and Exploration** – His voyages paved the way for future European expansion into Asia and the Americas, establishing new trade routes that fueled globalization.

**3. Navigation and Cartography** – The maps created from his expedition greatly improved European understanding of world geography and influenced future explorers.

**4. Cultural Exchange** – His encounters with various indigenous peoples contributed to the blending of cultures, albeit sometimes through violent means.

**5. Maritime Strategy** – His successful navigation of the Strait of Magellan demonstrated the importance of strategic naval passages, shaping global trade for centuries to come.

In conclusion, Ferdinand Magellan was a visionary navigator whose expedition forever changed humanity's perception of the world. His journey not only demonstrated the vastness of the planet but also set the stage for global trade, cultural exchanges, and further exploration. Despite his tragic death, his legacy endures, making him one of the most significant figures in the history of exploration.

# Martin Luther
Leader of the Protestant Reformation

Martin Luther was a German theologian, monk, and professor whose actions sparked the Protestant Reformation in the early 16th century. His challenge to the Catholic Church's practices, particularly the sale of indulgences, led to the formation of Protestant Christianity and forever changed the religious, political, and cultural landscape of Europe. His translation of the Bible into German made scripture accessible to the common people, reinforcing his belief in salvation through faith alone.

## Origin

Martin Luther was born on November 10, 1483, in Eisleben, in the Holy Roman Empire (modern-day Germany). He was the son of Hans and Margarethe Luther, a working-class family that sought to improve their social standing through hard work and education. His father was a miner who later became a leaseholder of copper mines and smelting operations, providing the family with some financial stability.

The political and religious climate of the late 15th century was dominated by the Catholic Church, which held significant power over both spiritual and secular matters. The Church's influence, along with the emerging Renaissance ideas of humanism and education, shaped the intellectual world that Martin Luther would later challenge.

## Childhood and Youth

Luther was raised in a strict household, where discipline and religious devotion were emphasized. His father had ambitions for him to become a lawyer, so Luther was sent to school in Mansfeld, Magdeburg, and later Eisenach, where he received a rigorous education in Latin, grammar, rhetoric, and philosophy.

In 1501, at the age of 17, he enrolled at the University of Erfurt, one of the leading universities in Germany. There, he completed his bachelor's degree in 1502 and his master's degree in 1505. Following his father's wishes, he began studying law, but a life-changing event altered his course. During a violent thunderstorm in 1505, Luther was nearly struck by lightning. In a moment of fear, he vowed to become a monk if he survived. True to his word, he abandoned his legal studies and entered the Augustinian Monastery in Erfurt.

## Adulthood

Luther quickly adapted to monastic life, dedicating himself to prayer, fasting, and theological study. He was ordained as a priest in 1507 and continued his education at the University of Wittenberg, earning his Doctor of Theology in 1512. He then became a professor of biblical studies at Wittenberg, where he gained a reputation for his deep knowledge of scripture and powerful preaching.

During this period, Luther became increasingly troubled by the Catholic Church's practices, particularly the sale of indulgences – payments made to the Church in exchange for the forgiveness of sins. In 1517, he famously nailed his "Ninety-Five Theses" to the door of Wittenberg Castle Church, challenging Church doctrine and sparking widespread debate.

His criticisms led to intense conflict with Church authorities. Pope Leo X demanded that Luther recant his statements, but he refused. In 1521, he was excommunicated and later declared an outlaw by Emperor Charles V at the Diet of Worms. Protected by Frederick the Wise, Elector of Saxony, Luther went into hiding at Wartburg Castle, where he translated the New Testament into German, making the Bible accessible to ordinary people.

Over the following years, Luther continued to preach, write, and reform Christian practices. He emphasized salvation through faith alone ("sola fide"), the authority of scripture ("sola scriptura"), and the priesthood of all believers, laying the theological foundations of Protestant Christianity.

## Private Life

Despite his monastic background, Luther left the clergy and married Katharina von Bora, a former nun, in 1525. Their marriage was unusual at the time but became a model for Protestant clerical families. They had six children and maintained a warm, lively household.

Luther's personal life reflected his beliefs in simplicity and family values. He enjoyed music, social gatherings, and discussions with friends and students. His home in Wittenberg became a center of theological debate and intellectual exchange.

Although he was deeply devoted to his faith, Luther was not without flaws. He was known for his fiery temper and controversial writings, particularly his later anti-Semitic statements, which have been the subject of extensive criticism and debate.

## Death

Luther's health declined in his later years due to heart disease and other ailments. He continued writing and preaching until his death on February 18, 1546, in his hometown of Eisleben. His final words reportedly were, "We are beggars: this is true." He was buried in Wittenberg's Castle Church, where his reformation had begun nearly three decades earlier.

His death marked the end of his personal influence, but his ideas continued to spread, shaping Protestantism and influencing generations of theologians and reformers.

## Character

Luther was a complex figure – courageous, passionate, and deeply committed to his faith. His willingness to defy powerful authorities demonstrated his belief in personal conviction and the pursuit of truth. He was an eloquent writer and speaker, capable of inspiring followers and challenging opponents with equal force.

However, his character also had its contradictions. He was at times harsh and intolerant of dissent, and his polemical style led to conflicts not only with the Catholic Church but also with other reformers. Despite his flaws, his dedication to religious reform and intellectual freedom left an indelible mark on history.

## Influence on Humanity

Martin Luther's impact on Christianity and world history cannot be overstated. His actions and writings led to profound changes that shaped religious, political, and cultural developments for centuries. Some of his key contributions include:

**1. The Protestant Reformation** – Luther's rejection of Catholic doctrine led to the formation of various Protestant denominations, reshaping Christianity forever.

**2. Bible Translation and Literacy** – By translating the Bible into German, he made scripture accessible to ordinary people, encouraging literacy and education.

**3. Religious Freedom and Individual Faith** – His teachings emphasized personal faith over institutional authority, influencing concepts of religious liberty and democracy.

**4. Challenging Church Authority** – His defiance of the Pope and the Catholic hierarchy set a precedent for questioning and reforming religious institutions.

**5. Influence on Western Thought** – His ideas contributed to the development of modern theology, ethics, and political philosophy.

---

In conclusion, Martin Luther was a pivotal figure whose courage, intellect, and faith reshaped Christianity and the world. His legacy endures in Protestant churches, religious freedoms, and the ongoing pursuit of truth and reform in all aspects of life. His story remains a testament to the power of ideas and the enduring impact of those who challenge the status quo.

# Elizabeth I
Queen of England and symbol of the "Golden Age"

Elizabeth I of England was one of the most influential and remarkable monarchs in history. Ruling for 44 years during the late 16th century, she presided over a golden age of English culture, exploration, and military success. Her reign, often called the Elizabethan Era, saw the defeat of the Spanish Armada, the flourishing of the English Renaissance, and the solidification of Protestant England. Despite intense challenges, both personal and political, Elizabeth navigated her rule with intelligence, charisma, and a deep commitment to her people.

## Origin

Elizabeth Tudor was born on September 7, 1533, at Greenwich Palace, the daughter of King Henry VIII and his second wife, Anne Boleyn. Her birth was initially met with great disappointment, as Henry VIII had desperately wanted a male heir. Anne Boleyn's inability to produce a son led to her downfall, and she was executed in 1536 when Elizabeth was just two years old. Following her mother's death, Elizabeth was declared illegitimate and removed from the line of succession.

Her father later married Jane Seymour, who gave birth to Prince Edward, and Elizabeth's place in the royal family remained uncertain. Despite her precarious status, she was given an education befitting a princess, ensuring she was well-prepared for any future role in governance.

## Childhood and Youth

Elizabeth spent much of her childhood at Hatfield House, where she received an extensive education. Guided by some of the greatest scholars of the time, including Roger Ascham, she became fluent in multiple languages, including Latin, Greek, French, and Italian. She also studied philosophy, history, and theology, developing a keen intellect that would later define her reign.

Her half-brother, Edward VI, ascended the throne after Henry VIII's death in 1547, but his reign was short-lived. Following Edward's death in

1553, Elizabeth's half-sister Mary I took the throne and attempted to restore Catholicism in England. Elizabeth, a Protestant, was viewed as a threat and was imprisoned in the Tower of London for a time. Though she was eventually released, her life remained in constant peril as she navigated the dangerous political landscape of her sister's rule.

## Adulthood

Mary I's death in 1558 brought Elizabeth to the throne at the age of 25. She inherited a country deeply divided by religious conflict, economic instability, and external threats. With remarkable political skill, she re-established Protestantism as England's official religion through the Elizabethan Religious Settlement, which sought to balance moderate Protestant and Catholic beliefs.

One of the defining moments of her reign came in 1588, when the Spanish Armada, sent by King Philip II of Spain, attempted to invade England. Against all odds, the English navy, aided by strategic weather conditions, defeated the Armada, solidifying England's status as a dominant naval power.

Elizabeth's reign also saw significant cultural achievements, as literature and the arts flourished. This era gave rise to William Shakespeare, Christopher Marlowe, and other literary giants whose works continue to shape English literature. The Queen's support for exploration led to the exploits of Sir Francis Drake, who circumnavigated the world, and Sir Walter Raleigh, who established early attempts at English colonization in North America.

## Private Life

Elizabeth famously never married, earning her the title "The Virgin Queen." Despite numerous marriage proposals and diplomatic courtships with European princes and noblemen, she remained steadfastly single. Her closest relationship was with Robert Dudley, Earl of Leicester, whom many suspected she loved but could not marry due to political complications.

Her decision to remain unmarried allowed her to retain absolute authority over her kingdom. She skillfully used the prospect of marriage as a political tool, forming alliances without committing to any particular suitor. Her court was filled with intrigue, yet she maintained control with a combination of charm, intelligence, and occasional ruthlessness.

She surrounded herself with trusted advisors, including William Cecil and Francis Walsingham, who helped her manage state affairs and defend against internal and external threats. Despite her powerful status, Elizabeth was known for her deep connection to her people, frequently engaging in public appearances and speeches that reinforced her image as the mother of England.

## Death

By the early 1600s, Elizabeth's health began to decline. She suffered from depression following the deaths of many of her closest friends and advisors, including Robert Dudley. In March 1603, she fell gravely ill and passed away on March 24 at Richmond Palace at the age of 69.

With no direct heir, she was succeeded by James VI of Scotland, the son of her cousin Mary, Queen of Scots. This peaceful transition of power united England and Scotland under one monarchy, setting the stage for the eventual formation of Great Britain.

Elizabeth was buried in Westminster Abbey, and her tomb bears the inscription, "Partner in throne and grave, here we sleep, Elizabeth and Mary, sisters in hope of the Resurrection."

## Character

Elizabeth I was a complex and multifaceted ruler. She was both charismatic and calculating, possessing an extraordinary ability to inspire loyalty while maintaining a firm grip on power. Her intelligence and education allowed her to navigate the treacherous political environment of her time, balancing the demands of religious factions, foreign powers, and domestic rivals.

Her image as the "Virgin Queen" was not just a personal choice but a political strategy that reinforced her authority and devotion to England. Despite facing constant threats, including assassination plots and conspiracies, she remained resolute and unshaken in her leadership.

Her speeches, including the famous Tilbury Speech before the battle with the Spanish Armada, showcased her ability to connect with her people and rally them in times of crisis. She possessed a sharp wit, a love for pageantry, and a keen understanding of the power of symbolism in maintaining her rule.

## Influence on Humanity

Elizabeth I's reign left an enduring legacy that shaped the course of English and world history. Her impact can be seen in several key areas:

**1. Religious Stability** – Her religious policies helped define Protestant England and reduced sectarian conflicts that had plagued the country before her rule.

**2. Expansion of the English Navy** – Under her leadership, England became a formidable naval power, which later enabled the growth of the British Empire.

**3. Cultural Flourishing** – The Elizabethan Age was a golden era for English literature, with the works of Shakespeare and others shaping the global literary canon.

**4. Early Exploration and Colonization** – Her support for explorers laid the groundwork for future English colonization efforts in North America.

**5. Model of Female Leadership** – As one of the most powerful female rulers in history, Elizabeth I set a precedent for strong, independent women in leadership roles.

In conclusion, Elizabeth I was not only a great monarch but also a symbol of resilience, intelligence, and dedication to her nation. Her reign ushered in a period of relative peace, artistic brilliance, and national pride, ensuring that she would be remembered as one of England's greatest and most beloved rulers.

# Francis Bacon
Philosopher and founder of the scientific method

Francis Bacon was a statesman, philosopher, scientist, and writer whose contributions laid the foundation for the modern scientific method. A visionary thinker, he championed empirical research and inductive reasoning, reshaping the way knowledge was pursued. His works on science, law, and politics influenced generations of intellectuals and laid the groundwork for the Enlightenment.

## Origin

Francis Bacon was born on January 22, 1561, in London, England, during the reign of Queen Elizabeth I. He was the youngest son of Sir Nicholas Bacon, who served as Lord Keeper of the Great Seal, and Anne Cooke Bacon, a highly educated woman with strong Puritan beliefs. His family's wealth and political connections provided him with early access to the royal court and the best educational opportunities available in England.

Bacon was born into a time of great political and intellectual transformation. The Renaissance had brought a revival of learning, and England was experiencing an age of exploration, religious upheaval, and scientific curiosity. These influences would later shape his thinking and fuel his quest for knowledge.

## Childhood and Youth

Francis Bacon showed exceptional intellectual promise from an early age. At the age of 12, he was sent to Trinity College, Cambridge, where he studied under some of the most distinguished scholars of the time. However, he grew disillusioned with the Aristotelian philosophy that dominated academia and began formulating his own ideas about empirical research.

After completing his studies at Cambridge, Bacon traveled to France in 1576 to work under Sir Amias Paulet, the English ambassador to the French court. His experiences in France exposed him to European political structures and court diplomacy, further broadening his worldview.

However, his stay in France was cut short when his father died in 1579, forcing him to return to England and seek financial stability.

## Adulthood

Upon returning to England, Bacon pursued a career in law, enrolling at Gray's Inn. By 1582, he was admitted to the bar and began working on legal cases. However, his true passion lay in philosophy and scientific inquiry.

In 1584, he entered Parliament as a member for Melcombe Regis and later represented several other constituencies. His political career was marked by his service under Queen Elizabeth I and, later, King James I, who appointed him Attorney General in 1613 and Lord Chancellor in 1618. Despite his political success, he was also accused of corruption and impeached in 1621, leading to his fall from grace.

Bacon's most significant contributions came in the form of his writings. His seminal work, "Novum Organum" (1620), outlined his new method of scientific inquiry, emphasizing inductive reasoning over the rigid deduction of Aristotelian thought. This approach, which called for observation, experimentation, and hypothesis-testing, laid the foundation for the modern scientific method.

Apart from philosophy, Bacon also wrote extensively on politics, law, and morality. His essays, compiled in "Essays" (1597, 1612, and 1625), provided keen insights into human behavior, governance, and ethics.

## Private Life

Bacon's personal life was marked by intellectual pursuits and social ambition. In 1606, he married Alice Barnham, the daughter of a wealthy London merchant. However, their marriage was not particularly affectionate, and there is little evidence of a close relationship between them.

Throughout his life, Bacon was deeply devoted to knowledge and writing, often prioritizing his intellectual endeavors over personal relationships. His friendships with notable figures such as the Earl of Essex and King James I played a crucial role in his career but also contributed to his political downfall.

Bacon's sexual orientation has been the subject of speculation. Some historians suggest that he may have had romantic relationships with men, based on contemporary accounts and his close relationships with male companions. However, no definitive evidence exists to confirm these claims.

## Death

Francis Bacon died on April 9, 1626, at the age of 65. Ironically, his death was the result of a scientific experiment. While traveling near Highgate, he attempted to test the effects of cold preservation by stuffing a chicken with snow. He caught pneumonia during the process and succumbed to the illness shortly after.

Despite his downfall in politics, Bacon remained intellectually active until his final days. He left behind a vast body of work that would influence generations of scientists, philosophers, and policymakers.

## Character

Bacon was an intellectual giant with an insatiable curiosity for knowledge. He was pragmatic, visionary, and determined to reform the way people understood the world. His scientific rigor and philosophical insights made him one of the most forward-thinking minds of his era.

However, he was also ambitious and politically astute, sometimes engaging in questionable dealings to secure favor at court. His impeachment for corruption in 1621 tarnished his reputation, but he never let it deter him from his intellectual pursuits.

Despite his fall from political grace, he remained dedicated to advancing human knowledge. His ability to think beyond the conventional frameworks of his time made him a revolutionary figure in philosophy and science.

## Influence on Humanity

Francis Bacon's contributions have had a profound and lasting impact on multiple fields. His ideas shaped the course of scientific inquiry, governance, and education. Some of his most significant influences include:

**1. The Scientific Method** – Bacon's emphasis on observation, experimentation, and inductive reasoning became the foundation of modern scientific inquiry. His methods influenced figures such as Isaac Newton and paved the way for the Enlightenment.

**2. Empiricism in Philosophy** – His work contributed to the development of empiricism, a school of thought that asserts that knowledge comes from sensory experience. This philosophy would later be expanded by thinkers like John Locke and David Hume.

**3. Legal and Political Thought** – Bacon's essays and legal writings influenced governance, ethics, and the structure of modern legal systems.

**4. Literary Contributions** – His essays remain widely read and admired for their wisdom, brevity, and keen observations of human nature.

**5. Influence on Technology and Innovation** – His vision of scientific progress as a means to improve human life inspired advancements in technology, engineering, and medicine.

---

In conclusion, Francis Bacon was not just a philosopher or politician – he was a revolutionary thinker who reshaped humanity's approach to knowledge. His contributions to science, philosophy, and law continue to influence intellectual thought and the pursuit of truth. His legacy endures as a testament to the power of reason and the endless potential of human inquiry.

# Galileo Galilei
Father of modern science and astronomy

Galileo Galilei was an Italian astronomer, physicist, and engineer whose groundbreaking discoveries laid the foundation for modern science. Often referred to as the "father of observational astronomy," he revolutionized our understanding of the cosmos with his telescope observations and championed the heliocentric theory of the solar system. His work not only advanced scientific knowledge but also challenged long-held beliefs, bringing him into conflict with the Catholic Church.

## Origin

Galileo Galilei was born on February 15, 1564, in Pisa, a city in the Grand Duchy of Tuscany (modern-day Italy). He was the eldest of six children in the Galilei family. His father, Vincenzo Galilei, was a musician, composer, and music theorist, while his mother, Giulia Ammannati came from a noble background.

Vincenzo's intellectual pursuits and critical approach to established knowledge greatly influenced Galileo's thinking. The Renaissance was in full swing, fostering a spirit of inquiry and discovery that would later shape Galileo's scientific endeavors.

## Childhood and Youth

Galileo received his early education at a monastery school in Vallombrosa, near Florence, where he displayed a keen intellect. His father encouraged him to pursue a medical career, leading him to enroll at the University of Pisa in 1581 to study medicine.

However, Galileo soon developed a passion for mathematics and natural philosophy. He abandoned his medical studies in favor of mathematics and physics, influenced by the works of Aristotle and Archimedes His first significant scientific discovery occurred in 1583 when he observed the isochronism of a pendulum, which later contributed to the development of more accurate timekeeping devices. By 1589, Galileo secured a position as a professor of mathematics at the University of Pisa, marking the beginning of his academic career. During this period, he conducted experiments challenging Aristotle's theories on motion, setting the stage for the development of classical mechanics.

## Adulthood

In 1592, Galileo moved to the University of Padua, where he taught geometry, mechanics, and astronomy for 18 years. This was a highly productive period during which he made significant contributions to kinematics, material science, and engineering.

By 1609, he had heard of a new invention from the Netherlands: the telescope. Improving upon the design, Galileo built his own version and turned it towards the heavens. What he saw would change the course of astronomy forever. His observations included:

- The rugged surface of the Moon, challenging the Aristotelian belief that celestial bodies were smooth and perfect.
- The four largest moons of Jupiter (now known as the Galilean moons), providing evidence that not all celestial bodies orbited the Earth.
- The phases of Venus, supporting the heliocentric model proposed by Copernicus.
- Countless stars in the Milky Way, revealing the vastness of the universe.

In 1610, he published "Sidereus Nuncius" ("The Starry Messenger"), detailing these discoveries. His findings earned him fame but also attracted the scrutiny of the Catholic Church, which upheld the geocentric model of the universe.

## Private Life

Galileo never married but had three children – two daughters, Virginia and Livia, and a son, Vincenzo – with a woman named Marina Gamba. Due to their illegitimate status, his daughters were placed in a convent, while Vincenzo was later legitimized. Despite his growing scientific reputation, Galileo struggled financially. His teaching positions provided limited income, and he often sought patronage from influential figures, including the Medici family in Florence. His relationship with his daughters, especially Virginia (who became Sister Maria Celeste), was deeply affectionate, as revealed in their surviving letters.

## Death

Galileo's later years were marked by his infamous trial by the Roman Catholic Inquisition. His advocacy for the heliocentric model led to accusations of heresy. In 1633, he was forced to recant his support for Copernican theory under the threat of severe punishment. He was sentenced to house arrest, where he remained for the rest of his life.

Despite his confinement, Galileo continued to work. In 1638, he published "Two New Sciences", summarizing his contributions to physics, particularly in mechanics and the study of motion.

He died on January 8, 1642, at the age of 77, in his villa in Arcetri, near Florence. He was blind by this time, yet his intellectual curiosity never waned.

## Character

Galileo was a man of immense intellect, curiosity, and perseverance. His relentless pursuit of truth often placed him at odds with powerful institutions, yet he remained committed to scientific inquiry. He was also a skilled communicator, using wit and persuasive arguments to defend his ideas. His ability to explain complex concepts in accessible language helped bridge the gap between scholars and the general public.

However, he could be combative, particularly when defending his theories. His sharp critiques of other scholars and his sometimes sarcastic tone made him as many enemies as admirers. Nevertheless, his unwavering dedication to the scientific method set him apart as a pioneer of modern science.

## Influence on Humanity

Galileo's impact on science and human thought is immeasurable. His contributions laid the foundation for future discoveries and reshaped humanity's understanding of the universe. His key influences include:

**1. Revolutionizing Astronomy** – By using the telescope to make systematic observations, Galileo provided evidence that challenged the traditional geocentric model.

**2. Foundations of Modern Physics** – His studies on motion and acceleration influenced Isaac Newton's work, leading to the formulation of classical mechanics.

**3. Scientific Methodology** – Galileo championed observation and experimentation over reliance on authority, establishing principles that remain central to scientific inquiry.

**4. Impact on the Church and Science Relationship** – His trial highlighted the tension between science and religion, paving the way for future debates on the role of evidence-based reasoning in human knowledge.

**5. Inspiration for Future Generations** – Scientists such as Newton, Einstein, and Hawking built upon Galileo's legacy, demonstrating the enduring relevance of his discoveries.

---

In conclusion, Galileo Galilei was more than just an astronomer – he was a visionary who challenged the status quo and reshaped humanity's understanding of the cosmos. His relentless pursuit of truth, despite opposition, established him as a foundational figure in the history of science. Today, his contributions continue to inspire scientists, educators, and thinkers around the world.

# William Shakespeare
The greatest playwright in English literature

William Shakespeare is widely regarded as the greatest playwright and poet in the English language. His works, which include tragedies, comedies, and historical plays, have influenced literature, theater, and storytelling for over four centuries. His ability to explore the human condition, combined with his mastery of poetic language, has cemented his legacy as a literary giant.

## Origin

William Shakespeare was born on April 23, 1564, in Stratford-upon-Avon, a market town in Warwickshire, England. He was the third of eight children born to John Shakespeare, a prosperous glove-maker and town official, and Mary Arden, the daughter of a wealthy landowner. His birth coincided with the Elizabethan era, a period of cultural flourishing and the rise of the English Renaissance.

Stratford-upon-Avon was a thriving town with a strong tradition of commerce and civic engagement. Shakespeare's family, though not of noble birth, enjoyed a comfortable life due to John Shakespeare's business and political connections. However, financial difficulties later troubled the family, possibly influencing Shakespeare's decision to leave for London in search of better opportunities.

## Childhood and Youth

Shakespeare likely attended the King's New School in Stratford, where he would have received a rigorous education in Latin, classical literature, rhetoric, and history. Though records of his schooling do not survive, the depth of classical knowledge displayed in his plays suggests he was well-educated.

Little is known about his teenage years, leading some scholars to refer to this period as the "lost years." It is speculated that he may have worked as a teacher, apprentice, or actor before his theatrical career began in earnest. His exposure to traveling theater troupes may have inspired his passion for drama and storytelling.

## Adulthood

By the late 1580s or early 1590s, Shakespeare had moved to London and begun working in the theater industry. His first known works were "Henry VI" (Parts 1, 2, and 3) and "Titus Andronicus", which established him as a playwright. By 1594, he was a founding member of the Lord Chamberlain's Men, a popular acting company.

Over the next two decades, Shakespeare wrote some of the most enduring plays in history, including:

- **Tragedies**: "Hamlet, Macbeth, Othello, King Lear, Romeo and Juliet".
- **Comedies**: "A Midsummer Night's Dream, Twelfth Night, Much Ado About Nothing, The Merchant of Venice".
- **Histories**: "Richard III, Henry V, Julius Caesar".

His works were performed at venues like The Theatre and later, the famous Globe Theatre, which was built in 1599 by his company. His plays gained immense popularity, attracting audiences from all social classes, from commoners to royalty.

In addition to his plays, Shakespeare wrote 154 sonnets and several narrative poems, including "Venus and Adonis" and "The Rape of Lucrece", showcasing his mastery of poetic form and deep understanding of human emotions.

## Private Life

In 1582, at just 18 years old, William Shakespeare married Anne Hathaway, who was eight years older than him. The couple had three children: Susanna (born 1583) and twins Hamnet and Judith (born 1585). Hamnet died at the age of 11, an event that may have influenced Shakespeare's later tragedies.

Despite his rising fame in London, Shakespeare maintained strong ties to Stratford, where his family resided. He acquired property there, including

New Place, one of the largest houses in the town. In 1613, he retired to Stratford, spending his final years with his family.

While there are numerous theories about Shakespeare's personal beliefs and relationships, much of his private life remains a mystery. Some scholars have speculated about his possible involvement in clandestine political or religious activities, but there is little concrete evidence.

## Death

Shakespeare died on April 23, 1616, at the age of 52. The cause of his death is unknown, though some accounts suggest he succumbed to an illness. He was buried in Holy Trinity Church in Stratford-upon-Avon, where his epitaph, allegedly written by him, warns against disturbing his remains.

His last will and testament divided his estate among his family and friends, famously leaving his "second-best bed" to his wife, Anne Hathaway – a bequest that has fueled much speculation about their relationship.

## Character

Shakespeare was a keen observer of human nature, which is evident in the depth and complexity of his characters. His ability to portray both the grandeur and flaws of humanity has made his works timeless.

He was also a shrewd businessman, involved in theater management and real estate investments. His financial success enabled him to retire comfortably, a rare feat for a playwright of his time.

Despite his literary genius, Shakespeare remains an enigmatic figure. Unlike many famous writers, he left behind no personal letters or diaries, and his true personality is inferred mainly from his works and contemporary accounts.

## Influence on Humanity

Shakespeare's impact on literature, language, and culture is immeasurable. His contributions include:

**1. Shaping the English Language** – Many words and phrases used today originated in his works, including "foregone conclusion, break the ice, all that glitters is not gold", and "wild-goose chase".

**2. Universal Themes** – His exploration of love, power, betrayal, ambition, and fate resonates across cultures and eras.

**3. Influencing Literature and Theater** – Writers from Charles Dickens to modern playwrights have drawn inspiration from his works.

**4. Adaptations and Interpretations** – His plays have been adapted into countless films, novels, and performances worldwide.

**5. Cultural Icon** – His legacy is celebrated annually through festivals, academic studies, and theatrical productions, ensuring his works remain relevant.

---

In conclusion, William Shakespeare was more than just a playwright; he was a literary architect who reshaped the world of storytelling. His genius lies in his ability to capture the essence of human emotion, making his works as compelling today as they were in the 16th century. His influence continues to shape literature, theater, and popular culture, cementing his status as one of the greatest writers in history.

# Johannes Kepler
Mathematician and pioneer of planetary motion theory

Johannes Kepler was a German astronomer, mathematician, and physicist who fundamentally transformed our understanding of planetary motion. He formulated the three laws of planetary motion, which provided the foundation for Newton's law of universal gravitation. His work not only confirmed the heliocentric model proposed by Copernicus but also established mathematical principles that guided future astronomical discoveries. Kepler's contributions extended beyond astronomy, influencing optics, mathematics, and the philosophy of science.

## Origin

Johannes Kepler was born on December 27, 1571, in Weil der Stadt, a small town in the Holy Roman Empire (modern-day Germany). He came from a humble background; his father, Heinrich Kepler, was a mercenary soldier, and his mother, Katharina Guldenmann, was a herbalist and healer. His family was of modest means, and his childhood was marked by financial struggles.

His birthplace, Weil der Stadt, was a part of the Duchy of Württemberg, an area influenced by Lutheran religious traditions. Kepler's Lutheran faith played a significant role in shaping his worldview, and throughout his life, he saw his scientific pursuits as a way to understand the divine order of the cosmos.

## Childhood and Youth

Kepler's early years were fraught with hardship. His father frequently traveled as a mercenary and eventually disappeared, leaving the family without stable financial support. His mother's reputation as a healer and her later accusation of witchcraft created additional social challenges.

Despite these difficulties, Kepler demonstrated exceptional intelligence from an early age. He attended the Latin school in Leonberg before securing a scholarship to the University of Tübingen in 1589. There, he studied theology, philosophy, and mathematics under the guidance of Michael Maestlin, a staunch advocate of the Copernican heliocentric model.

While at Tübingen, Kepler became deeply interested in astronomy and mathematics. Though originally intended for a clerical career, his mathematical talent led to his appointment as a mathematics teacher and astronomer in Graz, Austria, in 1594. This marked the beginning of his professional engagement with celestial studies.

## Adulthood

Kepler's career took a decisive turn when he was invited to work as an assistant to the renowned Danish astronomer Tycho Brahe in 1600. Brahe had compiled an extensive dataset of planetary observations, which Kepler used to develop his groundbreaking laws of planetary motion.

Following Brahe's death in 1601, Kepler succeeded him as the Imperial Mathematician to Emperor Rudolf II in Prague. Over the next decade, he meticulously analyzed Brahe's data, leading to the publication of his first two laws of planetary motion in "Astronomia Nova" (1609):

**1. The Law of Ellipses** – Planets orbit the Sun in elliptical paths, rather than perfect circles.

**2. The Law of Equal Areas** – A planet sweeps out equal areas in equal times as it moves along its orbit.

His third law, the Harmonic Law, which establishes a relationship between a planet's orbital period and its distance from the Sun, was published in "Harmonices Mundi" (1619). These laws revolutionized astronomy, providing the first accurate mathematical description of planetary motion.

Kepler also contributed significantly to optics. In 1604, he described the behavior of light in telescopes and lenses in his work "Astronomiae Pars Optica", laying the groundwork for future developments in optical science. His studies on the refraction of light helped improve telescope designs, including those used by Galileo Galilei.

In 1627, Kepler published the "Rudolphine Tables", which contained precise planetary tables based on Brahe's observations and Kepler's own calculations. These tables significantly improved the accuracy of celestial predictions and were used by astronomers for decades.

## Private Life

Kepler's personal life was marked by tragedy and resilience. In 1597, he married Barbara Müller, a wealthy widow. They had three children, but only one survived infancy. Barbara passed away in 1611, leaving Kepler devastated.

In 1613, he remarried to Susanna Reuttinger, with whom he had six more children. Although their marriage was reportedly more stable than his first, financial struggles and political turmoil made their life challenging.

Kepler also faced personal hardship when his mother, Katharina, was accused of witchcraft in 1615. He spent years defending her in court, eventually securing her release in 1621. This experience deepened his belief in rational inquiry over superstition.

## Death

Kepler's later years were spent in financial hardship, as political instability in the Holy Roman Empire disrupted his patronage. He continued to work on his astronomical studies, seeking additional support for his research.

On November 15, 1630, Johannes Kepler passed away in Regensburg at the age of 58. He died from a fever, likely brought on by exhaustion and illness. His burial site was later lost due to war and destruction, but his legacy endured through his scientific contributions.

## Character

Kepler was an inquisitive and deeply spiritual man who saw his scientific work as a means to understand God's design of the universe. He was meticulous in his research, willing to challenge established ideas in pursuit of truth. His determination, despite personal hardships and financial struggles, reflected his unwavering commitment to knowledge. Although often overshadowed by Galileo and Newton, Kepler was a revolutionary thinker who bridged the gap between classical and modern science. His intellectual humility and perseverance made him a respected figure among his contemporaries and later generations.

## Influence on Humanity

Kepler's impact on science and human thought is profound, with several key contributions:

**1. Laws of Planetary Motion** – His three laws provided the mathematical framework that enabled Isaac Newton to formulate the law of universal gravitation.

**2. Advancements in Astronomy** – By proving that planetary orbits were elliptical, Kepler overturned centuries of Aristotelian and Ptolemaic astronomy.

**3. Optical Science** – His work in optics laid the foundation for the development of telescopes and the study of light refraction.

**4. Mathematical Modeling** – Kepler introduced rigorous mathematical methods into astronomy, influencing the way scientists approach celestial mechanics.

**5. Impact on Scientific Methodology** – His reliance on empirical data and systematic analysis helped establish modern scientific inquiry.

In conclusion, Johannes Kepler was a pioneering scientist whose discoveries reshaped our understanding of the cosmos. His work laid the foundation for future astronomical and scientific breakthroughs, solidifying his place among the greatest minds in history. His unwavering dedication to discovery, even in the face of adversity, continues to inspire scientists and thinkers around the world.

# William Harvey
Discoverer of blood circulation

William Harvey was an English physician whose groundbreaking discovery of the circulation of blood revolutionized medical science. His meticulous experiments and observations laid the foundation for modern physiology and cardiology. Harvey's work challenged long-held medical beliefs and reshaped the understanding of human anatomy. His studies on blood circulation remain one of the most significant contributions to medical history.

## Origin

William Harvey was born on April 1, 1578, in Folkestone, Kent, England. He was the eldest of seven sons born to Thomas Harvey, a prosperous merchant, and Joan Halke. His father's business success allowed William to receive a high-quality education, positioning him for a prestigious career in medicine. His family belonged to England's rising merchant class, providing him with financial stability and opportunities for academic advancement.

Harvey was born during the Elizabethan era, a time of rapid scientific exploration and intellectual growth. England was emerging as a global power, and Renaissance ideals were encouraging a shift toward empirical research and inquiry. This environment played a significant role in shaping Harvey's approach to science and medicine.

## Childhood and Youth

Harvey's early education took place at King's School in Canterbury, where he displayed an early aptitude for learning, particularly in the sciences. At the age of 15, he enrolled at Gonville and Caius College, Cambridge, where he studied Latin, Greek, philosophy, and natural sciences. His classical education equipped him with the analytical skills necessary for his future medical career.

In 1599, he traveled to Italy to study medicine at the prestigious University of Padua, one of Europe's leading centers for medical education.

There, he trained under the renowned anatomist Hieronymus Fabricius, who had previously described the existence of valves in veins but had not determined their function. Harvey completed his medical degree in 1602, graduating with honors. His time in Padua exposed him to advanced medical theories and provided the foundation for his future research into circulation.

## Adulthood

After returning to England in 1602, Harvey settled in London and became a physician. He joined the Royal College of Physicians in 1607 and was later appointed as a physician at St. Bartholomew's Hospital. His reputation as an excellent clinician quickly grew, earning him a place as the personal physician to King James I in 1618 and later to King Charles I.

Harvey's most significant contribution to medicine was his discovery of the circulation of blood. In 1628, William Harvey published "Exercitatio Anatomica de Motu Cordis et Sanguinis in Animalibus" ("An Anatomical Study on the Motion of the Heart and Blood in Animals"), in which he systematically demonstrated that blood circulates through the body, driven by the heart's pumping action.

His research challenged the prevailing Galenic theory, which had suggested that blood was produced by the liver and consumed by the body rather than recirculated. Harvey's experiments, which included meticulous dissections and vivisections, provided empirical evidence that blood moves in a continuous loop through arteries and veins.

Despite initial resistance from conservative medical scholars, Harvey's findings gradually gained acceptance and transformed the field of physiology. His work laid the groundwork for later advancements in medicine, including the study of the cardiovascular system and the development of modern surgery.

## Private Life

William Harvey married Elizabeth Browne, the daughter of Lancelot Browne, a prominent physician, in 1604. The couple had no children, and Harvey's devotion to his work often took precedence over his personal life. His marriage provided him with connections to influential circles, further securing his position in the royal court.

Harvey was known for his reserved and diligent personality. He was deeply committed to his research and often spent long hours conducting experiments. His professional commitments took him across England and Europe, where he engaged with leading scientists and physicians of his time.

Despite his success, Harvey faced criticism and opposition. His revolutionary ideas about blood circulation contradicted long-established medical beliefs, leading some contemporaries to dismiss or ridicule his work. However, he remained steadfast in his convictions, confident in the accuracy of his observations and experiments.

## Death

Harvey spent his later years in quiet retirement, continuing his studies and writing. He suffered from declining health in his final years, possibly due to the stress of his work and the political upheavals of the English Civil War.

He passed away on June 3, 1657, at the age of 79, at his brother's home in Roehampton, London. He was buried in Hempstead, Essex. His death marked the loss of one of the most brilliant minds in medical history, but his work continued to inspire future generations of scientists.

## Character

Harvey was known for his analytical mind, methodical approach, and unwavering dedication to scientific discovery. His willingness to challenge established medical doctrines demonstrated his intellectual courage. He was meticulous in his experiments, emphasizing observation and empirical evidence over speculation.

Despite his professional achievements, Harvey remained humble and self-effacing. He never sought fame or wealth from his discoveries, choosing instead to focus on advancing medical knowledge. His work ethic and commitment to truth set him apart as one of the most influential figures in medical history.

## Influence on Humanity

William Harvey's contributions to science and medicine had a profound and lasting impact. His work reshaped medical understanding in several key areas:

**1. Revolutionizing Physiology** – By demonstrating the circulation of blood, Harvey overturned ancient medical theories and established a new foundation for the study of human physiology.

**2. Advancing Scientific Methodology** – His emphasis on experimentation, observation, and hypothesis testing influenced the development of modern scientific research.

**3. Influence on Surgery and Medicine** – His discoveries improved surgical techniques, diagnostics, and treatments related to the cardiovascular system.

**4. Inspiration for Future Scientists** – His work paved the way for later discoveries in cardiology, hematology, and modern medicine.

**5. Legacy in Medical Education** – His theories became a fundamental part of medical curricula and continue to be studied in medical schools worldwide.

In conclusion, William Harvey's discoveries revolutionized our understanding of human anatomy and laid the groundwork for modern medicine. His meticulous research methods and dedication to empirical science made him a pioneer in physiology. His legacy continues to shape medical education, research, and clinical practice, making him one of the most influential figures in the history of medicine.

# René Descartes
French philosopher and mathematician

René Descartes was a French philosopher, mathematician, and scientist whose contributions laid the foundation for modern philosophy and rationalism. His famous dictum, "Cogito, ergo sum" ("I think, therefore I am"), transformed epistemology and metaphysics, emphasizing doubt as a tool for acquiring knowledge. Descartes also played a crucial role in the development of analytical geometry, bridging the gap between algebra and geometry. His works influenced generations of thinkers and continue to shape philosophical discourse today.

## Origin

René Descartes was born on March 31, 1596, in La Haye en Touraine, a small town in central France that is now known as Descartes in his honor. He was born into a family of moderate nobility; his father, Joachim Descartes, was a lawyer and a member of the provincial parliament of Brittany, while his mother, Jeanne Brochard, died of tuberculosis shortly after his birth.

The Descartes family was well-respected, and although René was not born into wealth, he had access to education and opportunities that shaped his intellectual journey. His father's legal background exposed him to structured thinking and debate, which later influenced his philosophical approach.

## Childhood and Youth

Descartes' early education began at the Jesuit College of La Flèche, one of the most prestigious schools in France. He studied subjects such as Latin, logic, philosophy, mathematics, and physics. The Jesuit training emphasized Aristotelian philosophy and Scholasticism, but Descartes was already questioning traditional modes of thought, seeking a more systematic approach to knowledge.

Due to his delicate health, he was given special privileges, including permission to stay in bed later than his peers. This habit of morning reflection would remain with him throughout his life and contributed to his later methodological approach in philosophy.

In 1614, Descartes enrolled at the University of Poitiers, where he studied law, in accordance with his father's wishes. He received his law degree in 1616, but instead of pursuing a legal career, he decided to travel and explore the world in search of knowledge.

## Adulthood

Descartes' adulthood was marked by extensive travel, military service, and the pursuit of intellectual discovery. In 1618, he enlisted in the Dutch army of Maurice of Nassau, where he was introduced to the study of military engineering and applied mathematics. During this period, he met the scientist and mathematician Isaac Beeckman, who greatly influenced his thinking and encouraged his work in mathematics and physics.

In 1620, he left military service and traveled across Europe, visiting Bohemia, Germany, and Italy. These experiences deepened his philosophical inquiries and helped shape his ideas on skepticism and rationalism.

By 1628, Descartes settled in the Dutch Republic, where he would spend the next 20 years developing his most significant philosophical and scientific works. It was during this time that he formulated his method of systematic doubt, emphasizing the need to question all assumptions before accepting anything as true.

In 1637, he published "Discours de la méthode" ("Discourse on the Method"), in which he introduced his famous statement, "Cogito, ergo sum". The work outlined his approach to scientific and philosophical inquiry, advocating for a rational and mathematical understanding of the world. His most comprehensive philosophical work, "Meditations on First Philosophy" (1641), explored the nature of existence, the mind-body dualism, and the existence of God.

Descartes also made significant contributions to mathematics. His development of Cartesian coordinate geometry provided a way to represent geometric shapes using algebraic equations, paving the way for modern calculus and analytical geometry.

## Private Life

Despite his immense intellectual contributions, Descartes led a relatively private and reserved life. He never married but had a daughter, Francine, with a Dutch servant, Helena Jans van der Strom, in 1635. Tragically, Francine died of scarlet fever at the age of five, which deeply affected Descartes.

Descartes maintained correspondence with leading intellectuals of his time, including Princess Elisabeth of Bohemia, with whom he exchanged letters on philosophical and ethical issues. His relationships with students and scholars further shaped the intellectual landscape of Europe. His life in the Dutch Republic provided him with an atmosphere of intellectual freedom, where he could develop his ideas without fear of persecution. However, he remained cautious about publishing his works due to the growing conflict between science and religious doctrine.

## Death

In 1649, Descartes was invited to Sweden by Queen Christina, who was eager to learn from the great philosopher. He arrived in Stockholm and began tutoring the queen in philosophy. However, the harsh Scandinavian winter and the rigorous schedule imposed by the queen, which required early morning lessons, took a toll on his health. On February 11, 1650, Descartes died of pneumonia at the age of 53. Some historians have speculated that he may have been poisoned, but the official cause remains pneumonia. He was initially buried in Stockholm, but his remains were later moved to France and interred at the Abbey of Saint-Germain-des-Prés in Paris.

## Character

Descartes was known for his disciplined and independent mind. His ability to question traditional knowledge and seek rational explanations for natural phenomena set him apart as a true intellectual revolutionary. He was meticulous in his work, carefully constructing arguments and seeking clear, logical solutions to complex problems. Despite his skepticism, he was deeply religious and sought to reconcile his rationalist philosophy with his faith. His belief in the power of reason and mathematics shaped his approach to both scientific and metaphysical questions.

His reserved nature and preference for solitude allowed him to focus on his intellectual pursuits, but he also maintained strong connections with the intellectual elite of his time. His humility and caution in publishing controversial ideas reflected his awareness of the potential backlash from religious and academic authorities.

## Influence on Humanity

René Descartes' contributions had a profound impact on multiple disciplines, shaping the course of Western thought. His most significant influences include:

**1. Foundation of Modern Philosophy** – His method of systematic doubt and rational inquiry laid the groundwork for later philosophical movements, including Rationalism, Empiricism, and the Enlightenment.

**2. Advancements in Mathematics** – The Cartesian coordinate system provided a crucial link between algebra and geometry, forming the basis for analytical geometry and influencing modern calculus.

**3. Contributions to Science** – His mechanistic view of the universe and emphasis on mathematical descriptions of nature influenced physics, optics, and neuroscience.

**4. Mind-Body Dualism** – His concept of dualism, which distinguishes between the mind and body, became a central debate in philosophy, psychology, and cognitive science.

**5. Influence on Enlightenment Thinkers** – Philosophers such as Spinoza, Leibniz, and Kant built upon Descartes' ideas, further shaping modern epistemology and metaphysics.

In conclusion, René Descartes was a pioneering thinker whose ideas continue to shape philosophy, science, and mathematics. His relentless pursuit of knowledge through reason and skepticism established him as one of the greatest intellectual figures in history. His legacy endures as a testament to the power of rational inquiry and the enduring quest for truth.

# Oliver Cromwell
English statesman and Lord Protector

Oliver Cromwell was a pivotal figure in English history, leading the country through one of its most tumultuous periods – the English Civil War. As a military leader and later Lord Protector, he played a crucial role in the overthrow of the monarchy and the establishment of the Commonwealth. His rule remains one of the most controversial in British history, admired by some for promoting republican values and detested by others for his authoritarianism and military campaigns.

## Origin

Oliver Cromwell was born on April 25, 1599, in Huntingdon, England, into a family of minor gentry. He was the fifth child and only surviving son of Robert Cromwell, a member of Parliament and a prosperous landowner, and Elizabeth Steward. The Cromwells were a well-established family with connections to the powerful Tudor-era Thomas Cromwell, though Oliver's branch of the family had fallen into relative obscurity.

England at the time of Cromwell's birth was ruled by Queen Elizabeth I, who had solidified the Protestant Reformation. The country was deeply divided along religious and political lines, conflicts that would come to define Cromwell's future role in shaping the nation's destiny.

## Childhood and Youth

Cromwell's early education took place at Huntingdon Grammar School, where he was exposed to classical studies and the Puritanical beliefs that would later shape his political ideology. In 1616, he enrolled at Sidney Sussex College, Cambridge, a newly founded institution with strong Puritan influences. However, his time at Cambridge was cut short due to his father's death in 1617, forcing him to return home to manage family affairs.

Despite his noble lineage, Cromwell struggled financially during his early years. He married Elizabeth Bourchier in 1620, a match that provided him with connections to influential Puritan families. During this period, he faced bouts of depression and uncertainty, but he remained deeply religious, embracing Puritanism, which emphasized a personal relationship with God, moral discipline, and opposition to Catholic influences in the Church of England.

## Adulthood

Cromwell's political career began in 1628 when he was elected as a Member of Parliament for Huntingdon. Initially, he played a minor role in government, but as tensions between King Charles I and Parliament escalated, Cromwell's commitment to Puritanism and parliamentary sovereignty became more pronounced.

The outbreak of the English Civil War in 1642 marked a turning point in Cromwell's life. Initially serving as a captain in the Parliamentary army, he quickly rose through the ranks due to his exceptional leadership skills and military acumen. By 1644, he was instrumental in securing victory at the Battle of Marston Moor, and in 1645, he played a crucial role in the establishment of the New Model Army, which became the backbone of the Parliamentarian war effort.

In 1649, following the execution of King Charles I, England was declared a republic. Cromwell emerged as one of the most powerful figures in the newly established Commonwealth, leading military campaigns to subdue Royalist resistance in Ireland and Scotland. His conquest of Ireland (1649–1650) was particularly brutal, marked by the massacre of Royalist strongholds such as Drogheda and Wexford, actions that remain highly controversial.

By 1653, Cromwell had dissolved the Rump Parliament and, frustrated with the inefficacy of civilian rule, assumed the title of Lord Protector. As head of state, he ruled with near-monarchical authority, enforcing strict Puritan moral laws, promoting religious toleration (except for Catholics), and strengthening England's military presence abroad.

## Private Life

Despite his political and military prominence, Cromwell remained devoted to his family. He and his wife, Elizabeth, had nine children, and he maintained close relationships with them throughout his life. His letters to his children reveal a caring, affectionate father who took pride in their achievements and well-being.

He lived modestly relative to his power, preferring simple clothing and rejecting the opulent displays associated with monarchy. Though he wielded immense authority, he saw himself as a servant of God, believing that his actions were divinely ordained.

Cromwell's religious convictions deeply influenced his governance. He sought to create a godly society based on Puritan values, banning gambling, theater, and excessive celebration. His policies were aimed at moral reform, though they were often perceived as oppressive by those who did not share his Puritan beliefs.

## Death

Cromwell's health began to decline in 1658, possibly due to complications from malaria and kidney disease. On September 3, 1658, he passed away at Whitehall Palace in London, the anniversary of his victories at Dunbar and Worcester.

His death left England in a state of uncertainty. His son, Richard Cromwell, briefly succeeded him as Lord Protector but lacked his father's political and military skill. Within two years, the monarchy was restored under King Charles II in 1660. As a posthumous act of vengeance, Cromwell's body was exhumed in 1661, hanged, and beheaded, symbolizing the ultimate rejection of his rule.

## Character

Cromwell was a paradoxical figure — both deeply religious and ruthless in war, a man who sought liberty but ruled with an iron hand. His unwavering belief in divine providence guided his decisions, giving him a sense of righteousness that justified even his most controversial actions.

As a military leader, he was pragmatic and innovative, introducing disciplined tactics that modernized warfare. As a ruler, he was both an idealist and a realist, attempting to balance the principles of republicanism with the need for stability.

His leadership was marked by contradictions: he championed religious freedom for Protestants yet brutally suppressed Catholics in Ireland; he opposed monarchy but ruled as an autocrat; he dissolved parliaments while insisting on the supremacy of parliamentary government.

## Influence on Humanity

Cromwell's impact on history is profound and multifaceted. His key contributions include:

**1. Military Reforms** – His restructuring of the New Model Army influenced the future of military organization and professionalism.

**2. Republican Governance** – His leadership during the English Commonwealth laid the groundwork for later discussions on constitutional monarchy and democracy.

**3. Religious Toleration** – While controversial, his policies helped shape the long-term evolution of religious freedom in Britain.

**4. Expansion of English Power** – His foreign policies strengthened England's naval supremacy, setting the stage for its rise as a global power.

**5. Political Legacy** – His rule demonstrated both the possibilities and limitations of non-monarchical government, influencing political thought in Britain and beyond.

In conclusion, Oliver Cromwell remains one of the most divisive figures in British history. To some, he was a champion of liberty and godly rule; to others, he was a dictator and a zealot. Regardless of perspective, his influence on England's political evolution is undeniable, and his legacy continues to be debated to this day.

# John Locke
## The architect of modern liberalism

John Locke was an English philosopher and physician who played a crucial role in shaping modern political thought. Often regarded as the "Father of Liberalism," Locke's theories on government, human rights, and empiricism laid the foundation for constitutional democracy and the Enlightenment. His works, particularly "Two Treatises of Government" and "An Essay Concerning Human Understanding", remain influential in philosophy, political science, and law.

## Origin

John Locke was born on August 29, 1632, in Wrington, Somerset, England, during the reign of Charles I. He was baptized the same day at the village church. His father, also named John Locke, was a lawyer and military captain who fought for the Parliamentarians in the English Civil War. His mother, Agnes Keene, came from a respectable family and provided a nurturing influence during his early years.

Locke's family was of Puritan background, which shaped his early religious and moral outlook. His father's service in the Parliamentary army granted Locke opportunities for education and advancement, despite the family's modest wealth. The political turmoil of 17th-century England, marked by civil war, the execution of Charles I, and the rise of Oliver Cromwell, greatly influenced his later political philosophy.

## Childhood and Youth

Locke's early education took place at Westminster School in London, where he studied classical literature, Latin, Greek, and logic. He was an excellent student and benefited from a rigorous education that emphasized debate and critical thinking.

In 1652, he entered Christ Church, Oxford, where he studied philosophy, medicine, and natural sciences. Although Oxford's curriculum was still heavily focused on Aristotelian philosophy, Locke found inspiration in the works of modern thinkers such as René Descartes. His exposure to contemporary scientific advancements, including those of Robert Boyle and Thomas Sydenham, fueled his interest in empiricism and medicine. Locke's dissatisfaction with the rigid scholasticism of Oxford led him to explore experimental science. He became deeply involved with the Royal Society, a leading institution for scientific inquiry, where he engaged with prominent figures such as Robert Hooke and Isaac Newton.

## Adulthood

After completing his studies, Locke initially pursued a career in medicine. Under the mentorship of Thomas Sydenham, one of England's most respected physicians, he gained practical medical experience. Though he never formally practiced as a doctor, his medical knowledge earned him positions in political and aristocratic circles.

In 1667, Locke became the personal physician and advisor to Lord Ashley, later the Earl of Shaftesbury. This relationship proved pivotal in his intellectual and political career. Shaftesbury, a key opponent of absolute monarchy, introduced Locke to political affairs and involved him in drafting constitutional frameworks, including the "Fundamental Constitutions of Carolina", which aimed to establish a governance model for the American colony.

During the 1670s and 1680s, Locke's political and philosophical ideas began to crystallize. His opposition to the absolute rule of Charles II and James II made him a target of suspicion. After Shaftesbury's political downfall, Locke fled to the Netherlands in 1683, where he spent several years in exile. During this time, he wrote his most famous works, including "Two Treatises of Government", which justified resistance to tyranny and argued for the natural rights of life, liberty, and property.

In 1689, following the Glorious Revolution that deposed James II and installed William III and Mary II, Locke returned to England. He was appointed as a Commissioner of Appeals and became an advocate for religious tolerance and limited government.

## Private Life

Despite his public achievements, Locke led a relatively private life. He never married nor had children, dedicating himself entirely to intellectual pursuits. He suffered from chronic health issues, including asthma, which limited his mobility and dictated much of his routine.

Locke maintained close relationships with several influential figures, including philosopher Anthony Ashley Cooper (Earl of Shaftesbury) and scientist Robert Boyle. His friendships extended beyond politics and philosophy; he was known for his kindness and generosity, often assisting struggling scholars and engaging in lively correspondence with intellectuals across Europe.

He spent his later years at Oates, the estate of Sir Francis Masham, where he enjoyed a peaceful and studious retirement. During this period, he wrote extensively on theology, economics, and education, advocating for practical and empirical approaches to learning.

## Death

John Locke passed away on October 28, 1704, at the age of 72, at Oates in High Laver, Essex. His death was peaceful, and he remained engaged in philosophical discussions until his final days. He was buried in the local churchyard, and his epitaph emphasized his commitment to truth and reason.

Though he died relatively obscure compared to some of his contemporaries, his ideas would later become the cornerstone of modern liberal democracy.

## Character

Locke was known for his rational, calm, and deeply principled nature. He was meticulous in his arguments, always striving for clarity and logical consistency. His empirical approach to knowledge reflected his belief that human understanding should be based on experience rather than speculation.

He was a moderate and pragmatic thinker, advocating for tolerance and dialogue rather than radical revolution. His personal integrity and intellectual humility earned him respect across political and philosophical divides. Despite his non-confrontational demeanor, Locke was unwavering in his defense of liberty and the rule of law. His ability to balance reason with moral conviction made him one of the most influential figures of his time.

## Influence on Humanity

Locke's impact on the world is immeasurable. His contributions to philosophy, politics, and education laid the groundwork for the modern era. His most significant influences include:

**1. Political Philosophy** – "Two Treatises of Government" laid the foundation for constitutional democracy, profoundly influencing thinkers like Thomas Jefferson and shaping key historical documents such as the U.S. Declaration of Independence and the Bill of Rights.

**2. Empiricism** – "An Essay Concerning Human Understanding" laid the foundation for empiricism, asserting that knowledge is derived from sensory experience rather than innate ideas.

**3. Religious Tolerance** – Locke's writings on religious freedom influenced the development of secular governance and the separation of church and state.

**4. Education** – His "Thoughts Concerning Education" emphasized experiential learning and rational thinking, impacting modern educational philosophy.

**5. Economic Thought** – Locke's ideas on property and labor contributed to the development of classical liberal economic theory.

In conclusion, John Locke was a visionary who reshaped the way humanity thinks about governance, knowledge, and personal freedom. His works continue to inspire democratic movements, legal systems, and philosophical debates. His belief in reason, liberty, and the dignity of individuals ensures his place as one of the most influential thinkers in history.

# Antoni van Leeuwenhoek
The father of microbiology

Antoni van Leeuwenhoek was a Dutch scientist and tradesman who is widely regarded as the father of microbiology. Through his pioneering work in lens-making, he was the first to observe and document microscopic life, revealing the hidden world of microorganisms. His discoveries laid the foundation for microbiology and greatly advanced our understanding of biology, medicine, and natural sciences.

## Origin

Antoni van Leeuwenhoek was born on October 24, 1632, in Delft, a bustling trade city in the Dutch Republic (modern-day Netherlands). He came from a middle-class family; his father, Philips Antonysz van Leeuwenhoek, was a basket maker, and his mother, Margaretha Bel van den Berch, was from a well-respected brewing family. Delft was a center of commerce and craftsmanship, exposing young Antoni to various trades and skills that would later shape his scientific endeavors.

The 17th century, known as the Dutch Golden Age, was a period of great scientific and artistic advancement. The Netherlands was a hub of innovation, with scholars and artisans making remarkable contributions to various fields. It was in this intellectually stimulating environment that van Leeuwenhoek would make his mark on history.

## Childhood and Youth

Van Leeuwenhoek's early education was modest. He did not receive formal higher education or attend a university, unlike many of his scientific contemporaries. Instead, he was sent to a local school in Warmond, where he received a basic education in reading, writing, and arithmetic. His scientific knowledge would come later, through self-learning and keen observation.

At the age of 16, after the death of his father, van Leeuwenhoek moved to Amsterdam to apprentice as a draper's assistant. There, he learned about textiles, commerce, and lens-making, as magnifying glasses were commonly used by textile merchants to examine the quality of fabric. This exposure to optics sparked his lifelong fascination with lenses and microscopy.

## Adulthood

In 1654, van Leeuwenhoek returned to Delft and established his own drapery business. He became a successful and respected tradesman, serving as a civic official in various local administrative roles. Despite having no formal scientific training, his curiosity led him to experiment with lens-making and microscopy in his spare time.

Van Leeuwenhoek's meticulous craftsmanship allowed him to create some of the most powerful lenses of his time. Unlike the compound microscopes used by contemporary scientists, he developed single-lens microscopes with extraordinary magnification, reaching up to 300 times. These lenses enabled him to observe details of the natural world that had never been seen before.

His groundbreaking discoveries began in the 1670s when he started documenting microscopic organisms. In 1674, he observed single-celled organisms in pond water, describing them as "animalcules" (little animals). He later identified bacteria, sperm cells, red blood cells, and muscle fibers, among other microscopic structures. His meticulous records and illustrations provided the first glimpses of the microscopic world.

Van Leeuwenhoek's work gained recognition when he began corresponding with the Royal Society of London. Despite initial skepticism, his findings were eventually validated, earning him widespread acclaim. In 1680, he was elected as a fellow of the Royal Society, an exceptional achievement for a self-taught scientist.

## Private Life

Despite his scientific achievements, van Leeuwenhoek remained deeply rooted in his personal and civic life. He married Barbara de Mey in 1654, and they had five children, though only one survived to adulthood. His wife's death in 1666 was a significant personal loss, but he later remarried Cornelia Swalmius, with whom he shared a quiet and private life.

Van Leeuwenhoek was known to be a reserved and somewhat reclusive individual. Unlike many of his contemporaries, he never sought academic prestige or financial gain from his discoveries. Instead, he remained devoted to his work and his responsibilities as a civil servant in Delft. He declined offers to teach or travel, preferring to stay in his hometown and continue his microscopic observations.

His dedication to research was unwavering. He spent countless hours refining his lenses, observing specimens, and meticulously recording his findings. His reports to the Royal Society were written in Dutch rather than Latin, the scientific language of the time, emphasizing his practical and independent approach to science.

## Death

Antoni van Leeuwenhoek lived a long and productive life. He continued his scientific work well into his later years, making observations and refining his techniques even in his seventies and eighties.

He passed away on August 26, 1723, at the age of 90 in Delft. His cause of death was described as a rare condition, now known as Van Leeuwenhoek's disease, which caused involuntary muscle contractions. His burial took place in the Oude Kerk (Old Church) in Delft, where he was laid to rest in his beloved hometown.

Before his death, he ensured that his microscopes and research notes were preserved. His work continued to inspire future generations of scientists, leading to further advancements in microbiology and microscopy.

## Character

Van Leeuwenhoek was characterized by his meticulous attention to detail, insatiable curiosity, and independent spirit. He was a self-taught scientist who relied on careful observation rather than theoretical speculation. Unlike many scholars of his time, he was not interested in fame or formal academic recognition; instead, he focused solely on expanding knowledge through empirical evidence.

His perseverance and patience were remarkable. Crafting high-quality lenses required extraordinary skill, and he was known to spend weeks perfecting a single microscope. His ability to remain dedicated to his research, despite skepticism and limited formal training, demonstrated his intellectual resilience.

He was also known for his humility. Although he made some of the most significant discoveries in biological science, he never published books or sought personal accolades. His contributions were made quietly, through letters and communications with the scientific community.

## Influence on Humanity

Van Leeuwenhoek's discoveries had a profound and lasting impact on science and medicine. His key contributions include:

**1. Discovery of Microorganisms** – He was the first person to observe and describe bacteria, protozoa, and other microscopic life forms, laying the foundation for microbiology.

**2. Advancements in Microscopy** – His pioneering work in lens-making set new standards in optical technology, influencing future developments in microscopy.

**3. Contributions to Medicine** – His observations of red blood cells, sperm cells, and muscle fibers provided crucial insights into human biology and reproduction.

**4. Empirical Scientific Method** – His rigorous observational techniques emphasized empirical evidence over speculation, shaping the scientific method.

**5. Inspiration for Future Scientists** – His work influenced later scientists, including Louis Pasteur and Robert Koch, who expanded upon his findings to develop germ theory and microbiology.

In conclusion, Antoni van Leeuwenhoek was a visionary whose discoveries opened an entirely new dimension of the natural world. His dedication to scientific observation, despite lacking formal education, serves as a testament to the power of curiosity and perseverance. His contributions continue to shape biology, medicine, and technology, ensuring his place as one of the most influential scientists in history.

# Isaac Newton
Founder of classical mechanics

Isaac Newton was one of the most influential scientists in history, a mathematician, physicist, astronomer, and theologian whose discoveries laid the foundation for modern physics. His groundbreaking work in mathematics, optics, and gravity revolutionized scientific thought, shaping the way humanity understands the natural world. His "Philosophiæ Naturalis Principia Mathematica" introduced the laws of motion and universal gravitation, establishing the framework for classical mechanics.

## Origin

Isaac Newton was born on January 4, 1643 (December 25, 1642, in the Julian calendar) in Woolsthorpe, Lincolnshire, England. He was born prematurely, and his survival in infancy was uncertain. His father, also named Isaac Newton, was a prosperous farmer but died three months before Isaac's birth. His mother, Hannah Ayscough Newton, remarried when Isaac was three years old, leaving him in the care of his maternal grandparents while she moved to live with her new husband.

Newton's early years were marked by isolation and a sense of abandonment, which may have influenced his introspective and independent nature. He was raised in a rural farming community, but his talents lay far beyond agriculture. From an early age, he showed an aptitude for mechanics, constructing miniature windmills, sundials, and water clocks, hinting at the brilliant scientific mind he would later become.

## Childhood and Youth

Newton's formal education began at The King's School in Grantham, where he excelled in academics. Initially, he was uninterested in school, but after a personal rivalry with another student, he became determined to outperform his peers. His notebooks from this period reveal an intense curiosity and interest in various subjects, from mathematics to philosophy. At the age of 17, Newton's mother attempted to pull him out of school to manage the family farm, but he showed little interest in agriculture. Recognizing his potential, his schoolmaster and relatives persuaded his mother to allow him to pursue higher education.

In 1661, Newton entered Trinity College, Cambridge, as a subsizar (a student who paid reduced fees in exchange for serving wealthier students). At Cambridge, he studied the traditional curriculum but soon delved into the works of modern scientists such as Galileo Galilei, Johannes Kepler, and René Descartes. During this period, he developed his early ideas on calculus, optics, and gravity, although he kept much of his work private.

## Adulthood

Newton's academic career took off in 1665 when Cambridge closed due to the Great Plague. During his forced two-year retreat at Woolsthorpe, he conducted some of his most important early experiments. It was during this period that he formulated the laws of motion, the concept of gravity, and the principles of calculus. The famous story of an apple falling from a tree inspiring his theory of gravity likely stems from this time.

In 1667, Newton returned to Cambridge and was elected a Fellow of Trinity College. He became a professor of mathematics in 1669 and began his systematic study of optics. Through experiments with prisms, he demonstrated that white light was composed of a spectrum of colors, contradicting previous theories that light was a uniform entity. His most famous work, "Philosophiæ Naturalis Principia Mathematica" (1687), commonly referred to as the "Principia", provided the mathematical formulation of the laws of motion and universal gravitation. This work established Newton as the leading scientific thinker of his time and set the stage for the development of classical mechanics.

In 1696, Newton was appointed Warden of the Royal Mint, and in 1700, he became its Master, overseeing England's currency reform. His tenure was marked by his relentless pursuit of counterfeiters, displaying his characteristic precision and thoroughness.

## Private Life

Newton was intensely private and never married. He had few close relationships and dedicated most of his life to intellectual pursuits. Some historians suggest he may have had deep personal friendships, particularly with Swiss mathematician Nicolas Fatio de Duillier, though there is no concrete evidence of romantic involvement with anyone.

His personality was marked by periods of intense concentration and occasional bouts of paranoia and irritability. He engaged in bitter rivalries, most notably with German mathematician Gottfried Wilhelm Leibniz over the invention of calculus. Although both men developed calculus independently, a dispute arose over priority, leading to a long-lasting controversy in the mathematical community.

Newton's religious beliefs played a significant role in his life. He was deeply interested in theology and biblical prophecy, spending more time studying scripture than science in his later years. He was known to reject the doctrine of the Trinity, making him a heretic in the eyes of mainstream Christianity, though he kept these views largely private.

## Death

In his later years, Newton's health began to decline. He suffered from digestive problems and kidney stones, which caused great discomfort. Despite his ailments, he remained intellectually active and continued his work at the Royal Society and the Mint.

On March 31, 1727 (March 20 in the Julian calendar), Newton died in his sleep in London at the age of 84. He was buried in Westminster Abbey, an honor reserved for Britain's most distinguished individuals. His funeral was attended by many notable figures, reflecting the immense respect he had garnered during his lifetime.

## Character

Newton was a complex figure – brilliant yet reclusive, meticulous yet deeply spiritual. His relentless pursuit of knowledge and perfection made him one of the greatest minds in history. He was known for his intense focus, often working for days without sleep or food. Despite his genius, he could be highly sensitive to criticism, leading to conflicts with other intellectuals. His humility was often overshadowed by his competitive nature, as he was fiercely protective of his discoveries. However, his contributions to science were unparalleled, and he was recognized as one of the greatest thinkers of his time.

## Influence on Humanity

Newton's impact on science and humanity is immeasurable. His contributions include:

**1. Newtonian Mechanics** – His laws of motion and gravity provided the framework for classical mechanics, influencing physics for centuries.

**2. Calculus** – Although co-discovered with Leibniz, Newton's development of calculus became a fundamental tool in mathematics and engineering.

**3. Optics** – His studies on light and color laid the foundation for modern optical science.

**4. Astronomy** – His laws of motion and gravity explained planetary movements and celestial mechanics, influencing later astronomers such as Laplace and Einstein.

**5. Scientific Method** – Newton emphasized experimentation and mathematical analysis, shaping modern scientific inquiry.

**6. Engineering and Technology** – His principles underpin much of modern engineering, from space exploration to mechanical design.

**7. Monetary Reform** – His work at the Royal Mint stabilized England's currency and strengthened the financial system.

In conclusion, Isaac Newton was more than a scientist – he was a visionary whose discoveries transformed our understanding of the universe. His work continues to influence physics, mathematics, and engineering, making him one of the most important figures in the history of human knowledge. His relentless pursuit of truth and dedication to scientific principles ensure his legacy remains an enduring pillar of modern science.

# Peter the Great
## The Tsar who transformed Russia

Peter the Great was one of Russia's most influential rulers, responsible for modernizing the nation and turning it into a major European power. His extensive reforms in government, military, culture, and industry laid the foundations for Russia's imperial expansion and integration with the Western world. Peter's ambitious vision and relentless drive led him to reshape Russian society, often through drastic measures.

## Origin

Peter the Great, born Pyotr Alekseyevich Romanov, was born on June 9, 1672, in Moscow, Russia. He was the 14th child of Tsar Alexei I and his second wife, Natalia Naryshkina. His birth took place during a period of political instability in Russia, marked by power struggles between various noble factions and family members.

The Romanov dynasty had come to power in 1613 after the Time of Troubles, a period of chaos following the death of the last Rurikid tsar. By the time of Peter's birth, Russia was still a relatively backward, feudal society with limited exposure to Western technological and cultural advancements.

## Childhood and Youth

Peter's childhood was tumultuous. His father, Tsar Alexei, died in 1676 when Peter was just four years old. His elder half-brother, Fyodor III, became tsar but ruled only briefly before dying in 1682. This led to a power struggle between Peter's supporters and those backing his half-sister Sophia and her faction, the Miloslavskys.

In 1682, a violent coup led by the elite military corps known as the Streltsy placed Sophia as regent while Peter and his half-brother Ivan V were declared co-tsars. Sophia ruled in their name but maintained firm control over the government. Peter spent much of his youth away from the Kremlin, living in the village of Preobrazhenskoye, where he developed an interest in military training and Western-style learning.

In 1689, at the age of 17, Peter successfully overthrew Sophia and took direct control of the government. His co-tsar, Ivan V, was weak and sickly, and Peter became the dominant ruler. When Ivan died in 1696, Peter officially became the sole ruler of Russia.

## Adulthood

Peter embarked on an ambitious campaign to modernize Russia. He undertook extensive military, administrative, and economic reforms, many inspired by his travels across Europe.

In 1697-1698, Peter led the "Grand Embassy," a diplomatic mission to Western Europe. Traveling incognito, he visited the Netherlands, England, and other European countries, studying shipbuilding, military techniques, and governance. He sought to learn from the West and recruit experts to help modernize Russia. The trip had a profound impact on him, reinforcing his determination to reform Russia.

One of Peter's most significant achievements was modernizing the Russian military. He built a powerful navy from scratch, inspired by the shipbuilding techniques he had observed in the Netherlands and England. He also reorganized the army, implementing new training methods, modern weapons, and standardized uniforms.

His military prowess was demonstrated in the Great Northern War (1700-1721) against Sweden. After initial defeats, Peter restructured his forces and secured a decisive victory at the Battle of Poltava in 1709. The war ultimately led to Russia's dominance in the Baltic region and its emergence as a major European power.

Peter introduced sweeping changes to Russian society, forcing the nobility to adopt Western dress and customs. He moved the capital from Moscow to the newly built city of St. Petersburg in 1703, envisioning it as a "window to the West."

To strengthen his control, he restructured the Russian government, establishing the Table of Ranks, which allowed commoners to rise through state service. He also introduced a merit-based civil service, reducing the power of hereditary aristocrats. Economically, Peter promoted industrialization, established new manufacturing centers, and encouraged foreign experts to develop Russia's infrastructure.

## Private Life

Peter's personal life was as eventful as his reign. He was married twice. His first marriage, arranged by his mother, was to Eudoxia Lopukhina in 1689. The marriage was unhappy, and in 1698, Peter forced Eudoxia to become a nun, effectively ending their union.

In 1707, he married Catherine I, a former peasant and servant of his household. She became his closest confidante and was crowned Empress after his death. Together, they had numerous children, though few survived to adulthood.

Peter had a strained relationship with his eldest son, Alexei, from his first marriage. Displeased with Alexei's opposition to his reforms, Peter accused him of treason. In 1718, Alexei was arrested, tortured, and sentenced to death. He died in prison, likely due to his injuries.

## Death

Peter the Great died on February 8, 1725, at the age of 52. His health had deteriorated due to the stress of his rigorous lifestyle and multiple illnesses. His final illness was likely caused by complications from a bladder infection or kidney failure.

His death left Russia in a state of uncertainty, as he had not officially named a successor. His wife, Catherine I, was eventually proclaimed Empress, continuing his legacy of reform.

## Character

Peter was a complex and often contradictory figure. He was visionary yet ruthless, pragmatic yet impulsive. His determination to modernize Russia led him to implement radical changes, but his methods were often harsh. He had an insatiable curiosity and was deeply involved in his projects, from shipbuilding to city planning.

He was known for his hands-on approach – personally working as a shipbuilder, participating in battles, and engaging in practical learning. Despite his intelligence and energy, he could be cruel, particularly toward those who resisted his reforms.

Peter was also known for his unorthodox and often wild behavior. He enjoyed festivities, practical jokes, and had little regard for courtly etiquette. His ability to blend discipline with informality made him both respected and feared.

## Influence on Humanity

Peter's impact on Russia and the world was immense:

**1. Modernization of Russia** – His reforms transformed Russia into a centralized, bureaucratic state, aligning it with Western Europe.

**2. Military Strength** – His creation of a modern army and navy established Russia as a dominant power in Europe.

**3. Economic Growth** – His industrial policies laid the foundation for Russia's future economic development.

**4. Cultural Westernization** – His promotion of Western customs and education influenced Russian culture for centuries.

**5. Legacy of St. Petersburg** – The city remains one of Russia's most important cultural and economic centers.

In conclusion, Peter the Great was a towering figure who reshaped Russia and its role in the world. His relentless drive for modernization, military expansion, and cultural transformation set Russia on a path that would shape its history for centuries. Though his methods were often ruthless, his vision and reforms solidified his place as one of history's most influential rulers.

# Johann Sebastian Bach
## The Master of Baroque Music

Johann Sebastian Bach is widely regarded as one of the greatest composers of all time. His intricate compositions, deep understanding of harmony, and technical mastery revolutionized Western music, particularly during the Baroque era. Bach's work laid the foundation for many later composers and remains a cornerstone of classical music today. His compositions, ranging from orchestral suites to sacred cantatas, continue to inspire musicians and audiences alike.

### Origin

Johann Sebastian Bach was born on March 31, 1685 (March 21 under the Julian calendar), in Eisenach, a small town in the Duchy of Saxe-Eisenach (modern-day Germany). He came from a distinguished musical family, with generations of musicians preceding him. His father, Johann Ambrosius Bach, was a town musician who played the violin and trumpet, while his mother, Maria Elisabeth Lämmerhirt, also came from a family of musicians. The Bach family had been involved in music for several generations, and Johann Sebastian was surrounded by music from birth. This rich musical heritage played a crucial role in shaping his talent and dedication to the art form.

### Childhood and Youth

Bach's childhood was filled with both music and hardship. At the age of nine, he lost his mother, and less than a year later, his father also passed away. Orphaned at the age of ten, he was sent to live with his eldest brother, Johann Christoph Bach, in Ohrdruf. Johann Christoph was an organist and provided Bach with his first formal musical training, exposing him to keyboard music and composition.

Bach demonstrated immense talent at a young age, often secretly copying music from his brother's collection at night. This dedication helped him develop an exceptional understanding of counterpoint and harmony. In 1700, he was awarded a scholarship to study at the prestigious St.

Michael's School in Lüneburg, where he continued to refine his skills in composition, performance, and choral singing.

During his time in Lüneburg, he was influenced by the works of composers such as Johann Jakob Froberger, Dieterich Buxtehude, and Johann Pachelbel. His exposure to the vibrant musical culture of northern Germany helped shape his future compositions.

## Adulthood

Bach's professional career began in 1703 when he was appointed as a court musician in Weimar. Later that year, he secured a position as the organist of the New Church in Arnstadt. Though he was well respected for his musical abilities, his time in Arnstadt was marked by conflict with church authorities due to his unorthodox compositions and long, unauthorized absences.

In 1707, he moved to Mühlhausen to serve as an organist at St. Blasius Church. It was here that he married his first wife, Maria Barbara Bach, who was also his second cousin. The couple had several children, some of whom would go on to become composers themselves, including Carl Philipp Emanuel Bach and Wilhelm Friedemann Bach.

In 1708, Bach returned to Weimar, where he was appointed as court organist and later became concertmaster. During his time in Weimar, he composed some of his most famous organ works, including "Toccata and Fugue in D Minor" and "Prelude and Fugue in C Major". His reputation as an organ virtuoso grew, attracting students and admirers from across Germany.

In 1717, Bach accepted the prestigious position of Kapellmeister (music director) at the court of Prince Leopold of Anhalt-Köthen. This period was highly productive, as he composed many instrumental works, including the "Brandenburg Concertos", "The Well-Tempered Clavier", and numerous violin and keyboard sonatas.

## Private Life

Bach's personal life was deeply intertwined with his music. His first wife, Maria Barbara, passed away suddenly in 1720 while he was away on a trip with Prince Leopold. Devastated by her death, Bach remarried in 1721 to Anna Magdalena Wilcke, a talented soprano singer who provided him with great support. Together, they had thirteen children, though many did not survive infancy.

Anna Magdalena played an essential role in preserving Bach's compositions and assisting with his work. She also compiled the "Notebook for Anna Magdalena Bach", a collection of musical pieces for keyboard practice, some of which were composed by Bach himself.

Despite his growing fame, Bach lived a relatively modest life, focusing on his duties as a composer, teacher, and performer. His deep Lutheran faith was central to his life and heavily influenced his sacred compositions, including the "Mass in B Minor" and the "St. Matthew Passion".

## Death

In his later years, Bach suffered from deteriorating eyesight, which was exacerbated by an unsuccessful eye surgery performed by a traveling British doctor. His health continued to decline, and he ultimately passed away on July 28, 1750, at the age of 65. The exact cause of his death remains uncertain, but it is believed to have been related to complications from diabetes and the failed eye surgery.

Bach was buried in an unmarked grave at St. John's Cemetery in Leipzig, though his remains were later moved to St. Thomas Church, where he had served as the director of music for the last 27 years of his life.

## Character

Bach was known for his discipline, deep religiosity, and intense work ethic. He was a perfectionist who demanded the highest standards from himself and his students. Despite facing conflicts with employers and church authorities, he remained steadfast in his artistic vision.

He was also a devoted family man, and his letters reveal his love for his children and his deep faith in God. Unlike some of his contemporaries who sought fame and fortune, Bach composed music for the glory of God and the enrichment of human experience.

Though he was not widely recognized outside of Germany during his lifetime, his influence grew exponentially after his death, as later composers such as Mozart, Beethoven, and Chopin admired and studied his work.

## Influence on Humanity

Bach's impact on the world of music is unparalleled. His contributions include:

**1. Development of Counterpoint** – Bach perfected the use of counterpoint, creating intricate musical textures that remain a fundamental aspect of Western music.

**2. Harmonic Innovations** – His exploration of harmonic progressions and modulations influenced generations of composers.

**3. Keyboard Music** – His works for harpsichord and organ, such as "The Well-Tempered Clavier", remain essential study material for pianists and organists.

**4. Sacred Music** – His choral works, including "The St. Matthew Passion" and "Mass in B Minor", are among the most revered religious compositions.

**5. Musical Structure** – His fugues, canons, and suites established new standards for musical composition and form.

**6. Inspiration to Future Generations** – Beethoven, Mozart, and countless others studied and admired Bach's compositions, incorporating his techniques into their own works.

In conclusion, Johann Sebastian Bach was not only a composer but a musical architect whose influence has shaped centuries of music. His works continue to be performed, studied, and revered worldwide, ensuring that his legacy endures as one of the greatest minds in the history of music.

# Voltaire

Enlightenment philosopher who
advocated for freedom of speech and religion

---

Voltaire, born François-Marie Arouet, was one of the most influential writers and philosophers of the Enlightenment era. His sharp wit, keen intellect, and relentless advocacy for freedom of speech, religious tolerance, and social justice made him a formidable critic of established institutions. Through his prolific writings – ranging from plays and poems to philosophical treatises and historical analyses – Voltaire helped shape modern thought and inspired generations of revolutionaries and intellectuals.

## Origin

François-Marie Arouet, later known as Voltaire, was born on November 21, 1694, in Paris, France, as the youngest of five children in a middle-class family. His father, François Arouet, was a notary and a minor treasury official, while his mother, Marie Marguerite Daumard, came from a noble background. Though his family was not wealthy, they were well-connected, which allowed young François access to the finest education.

Voltaire's birthplace, late 17th-century France, was a society steeped in rigid class structures, religious orthodoxy, and absolute monarchy under King Louis XIV. These elements would later become the targets of his sharp criticism and reformist ideals.

## Childhood and Youth

As a child, Voltaire displayed remarkable intelligence and an insatiable curiosity for literature and philosophy. At the age of ten, he was sent to the prestigious Jesuit school Collège Louis-le-Grand in Paris, where he studied classical languages, rhetoric, and philosophy. The Jesuits provided him with a rigorous education, but their strict religious teachings also exposed him to the dogma that he would later challenge.

Despite his father's wish for him to become a lawyer, Voltaire was drawn to the literary world. He frequented the salons of Paris, where intellectuals, writers, and aristocrats debated politics, philosophy, and literature. He quickly became known for his wit and sharp tongue, skills that would define his literary career.

After completing his formal education, he worked briefly in a notary's office, but his distaste for legal work led him to pursue a literary life. His satirical wit, however, soon landed him in trouble.

## Adulthood

Voltaire's early adulthood was marked by controversy. In 1717, at the age of 23, he was imprisoned in the Bastille for nearly a year due to satirical verses he wrote mocking the French monarchy. It was during this imprisonment that he adopted the pen name "Voltaire." Scholars believe the name was an anagram of "Arouet le jeune" (Arouet the younger), though its exact origin remains debated.

Upon his release, Voltaire became one of the most famous writers in France. His play "Oedipe" (1718) was a great success, establishing him as a dramatist. However, his sharp criticism of government officials and religious authorities continued to provoke backlash. In 1726, after a quarrel with the aristocratic Chevalier de Rohan, Voltaire was exiled to England.

During his three-year stay in England, he was profoundly influenced by British constitutional monarchy, religious tolerance, and the works of John Locke and Isaac Newton. These ideas would later shape his philosophical outlook and reformist writings.

Upon returning to France in 1729, Voltaire focused on history, science, and philosophy. His book "Letters on the English" (1734) praised British political and intellectual freedoms while criticizing French society. The book was banned, and Voltaire was forced to flee Paris, taking refuge in the Château de Cirey with his mistress, Émilie du Châtelet.

Throughout the 1740s and 1750s, Voltaire's fame grew, and he became an adviser to several European rulers, including Frederick the Great of Prussia and Catherine the Great of Russia. His most famous philosophical work, "Candide" (1759), satirized optimism, religious hypocrisy, and political corruption.

## Private Life

Voltaire never married, but he had significant relationships throughout his life. His most famous romantic and intellectual partnership was with Émilie du Châtelet, a brilliant mathematician and physicist. They lived together for nearly 15 years, engaging in scientific and philosophical discussions while supporting each other's work.

After Émilie's death in 1749, Voltaire moved to Prussia at the invitation of Frederick the Great. However, their relationship soured, and Voltaire eventually settled in Ferney, near the Swiss border, where he spent the last 20 years of his life.

Despite his immense wealth and influence, Voltaire lived relatively simply. He devoted much of his fortune to supporting persecuted individuals, promoting education, and aiding the poor. He corresponded with intellectuals across Europe, becoming a symbol of the Enlightenment.

## Death

Voltaire returned to Paris in 1778, where he was hailed as a hero by the intellectual elite. However, his health declined rapidly, and he died on May 30, 1778, at the age of 83.

Because of his criticism of the Catholic Church, he was denied a Christian burial in Paris. His remains were secretly taken to Champagne and buried in a monastery. In 1791, during the French Revolution, his body was exhumed and placed in the Panthéon, where it remains today as a tribute to his contributions to French thought and liberty.

## Character

Voltaire was a man of paradoxes – fiercely independent yet eager to influence rulers, deeply skeptical yet hopeful for human progress. He was known for his sharp wit, relentless criticism of injustice, and his ability to provoke change through satire.

He was not just a thinker but a man of action, working to free wrongly imprisoned individuals and advocating for religious tolerance. His commitment to reason and justice made him a beacon of the Enlightenment.

Despite his humor and charm, Voltaire could be difficult and argumentative. He often clashed with rivals, but his willingness to challenge authority ensured that his ideas remained relevant.

## Influence on Humanity

Voltaire's impact on the world is immeasurable. His legacy includes:

**1. Freedom of Speech** – His defense of free expression influenced the formation of modern democratic principles.

**2. Religious Tolerance** – He challenged religious persecution and promoted the idea of secular governance.

**3. Political Thought** – His critiques of monarchy and advocacy for individual rights influenced the American and French Revolutions.

**4. Scientific Advancement** – His support for reason and empiricism contributed to the progress of the Enlightenment.

**5. Literary Excellence** – His plays, essays, and novels remain masterpieces of satire and philosophical literature.

In conclusion, Voltaire was more than a writer – he was a revolutionary thinker who shaped the modern world. His relentless pursuit of truth, justice, and reason continues to inspire those who challenge oppression and advocate for freedom. His legacy endures as a cornerstone of the Enlightenment and a guiding force for progress.

# Benjamin Franklin

Scientist, politician, and Founding Father of the USA

Benjamin Franklin was one of the most influential figures in American history. A statesman, scientist, inventor, writer, and diplomat, Franklin embodied the spirit of the Enlightenment and played a crucial role in shaping the United States. His contributions spanned multiple fields, from his groundbreaking experiments with electricity to his work in diplomacy and governance. His wisdom, wit, and scientific ingenuity made him a legendary figure whose legacy continues to impact humanity.

## Origin

Benjamin Franklin was born on January 17, 1706, in Boston, Massachusetts, then a British colony. He was the fifteenth of seventeen children born to Josiah Franklin, a candle and soap maker, and Abiah Folger. The Franklin family was of modest means, and young Benjamin's early life was shaped by hard work and frugality.

His father, Josiah, had emigrated from England in 1683 and established himself as a tradesman in Boston. His mother, Abiah, was of Puritan heritage, which influenced Franklin's values of diligence, self-improvement, and moral responsibility. Though he was born into a relatively humble family, Franklin's insatiable curiosity and intelligence set him apart from an early age.

## Childhood and Youth

Franklin's formal education was brief. He attended the Boston Latin School for only two years before being withdrawn due to financial constraints. His father intended for him to enter the clergy, but the cost of further education was too great. Instead, Franklin was apprenticed to his older brother, James, who ran a printing press and published "The New-England Courant".

Working in his brother's shop, Franklin developed a love for reading and writing. He secretly submitted essays under the pseudonym "Silence Dogood," which were published in the newspaper. These essays, filled with wit and social commentary, earned him local recognition but also led to tensions with his brother. At age 17, Franklin left Boston and traveled to Philadelphia, seeking greater opportunities.

In 1723, Franklin arrived in Philadelphia with little money but great ambition. He worked for a local printer and later traveled to London in 1724, hoping to expand his skills. After a challenging period in London, where he struggled to establish himself, he returned to Philadelphia in 1726 and set about building his career.

## Adulthood

Franklin's adult life was marked by remarkable achievements in multiple fields. In 1728, he established his own printing business, and by 1730, he became the publisher of "The Pennsylvania Gazette". His newspaper gained widespread readership and became a platform for public discourse. In 1732, he began publishing "Poor Richard's Almanack", a widely popular annual filled with proverbs, practical advice, and humor.

Franklin's curiosity and intellect led him to scientific experimentation. His most famous work involved electricity, particularly his 1752 kite experiment, which demonstrated that lightning was a form of electricity. This experiment laid the groundwork for modern electrical science and led to his invention of the lightning rod, which protected buildings from lightning strikes.

His other notable inventions included:

- **Bifocal Glasses** – Eyeglasses with lenses for both near and far vision.
- **Franklin Stove** – A more efficient heating stove.
- **Armonica** (Glass Harmonica) – A musical instrument that gained popularity in the 18th century.
- **Swim Fins** – Designed to improve swimming efficiency.

Franklin's influence extended beyond science. He was deeply involved in colonial and national politics. He played a crucial role in drafting the Albany Plan of Union in 1754, an early proposal for a unified colonial government. Later, he was instrumental in advocating for American independence.

During the American Revolution, Franklin served as a diplomat in France, securing critical military and financial support from the French government. His charm, wit, and negotiation skills helped solidify France's alliance with the United States, contributing significantly to the war effort.

He also participated in drafting the Declaration of Independence in 1776 and later helped negotiate the Treaty of Paris in 1783, which ended the Revolutionary War.

In 1787, Franklin played a key role in shaping the U.S. Constitution as one of the delegates at the Constitutional Convention. Though he was in his 80s by then, his wisdom and conciliatory approach helped bridge differences between factions.

## Private Life

Franklin married Deborah Read in 1730. Their relationship was unconventional; they never had a formal wedding ceremony but remained committed partners for decades. They had two children together, Francis Folger Franklin, who tragically died of smallpox at age four, and Sarah Franklin Bache, who carried on Franklin's legacy of public service.

Franklin also had an illegitimate son, William Franklin, who later became a Loyalist and opposed the American Revolution. Their political differences led to an estrangement that lasted until Franklin's death.

Throughout his life, Franklin was known for his sociability and extensive network of friends, both in America and Europe. He was a founder of the American Philosophical Society, a member of the Freemasons, and an advocate for public libraries and education.

## Death

Benjamin Franklin died on April 17, 1790, at the age of 84. His funeral in Philadelphia was attended by thousands, reflecting the immense respect he commanded. His will left generous donations to education and public institutions, reinforcing his lifelong commitment to civic improvement. His famous epitaph, which he had written earlier in life, compared his body to an old book that had served its purpose, suggesting a belief in the afterlife and intellectual legacy.

## Character

Franklin was known for his practicality, intelligence, humor, and relentless pursuit of self-improvement. His famous "13 Virtues" included principles such as industry, humility, and frugality, which he sought to embody throughout his life. He valued education, innovation, and public service, and his actions reflected these ideals.

Despite his achievements, Franklin was also pragmatic and aware of his own flaws. He was adaptable, capable of changing his views when necessary, and skilled at diplomacy and compromise.

## Influence on Humanity

Franklin's impact on history is immeasurable. His contributions include:

**1. Scientific Discoveries** – His work on electricity paved the way for future research.

**2. Political Foundations** – He helped shape the principles of American democracy and diplomacy.

**3. Education and Literacy** – He established public libraries, the University of Pennsylvania, and promoted scientific inquiry.

**4. Press and Free Speech** – His work in journalism set high standards for press freedom.

**5. Public Institutions** – He contributed to the creation of fire departments, postal services, and civic organizations.

In conclusion, Benjamin Franklin was a towering figure whose intellect, ambition, and civic spirit transformed society. His legacy lives on in science, politics, and public service, making him one of the most extraordinary figures in American and world history.

# Jean-Jacques Rousseau
The philosopher of freedom and democracy

Jean-Jacques Rousseau was one of the most influential thinkers of the Enlightenment, whose ideas shaped modern political philosophy, education, and literature. His works, including "The Social Contract" and "Emile", challenged the existing structures of authority and emphasized individual freedom, the social contract, and natural human goodness. His philosophy deeply influenced the French Revolution and the development of modern democracy.

## Origin

Jean-Jacques Rousseau was born on June 28, 1712, in Geneva, which was then an independent republic. His father, Isaac Rousseau, was a watchmaker, and his mother, Suzanne Bernard, came from a wealthy family. Tragically, Suzanne died of childbirth complications just days after Jean-Jacques was born.

Geneva was a city-state known for its Protestant values and emphasis on civic duty, and Rousseau was raised in an environment that valued education and moral responsibility. However, his early years were marked by instability, which significantly shaped his later views on society and human nature.

## Childhood and Youth

Rousseau's childhood was difficult and tumultuous. After his mother's death, he was raised primarily by his father, who instilled in him a love for reading. They would read books together, including classical literature and Plutarch's "Lives", which deeply influenced Rousseau's moral and political philosophy.

At the age of ten, his father fled Geneva after a dispute, leaving Jean-Jacques in the care of an uncle. He was soon apprenticed to an engraver, but he disliked the harsh conditions and discipline. At sixteen, Rousseau ran away from Geneva and traveled through France and Italy, taking on various jobs as a servant, tutor, and secretary.

During this period, he converted to Catholicism under the influence of Madame de Warens, a noblewoman who became his mentor and benefactor. She provided him with an education and introduced him to music, philosophy, and literature.

## Adulthood

In his early adulthood, Rousseau moved to Paris in 1742, where he sought to establish himself as a composer and intellectual. He became acquainted with leading Enlightenment figures such as Denis Diderot and contributed to the "Encyclopédie", writing about music and political philosophy.

His breakthrough came in 1750 with his "Discourse on the Arts and Sciences", in which he argued that civilization had corrupted humanity's natural goodness. This essay won him fame and recognition, though it also sparked controversy.

In 1755, he published "Discourse on the Origin and Basis of Inequality Among Men", where he introduced the concept of the "noble savage" and critiqued private property as a source of social inequality. This work laid the groundwork for his later political philosophy.

His most famous work, "The Social Contract" (1762), argued that legitimate political authority derives from the collective will of the people, rather than divine right or hereditary rule. He also published "Emile", a treatise on education that emphasized the importance of nurturing children's natural instincts rather than imposing rigid structures.

Due to the controversial nature of his writings, Rousseau faced persecution. Both "Emile" and "The Social Contract" were banned in France and Geneva, forcing him to flee. He sought refuge in Switzerland, Prussia, and eventually England, where he briefly stayed with the philosopher David Hume before their relationship soured.

## Private Life

Rousseau's personal life was marked by contradictions and hardships. He never married but had a long-term relationship with Thérèse Levasseur, a domestic servant. Together, they had five children, all of whom Rousseau abandoned to a foundling hospital, an act that later drew heavy criticism, given his philosophical emphasis on education and child-rearing.

Despite his intellectual brilliance, Rousseau struggled with paranoia and social alienation. He had frequent conflicts with other Enlightenment thinkers, including Voltaire and Diderot, and often believed he was the victim of conspiracies against him.

His later years were spent in relative isolation, as he wandered through France and Switzerland, working on his autobiographical writings. His "Confessions", completed in 1770, provided an intimate look at his life and thoughts, setting a new precedent for personal introspection in literature.

## Death

Jean-Jacques Rousseau died on July 2, 1778, at the age of 66. The exact cause of his death remains unclear, though it was reported to be due to a stroke or kidney disease. Some have speculated that he may have taken his own life due to his increasing paranoia and emotional distress.

He was initially buried on the Île des Peupliers, but during the French Revolution, his remains were moved to the Panthéon in Paris, where he was honored as a revolutionary thinker whose ideas helped inspire the movement.

## Character

Rousseau was a deeply introspective and emotional thinker. Unlike many of his contemporaries who emphasized rationality and scientific inquiry, he placed a strong emphasis on emotion, intuition, and the natural state of human beings. He was a passionate writer, and his works often carried a deeply personal and poetic quality.

However, he was also known for his difficult personality, intense self-doubt, and distrust of others. His tendency toward paranoia led to conflicts with many intellectual figures of his time. Despite his social struggles, his work displayed a profound belief in human goodness and the potential for a just and fair society.

## Influence on Humanity

Rousseau's impact on political philosophy, education, and literature is immense. His contributions include:

**1. Political Philosophy** – "The Social Contract" laid the foundation for modern democracy and influenced revolutionary movements, particularly the French Revolution and later democratic theories.

**2. Educational Theory** – His book "Emile" transformed ideas about child education, emphasizing experiential learning and emotional development.

**3. Critique of Inequality** – His "Discourse on Inequality" provided one of the earliest critiques of economic and social disparities, influencing socialist and anarchist thought.

**4. Romanticism** – His emphasis on emotion and nature inspired the Romantic movement, which rejected the rigid rationalism of the Enlightenment.

**5. Autobiography** – His "Confessions" pioneered the modern autobiographical genre, influencing personal and literary narratives.

In conclusion, Jean-Jacques Rousseau was a revolutionary thinker who challenged established norms and reshaped ideas about government, society, and human nature. His legacy continues to inspire debates on democracy, education, and personal freedom, ensuring his place as one of history's most influential philosophers.

# Adam Smith
The father of modern economics

Adam Smith was a Scottish economist, philosopher, and author who is widely regarded as the father of modern economics. His seminal work, "The Wealth of Nations", laid the foundation for classical economic theory and introduced concepts such as the division of labor, the invisible hand, and free markets. His ideas profoundly influenced economic thought, shaping policies and systems that continue to guide global economies today.

## Origin

Adam Smith was born on June 5, 1723, in Kirkcaldy, a small coastal town in Scotland. He was the son of Adam Smith Sr., a customs official, and Margaret Douglas. Unfortunately, his father died just a few months before Adam's birth, leaving his mother to raise him alone.

Kirkcaldy, though a relatively small town, was a thriving center of commerce and industry, which may have influenced Smith's interest in economics. His mother played a crucial role in his upbringing, ensuring he received a strong education that would prepare him for a distinguished career.

## Childhood and Youth

Smith was an intellectually curious child with a keen interest in books and learning. At the age of 14, he was sent to the University of Glasgow, where he studied moral philosophy under the renowned professor Francis Hutcheson. Hutcheson's ideas about individual liberty and ethical considerations in economics had a lasting impact on Smith's thinking.

In 1740, at the age of 17, Smith won a scholarship to Balliol College, Oxford, where he continued his studies. However, he was critical of the education system at Oxford, believing that it was outdated and uninspiring compared to the more dynamic learning environment at Glasgow. During his time at Oxford, he focused on self-directed learning, studying classical literature, logic, and economic theories.

## Adulthood

After completing his studies, Smith returned to Scotland and began delivering public lectures. In 1751, he was appointed a professor of logic at the University of Glasgow, and the following year, he became a professor of moral philosophy. His lectures covered subjects such as ethics, jurisprudence, and economics, and he quickly gained a reputation as an engaging and insightful teacher.

In 1759, Smith published "The Theory of Moral Sentiments", which explored human emotions, morality, and social relationships. The book established his philosophical outlook and provided a moral foundation for his later economic theories. He argued that human behavior was guided by sympathy and a sense of justice, rather than purely self-interest.

Smith's growing reputation led to an invitation to become a tutor for the Duke of Buccleuch, a position that took him on an extensive tour of Europe from 1764 to 1766. During his travels, he met leading intellectuals, including Voltaire, François Quesnay, and Anne Robert Jacques Turgot, whose economic theories influenced his thinking.

After returning to Scotland, Adam Smith spent ten years writing his magnum opus, "An Inquiry into the Nature and Causes of the Wealth of Nations," which was published in 1776. The book was a groundbreaking analysis of economic principles, advocating for free markets, limited government intervention, and the importance of competition in promoting prosperity.

## Private Life

Despite his immense intellectual contributions, Smith led a relatively private and modest life. He never married and had no known romantic relationships. Instead, he remained devoted to his mother, with whom he lived for most of his life. He was described as gentle, reserved, and somewhat absent-minded, often lost in thought about economic or philosophical matters.

Smith had a small but close circle of friends, including Scottish Enlightenment thinkers such as David Hume, James Watt, and Adam Ferguson. His friendships with these intellectuals helped shape his ideas and allowed him to engage in stimulating discussions about philosophy, economics, and politics.

He was known for his generosity and kindness, often helping students and colleagues in need. Despite his reputation as a leading economist, he was not wealthy and lived a relatively simple life. His personal habits reflected his philosophical beliefs in moderation and practical wisdom.

## Death

In his later years, Smith continued to refine his ideas and engage in intellectual discourse. In 1778, he was appointed Commissioner of Customs for Scotland, a position that provided him with financial security and allowed him to contribute to economic policy.

Smith's health began to decline in the early 1790s, and he suffered from what was believed to be a severe illness. He passed away on July 17, 1790, at the age of 67 in Edinburgh. Before his death, he ordered many of his unpublished manuscripts to be burned, leaving only a limited selection of his personal notes and correspondences.

## Character

Smith was known for his intellectual rigor, humility, and moral integrity. Unlike many public intellectuals of his time, he did not seek fame or fortune, choosing instead to focus on his work and scholarship. He was deeply compassionate and believed that economic policies should serve the greater good, rather than just benefiting the wealthy elite.

His philosophy combined a belief in free markets with a strong sense of morality. He saw the market as a means of creating wealth and prosperity but also emphasized the importance of ethical behavior and social responsibility. He argued that self-interest, when properly regulated by competition and legal frameworks, could lead to beneficial outcomes for society as a whole.

Smith was also known for his dry wit and eccentricities. He had a habit of speaking to himself while walking and was often so engrossed in his thoughts that he would forget his surroundings. Despite his absent-minded nature, he was widely respected for his wisdom and insight.

## Influence on Humanity

Adam Smith's impact on economic thought and policy cannot be overstated. His ideas shaped the principles of capitalism and continue to influence economic policies worldwide. Some of his key contributions include:

**1. The Invisible Hand** – Smith introduced the concept of the invisible hand, arguing that individual self-interest in a competitive market leads to beneficial societal outcomes.

**2. Free Markets** – He advocated for minimal government intervention in the economy, arguing that free markets are the most efficient way to allocate resources.

**3. Division of Labor** – Smith highlighted the importance of specialization and the division of labor in increasing productivity and economic growth.

**4. Role of Government** – While he supported free markets, he also recognized the need for government to enforce laws, protect property rights, and provide public goods.

**5. Impact on Political Economy** – His ideas influenced economic liberalism, shaping policies in countries such as the United States and Britain, and laid the foundation for modern capitalism.

**6. Legacy in Economic Thought** – His work inspired economists such as David Ricardo, John Stuart Mill, and later, Friedrich Hayek and Milton Friedman.

In conclusion, Adam Smith was not only an economist but also a philosopher whose ideas transformed the way societies understand markets, trade, and economic development. His work remains a fundamental part of economic theory and policy, ensuring his place as one of the most influential thinkers in history.

# Immanuel Kant

Enlightenment Philosopher known for his work on ethics and metaphysics

Immanuel Kant was one of the most influential philosophers in Western thought. His work in metaphysics, epistemology, ethics, and aesthetics redefined the scope and limits of human knowledge, shaping philosophical discourse for centuries. Kant's "Critique of Pure Reason" revolutionized philosophy by exploring the relationship between human experience and knowledge. His ideas on morality, autonomy, and the categorical imperative continue to guide ethical and political theory.

## Origin

Immanuel Kant was born on April 22, 1724, in Königsberg, a city in East Prussia (now Kaliningrad, Russia). He was the fourth of nine children in a modest but hardworking family. His father, Johann Georg Kant, was a harness maker, and his mother, Anna Regina Reuter, was known for her devout religious beliefs and emphasis on moral education. Königsberg was an intellectual and commercial hub of Prussia, fostering a vibrant academic atmosphere. Though his family had limited financial means, they valued education, which set Kant on the path to becoming one of the greatest philosophers in history.

## Childhood and Youth

Kant's early life was shaped by the strict discipline of his Pietist upbringing. He attended the Collegium Fridericianum, a Lutheran school that emphasized religious devotion, classical languages, and moral discipline. The rigorous education instilled in him a strong work ethic and an appreciation for structured thinking.

Despite his family's financial struggles, Kant excelled in school, showing an aptitude for philosophy, mathematics, and natural sciences. At the age of 16, he enrolled at the University of Königsberg (Albertina) to study philosophy, theology, and physics. During his university years, he was influenced by thinkers such as Christian Wolff and Isaac Newton, whose ideas would later shape his critical philosophy.

Tragedy struck in 1746 when Kant's father died, leaving him in financial hardship. Unable to continue his studies immediately, he worked as a private tutor for nearly a decade, teaching children of noble and wealthy families while continuing his intellectual pursuits.

## Adulthood

Kant returned to academia in 1755, earning his doctorate and beginning his career as a lecturer at the University of Königsberg. For over fifteen years, he taught a wide range of subjects, including logic, metaphysics, mathematics, physics, and anthropology. His early works, such as "Universal Natural History and Theory of the Heavens" (1755), reflected his admiration for Newtonian physics and rationalist philosophy.

By the 1770s, Immanuel Kant began formulating his critical philosophy, which culminated in his seminal work, "Critique of Pure Reason" (1781). This groundbreaking work examined the limitations and capabilities of human reason, arguing that knowledge arises from both sensory experience ("a posteriori") and inherent structures of the mind ("a priori"). He proposed that while we can never know things as they are ("noumena"), we can understand them as they appear to us ("phenomena").

Kant followed this with "Critique of Practical Reason" (1788), which laid the foundation for his moral philosophy, and "Critique of Judgment" (1790), which explored aesthetics and teleology. His ethical theory, based on the categorical imperative – the idea that moral actions should be universalizable – became one of the most significant contributions to moral philosophy.

Throughout his career, Kant maintained an unwavering commitment to teaching, mentoring students, and engaging in philosophical debates. His influence extended beyond Germany, shaping the works of later thinkers such as Hegel, Schopenhauer, and Nietzsche.

## Private Life

Kant led an exceptionally disciplined and structured life. He never married and had no known romantic relationships. He was highly regimented in his daily routine, famously taking walks at the exact same time each day, to the point that locals reportedly set their clocks by his movements.

Despite his reserved nature, Kant enjoyed intellectual discussions and maintained friendships with colleagues and students. He was known for his hospitality and engaging conversation, though he avoided unnecessary travel, preferring to stay in Königsberg for most of his life.

His financial situation improved later in life due to the success of his publications and university salary, allowing him to live comfortably and dedicate himself entirely to philosophical inquiry.

## Death

In his later years, Kant's health deteriorated, and he suffered from memory loss and physical frailty. His decline was gradual, and by 1803, he had largely withdrawn from public life. He passed away on February 12, 1804, at the age of 79.

Kant's last words were reportedly "Es ist gut" ("It is good"), reflecting his philosophical acceptance of life's end. He was buried in the Königsberg Cathedral, and his grave remains a site of pilgrimage for philosophers and admirers of his work.

## Character

Kant was known for his rigorous intellect, humility, and disciplined lifestyle. He was deeply committed to truth-seeking and intellectual honesty, refusing to compromise his philosophical principles for popularity or material gain. Though often portrayed as austere, he had a dry wit and enjoyed engaging with others in philosophical debate.

His moral philosophy was deeply rooted in duty and rationality, emphasizing ethical consistency and universal moral laws. He championed enlightenment ideals, encouraging independent thought, education, and the courage to use one's reason ("sapere aude").

Kant's dedication to routine and structure was legendary, and his meticulous approach to both life and philosophy reflected his belief in the power of rational order. His unwavering commitment to academia and teaching left a lasting impact on generations of scholars.

# Influence on Humanity

Kant's influence on philosophy and human thought is immeasurable. His contributions include:

**1. Epistemology and Metaphysics** – His "Critique of Pure Reason" revolutionized how knowledge and perception are understood, laying the groundwork for modern epistemology.

**2. Ethics and Morality** – The categorical imperative remains a cornerstone of deontological ethics, shaping contemporary moral philosophy and human rights discourse.

**3. Political Philosophy** – His ideas on perpetual peace and cosmopolitanism influenced democratic ideals, international relations, and political philosophy.

**4. Aesthetics and Art Theory** – His "Critique of Judgment" provided foundational insights into beauty, taste, and artistic interpretation.

**5. Education and the Enlightenment** – His advocacy for reason, education, and critical thinking inspired generations of scholars and educators.

**6. Impact on Later Philosophers** – Kant's work deeply influenced figures such as Hegel, Marx, Schopenhauer, Nietzsche, and contemporary philosophers like Rawls and Habermas.

In conclusion, Immanuel Kant's intellectual legacy is one of the most profound in history. His relentless pursuit of knowledge, commitment to moral philosophy, and critical examination of human reason continue to shape the way we think about the world. His work remains essential to modern philosophy, ethics, and political thought, ensuring his place among the greatest minds of all time.

# George Washington
## First U.S. president and leader of the American Revolution

George Washington, often referred to as the "Father of His Country," was a military commander, statesman, and the first President of the United States. He played a key role in the American Revolution, the drafting of the U.S. Constitution, and the establishment of the young republic. His leadership, integrity, and dedication to democratic principles set a precedent for future leaders.

## Origin

George Washington was born on February 22, 1732, in Westmoreland County, Virginia, then a British colony. He was the son of Augustine Washington, a prosperous planter and businessman, and Mary Ball Washington. His family was part of the colonial gentry, with strong connections to land ownership and local politics.

Washington's ancestors were English, and his great-grandfather had settled in Virginia in the mid-1600s. Though his family was not among the wealthiest in the colony, they were respected and influential, giving young George opportunities for social mobility and leadership.

## Childhood and Youth

Washington spent his early years on his family's plantation, absorbing lessons in agriculture, business, and colonial society. His formal education was limited, consisting primarily of home tutoring and some schooling in basic mathematics, reading, and writing. Unlike many of his contemporaries who studied abroad, Washington never received a classical European education.

At the age of 11, Washington's father passed away, leaving much of the family's wealth and land to his half-brothers. This forced young George to take on responsibilities at an early age. His older brother, Lawrence Washington, became a mentor and exposed him to Virginia's elite circles.

In his teenage years, Washington developed a passion for surveying and cartography. He secured a job as a surveyor for Lord Fairfax, traveling through the rugged frontier and gaining valuable experience in land management and military strategy. These early experiences shaped his resilience and leadership abilities.

## Adulthood

Washington's military career began in 1752 when he was appointed a major in the Virginia militia. His leadership skills were tested during the French and Indian War (1754–1763), where he served under British command. His bravery and strategic thinking earned him a reputation as a capable leader, though he also experienced setbacks, such as the failed expedition at Fort Necessity.

Following the war, Washington returned to Mount Vernon, his plantation, and focused on agricultural pursuits. However, the growing tensions between the American colonies and Great Britain soon called him back into public service.

In 1775, as dissatisfaction with British rule grew, Washington was appointed Commander-in-Chief of the Continental Army. Leading an untrained and poorly equipped force, he orchestrated key victories, including the crossing of the Delaware River and the Battle of Yorktown. His ability to inspire troops, manage resources, and navigate political challenges was instrumental in securing American independence.

After the war, Washington was unanimously elected as the first President of the United States in 1789. He established many precedents for the office, including the cabinet system, the two-term tradition, and the principle of a peaceful transfer of power. His presidency was marked by efforts to stabilize the new nation, including the establishment of a national bank, maintaining neutrality in foreign conflicts, and fostering unity among states.

Washington voluntarily stepped down after two terms, reinforcing the idea that leadership should be a temporary service rather than a lifetime position.

## Private Life

Washington married Martha Custis, a wealthy widow, in 1759. Their marriage provided financial security and social status, though they had no children of their own. Washington became a father figure to Martha's children from her previous marriage and cared deeply for his extended family.

His estate, Mount Vernon, was his lifelong passion. Washington was an innovative farmer, experimenting with crop rotation and new agricultural techniques. Despite owning enslaved people, he expressed growing discomfort with slavery later in life and made provisions in his will for their emancipation upon Martha's death.

Washington valued personal discipline, often waking early to manage his affairs. He enjoyed horseback riding, hunting, and socializing with guests, though he was known for his reserved demeanor.

## Death

On December 12, 1799, Washington fell ill after riding through cold, wet conditions. His condition worsened rapidly, and on December 14, he passed away at Mount Vernon. His final words were reported to be, "Tis well."

His death was mourned across the nation, and he was widely eulogized as a leader of unmatched integrity and dedication to the Republic. He was buried at Mount Vernon, which remains a national historic site.

## Character

Washington was known for his steadfastness, humility, and sense of duty. He believed in leading by example, often placing the nation's interests above his own. His reluctance to hold power indefinitely demonstrated his commitment to republican values, distinguishing him from many rulers of his time.

Though not a brilliant orator or scholar, Washington's leadership was marked by practicality, perseverance, and an ability to unify people with different interests. He was deeply aware of his legacy and conducted himself with an almost theatrical sense of dignity and decorum.

Despite his virtues, Washington was not without flaws. His initial reluctance to address slavery and his struggles with managing political factions revealed the complexities of his era. However, his ability to navigate challenges with wisdom and restraint solidified his reputation as an exemplary leader.

## Influence on Humanity

Washington's influence extends far beyond his lifetime. His contributions include:

**1. Establishing American Democracy** – His leadership in the Revolutionary War and presidency laid the foundation for the United States' democratic institutions.

**2. Presidential Precedents** – His voluntary resignation after two terms set an enduring standard for executive leadership.

**3. Military Strategy** – His innovative tactics in guerrilla warfare and strategic retreats influenced future military doctrine.

**4. National Unity** – His emphasis on national identity and unity helped bind the fledgling states into a coherent nation.

**5. Moral Leadership** – His decision to free his enslaved workers in his will signaled an evolving stance on human rights and justice.

In conclusion, George Washington was not just the first President of the United States – he was a visionary leader who shaped the nation's identity. His principles of duty, humility, and commitment to democratic governance continue to inspire leaders around the world. His legacy remains a testament to the power of integrity and service in shaping a nation's destiny.

# James Watt
## Developer of the steam engine

James Watt was a Scottish inventor, mechanical engineer, and chemist whose improvements to the steam engine revolutionized industry and transportation. His innovations significantly increased the efficiency of steam power, playing a pivotal role in the Industrial Revolution. Watt's work laid the foundation for modern engineering and energy production, shaping the course of technological progress.

## Origin

James Watt was born on January 19, 1736, in Greenock, Scotland, a bustling port town on the River Clyde. He was the eldest of five surviving children born to James Watt Sr., a prosperous shipbuilder and merchant, and Agnes Muirhead, who came from a well-educated family. Watt's father was also involved in local government, giving young James exposure to business and mechanical trade from an early age.

Scotland in the 18th century was a center of Enlightenment thought, with major advancements in philosophy, science, and engineering. This intellectual atmosphere influenced Watt's development as an innovator and problem-solver.

## Childhood and Youth

As a child, Watt was frail and often in poor health, leading him to be homeschooled by his mother. Despite these challenges, he displayed an early talent for mechanics and mathematics. His father's workshop provided him with hands-on experience, where he developed skills in metalworking, measuring instruments, and model-making.

At the age of 17, Watt traveled to Glasgow, where he sought formal training in instrument-making. In 1755, he moved to London and apprenticed with a maker of mathematical instruments. The intense workload and long hours took a toll on his health, but he persevered and became highly skilled in precision engineering.

Upon returning to Glasgow in 1756, Watt set up a workshop at the University of Glasgow, where he repaired and manufactured scientific instruments. His interactions with university professors, including Joseph Black, exposed him to cutting-edge scientific research, particularly in thermodynamics and energy efficiency.

## Adulthood

Watt's breakthrough came in 1764 when he was asked to repair a model of Thomas Newcomen's steam engine. He quickly realized that Newcomen's design was highly inefficient, wasting vast amounts of energy. Over the next several years, Watt conducted experiments to improve steam engine performance.

In 1765, he devised a revolutionary concept – the separate condenser. By condensing steam in a separate chamber rather than within the main cylinder, Watt dramatically increased the engine's efficiency and reduced fuel consumption. However, he lacked the financial resources to build a working model.

To fund his project, Watt partnered with John Roebuck, an industrialist, but financial difficulties delayed progress. In 1775, Watt secured a partnership with Matthew Boulton, a wealthy businessman and manufacturer. With Boulton's support, Watt perfected his steam engine design and successfully patented it in 1769.

The Watt-Boulton steam engine became commercially viable in the 1770s, and by the 1780s, it was transforming industries such as mining, textile manufacturing, and transportation. Watt continued refining his invention, introducing the sun-and-planet gear system, which converted reciprocating motion into rotary motion – crucial for powering mills and factories.

By the end of the 18th century, Watt's steam engine was widely adopted across Britain and Europe, fueling the rapid expansion of industry and commerce. His contributions extended beyond steam power, as he also developed the concept of horsepower and contributed to early work in thermodynamics.

## Private Life

Watt married his first wife, Margaret Miller, in 1764, and they had several children. Tragically, Margaret died in 1773, leaving Watt devastated. He remarried in 1776 to Ann MacGregor, who provided him with emotional stability and support during his most productive years.

Watt was deeply committed to his work, often spending long hours in his workshop. However, he also had a close circle of friends, including leading scientists and engineers of his time, such as Erasmus Darwin and Joseph Priestley. He was a founding member of the Lunar Society, an influential group of intellectuals who discussed scientific advancements and industrial innovations.

Despite his wealth and fame, Watt remained modest and preferred a quiet life away from public attention. He enjoyed gardening and reading, often retreating to his home to engage in private experiments.

## Death

James Watt retired from active engineering in the early 1800s, though he continued to advise on scientific and industrial matters. He spent his final years at Heathfield Hall, his estate near Birmingham.

He passed away peacefully on August 25, 1819, at the age of 83. He was buried in Handsworth Cemetery, where his contributions to engineering and industry were honored by future generations.

## Character

Watt was known for his perseverance, intellectual curiosity, and meticulous attention to detail. He was a perfectionist, often delaying projects until he was satisfied with the results. Despite moments of self-doubt, his persistence ultimately led to some of the most important technological advancements of his time.

He was also deeply ethical, refusing to exploit his patents unfairly and often advising others on engineering improvements. While he was sometimes reserved and private, he had a generous spirit and valued collaboration over competition.

Watt's ability to blend theoretical knowledge with practical engineering solutions made him a transformative figure in the industrial world. His legacy was built not just on invention but on his ability to refine and commercialize technology that reshaped the global economy.

## Influence on Humanity

James Watt's contributions to engineering and industry were profound, leading to several key advancements:

**1. The Industrial Revolution** – His improvements to the steam engine powered factories, mines, and transportation, fueling economic growth and industrial expansion.

**2. Steam Power in Transportation** – His innovations led to the development of steam-powered locomotives and ships, revolutionizing travel and trade.

**3. Concept of Horsepower** – Watt introduced the term "horsepower" to quantify engine performance, a standard still used in engineering today.

**4. Energy Efficiency and Thermodynamics** – His work on steam energy efficiency laid the groundwork for modern thermodynamics and mechanical engineering.

**5. Influence on Future Engineers** – Watt's ideas inspired future inventors, including George Stephenson and Robert Fulton, who further developed steam-powered transportation.

**6. Economic and Social Transformation** – His contributions accelerated urbanization, changed labor dynamics, and helped create the modern industrial economy.

In conclusion, James Watt's ingenuity and engineering brilliance played a fundamental role in shaping the modern world. His contributions to steam power, energy efficiency, and industrial technology continue to influence engineering and economic development. His legacy remains a testament to the power of human innovation and perseverance.

# Thomas Jefferson

Third U.S. president and
author of the Declaration of Independence

---

Thomas Jefferson was one of the most influential figures in American history, serving as the principal author of the Declaration of Independence and the third President of the United States. A polymath, Jefferson was also an accomplished architect, inventor, and philosopher. His vision for a nation built on democratic principles, education, and individual liberty continues to shape American society.

---

## Origin

Thomas Jefferson was born on April 13, 1743, in Shadwell, Virginia, then a British colony. He was the third of ten children born to Peter Jefferson, a successful planter and surveyor, and Jane Randolph, a member of one of Virginia's most prominent families. The Jeffersons were part of the colonial gentry, affording young Thomas access to wealth, education, and political connections.

Virginia in the mid-18th century was a growing and influential colony, shaped by tobacco farming, slavery, and a rigid class system. These influences would play a significant role in Jefferson's later political and moral beliefs, as he navigated the contradictions between his ideals of liberty and his own status as a slave owner.

---

## Childhood and Youth

Jefferson grew up on his family's plantation, Shadwell, in the rolling hills of Virginia. As a child, he was fascinated by nature, music, and literature. His father instilled in him a strong work ethic and a love for learning. When Peter Jefferson died in 1757, the 14-year-old Thomas inherited a significant amount of land, wealth, and enslaved people.

Jefferson was sent to study under Reverend James Maury, a respected clergyman, where he excelled in Latin, Greek, and classical philosophy. In 1760, he enrolled at the College of William & Mary in Williamsburg, where he was introduced to Enlightenment ideals. He studied law under the tutelage of George Wythe, one of the most esteemed legal minds in colonial America. During his studies, Jefferson developed a deep appreciation for reason, science, and political theory, all of which influenced his later writings and policies.

After completing his education, Jefferson was admitted to the Virginia bar in 1767 and began practicing law, representing clients in land disputes and inheritance cases. His legal career was short-lived, as he soon became immersed in politics.

## Adulthood

Jefferson's political career began in 1769 when he was elected to the Virginia House of Burgesses. He quickly aligned himself with the growing movement for American independence, advocating for colonial rights and resistance against British rule.

In 1774, he authored "A Summary View of the Rights of British America," in which he outlined his opposition to British taxation and monarchy. The pamphlet gained widespread attention and established Jefferson as a leading voice in the revolutionary cause.

In 1775, as tensions escalated, Jefferson was selected as a delegate to the Second Continental Congress. In June 1776, he was tasked with drafting the Declaration of Independence. Drawing on Enlightenment principles, Jefferson articulated the natural rights of life, liberty, and the pursuit of happiness, framing the American colonies' case for separation from Britain.

The Declaration, adopted on July 4, 1776, became the cornerstone of American democracy and inspired revolutions worldwide.

Jefferson served as Governor of Virginia from 1779 to 1781, during which he faced challenges in defending the state against British invasions. Following the war, he focused on legislative reforms, advocating for religious freedom, education, and the abolition of primogeniture.

From 1785 to 1789, Jefferson served as U.S. Minister to France, witnessing the early stages of the French Revolution and deepening his commitment to republican ideals.

Elected as the third President of the United States in 1800, Jefferson's presidency was marked by major achievements and controversies:

- **Louisiana Purchase** (1803): He doubled the size of the U.S. by acquiring the Louisiana Territory from France.
- **Lewis and Clark Expedition** (1804-1806): He commissioned an expedition to explore the western frontier.
- **Embargo Act** (1807): In response to British and French interference in American trade, Jefferson imposed an embargo that ultimately hurt the U.S. economy.

Despite these accomplishments, his presidency was also marred by tensions over slavery, Native American policies, and increasing partisan divisions.

## Private Life

Jefferson married Martha Wayles Skelton in 1772, and they had six children, though only two survived to adulthood. Their marriage was marked by mutual affection, but Martha's death in 1782 devastated Jefferson. He never remarried.

Jefferson's personal life was complicated by his relationship with Sally Hemings, an enslaved woman at Monticello. Evidence suggests that Jefferson fathered several of her children, though he never publicly acknowledged them. This contradiction between his public advocacy for liberty and his private life as a slave owner remains one of the most debated aspects of his legacy.

He was also a passionate architect and scholar, designing Monticello and founding the University of Virginia, which he considered one of his greatest achievements.

## Death

Thomas Jefferson died on July 4, 1826, the 50th anniversary of the Declaration of Independence. Remarkably, John Adams, his longtime political rival and friend, died on the same day. Jefferson was 83 years old. He was buried at Monticello, and his self-written epitaph highlighted three accomplishments: authoring the Declaration of Independence, founding the University of Virginia, and crafting Virginia's Statute for Religious Freedom – leaving out his presidency.

## Character

Jefferson was a man of intellect, curiosity, and contradictions. He championed democracy, freedom, and education but remained a slaveholder. He valued reason and scientific inquiry but was deeply spiritual. He could be both pragmatic and idealistic, shaping his policies based on the evolving needs of the nation.

His reserved and introspective nature sometimes made him an elusive figure, yet he was deeply committed to public service. His ability to balance political philosophy with practical governance made him one of the most influential figures of his era.

## Influence on Humanity

Jefferson's legacy extends far beyond his time:

**1. Democratic Ideals** – His writings influenced revolutions in France and Latin America.

**2. Religious Freedom** – His Virginia Statute for Religious Freedom helped establish the separation of church and state.

**3. Expansion of the U.S.** – The Louisiana Purchase set the stage for America's westward expansion.

**4. Education and Knowledge** – The University of Virginia remains a testament to his belief in public education.

**5. Human Rights and Liberties** – His principles in the Declaration of Independence continue to inspire global movements for freedom and equality.

In conclusion, Thomas Jefferson was a visionary leader whose contributions to democracy, governance, and education continue to shape the modern world. Though his legacy is complex and filled with contradictions, his impact on American society and global political thought is undeniable.

# Antoine Laurent de Lavoisier
## The Father of Modern Chemistry

Antoine Laurent de Lavoisier was a pioneering French chemist whose discoveries revolutionized the field of chemistry and laid the foundation for modern chemical sciences. Known for establishing the law of conservation of mass, recognizing and naming oxygen and hydrogen, and reforming chemical nomenclature, Lavoisier transformed alchemy into a structured and systematic science. His work remains central to scientific progress, and his impact extends beyond chemistry into fields such as biology and physics.

## Origin

Antoine Laurent de Lavoisier was born on August 26, 1743, in Paris, France, into a wealthy and influential family. His father, Jean-Antoine Lavoisier, was a lawyer and financier, while his mother, Émilie Punctis, came from a well-established bourgeois family. Lavoisier's privileged upbringing provided him with access to the best education and an early exposure to intellectual and scientific pursuits.

The 18th century in France was a period of scientific and intellectual enlightenment. The works of René Descartes, Isaac Newton, and other great thinkers heavily influenced the European scientific community, and Lavoisier was raised in an environment that encouraged rational inquiry and systematic experimentation.

## Childhood and Youth

Lavoisier exhibited an early interest in the natural sciences and showed exceptional academic ability. At the age of 11, he enrolled at the Collège des Quatre-Nations, also known as the Collège Mazarin, one of Paris's most prestigious institutions. There, he excelled in mathematics, chemistry, botany, and astronomy.

His teachers recognized his intellectual potential, and he was particularly influenced by the geologist Jean-Étienne Guettard, who introduced him to the study of minerals and the classification of natural substances. This exposure ignited Lavoisier's passion for scientific discovery.

Despite his love for science, Lavoisier followed his father's wishes and pursued a law degree at the University of Paris. He earned his law degree in 1764, but his true calling remained in the sciences. While fulfilling his legal studies, he continued to study chemistry and physics in his spare time, attending lectures at the Academy of Sciences and collaborating with leading scientists of the time.

## Adulthood

After completing his law degree, Lavoisier chose to dedicate his life to scientific research. In 1768, at the age of 25, he was elected to the prestigious French Academy of Sciences, a remarkable achievement for such a young scholar. His early research focused on geology, water analysis, and the improvement of urban sanitation.

Lavoisier's most significant contributions came in the field of chemistry. He systematically debunked the centuries-old phlogiston theory, which held that a mysterious substance called "phlogiston" was released during combustion. Through meticulous experimentation, he demonstrated that combustion and respiration were processes involving oxygen, which he named from the Greek words for "acid-former."

In 1778, he identified and named hydrogen, recognizing it as a fundamental element in the composition of water. His studies on air and gases helped establish the concept of chemical elements and led to a deeper understanding of oxidation and combustion.

In 1789, Antoine Lavoisier published "Traité Élémentaire de Chimie" ("Elementary Treatise on Chemistry"), widely regarded as the first modern chemistry textbook. It introduced a systematic method of chemical nomenclature, which standardized chemical terminology and established the basis for modern chemical classification.

Lavoisier's expertise was not limited to academia. He was appointed as a tax collector for the "Ferme Générale", a private tax-collection agency, which allowed him to fund his scientific research. He used his position to implement agricultural and economic reforms, improve public sanitation, and contribute to better urban planning in Paris.

During the American Revolutionary War, he worked with the French government to improve the manufacture of gunpowder, significantly increasing its quality and production capacity.

## Private Life

Lavoisier married Marie-Anne Paulze in 1771 when she was just 13 years old. Despite her young age, she became an indispensable partner in his scientific endeavors. Highly intelligent and well-educated, Marie-Anne learned chemistry, Latin, and English to assist her husband. She translated important scientific works, illustrated his experiments, and conducted research alongside him.

Their home became a center for scientific discussions, hosting intellectuals and scientists such as Joseph Priestley, Benjamin Franklin, and Pierre-Simon Laplace. Marie-Anne's contributions played a crucial role in Lavoisier's research, and she later became an advocate for preserving his legacy after his tragic death.

## Death

Lavoisier's successful career and association with the "Ferme Générale" made him a target during the French Revolution. The tax collection system he worked for was deeply unpopular, and despite his efforts to reform it, he was branded as an enemy of the people.

On May 8, 1794, at the height of the Reign of Terror, Lavoisier was arrested and swiftly tried by the Revolutionary Tribunal. The judge reportedly declared, "The Republic has no need of scientists." He was executed by guillotine on the same day, at the age of 50.

His death was widely condemned in the scientific community, and years later, his reputation was rehabilitated. The French government officially recognized his contributions, and his legacy was firmly established as one of the most important figures in the history of science.

## Character

Lavoisier was known for his meticulous approach to scientific research, his analytical thinking, and his commitment to empirical evidence. He was disciplined, methodical, and deeply passionate about scientific inquiry.

Despite his wealth and status, he remained dedicated to the betterment of society. He believed in using science for the public good, advocating for better sanitation, agricultural improvements, and economic policies that benefited the general population.

His ability to challenge established beliefs, conduct rigorous experiments, and apply scientific principles to practical problems set him apart as a true pioneer of modern chemistry.

## Influence on Humanity

Lavoisier's impact on science and humanity is immeasurable. His key contributions include:

**1. Law of Conservation of Mass** – He established that matter is neither created nor destroyed in chemical reactions, forming the foundation of modern chemistry.

**2. Identification of Oxygen and Hydrogen** – He named and characterized these elements, revolutionizing our understanding of combustion and respiration.

**3. Modern Chemical Nomenclature** – His system of naming elements and compounds brought clarity and standardization to chemistry.

**4. First Chemistry Textbook** – "Traité Élémentaire de Chimie" became the basis for modern chemical education.

**5. Industrial and Public Reforms** – His work in improving gunpowder production, agriculture, and urban sanitation had lasting impacts beyond chemistry.

In conclusion, Antoine Laurent de Lavoisier was not only a brilliant chemist but also a visionary who transformed science through systematic research and empirical rigor. His contributions continue to shape chemistry, physics, and engineering, making him one of the most significant figures in scientific history.

# Mayer Amschel Rothschild

Founder of an influential financial dynasty

Mayer Amschel Rothschild was a German-Jewish banker and entrepreneur who laid the foundation for one of the most influential banking dynasties in history. His innovative approach to finance, business acumen, and strategic vision transformed the Rothschild family into a powerful force in international banking. By establishing a network of financial institutions across Europe, he created a model that would shape global finance for centuries.

## Origin

Mayer Amschel Rothschild was born on February 23, 1744, in the Jewish ghetto of Frankfurt, Germany. He was the fourth of eight children in a modest Jewish family. His father, Amschel Moses Rothschild, was a money changer and trader who dealt in currency exchange and minor banking services. His mother, Schönche Rothschild, played a crucial role in raising the family within the constraints of the ghetto's rigid social structure.

The Jewish community in Frankfurt lived under strict regulations, confined to the narrow, overcrowded streets of the Judengasse (Jewish alley). Despite these restrictions, the Rothschild family emphasized education, religious values, and business acumen, all of which shaped Mayer's future success.

## Childhood and Youth

Mayer Amschel Rothschild's early years were marked by hardship and limited opportunities due to the discriminatory laws imposed on Jews in 18th-century Germany. However, he received a basic education in Jewish law and finance and was taught the importance of diligence and resourcefulness.

At the age of 12, Mayer was sent to Hanover to apprentice at the banking house of Simon Wolf Oppenheimer. This experience exposed him to the world of finance, banking, and trade, providing him with valuable skills in money lending, investment, and currency exchange. He developed a keen understanding of international finance and trade networks, skills that would later serve him in building his own banking empire.

Upon his father's death in 1755, Mayer returned to Frankfurt and took over the family business. He initially worked as a coin dealer and trader, specializing in rare coins and collectibles. His reputation for honesty and financial acumen grew, attracting the attention of powerful clients, including members of the nobility.

## Adulthood

Mayer's breakthrough came when he established strong ties with Prince William IX of Hesse-Kassel, one of the wealthiest rulers in Europe. Through his dealings with the prince's court, he gained access to significant capital and developed expertise in government financing and military funding.

During the Napoleonic Wars (1803–1815), Rothschild played a crucial role in financing Britain's war effort against France. He utilized a sophisticated network of couriers and secret channels to transfer money across Europe, ensuring that funds reached their intended recipients efficiently. This innovative approach allowed him to circumvent political and military obstacles, solidifying his reputation as a trusted financial partner.

To expand his influence, Mayer strategically placed his five sons in key financial centers:

- Amschel Mayer Rothschild in Frankfurt
- Salomon Mayer Rothschild in Vienna
- Nathan Mayer Rothschild in London
- Carl Mayer Rothschild in Naples
- James Mayer Rothschild in Paris

This network allowed the Rothschild family to dominate European banking, facilitating cross-border transactions and providing financial services to monarchs, governments, and businesses. The family's ability to act as an international bank laid the groundwork for modern financial institutions.

Mayer introduced several groundbreaking financial practices that revolutionized banking:

**1. Syndicated Loans**: He pioneered large-scale government loans, enabling nations to fund wars and infrastructure projects.

**2. Bond Markets**: His family played a significant role in developing the international bond market.

**3. Confidential Financial Networks**: He created a system of private couriers and coded messages to ensure secure communication.

**4. Diversification**: The Rothschilds invested in various industries, including mining, railroads, and infrastructure, ensuring long-term financial stability.

## Private Life

Mayer Amschel Rothschild married Guttle Schnapper in 1770, and together they had ten children. Guttle played a crucial role in managing family affairs and maintaining the Rothschild legacy. Their children were raised with a strong emphasis on discipline, education, and loyalty to family business interests.

Unlike many wealthy individuals of his time, Mayer lived modestly and maintained a strong sense of Jewish identity. He was a devoted family man and instilled values of unity, integrity, and perseverance in his children. He also supported Jewish causes, funding schools, synagogues, and charities to improve conditions within the Jewish community.

## Death

Mayer Amschel Rothschild passed away on September 19, 1812, at the age of 68. His death marked the end of an era, but his carefully structured financial empire continued to thrive under the leadership of his sons.

He was buried in the Jewish cemetery in Frankfurt, and his legacy was carried forward by his descendants, who expanded the family's banking empire across Europe and beyond.

## Character

Mayer Amschel Rothschild was known for his intelligence, pragmatism, and discretion. He valued secrecy and operated behind the scenes, ensuring that his financial transactions remained secure and confidential. His ability to analyze risk, navigate complex political landscapes and adapt to changing economic conditions made him a formidable figure in the financial world.

He remained true to his faith and his family and made his decisions on that basis. His emphasis on family unity and long-term planning ensured that his descendants upheld the Rothschild legacy for generations.

## Influence on Humanity

Mayer Amschel Rothschild's influence extended far beyond his own lifetime. His contributions to banking and finance shaped the modern financial system in numerous ways:

**1. Creation of an International Banking System** – The Rothschild network set the standard for multinational banking operations.

**2. Development of Government Bonds** – He pioneered the use of government-backed securities, influencing how nations finance their economies.

**3. Modern Financial Communications** – His system of confidential couriers and coded messages laid the groundwork for secure banking communications.

**4. Philanthropy and Jewish Advancement** – He supported numerous educational and religious initiatives, promoting social mobility and economic empowerment within Jewish communities.

**5. Economic Stability** – His financial strategies helped stabilize economies during times of war and political upheaval.

The Rothschild dynasty continued to flourish long after Mayer's death, expanding into industries such as railroads and mining. The Rothschilds' unprecedented financial power in the 18th and 19th centuries attracted both admiration and criticism, as the extreme concentration of wealth led to increased social inequality.

Critics also accuse Mayer Amschel Rothschild and his family of exerting political influence through their financial power and influencing governments through loans and financial support. They were often accused of using conflicts to their advantage by financing wars, making them a symbol of "secret control" of politics and the economy in the eyes of many.

---

In conclusion, Mayer Amschel Rothschild was a visionary who transformed the banking world. His strategic approach to finance, emphasis on family unity, and commitment to innovation ensured his legacy would endure for centuries. His contributions to banking and global finance continue to shape the modern world, making him one of the most significant figures in financial history.

# Edward Jenner
## The Pioneer of Vaccination

Edward Jenner was an English physician and scientist best known for developing the world's first vaccine, which laid the foundation for modern immunology. His discovery of the smallpox vaccine not only saved millions of lives but also led to the eventual eradication of smallpox. Jenner's work remains one of the most significant achievements in medical history, demonstrating the power of scientific observation, experimentation, and perseverance. This biography explores his life, groundbreaking discoveries, and his lasting impact on humanity.

## Origin

Edward Jenner was born on May 17, 1749, in Berkeley, Gloucestershire, England. He was the eighth of nine children in a family deeply rooted in the church and education. His father, Reverend Stephen Jenner, was the vicar of Berkeley, and his mother, Sarah Jenner, was devoted to raising their children.

From an early age, Jenner displayed intellectual curiosity, particularly about the natural world. Growing up in a rural setting, he developed a fascination with biology, medicine, and natural sciences. His childhood environment provided him with early exposure to country medicine, which would later influence his revolutionary ideas in vaccination and immunology.

## Childhood and Youth

Jenner's early education took place at a local school in Wotton-under-Edge before he moved to Cirencester Grammar School, where he excelled in science and Latin. As a young boy, he became fascinated with medicine, often accompanying local doctors on their rounds.

At the age of 13, he was apprenticed to a surgeon in Chipping Sodbury, a small town near Bristol. Under the guidance of this country physician, Jenner gained firsthand experience in anatomy, surgical techniques, and patient care. His apprenticeship lasted seven years, during which he learned about common diseases, treatments, and the practice of inoculation – a rudimentary method of protecting against smallpox by exposing individuals to a mild form of the disease. Jenner's keen observational skills and deep interest in medical advancements prompted him to pursue formal studies in London, where he would train under some of the greatest medical minds of his time.

## Adulthood

In 1770, Jenner traveled to London to train under John Hunter, a renowned surgeon and scientist at St. George's Hospital. Hunter, known for his emphasis on empirical research and experimentation, encouraged Jenner to approach medicine with a scientific and inquisitive mindset He famously advised Jenner, "Don't think – try."

Jenner's years in London exposed him to cutting-edge medical knowledge, but he eventually returned to Berkeley in 1773 to establish his own medical practice. There, he became a respected country doctor, treating patients from all walks of life while continuing his scientific inquiries.

During his time in rural England, Jenner observed that milkmaids who had contracted cowpox, a mild disease affecting cows, seemed to be immune to smallpox – a deadly disease that had devastated populations for centuries. Intrigued by this phenomenon, he hypothesized that exposure to cowpox could provide protection against smallpox.

To test his theory, in 1796, Jenner performed a historic experiment. He took pus from a cowpox lesion on a milkmaid named Sarah Nelmes and inoculated an eight-year-old boy named James Phipps, the son of his gardener. After a few weeks, Jenner exposed Phipps to smallpox, but the boy did not develop the disease – proving Jenner's hypothesis correct.

Jenner called his procedure "vaccination", derived from the Latin word vacca (meaning "cow"). He published his findings in 1798 under the title An Inquiry into the Causes and Effects of the Variolae Vaccinae. His work revolutionized preventive medicine, offering a safer and more effective alternative to the existing method of variolation (inoculation with smallpox virus), which often led to severe illness or death.

Initially, Jenner's work faced skepticism from the medical community, but over time, vaccination gained widespread acceptance. Governments and physicians around the world began implementing smallpox vaccination programs, dramatically reducing the incidence of the disease.

By 1801, Jenner's work was officially recognized, and he received funding from the British government to promote vaccination. His discovery was later adopted globally, ultimately leading to the World Health Organization's (WHO) declaration of smallpox eradication in 1980 – one of the greatest medical achievements in history.

## Private Life

Edward Jenner led a modest and fulfilling personal life. In 1788, he married Catherine Kingscote, with whom he had three children. Their marriage was loving and supportive, though they faced hardships, including the loss of one of their children at a young age.

Jenner was a member of the Royal Society. Despite his fame, Jenner remained humble and dedicated to his patients. He continued practicing medicine in Berkeley, preferring the quiet life of a country doctor over the limelight of the medical elite in London.

Beyond medicine, Jenner was a passionate naturalist. He studied birds, fossils, and the natural environment, even contributing to early research on cuckoo bird behavior. His love for nature reflected his scientific curiosity and deep appreciation for the world around him.

## Death

Jenner's later years were marked by health issues and personal losses, including the death of his wife. Despite this, he continued his work in vaccination and medical education until his final years. On January 26, 1823, Edward Jenner passed away at the age of 73 from a stroke. He was buried in Berkeley, Gloucestershire, where his contributions to medicine are still honored today.

## Character

Jenner was a modest yet determined scientist, distinguished by his keen observational skills and methodical approach to research. Despite facing significant skepticism and opposition, he remained steadfast in his convictions and worked tirelessly to promote vaccination. His willingness to challenge established medical beliefs and his dedication to scientific rigor made him a true innovator.

He was not driven by a desire for fame but saw his work as a service to humanity. His humility and deep compassion for his patients earned him a reputation as a beloved physician and a highly respected member of society.

## Influence on Humanity

Edward Jenner's discovery of vaccination transformed public health and medicine, saving countless lives and paving the way for modern immunology. His work directly led to:

**1. The Eradication of Smallpox** (1980) – A disease that once killed millions was completely eliminated.

**2. The Development of Vaccines for Other Diseases** – Inspired later vaccines for polio, measles and influenza.

**3. Global Public Health Programs** – Vaccination is now a fundamental strategy in disease prevention worldwide.

**4. Scientific Advancements in Immunology** – His research laid the groundwork for modern immunology and virology.

Jenner's legacy continues in vaccination efforts worldwide, ensuring that future generations remain protected from deadly infectious diseases.

---

Edward Jenner was not just a physician but a visionary scientist whose discovery changed the course of history. His invention of vaccination remains one of medicine's greatest achievements, saving millions of lives and shaping modern healthcare. His legacy of scientific innovation, compassion, and dedication to humanity will be remembered for generations to come.

# Wolfgang Amadeus Mozart
Composer and child prodigy of music

Wolfgang Amadeus Mozart was one of the greatest composers in Western music history. A child prodigy who astonished audiences across Europe, he composed over 600 works spanning symphonies, operas, chamber music, and choral compositions. His genius reshaped classical music, setting the standard for melody, harmony, and orchestration. Despite his short life, Mozart's influence on music remains unparalleled, inspiring composers for centuries.

## Origin

Wolfgang Amadeus Mozart was born on January 27, 1756, in Salzburg, then part of the Holy Roman Empire (modern-day Austria). He was the youngest of seven children, though only he and his sister Maria Anna ("Nannerl") survived infancy. His father, Leopold Mozart, was a respected composer, violinist, and music teacher, while his mother, Anna Maria Mozart, came from a middle-class background.

Leopold recognized Wolfgang's extraordinary talent at an early age and became his primary instructor, nurturing his musical abilities and guiding his early career. The Mozart family was deeply immersed in music, creating an environment that fostered young Wolfgang's rapid development.

## Childhood and Youth

From the age of three, Mozart displayed an uncanny ability to recognize and reproduce musical notes. By five, he was composing short pieces and performing for European nobility. His father began taking him and Nannerl on tours across Europe, showcasing their remarkable talents.

Between 1762 and 1773, Mozart performed in cities including Munich, Vienna, Paris, London, and Rome. He played before royals such as Empress Maria Theresa and King George III. Audiences were stunned by his ability to play the harpsichord and violin effortlessly while improvising complex compositions on the spot.

During his time in Italy, Mozart was honored by Pope Clement XIV, who awarded him the Order of the Golden Spur. He also transcribed "Miserere" by Gregorio Allegri after hearing it only once, demonstrating his remarkable musical memory.

Despite his growing reputation, Mozart struggled to find stable employment, often relying on commissions and freelance work. By his teenage years, he was composing symphonies, operas, and sacred music, showcasing a maturity beyond his years.

## Adulthood

As he transitioned into adulthood, Mozart sought greater independence, frequently clashing with his employer, Archbishop Colloredo of Salzburg. Dissatisfied with his restrictive position, he left Salzburg in 1781 and moved to Vienna, where he hoped to establish himself as a freelance composer and performer.

Vienna proved to be both a place of triumph and hardship. Mozart gained recognition for his operas, symphonies, and piano concertos, securing a small but dedicated patronage. Some of his most celebrated works from this period include:

- **The Marriage of Figaro** (1786)
- **Don Giovanni** (1787)
- **Eine kleine Nachtmusik** (1787)
- **Symphony No. 40 in G minor** (1788)
- **Così fan tutte** (1790)

Despite his success, Mozart's financial situation was often precarious. Unlike many court musicians, he lacked a stable salary and relied on inconsistent commissions. His extravagant lifestyle and poor financial management contributed to ongoing financial struggles.

## Private Life

In 1782, Mozart married Constanze Weber, a singer from a musical family. Though their marriage faced challenges, including financial difficulties and the loss of several children, they shared a deep bond. Constanze supported Mozart's career, handling his finances and ensuring his works were published after his death.

The couple had six children, though only two survived to adulthood. Mozart adored his family, often expressing his affection in playful letters filled with humor and warmth.

Mozart's social circle included prominent composers and intellectuals such as Joseph Haydn, who greatly admired his work. The two shared mutual respect, with Haydn famously telling Leopold Mozart, "Your son is the greatest composer I know."

## Death

In late 1791, Mozart fell seriously ill while working on his final composition, "Requiem in D minor". He was overwhelmed with fatigue, fever, and swelling, yet continued composing until he could no longer write.

On December 5, 1791, at the age of 35, Mozart passed away in Vienna. The exact cause of his death remains a subject of debate, with theories ranging from rheumatic fever to kidney failure or poisoning. His funeral was modest, and he was buried in an unmarked grave, as was customary for middle-class citizens at the time.

His unfinished "Requiem" was later completed by his student Franz Xaver Süssmayr, and it remains one of his most profound and moving compositions.

## Character

Mozart was known for his charismatic personality, sharp wit, and mischievous sense of humor. His letters reveal a playful and affectionate man who found joy in life, despite its hardships.

He was also deeply passionate about music, often composing with intense focus and determination. His ability to blend technical mastery with emotional depth made his music profoundly expressive. Despite his genius, Mozart was not a shrewd businessman. His financial troubles were exacerbated by his generosity, as he often lent money to friends and lived beyond his means. Nevertheless, he remained dedicated to his art, prioritizing creativity over financial gain.

# Influence on Humanity

Mozart's impact on music and culture is immeasurable. His contributions include:

**1. Evolution of Classical Music** – Mozart expanded the boundaries of symphony, opera, and chamber music, setting new standards for structure, orchestration, and thematic development. His work bridged the Baroque and Romantic eras, influencing composers like Beethoven and Schubert.

**2. Innovations in Opera** – His operas transformed the genre by blending drama, humor, and musical complexity. "The Marriage of Figaro" and "Don Giovanni" revolutionized opera's dramatic potential, emphasizing character development and social commentary.

**3. Mastery of Form and Harmony** – Mozart refined sonata-allegro form, enriched harmonic progressions, and perfected counterpoint, influencing generations of composers.

**4. Inspiration for Future Composers** – Beethoven, who studied Mozart's works, was profoundly inspired by his style. Romantic composers such as Chopin, Liszt, and Brahms also drew inspiration from his compositions.

**5. Cultural Legacy** – Mozart's music remains widely performed and beloved worldwide. His melodies are instantly recognizable, and his influence extends beyond classical music into film, literature, and popular culture.

**6. Contributions to Music Education** – Mozart's compositions are fundamental in music education, serving as essential studies for students of piano, violin, and orchestration.

In conclusion, Wolfgang Amadeus Mozart was a musical genius whose work continues to captivate and inspire. His ability to blend technical brilliance with profound emotion cemented his status as one of history's greatest composers. Though his life was tragically short, his music remains immortal, a testament to the boundless power of artistic expression.

# John Dalton
Chemist and founder of atomic theory

John Dalton was an English scientist, chemist, and physicist who laid the groundwork for modern atomic theory. His contributions to chemistry, particularly his proposal that matter is composed of indivisible atoms, revolutionized scientific understanding. In addition to his work in atomic theory, Dalton made significant advances in meteorology and the study of color blindness, a condition sometimes referred to as "Daltonism" in his honor. His disciplined approach to science and unwavering commitment to empirical evidence made him one of the most influential figures in the development of modern chemistry and physics.

## Origin

John Dalton was born on September 6, 1766, in Eaglesfield, a small village in Cumberland, England (now part of Cumbria). He was born into a Quaker family, which emphasized simplicity, hard work, and education. His parents, Joseph Dalton and Deborah Greenup, were modest weavers, and their Quaker beliefs played a crucial role in shaping his values and dedication to learning.

Dalton's early environment was rural and relatively isolated from mainstream academic institutions. However, the Quakers encouraged intellectual pursuits, fostering an environment where scientific inquiry was respected. His upbringing instilled in him a strong sense of discipline and self-reliance, traits that would define his career in science.

## Childhood and Youth

Dalton showed an early aptitude for mathematics and science. He attended a Quaker school in Eaglesfield, where his intelligence and curiosity stood out. By the age of 12, he was already assisting in teaching younger students. At 15, he moved to Kendal to work as a teacher at a Quaker boarding school. During his time in Kendal, Dalton was influenced by Elihu Robinson and John Gough, two prominent Quakers with strong scientific backgrounds. Gough, who was blind, introduced Dalton to experimental science and meteorology. Under their guidance, Dalton honed his skills in observation, experimentation, and logical reasoning.

While still in his late teens, Dalton began conducting experiments in meteorology, a subject that would remain a lifelong passion. He meticulously recorded weather patterns, making detailed observations of temperature, barometric pressure, and humidity. His early work in meteorology laid the foundation for his later scientific contributions.

## Adulthood

In 1793, at the age of 27, Dalton moved to Manchester, where he was appointed as a tutor at New College, a Dissenting academy that provided higher education to nonconformists. During this period, he published his first book, "Meteorological Observations and Essays", which reflected his deep interest in atmospheric science. Though the book did not gain widespread attention at the time, it demonstrated his commitment to rigorous scientific study.

Dalton's most groundbreaking work came in the early 1800s when he formulated the first modern atomic theory. Prior to his work, the concept of atoms was largely philosophical. Through systematic experimentation, Dalton proposed that:

- All matter is composed of small, indivisible particles called atoms.
- Atoms of the same element are identical in mass and properties, while atoms of different elements have different masses and properties.
- Atoms combine in fixed ratios to form compounds.
- Chemical reactions involve the rearrangement of atoms but do not create or destroy them.

These principles, published in his 1808 book "A New System of Chemical Philosophy", provided a systematic explanation of chemical composition and reactions. His atomic theory became the foundation of modern chemistry and influenced the development of the periodic table and molecular theory.

Dalton also made pioneering contributions to the study of color blindness, a condition he personally had. In 1794, he published the first scientific paper describing the condition, theorizing that color blindness was caused by a defect in the fluid of the eye. While his specific hypothesis was later disproven, his research helped lay the groundwork for the modern understanding of color vision deficiencies. As a result, color blindness is sometimes referred to as "Daltonism" in his honor.

## Private Life

Despite his scientific achievements, Dalton lived a modest and largely solitary life. He never married and had no known romantic relationships. He remained devoted to his research and teaching, valuing knowledge and scientific inquiry above social status or wealth. His personal habits were simple, and he maintained a disciplined routine. He was known to dress plainly and adhered to the Quaker principles of humility and integrity. Although he achieved significant recognition during his lifetime, he never sought fame or financial gain from his discoveries.

Dalton's students and colleagues described him as reserved but kind, with a deep commitment to education and scientific progress. He preferred to spend his time conducting experiments and meticulously recording data rather than engaging in social activities.

## Death

John Dalton suffered a series of strokes in his later years, which gradually impaired his mobility and speech. Despite his declining health, he continued his scientific work, even making observations until his final days. He passed away on July 27, 1844, at the age of 77 in Manchester. His death was widely mourned, and he was given a public funeral attended by thousands. In recognition of his contributions, his brain was examined posthumously to study the physiological basis of color blindness. Dalton was buried in Ardwick Cemetery in Manchester, and his legacy was honored with statues and commemorations in scientific institutions around the world.

## Character

Dalton was known for his integrity, humility, and relentless dedication to science. His Quaker upbringing influenced his ethical approach to research, emphasizing honesty and precision in his work. He was methodical, rarely making speculative claims without solid experimental evidence. Despite his intellectual prowess, he remained unassuming and avoided personal glory. He was deeply respected by his peers for his kindness, sincerity, and commitment to truth. His meticulous approach to recording data set a high standard for future scientists, reinforcing the importance of empirical evidence in scientific discovery.

## Influence on Humanity

John Dalton's impact on science and humanity is profound. His contributions include:

**1. Foundation of Modern Chemistry** – His atomic theory revolutionized the understanding of chemical reactions and matter, influencing generations of scientists.

**2. Advancements in Meteorology** – His work in atmospheric science helped establish meteorology as a scientific discipline.

**3. Study of Color Blindness** – His research on vision deficiencies contributed to ophthalmology and color perception studies.

**4. Scientific Methodology** – His emphasis on empirical observation and systematic experimentation set standards for scientific inquiry.

**5. Education and Mentorship** – As a lifelong teacher, he inspired countless students and contributed to the growth of scientific education in England.

Dalton's atomic theory provided the foundation for modern chemistry and physics, influencing groundbreaking discoveries such as Mendeleev's periodic table, Rutherford's nuclear model, and the development of quantum mechanics.

---

In conclusion, John Dalton's relentless pursuit of knowledge and commitment to scientific accuracy transformed multiple fields of study. His discoveries continue to shape the way scientists understand matter, weather, and human physiology. Though he lived a humble life, his contributions left an indelible mark on humanity, solidifying his place among the greatest scientific minds in history.

# Napoleon Bonaparte
French emperor and reformer of Europe

Napoleon Bonaparte was one of the most influential military and political leaders in history. Rising to power during the turbulent years of the French Revolution, he established himself as Emperor of France and reshaped European politics, warfare, and governance. His military genius, legal reforms, and administrative innovations had a lasting impact on the modern world. However, his ambition and relentless pursuit of power also led to conflicts that engulfed much of Europe.

## Origin

Napoleon Bonaparte was born on August 15, 1769, in Ajaccio, Corsica, an island that had been transferred from Genoese to French control just a year before his birth. He was the second of eight children born to Carlo Maria di Buonaparte and Letizia Ramolino. His family belonged to the minor Corsican nobility but was not wealthy. Corsica was a land of political turmoil, and Napoleon's early years were shaped by his father's political involvement in the resistance against French rule. Despite this, Carlo eventually aligned with the French administration, securing scholarships for his sons, which allowed Napoleon to receive a formal education in mainland France.

## Childhood and Youth

Napoleon left Corsica at the age of nine to study in France. He attended the military academy at Brienne-le-Château, where he excelled in mathematics and military strategy but struggled with social integration due to his Corsican accent and outsider status. His determination and intelligence, however, earned him a place at the prestigious École Militaire in Paris.

In 1785, at the age of 16, Napoleon graduated as a second lieutenant in the French artillery. His early career was marked by extensive study of classical military campaigns and a growing awareness of the political instability in France. He initially identified as a Corsican nationalist, but over time, his allegiance shifted toward the French Republic.

## Adulthood

Napoleon's military career gained momentum during the French Revolution. In 1793, he played a crucial role in recapturing the city of Toulon from royalist forces, earning a promotion to brigadier general at just 24 years old. His strategic brilliance and leadership abilities became evident in his campaigns in Italy and Egypt.

By 1799, France was in political disarray. Napoleon capitalized on this instability and staged a coup d'état on November 9, 1799, establishing himself as First Consul of France. By 1804, he had consolidated power and declared himself Emperor of the French, marking the beginning of the Napoleonic era.

Napoleon's reign was defined by nearly continuous military conflict. His campaigns across Europe showcased his tactical ingenuity, particularly at battles such as Austerlitz (1805), Jena-Auerstedt (1806), and Wagram (1809). At its height, the French Empire dominated most of continental Europe.

However, his invasion of Russia in 1812 marked the beginning of his downfall. The harsh winter and logistical failures devastated his army. This setback, combined with growing opposition from European coalitions, led to his defeat in 1814. He was exiled to the island of Elba but made a dramatic return to power in 1815 during the Hundred Days. His final defeat at the Battle of Waterloo later that year resulted in his permanent exile to Saint Helena.

## Private Life

Napoleon's personal life was as complex as his political career. He married Joséphine de Beauharnais in 1796, a union that brought him into elite French society. However, their marriage was childless, and in 1810, he divorced her to marry Marie Louise of Austria, with whom he had a son, Napoleon II.

Despite his military and political engagements, Napoleon maintained a keen interest in literature, science, and governance. He was deeply involved in shaping the legal and educational systems of France, and his reforms extended beyond his own era.

# Death

After his defeat at Waterloo in 1815, Napoleon was exiled to the remote island of Saint Helena in the South Atlantic. He spent his final years under British supervision, dictating his memoirs and reflecting on his legacy.

He died on May 5, 1821, at the age of 51, likely from stomach cancer, though some theories suggest he may have been poisoned. His body was later moved to Les Invalides in Paris in 1840, where he remains entombed in a grand monument.

# Character

Napoleon was a paradoxical figure – brilliant yet ruthless, pragmatic yet idealistic. His confidence, strategic mind, and extraordinary memory enabled him to command loyalty from his troops and allies. He was known for his relentless work ethic, often sleeping only a few hours a night.

Despite his many achievements, Napoleon's ambition often led to overreach. His authoritarian rule, censorship, and suppression of dissent contrasted with his advocacy for meritocracy and legal reform. His ability to inspire devotion and fear in equal measure made him one of history's most complex leaders.

# Influence on Humanity

Napoleon's impact on the world is vast and multifaceted. His contributions include:

**1. The Napoleonic Code** – His legal code standardized laws across France and influenced legal systems worldwide, emphasizing equality before the law and the protection of property rights.

**2. Military Strategy** – His battlefield tactics and organizational reforms revolutionized modern warfare and are still studied in military academies today.

**3. European Political Reshaping** – His conquests redrew the map of Europe, leading to the eventual rise of nation-states.

**4. Modernizing Institutions** – He reformed education, finance, and administration, laying the groundwork for modern governance in France and beyond.

**5. Inspiration for Future Leaders** – Figures such as Adolf Hitler and Charles de Gaulle drew lessons from his leadership, either as a model or a warning.

---

In conclusion, Napoleon Bonaparte was a visionary leader whose military and political legacy continues to shape the world. His ambition, reforms, and strategies left an indelible mark on history, making him one of the most studied figures in military and political history. Whether admired or criticized, his influence on humanity remains undeniable.

# Ludwig van Beethoven
Composer and pioneer of Romantic music

Ludwig van Beethoven was one of the most influential and celebrated composers in Western music history. His works bridged the Classical and Romantic eras, redefining the possibilities of musical expression. Despite immense personal hardships, including progressive hearing loss, Beethoven composed some of the most profound and enduring music ever written. His symphonies, sonatas, and concertos continue to inspire musicians and audiences worldwide.

## Origin

Ludwig van Beethoven was born on December 17, 1770, in Bonn, a city in the Electorate of Cologne, part of the Holy Roman Empire (modern-day Germany). His grandfather, Ludwig van Beethoven, was a respected musician who had risen to prominence in Bonn. His father, Johann van Beethoven, was a court musician and singer, while his mother, Maria Magdalena Keverich, was known for her kind and gentle nature. The Beethoven family had a modest social standing, but music was an essential part of their identity. Johann, recognizing his son's talent, sought to mold Ludwig into a prodigy akin to Wolfgang Amadeus Mozart. However, Johann's methods were harsh, and his heavy drinking often made home life difficult.

## Childhood and Youth

Beethoven's early musical training was rigorous and often harsh. His father would wake him at night to practice the piano, sometimes beating him for mistakes. Despite this, young Ludwig displayed extraordinary talent, giving his first public performance at the age of seven. By the time he was a teenager, Beethoven was studying under renowned musicians such as Christian Gottlob Neefe, who recognized his prodigious abilities and introduced him to the works of Johann Sebastian Bach. At 13, Beethoven was appointed assistant court organist, a remarkable achievement for someone so young. In 1787, Beethoven traveled to Vienna, hoping to study with Mozart. However, he was forced to return home when his mother fell ill and died of tuberculosis. This tragic event thrust him into the role of caretaker for his younger siblings, further complicating his development as a musician.

## Adulthood

In 1792, Beethoven moved permanently to Vienna, the musical capital of Europe. There, he studied with Joseph Haydn and later took instruction from Antonio Salieri. Vienna provided him with the opportunity to perform for aristocrats, gaining a reputation as a virtuoso pianist with an intense, expressive style.

By the late 1790s, Beethoven had established himself as one of the most sought-after composers in Vienna. His early compositions, including the "Piano Sonatas Op. 2" and "Symphony No. 1," demonstrated his mastery of Classical forms while subtly hinting at his innovative musical style.

Around 1801, Beethoven began to notice symptoms of hearing loss, a devastating condition for a musician. By 1802, he wrote the "Heiligenstadt Testament", a letter expressing his despair over his worsening deafness and his determination to continue composing.

Despite his struggles, Beethoven entered his "Heroic Period," producing groundbreaking works such as:

- **Symphony No. 3 "Eroica"** (1803) – A revolutionary composition that expanded the boundaries of symphonic form.
- **Symphony No. 5** (1808) – Featuring the iconic four-note motif, it symbolized triumph over adversity.
- **Piano Concerto No. 5 "Emperor"** (1811) – One of the greatest concertos ever written.

As his hearing deteriorated further, Beethoven relied on conversation books to communicate. Yet, his compositions became even more profound, culminating in his late masterpieces.

## Private Life

Beethoven never married, though he had deep, sometimes turbulent relationships with several women. Among them was the mysterious

"Immortal Beloved," whose identity remains a subject of speculation. Some believe she was Antonie Brentano, while others argue she was Josephine Brunsvik.

Despite his genius, Beethoven was known for his erratic behavior and struggles with personal relationships. He had a fiery temper and could be both charming and abrasive. His household was often in disarray, and he frequently quarreled with friends and patrons.

Beethoven was deeply devoted to his nephew, Karl, whom he attempted to raise after the death of his brother. However, his strict and controlling nature led to a strained relationship, culminating in Karl's attempted suicide.

## Death

In his final years, Beethoven suffered from severe health problems, including liver disease and chronic stomach ailments. His deafness was total by the 1820s, yet he continued composing some of his greatest works, including "Symphony No. 9 (Choral)" in 1824, which introduced the "Ode to Joy" theme.

Beethoven died on March 26, 1827, at the age of 56. His funeral in Vienna was attended by thousands, a testament to his immense influence and popularity.

His final words are believed to have been, "Pity, pity – too late!" – possibly referring to the late arrival of wine from a friend.

## Character

Beethoven was a man of contrasts – both deeply sensitive and fiercely independent. He was known for his unwavering dedication to his art, refusing to compromise his musical vision even when faced with financial struggles and physical suffering.

His determination in the face of adversity, especially his ability to compose masterpieces despite deafness, made him a symbol of resilience and artistic integrity. He was deeply philosophical, often contemplating themes of freedom, humanity, and individualism in his music.

Though he could be difficult and temperamental, Beethoven was also deeply compassionate. His compositions express a vast range of human emotion, from profound sorrow to ecstatic joy, reflecting his deep empathy for the human experience.

## Influence on Humanity

Beethoven's contributions to music and culture are immeasurable. His legacy includes:

**1. Evolution of Classical Music** – Beethoven pushed the boundaries of musical form, expanding the symphony, sonata, and concerto beyond their Classical constraints. His works paved the way for the Romantic era, influencing composers such as Brahms, Wagner, and Mahler.

**2. Symphony No. 9 and Universal Brotherhood** – His "Ninth Symphony", with its "Ode to Joy" finale, became a symbol of universal brotherhood and freedom. It was later adopted as the European Union's anthem, underscoring its enduring message of unity.

**3. Inspiration for Future Composers** – From Chopin to Tchaikovsky, countless composers have drawn inspiration from Beethoven's innovations in harmony, rhythm, and orchestration.

**4. Triumph Over Adversity** – His ability to compose masterpieces despite deafness remains one of the most inspiring stories in artistic history.

**5. Cultural and Political Impact** – Beethoven's music was used to symbolize resistance against oppression, from 19th-century revolutionary movements to World War II resistance efforts.

In conclusion, Ludwig van Beethoven was not just a composer; he was a force of nature whose music redefined what was possible in the art form. His works continue to move and inspire generations, proving that true genius transcends hardship and time. His legacy is a testament to the power of human creativity, perseverance, and the eternal quest for artistic expression.

# Simón Bolívar
## The Liberator of South America

Simón Bolívar was one of the most influential figures in Latin American history. Known as "El Libertador" (The Liberator), he played a crucial role in the independence movements of several South American nations, including Venezuela, Colombia, Ecuador, Peru, and Bolivia. A visionary leader, Bolívar sought to unite the liberated territories into a single nation, Gran Colombia, but his dream was ultimately unfulfilled. Despite the challenges and betrayals he faced, Bolívar remains a symbol of freedom and resistance. His legacy continues to shape political and social thought in Latin America.

## Origin

Simón José Antonio de la Santísima Trinidad Bolívar y Palacios was born on July 24, 1783, in Caracas, in what was then the Captaincy General of Venezuela, a Spanish colony. He was born into an aristocratic Creole family of Spanish descent, which granted him access to wealth, education, and social prestige.

His father, Juan Vicente Bolívar y Ponte, was a wealthy landowner and a colonel in the Spanish militia, while his mother, María de la Concepción Palacios y Blanco, came from a noble family. The Bolívar family was heavily involved in colonial politics and owned extensive landholdings, which provided young Simón with financial security but also exposed him to the political struggles of the time.

## Childhood and Youth

Bolívar's childhood was marked by tragedy. His father died when he was just three years old, and his mother passed away when he was nine. Orphaned at an early age, he was placed under the care of his uncles and a family tutor, Simón Rodríguez, who became a crucial influence in his intellectual and ideological development.

Rodríguez introduced Bolívar to Enlightenment philosophy, including the works of Voltaire, Rousseau, and Montesquieu. These ideas would later shape Bolívar's vision for independence and republicanism.

At 16, Bolívar was sent to Spain for further education. While in Madrid, he was exposed to European politics and society. He married María Teresa Rodríguez del Toro y Alaysa in 1802, but she tragically died of yellow fever less than a year later. Heartbroken, Bolívar vowed never to remarry, instead dedicating his life to political and military pursuits.

In 1804, Bolívar traveled to France, where he witnessed the rule of Napoleon Bonaparte. He was deeply inspired by Napoleon's rise but later became critical of his authoritarian tendencies. His experiences in Europe solidified his desire to free South America from Spanish rule.

## Adulthood

Bolívar returned to Venezuela in 1807, just as revolutionary sentiments were growing across Latin America. In 1810, he joined the movement that declared Venezuela's independence from Spain. However, early efforts were met with failure, and Spanish forces recaptured Venezuela in 1812.

After regrouping in New Granada (modern Colombia), Bolívar launched a series of campaigns to liberate South America. His most famous military achievement was the "Admirable Campaign" (1813), which led to the temporary liberation of Venezuela. However, political instability and Spanish counterattacks forced him into exile in the Caribbean.

Bolívar's most remarkable military feat came in 1819 when he led a daring march across the Andes Mountains to surprise Spanish forces in present-day Colombia. His victory at the Battle of Boyacá secured Colombia's independence. Over the next few years, he continued to lead campaigns across the continent, eventually liberating Ecuador, Peru, and Bolivia, the latter of which was named in his honor.

After securing independence, Bolívar sought to unify the liberated territories into a single republic, known as Gran Colombia, encompassing present-day Venezuela, Colombia, Ecuador, and Panama. He served as president but struggled to maintain unity among the various factions.

Internal conflicts, regional rivalries, and opposition to his authority led to the fragmentation of his vision.

In 1826, Bolívar convened the Congress of Panama, aiming to establish a federation of Latin American nations. However, his dream of a united South America was ultimately undone by political divisions and resistance from local leaders.

## Private Life

Despite his deep commitment to political and military affairs, Bolívar had a personal life marked by passion and complexity. After the death of his wife, he never remarried, but he had numerous romantic relationships. His most well-known companion was Manuela Sáenz, an Ecuadorian revolutionary who became his confidante and political ally. She played a crucial role in his life, even saving him from an assassination attempt in 1828. Bolívar was known for his charisma, intelligence, and persuasive oratory. He maintained close relationships with many political and intellectual figures of his time, including Francisco de Paula Santander, Antonio José de Sucre, and José de San Martín, though these alliances often turned into rivalries.

## Death

By the early 1830s, Bolívar's health was in decline, and his political dreams were crumbling. Gran Colombia had fractured, and he faced growing opposition from former allies. Disillusioned and exhausted, he resigned from the presidency in 1830 and planned to retire in exile. On December 17, 1830, Simón Bolívar died of tuberculosis in Santa Marta, Colombia, at the age of 47. He had lost much of his political influence, and his final years were spent in isolation. However, his legacy would grow after his death, as subsequent generations recognized his contributions to Latin American independence.

## Character

Bolívar was a man of immense vision, ambition, and determination. He was deeply influenced by Enlightenment ideals and believed in the principles of liberty, equality, and justice. His charisma and leadership inspired thousands to join the independence movement, and his military genius led to the liberation of an entire continent.

However, Bolívar's authoritarian tendencies and belief in strong central rule often put him at odds with democratic principles. He struggled with balancing power and liberty, sometimes resorting to harsh measures to maintain order. Despite this, his commitment to the cause of independence never wavered.

## Influence on Humanity

Simón Bolívar's impact on the world extends far beyond his lifetime. His contributions include:

**1. Independence of South America** – He played a key role in liberating Venezuela, Colombia, Ecuador, Peru, and Bolivia from Spanish rule.

**2. Political Thought** – His writings and speeches continue to influence Latin American political philosophy.

**3. Symbol of Resistance** – He remains a symbol of freedom and anti-imperialism in Latin America.

**4. National Identity** – Many Latin American countries celebrate Bolívar as a national hero, and his name is enshrined in countless institutions, streets, and monuments.

**5. Legacy in Leadership** – His vision for a united Latin America inspired future leaders, though his dream of regional unity remains elusive.

In conclusion, Simón Bolívar was a visionary leader whose courage and determination reshaped the history of South America. While his dream of a unified continent was never fully realized, his influence endures in the political, social, and cultural fabric of Latin America. His legacy as "El Libertador" remains a beacon of hope for those who seek freedom and justice.

# Louis Daguerre
Pioneer of photography

Louis Daguerre was a French artist, chemist, and physicist who revolutionized visual representation with the invention of the daguerreotype, the first practical method of photography. His discovery opened the door to modern photography, capturing history, art, and personal moments in ways never before possible. His work laid the foundation for the photographic industry, influencing science, journalism, and the arts.

## Origin

Louis-Jacques-Mandé Daguerre was born on November 18, 1787, in Cormeilles-en-Parisis, a small town north of Paris, France. He was born into a modest but respectable family. His father, a clerk in the local government, encouraged creativity and craftsmanship, which greatly influenced young Louis.

France in the late 18th century was experiencing political and social upheaval, with the French Revolution reshaping its institutions and way of life. Growing up in such an era exposed Daguerre to radical ideas in art and science, setting the stage for his later innovations.

## Childhood and Youth

As a child, Daguerre displayed an early aptitude for art and design. He had a particular fascination with light and its effects, which would later become central to his work in photography. His interest in artistic techniques led him to study painting, stage design, and theatrical effects, fields that required a deep understanding of lighting and perspective.

Daguerre's talent in painting, especially in scenic illusions, gained him recognition in artistic circles. His early career was devoted to working as an apprentice to prominent painters in Paris, where he honed his skills in theatrical design. He eventually worked for the famed panorama artist Pierre Prévost, creating large-scale, immersive paintings that simulated real-life scenes. During his youth, he was drawn to scientific experimentation, particularly in optics and light manipulation. His artistic and scientific interests converged in his later work, leading him toward groundbreaking discoveries in photography.

## Adulthood

In the 1820s, Daguerre became renowned for his work in dioramas, an innovative form of theatrical entertainment that used large, semi-transparent paintings illuminated with changing light effects to create a sense of movement and realism. He opened the Diorama Theatre in Paris in 1822, which became a popular attraction. These immersive experiences captivated audiences and demonstrated Daguerre's expertise in manipulating light and illusion. His work in dioramas led him to explore new ways of capturing light more permanently. This quest brought him into contact with Joseph Nicéphore Niépce, a fellow French inventor who had been experimenting with early photographic processes. Niépce had successfully created the first known photograph in the 1820s but struggled with long exposure times and image permanence. After Niépce's death in 1833, Daguerre continued their collaborative research, improving upon Niépce's heliographic techniques. Through meticulous experimentation, Daguerre discovered a process that dramatically reduced exposure times and produced detailed, fixed images.

By 1837, he successfully developed the daguerreotype process, which used a silver-plated copper sheet coated with light-sensitive chemicals. The image was exposed in a camera obscura, then developed using mercury vapor and fixed with a salt solution, making it permanent. This process created sharp, highly detailed images, unlike anything seen before. Recognizing the revolutionary nature of his invention, Daguerre sought government support. In 1839, the French Academy of Sciences publicly announced his invention, and the French government acquired the rights, making it freely available to the public. This move ensured the rapid spread of photography across the world.

## Private Life

Daguerre maintained a relatively private life, focusing intensely on his artistic and scientific pursuits. He married Louise Georgina Arrowsmith, with whom he had children, but little is documented about his family life.

Despite his fame, Daguerre remained humble, dedicating most of his time to perfecting his work rather than seeking personal recognition. His work in photography overshadowed his earlier contributions to theater and diorama art, but he remained proud of his artistic roots. After the public release of the daguerreotype process, Daguerre retreated from the spotlight and spent his later years in Bry-sur-Marne, a quiet town near Paris, where he continued his artistic and scientific pursuits in relative obscurity.

## Death

Louis Daguerre passed away on July 10, 1851, at the age of 63. Though his contributions to photography were immense, he did not live to see the full extent of photography's global impact. His death marked the end of an era, but his invention endured, paving the way for new advancements in imaging technology. In recognition of his achievements, his name was engraved on the Eiffel Tower alongside other great French scientists and inventors.

## Character

Daguerre was known for his curiosity, persistence, and artistic sensibility. He was a visionary who saw the potential of combining science and art to create something revolutionary. His willingness to experiment and his meticulous attention to detail set him apart from his contemporaries. He was also highly strategic, understanding the importance of securing government support for his invention. Unlike many inventors who struggled to commercialize their discoveries, Daguerre ensured that photography became widely accessible, allowing it to flourish as an industry.

Despite his achievements, Daguerre remained a modest figure, preferring to focus on his work rather than seek the limelight. His passion for light and visual storytelling remained central to his life's work.

## Influence on Humanity

Louis Daguerre's impact on the world was profound. His invention of the daguerreotype marked the beginning of photography as a practical and artistic medium. His contributions include:

**1. Revolutionizing Visual Documentation** – The daguerreotype allowed for the accurate capture of people, landscapes, and events, preserving moments in history for future generations.

**2. Advancing Scientific Discovery** – Photography became an essential tool in astronomy, medicine, and anthropology, enabling precise documentation and analysis.

**3. Democratizing Art and Portraiture** – Before photography, portrait painting was a privilege of the wealthy. The daguerreotype made personal portraiture accessible to the middle class.

**4. Influence on Modern Photography** – While the daguerreotype was eventually replaced by newer photographic techniques, it laid the groundwork for the development of film, digital photography, and imaging technologies.

**5. Cultural and Historical Impact** – Photography became an integral part of journalism, education, and artistic expression, shaping how humanity records and perceives the world.

---

In conclusion, Louis Daguerre was a pioneer whose work forever changed the way humans capture and preserve reality. His relentless pursuit of light and image-making led to one of the most significant inventions in history. Today, every photograph taken – whether on film, digital cameras, or smartphones – owes something to his groundbreaking discovery. His legacy endures in every snapshot, reminding the world of the transformative power of innovation and vision.

# Michael Faraday
Discoverer of electromagnetic induction

Michael Faraday was a pioneering scientist whose discoveries in electromagnetism and electrochemistry revolutionized the fields of physics and engineering. He made crucial contributions to our understanding of electricity, laying the groundwork for modern technologies such as electric motors, transformers, and generators. Despite lacking a formal education, Faraday's relentless curiosity, dedication, and ingenuity led him to become one of the most influential scientists of all time. His discoveries not only shaped the scientific world but also had a profound impact on industry, communication, and modern society.

## Origin

Michael Faraday was born on September 22, 1791, in Newington Butts, a small village near London, England. He was the third of four children in a humble family. His father, James Faraday, was a blacksmith, while his mother, Margaret Hastwell Faraday, was a devoted homemaker who ensured her children were raised with strong moral values.

Faraday's family belonged to the Sandemanian Christian sect, a branch of Protestantism that emphasized humility, simplicity, and strong faith. This religious upbringing deeply influenced his character, shaping his ethical outlook and his lifelong commitment to integrity and modesty.

## Childhood and Youth

Faraday's early life was marked by poverty and limited access to formal education. Unlike many of his scientific contemporaries, he did not attend a prestigious university. Instead, he received a basic education at a local school and had to leave formal schooling at an early age to help support his family.

At the age of 14, Faraday was apprenticed to a local bookbinder and bookseller, George Riebau. This apprenticeship proved to be a turning point in his life. While working in the shop, he had access to numerous scientific books, including Jane Marcet's "Conversations on Chemistry" and Isaac Watts' "Improvement of the Mind." Faraday avidly read these books, developing a passion for science and experimentation.

His enthusiasm for chemistry and physics grew, and he began conducting small experiments at home. Inspired by his readings, he attended public lectures by renowned scientists, including Humphry Davy, at the Royal Institution. Faraday took meticulous notes and even bound them into a personal volume, which he later used to secure a position as Davy's assistant.

## Adulthood

In 1812, Faraday sent his carefully compiled lecture notes to Sir Humphry Davy, one of Britain's leading chemists. Impressed by Faraday's dedication, Davy offered him a job as a laboratory assistant at the Royal Institution in 1813. This opportunity allowed Faraday to immerse himself in scientific research, and he quickly gained hands-on experience in experimental chemistry.

Faraday accompanied Davy on a European scientific tour from 1813 to 1815, visiting France and Italy and meeting distinguished scientists such as André-Marie Ampère and Alessandro Volta. This journey exposed him to cutting-edge research and significantly broadened his scientific knowledge.

In 1821, inspired by Hans Christian Ørsted's discovery that an electric current could produce a magnetic field, Faraday began his pioneering experiments in electromagnetism. He discovered that a wire carrying an electric current could move around a magnet, demonstrating the principle of electromagnetic rotation. This experiment laid the foundation for electric motors and generators.

In 1831, Faraday made his most significant discovery – electromagnetic induction. He found that a changing magnetic field could induce an electric current in a conductor, a principle that became the basis for the modern generation of electricity. His work led to the development of transformers and dynamos, making large-scale electricity production possible.

Faraday also made groundbreaking contributions to electrochemistry. He formulated the laws of electrolysis, which describe how electric current causes chemical reactions in liquids. His discoveries paved the way for advances in battery technology and industrial electroplating. In addition to these achievements, Faraday discovered benzene, a fundamental hydrocarbon used in the chemical industry. His contributions to chemistry, along with his work in electromagnetism, solidified his reputation as one of the greatest experimental scientists of all time.

## Private Life

Despite his scientific fame, Faraday remained a humble and private individual. In 1821, he married Sarah Barnard, the daughter of a Sandemanian minister. Their marriage was a happy and supportive one, though they had no children. Faraday's deep religious beliefs influenced his personal and professional life. He refused to engage in lucrative military research, believing that science should serve humanity rather than destruction. He also turned down a knighthood and other honorary titles, preferring to be addressed simply as "Mr. Faraday."

Throughout his life, Faraday valued knowledge for its own sake and remained dedicated to public education. He delivered the famous Christmas Lectures at the Royal Institution, engaging audiences with clear and exciting demonstrations of scientific principles. His ability to explain complex scientific ideas in simple terms made him an exceptional educator.

## Death

By the 1850s, Faraday's health began to decline, and he gradually withdrew from active research. He suffered from memory loss and fatigue, likely due to prolonged exposure to chemicals during his early experiments. On August 25, 1867, Michael Faraday passed away peacefully at the age of 75 at his home in Hampton Court. In accordance with his humble nature, he declined burial in Westminster Abbey, choosing instead to be laid to rest in a simple grave in Highgate Cemetery.

## Character

Faraday was known for his humility, integrity, and dedication to scientific discovery. Unlike many scientists of his time, he was not motivated by wealth or prestige. He refused offers of knighthood and government positions, believing that his duty was to advance knowledge rather than seek personal gain.

His work ethic was extraordinary, and he was deeply committed to experimental rigor. He meticulously documented his findings, ensuring that future generations could build upon his research. His kindness and generosity also earned him the admiration of his peers and students.

## Influence on Humanity

Michael Faraday's discoveries transformed the world. His contributions include:

**1. Electromagnetic Induction** – The foundation of electric power generation, leading to the development of transformers, generators, and electrical grids.

**2. Electromagnetic Rotation** – The principle behind electric motors, revolutionizing transportation and industry.

**3. Laws of Electrolysis** – Fundamental to electrochemistry, paving the way for advancements in batteries and industrial chemistry.

**4. Public Education** – His lectures and outreach efforts helped popularize science and inspire future generations of scientists, including James Clerk Maxwell and Albert Einstein.

**5. Scientific Methodology** – His meticulous approach to experimentation set a high standard for future researchers.

Faraday's legacy lives on in the modern world, from the electricity that powers our homes to the batteries in our devices. His work laid the foundation for electrical engineering, telecommunications, and countless technological advancements.

In conclusion, Michael Faraday was a self-taught genius whose contributions to science changed the world. His humility, passion for knowledge, and dedication to the betterment of humanity make him one of history's greatest scientists. His legacy continues to inspire, proving that curiosity, perseverance, and integrity can lead to extraordinary discoveries.

# Charles Babbage
## The Father of the Computer

Charles Babbage was an English mathematician, inventor, and mechanical engineer who is widely regarded as the "Father of the Computer." His pioneering work on mechanical computation laid the foundation for modern computing. Despite facing financial and technical challenges that prevented his ambitious designs from being fully realized during his lifetime, Babbage's concepts of programmable machines, automatic calculations, and mechanical computing devices influenced future generations of scientists and engineers. His legacy continues to shape the world of technology.

## Origin

Charles Babbage was born on December 26, 1791, in London, England. He was the son of Benjamin Babbage, a wealthy banker and merchant, and Elizabeth Plumleigh Teape. His family belonged to Britain's prosperous middle class, affording him access to a privileged education and financial stability that allowed him to pursue scientific interests.

Babbage's birthplace, London, was a hub of intellectual and industrial development in the late 18th century. This environment fostered scientific inquiry and technological advancements, shaping his curiosity and future endeavors.

## Childhood and Youth

Babbage showed an early interest in mathematics and problem-solving. As a child, he suffered from poor health, leading his family to arrange private tutoring for him rather than enrolling him in traditional schools. His private tutors provided him with a strong foundation in mathematics, enabling him to excel in the subject.

At the age of 16, Babbage attended the Holmwood Academy in Middlesex, where he studied contemporary mathematical theories. Recognizing his exceptional talent, he was later admitted to Trinity College, Cambridge, in 1810. However, he was dissatisfied with the outdated mathematical curriculum, which lagged behind developments in continental Europe.

To supplement his studies, Babbage and a group of like-minded students formed the Analytical Society, aiming to modernize British mathematics by introducing advanced European concepts. His academic pursuits eventually led him to switch to Peterhouse, Cambridge, where he graduated with top honors in 1814.

## Adulthood

After graduating from Cambridge, Babbage devoted himself to mathematics, mechanical engineering, and scientific research. He was appointed as a lecturer at the Royal Institution in 1816 and became a Fellow of the Royal Society in 1817, solidifying his status as a leading intellectual of his time.

Babbage made significant contributions to mathematics, particularly in calculus, numerical analysis, and cryptography. However, his most remarkable achievements were in mechanical computation, where he aimed to automate complex calculations that were previously performed manually.

One of Babbage's most ambitious projects was the Difference Engine, a mechanical calculator designed to compute polynomial functions and generate mathematical tables with high accuracy. In 1822, he presented the idea to the Royal Astronomical Society, highlighting how it could eliminate human errors in mathematical calculations used in navigation and engineering.

The British government granted him funding to build the Difference Engine, but the project encountered numerous obstacles, including financial difficulties, engineering limitations, and political opposition. By 1833, the project was abandoned due to escalating costs and technical challenges.

Undeterred by the failure of the Difference Engine, Babbage embarked on an even more ambitious project – the Analytical Engine. Unlike the Difference Engine, which was limited to specific calculations, the Analytical Engine was designed as a general-purpose computing device, featuring:

- A "store" for memory (analogous to modern RAM)
- A "mill" for processing arithmetic operations (similar to a CPU)
- Punch cards for input and programming (inspired by Jacquard loom technology)
- Conditional branching and loops, resembling modern programming concepts

Although Babbage never built a working model of the Analytical Engine, his visionary ideas closely resembled modern computer architecture, making him a true pioneer in computational theory.

## Private Life

In 1814, Babbage married Georgiana Whitmore, with whom he had eight children. Tragically, only three of their children survived to adulthood. The loss of his wife and several of his children deeply affected Babbage, leading to periods of grief and isolation.

Despite his scientific genius, Babbage was known for his eccentricity and impatience with bureaucracy. He frequently clashed with government officials and colleagues, which hindered his ability to secure consistent funding for his projects.

Beyond his work in mathematics and computing, Babbage had diverse interests. He was a strong advocate for industrial automation, an outspoken critic of inefficiency, and a researcher in various fields, including railway safety and postal system improvements.

## Death

Charles Babbage passed away on October 18, 1871, at the age of 79. He died in London and was buried at Kensal Green Cemetery.

At the time of his death, much of his work remained unfinished, and his contributions were not widely recognized. However, his notebooks and blueprints were later studied by engineers and scientists, leading to a renewed appreciation of his pioneering ideas.

In a remarkable effort to honor his legacy, the Science Museum in London built a fully functional model of the Difference Engine in 1991, proving that Babbage's designs were indeed feasible with 19th-century technology.

## Character

Babbage was a brilliant but often misunderstood figure. His keen intellect and relentless drive for perfection sometimes led to conflicts with colleagues and patrons. He was highly ambitious and had little patience for those who did not share his vision for progress and automation. Despite his difficult personality, Babbage was deeply committed to scientific advancement and innovation. He was a polymath, constantly exploring new ideas and pushing the boundaries of technology. His eccentricity was matched by his generosity – he mentored young scientists and actively promoted education and reform in engineering and mathematics.

## Influence on Humanity

Babbage's influence extends far beyond his own time. His concepts of mechanical computation and programmable machines laid the groundwork for the digital revolution. His contributions include:

**1. Foundations of Modern Computing** – His ideas about memory, processing, and programming closely resemble the architecture of modern computers.

**2. Inspiration for Future Scientists** – Alan Turing, the father of modern computing, was inspired by Babbage's work when developing theoretical computing models.

**3. Advancements in Automated Calculation** – His designs influenced later mechanical calculators and early computational devices used in engineering and navigation.

**4. Mathematical and Engineering Legacy** – His contributions to numerical analysis, cryptography, and mechanical engineering continue to inform scientific research and technology development.

**5. Recognition in the Digital Age** – Babbage's name is now celebrated in the fields of computer science and engineering, with institutions, awards, and programming languages honoring his legacy.

In conclusion, Charles Babbage was a visionary ahead of his time. Although he did not see his machines fully realized, his work laid the foundation for the digital age. Today, computers, smartphones, and automated systems owe their existence to his pioneering ideas. His legacy is a testament to human ingenuity and the relentless pursuit of knowledge, proving that true innovation often transcends its own era.

# Abraham Lincoln

U.S. president who led the country during the
Civil War and abolished slavery

Abraham Lincoln, the 16th President of the United States, is widely regarded as one of the greatest leaders in American history. His leadership during the Civil War, his unwavering commitment to the Union, and his role in the abolition of slavery define his legacy. Despite facing immense personal and political challenges, Lincoln preserved the United States as a unified nation and laid the foundation for a more just society. His speeches, policies, and vision for democracy continue to inspire generations.

## Origin

Abraham Lincoln was born on February 12, 1809, in a one-room log cabin in Hardin County (now LaRue County), Kentucky. He was the second child of Thomas Lincoln and Nancy Hanks Lincoln. His family was of modest means, and life on the frontier was filled with hardships.

Lincoln's ancestry traces back to Samuel Lincoln, who emigrated from England to the American colonies in the 17th century. His father, Thomas, was a farmer and carpenter, but frequent land disputes and financial instability forced the family to relocate multiple times. The Lincolns eventually settled in southern Indiana in 1816, seeking better opportunities.

## Childhood and Youth

Lincoln's childhood was marked by tragedy and struggle. In 1818, when he was just nine years old, his mother, Nancy Hanks Lincoln, died of milk sickness, a disease caused by drinking contaminated milk. This loss deeply affected young Abraham and instilled in him a sense of resilience and responsibility. His father remarried Sarah Bush Johnston, a kind and nurturing woman who encouraged Lincoln's education. Though formal schooling was scarce, Lincoln was an avid reader and largely self-taught. He borrowed books from neighbors, including "The Life of George Washington" and "The Bible", which shaped his moral and intellectual outlook.

Lincoln worked on the family farm, splitting logs for fences and performing other manual labor. His experiences of hardship and labor instilled in him a deep understanding of the struggles of common people, which later influenced his political philosophy. As a teenager, Lincoln developed a reputation for his storytelling, wit, and strong sense of justice. By the time he reached adulthood, he had developed a thirst for knowledge and a drive to improve his circumstances.

## Adulthood

In 1830, Lincoln moved to Illinois, where he worked various jobs, including as a store clerk, rail-splitter, and surveyor. In 1832, he served briefly in the Black Hawk War, though he saw little combat. Following his service, he ran for the Illinois state legislature but was defeated. However, his political aspirations remained strong.

Lincoln studied law on his own, passing the bar examination in 1836. He established a legal practice in Springfield, Illinois, where he gained a reputation for honesty and eloquence. His ability to connect with juries and his persuasive speeches earned him the nickname "Honest Abe."

His political career gained momentum when he was elected to the Illinois House of Representatives in 1834. As a legislator, he opposed slavery's expansion but initially focused on economic development and infrastructure improvements.

Lincoln's national prominence grew during his 1858 debates with Stephen Douglas, his opponent in the Illinois Senate race. Although he lost the election, his powerful arguments against slavery's expansion caught the attention of the nation.

In 1860, Lincoln was nominated as the Republican candidate for President of the United States. His moderate stance on slavery, coupled with his appeal to both Northern and Western voters, helped him win the election. His victory, however, was met with immediate resistance from Southern states, leading to the secession crisis. Lincoln took office on March 4, 1861, amid the growing threat of secession. The Confederate attack on Fort Sumter in April 1861 marked the beginning of the Civil War. Lincoln's leadership during this period was defined by his steadfast commitment to preserving the Union.

Throughout the war, Lincoln navigated political divisions, military setbacks, and personal losses. He faced criticism from both abolitionists, who demanded immediate emancipation, and conservatives, who sought a negotiated peace.

On January 1, 1863, Lincoln issued the Emancipation Proclamation, declaring freedom for enslaved people in Confederate-held territories. Though it did not immediately end slavery, it shifted the war's purpose toward a moral crusade for human rights and strengthened Union support among abolitionists and African Americans.

Under Lincoln's leadership, the Union army achieved key victories, including the Battle of Gettysburg and the capture of Atlanta. His Gettysburg Address in 1863 eloquently reaffirmed the principles of democracy and national unity.

In 1864, Lincoln was re-elected as President. He championed the passage of the 13th Amendment, which abolished slavery in the United States.

## Private Life

Lincoln married Mary Todd in 1842. The couple had four sons, but only one, Robert Todd Lincoln, survived into adulthood. Lincoln's personal life was marked by profound sorrow, as he and Mary endured the deaths of three of their children. Mary Todd Lincoln was a complex figure, deeply devoted to her husband but also prone to mood swings and depression. The couple's marriage faced challenges, especially due to the pressures of the Civil War and personal tragedies. Despite his demanding political career, Lincoln was known for his humor, love of storytelling, and deep empathy. He often visited soldiers in hospitals and sought ways to connect with everyday Americans.

## Death

On April 14, 1865, just days after the Confederate surrender at Appomattox Court House, Lincoln was assassinated by John Wilkes Booth at Ford's Theatre in Washington, D.C. He died the following morning, April 15, 1865. His assassination shocked the nation, and he was mourned as a martyr for liberty and national unity. His funeral procession traveled across multiple states, drawing immense crowds who paid tribute to the fallen leader.

## Character

Lincoln's character was defined by resilience, humility, and deep moral conviction. He was a self-made man who rose from poverty to lead the nation during its most trying times. His ability to empathize with people from all walks of life made him a unifying figure. His integrity and honesty earned him widespread respect, even among political opponents. He was known for his patience, sense of humor, and capacity for forgiveness, qualities that made him an effective and compassionate leader.

## Influence on Humanity

Lincoln's influence extends far beyond his lifetime. His leadership during the Civil War preserved the United States and ended slavery, reshaping the course of history. His legacy includes:

**1. The Abolition of Slavery** – His efforts led to the passage of the 13th Amendment, ending slavery in America.

**2. Strengthening Democracy** – His commitment to government "of the people, by the people, for the people" remains a defining principle of democracy.

**3. Moral Leadership** – He set a standard for political leadership based on integrity, compassion, and unity.

**4. Inspiration for Civil Rights Movements** – His vision for equality inspired future leaders, including Martin Luther King Jr.

In conclusion, Abraham Lincoln's legacy as a leader, emancipator, and unifier endures. His vision for freedom and democracy continues to guide nations and inspire individuals seeking justice and equality worldwide.

# Charles Darwin
## The Father of Evolutionary Theory

Charles Darwin was an English naturalist, geologist, and biologist best known for his contributions to the theory of evolution by natural selection. His groundbreaking work, "On the Origin of Species," revolutionized scientific understanding of life's diversity and laid the foundation for modern evolutionary biology. Despite facing considerable controversy in his time, Darwin's ideas have profoundly influenced science, philosophy, and society.

### Origin

Charles Robert Darwin was born on February 12, 1809, in Shrewsbury, England, into a wealthy and well-connected family. His father, Robert Darwin, was a prominent physician, while his mother, Susannah Wedgwood, came from the famous Wedgwood pottery family. His paternal grandfather, Erasmus Darwin, was a respected physician and naturalist who speculated on evolutionary ideas decades before Charles would develop his own theories.

Raised in an environment that valued education, intellectual inquiry, and financial security, Darwin had the resources and support to pursue his academic interests. His family's affluence provided him with a privileged upbringing and access to some of the best schools in England.

### Childhood and Youth

Darwin showed an early interest in nature and collecting specimens, often gathering insects, shells, and rocks. He was an inquisitive child but not an exceptional student in traditional academic subjects. He attended Shrewsbury School, where he struggled with rote learning but excelled in observation and curiosity-driven study.

In 1825, at the age of 16, Darwin was sent to the University of Edinburgh to study medicine. However, he found the subject unappealing, particularly the surgical procedures, which he found distressing. While at Edinburgh, he became involved with natural history societies, learned taxidermy, and was introduced to scientific debates, including discussions on evolution.

Recognizing that Darwin had no passion for medicine, his father sent him to Christ's College, Cambridge, in 1828, intending for him to become a clergyman. Although he did not embrace theology, he excelled in botany and natural sciences, developing a close relationship with Professor John Stevens Henslow, who became a mentor and encouraged his interest in natural history.

## Adulthood

Darwin's life changed dramatically when he was invited to join the HMS "Beagle" as a naturalist on a five-year voyage (1831–1836) to survey South America and other parts of the world. The expedition, led by Captain Robert FitzRoy, provided Darwin with firsthand experience of diverse ecosystems and geological formations.

During the voyage, he collected thousands of specimens and made detailed observations that laid the groundwork for his evolutionary theories. The Galápagos Islands were particularly influential in shaping his ideas, as he noted the variations in species, such as finches, across different islands.

After returning to England in 1836, Darwin spent the next two decades analyzing his findings, consulting with other scientists, and refining his ideas on evolution. Influenced by the work of Thomas Malthus on population growth, he developed the principle of natural selection, proposing that species evolve over time due to the survival and reproduction of individuals with advantageous traits.

In 1859, he published "On the Origin of Species", in which he presented extensive evidence for evolution by natural selection. The book was met with both acclaim and controversy, challenging traditional religious views on creation while laying the foundation for modern evolutionary biology.

Darwin continued to publish influential works, including "The Descent of Man" (1871), which applied his theory to human evolution, and "The Expression of the Emotions in Man and Animals" (1872), exploring the biological basis of emotions.

## Private Life

In 1839, Darwin married his cousin, Emma Wedgwood, with whom he had ten children. Their marriage was affectionate and intellectually stimulating, though Emma was deeply religious, which created tensions given Darwin's increasingly secular scientific views.

Despite his professional success, Darwin suffered from chronic illnesses, including digestive problems, fatigue, and anxiety. His health struggles often confined him to his home in Down House, where he continued his scientific work in relative isolation.

Darwin was a devoted father and took an active role in his children's upbringing. He was also deeply compassionate, supporting various social causes, including the abolition of slavery.

## Death

Charles Darwin died on April 19, 1882, at the age of 73. He was buried in Westminster Abbey, an honor rarely given to a scientist, signifying his immense contributions to human knowledge.

Though his work was initially met with resistance, by the time of his death, evolutionary theory had gained significant acceptance in scientific circles. His ideas continued to influence biology, anthropology, and genetics in the decades that followed.

## Character

Darwin was known for his humility, patience, and meticulous approach to science. He was not a combative or confrontational figure but rather a careful observer who let evidence guide his conclusions.

Despite his revolutionary ideas, he avoided direct public debates on religious and scientific controversies. He preferred to let his work speak for itself and allowed others, such as Thomas Huxley, to defend his theories against critics.

His commitment to scientific integrity and the pursuit of truth made him a highly respected figure in the scientific community. He was also deeply empathetic, showing kindness to friends, family, and colleagues, even in disagreement.

## Influence on Humanity

Darwin's impact on the world is immeasurable. His contributions include:

**1. The Foundation of Evolutionary Biology** – His theory of natural selection remains the cornerstone of modern biology, influencing fields such as genetics, ecology, and paleontology.

**2. Advancing Scientific Thought** – Darwin's emphasis on empirical evidence and systematic observation set new standards for scientific methodology.

**3. Challenging Religious Doctrine** – His work reshaped humanity's understanding of origins, leading to ongoing debates between science and religion.

**4. Influencing Social and Political Thought** – His ideas were applied to various disciplines, though some misused them in pseudoscientific theories such as Social Darwinism.

**5. A Lasting Legacy in Genetics** – The rediscovery of Gregor Mendel's work on heredity in the early 20th century confirmed and expanded upon Darwin's ideas, leading to the modern synthesis of evolution and genetics.

In conclusion, Charles Darwin's discoveries fundamentally changed the way humans perceive life and our place in the natural world. His legacy continues to shape scientific research, philosophy, and education, ensuring that his influence endures for generations to come.

# Otto von Bismarck
Founder of the German Empire

Otto von Bismarck was one of the most influential statesmen in modern history, known for unifying Germany and shaping the course of European politics in the late 19th century. As the first Chancellor of the German Empire, he masterfully used diplomacy, war, and strategic alliances to forge a powerful and unified Germany. His policies, known as "Realpolitik", emphasized pragmatic governance over ideological considerations, earning him the nickname the "Iron Chancellor".

## Origin

Otto Eduard Leopold von Bismarck was born on April 1, 1815, in Schönhausen, a town in the Kingdom of Prussia (modern-day Germany). He was born into a Junker family, the landowning aristocracy of Prussia, which had a strong tradition of military service and bureaucratic administration.

His father, Karl Wilhelm Ferdinand von Bismarck, was a nobleman and a former Prussian military officer, while his mother, Wilhelmine Mencken, came from a more intellectual and bureaucratic background. The combination of his father's conservative aristocratic values and his mother's refined intellect played a crucial role in shaping Bismarck's character and political outlook.

## Childhood and Youth

Bismarck was raised in a privileged yet disciplined environment. As a child, he was known for his intelligence and independent streak but was not always academically inclined. He attended the prestigious Plamann Institute in Berlin and later the Friedrich-Wilhelm Gymnasium.

In 1832, he enrolled at the University of Göttingen to study law. Though he was more interested in socializing and dueling than in academics, he gained valuable insights into politics and state affairs. He later continued his legal studies at the University of Berlin.

After completing his education, Bismarck entered the Prussian civil service. However, bureaucratic work did not satisfy him, and he soon withdrew to manage his family estate in Pomerania. There, he developed a deep appreciation for rural aristocratic life and became more involved in political affairs.

## Adulthood

Bismarck's political career began in earnest in 1847 when he was elected as a delegate to the Prussian legislature. A staunch conservative, he opposed liberal movements and democratic reforms, believing in the supremacy of the monarchy and the traditional aristocratic order.

During the revolutionary upheavals of 1848, Bismarck aligned himself with the conservative faction, advocating for a strong Prussian state rather than a unified German democracy. His loyalty to the monarchy earned him the trust of King Frederick William IV and later his successor, King Wilhelm I.

In 1862, Bismarck was appointed Prime Minister of Prussia and Minister of Foreign Affairs by King Wilhelm I. He quickly consolidated power and pursued an aggressive foreign policy aimed at uniting the German states under Prussian leadership.

Through a series of wars, Bismarck achieved his goal:

**1. The Danish War** (1864): Prussia and Austria fought together against Denmark, gaining control of the territories of Schleswig and Holstein.

**2. The Austro-Prussian War** (1866): Bismarck orchestrated a conflict with Austria, decisively defeating it at the Battle of Königgrätz. This victory established Prussia as the dominant German power and led to the formation of the North German Confederation.

**3. The Franco-Prussian War** (1870-1871): Bismarck engineered a war with France, using nationalist sentiment to rally the German states. The stunning victory against France led to the proclamation of the German Empire in 1871, with Wilhelm I crowned as the first German Emperor.

As Chancellor of the newly unified German Empire, Bismarck focused on maintaining stability and consolidating power. His domestic policies included:

- **Kulturkampf** (Culture Struggle): An anti-Catholic campaign aimed at reducing the influence of the Catholic Church in Germany.
- **Anti-Socialist Laws**: Measures to suppress socialist movements, though he simultaneously introduced social welfare programs such as pensions and health insurance to undermine their appeal.
- **Diplomatic Strategy**: Bismarck sought to prevent European conflicts by forming alliances, including the "Triple Alliance" with Austria-Hungary and Italy.

## Private Life

Bismarck married Johanna von Puttkamer in 1847, a deeply religious and devoted woman who provided him with emotional stability throughout his political career. Their marriage was marked by mutual affection and respect, and they had three children.

Despite his public image as a stern and pragmatic leader, Bismarck was deeply attached to his family. He enjoyed reading, hunting, and spending time on his estate in Friedrichsruh. His letters to his wife reveal a more sensitive and affectionate side that contrasted with his political persona.

## Death

Bismarck's dominance in German politics ended in 1890 when he was dismissed by Emperor Wilhelm II, who sought to assert his own authority. In his later years, he lived in retirement, writing his memoirs and reflecting on his career.

He died on July 30, 1898, at the age of 83 in Friedrichsruh. Though he had fallen out of favor with the German leadership, he was widely revered by the public, and his legacy as the unifier of Germany remained intact.

## Character

Bismarck was a master strategist, known for his ability to manipulate political situations to his advantage. He was pragmatic, ruthless when necessary, but also capable of remarkable foresight and adaptability. Despite his autocratic tendencies, he had a keen sense of humor and often used sarcasm to disarm opponents. His complex personality made him both feared and respected by allies and adversaries alike.

He believed in power politics and had little patience for ideological debates. His guiding principle was "Realpolitik" – the idea that politics should be based on practical considerations rather than moral or ideological doctrines.

## Influence on Humanity

Bismarck's impact on the world was profound and enduring. His contributions include:

**1. German Unification** – He transformed Germany from a collection of fragmented states into a powerful empire, altering the balance of power in Europe.

**2. Modern Statecraft** – His diplomatic strategies influenced global politics and international relations, shaping alliances that lasted for decades.

**3. Social Welfare Reforms** – His introduction of pensions, health insurance, and workers' rights laid the foundation for modern social security systems.

**4. Geopolitical Legacy** – His alliances and territorial rearrangements influenced European conflicts, including the eventual path to World War I.

**5. Pragmatic Leadership** – His philosophy of "Realpolitik" became a model for leaders seeking to balance power, strategy, and governance.

In conclusion, Otto von Bismarck was a statesman of unparalleled influence, whose political acumen reshaped Europe. His ability to balance war, diplomacy, and governance made him one of history's most effective leaders. Though his empire would later face challenges, his legacy as the architect of German unity and modern statecraft remains unmatched.

# Karl Marx
Founder of Marxism and critic of capitalism

Karl Marx was a German philosopher, economist, historian, sociologist, and political theorist whose revolutionary ideas profoundly influenced the course of world history. His theories on capitalism, class struggle, and historical materialism laid the groundwork for socialism and communism. Marx's most influential work, "The Communist Manifesto", co-authored with Friedrich Engels, and "Das Kapital" remain cornerstone texts in political and economic thought. His legacy continues to shape global discourse on economic systems, social justice, and revolutionary movements.

## Origin

Karl Heinrich Marx was born on May 5, 1818, in Trier, in the Kingdom of Prussia (now part of Germany). His family was of Jewish descent, but his father, Heinrich Marx, converted to Lutheran Protestantism to continue practicing law, as Jews faced significant legal restrictions in Prussia. Karl's mother, Henriette Pressburg, came from a wealthy Dutch Jewish family.

Marx grew up in a relatively comfortable middle-class environment, receiving a solid education that prepared him for a life of intellectual and political inquiry. Trier, a historic city on the banks of the Moselle River, was a hub of political activity and debate, exposing Marx to ideas about social justice and reform from an early age.

## Childhood and Youth

As a child, Marx displayed a strong intellect and curiosity. His father encouraged his education, hoping that Karl would follow in his footsteps as a lawyer. Marx attended the Friedrich-Wilhelm Gymnasium in Trier, where he excelled in literature, history, and philosophy.

In 1835, at the age of 17, Marx enrolled at the University of Bonn to study law, but he quickly became more interested in philosophy and literature. His time at Bonn was marked by a rebellious streak; he joined student clubs and got into duels, leading his father to transfer him to the University of Berlin in 1836, where he would come under the influence of the Young Hegelians, a group of radical thinkers inspired by the philosophy of Georg Wilhelm Friedrich Hegel.

At Berlin, Marx immersed himself in philosophy, particularly Hegelian dialectics. He studied the works of Immanuel Kant, Ludwig Feuerbach, and David Ricardo, gradually developing his own ideas about history, economics, and society. By the time he completed his doctoral dissertation in 1841, Marx had already begun formulating the philosophical and political ideas that would define his later work.

## Adulthood

Marx initially pursued an academic career but found his radical views at odds with the Prussian government. Unable to secure a teaching position, he turned to journalism, writing for the "Rheinische Zeitung", a liberal newspaper in Cologne. His articles, which criticized Prussian policies and advocated for press freedom, led to the newspaper's suppression in 1843.

Facing increasing government censorship, Marx moved to Paris, where he became involved with socialist and communist groups. It was in Paris that he met Friedrich Engels, who would become his lifelong collaborator and intellectual partner. Together, they developed the concept of historical materialism, arguing that economic structures determine social and political conditions.

Marx's political writings and activism led to his expulsion from France in 1845. He moved to Brussels, where he and Engels co-authored "The Communist Manifesto" (1848). This seminal work called for the working class (proletariat) to rise against the bourgeoisie and establish a classless, communist society. The revolutions of 1848, which swept across Europe, seemed to confirm Marx's theories, but they ultimately failed, forcing him into exile once again.

In 1849, Marx settled in London, where he would spend the rest of his life. He continued his activism but focused primarily on his scholarly work. In the British Museum, he researched and wrote "Das Kapital", his magnum opus on capitalism's inner workings and inherent contradictions. The first volume was published in 1867, but Marx did not live to complete the subsequent volumes, which Engels later compiled and published posthumously.

Despite his intellectual contributions, Marx lived in poverty for much of his time in London, relying on financial support from Engels. His radical ideas kept him at odds with the British authorities, and his writings were largely ignored by mainstream intellectual circles during his lifetime.

## Private Life

Marx married Jenny von Westphalen, an aristocratic woman from a politically liberal family, in 1843. Their marriage was characterized by deep affection and shared intellectual pursuits, but also financial hardship. The couple had seven children, though only three survived into adulthood due to poor living conditions.

Marx's family life was strained by their constant financial struggles. Jenny often suffered from illness, and their children's deaths deeply affected them. Despite his poverty, Marx continued his work, prioritizing his intellectual pursuits over financial stability.

His relationships extended beyond his family, particularly with Engels, who not only supported him financially but also helped refine and spread his ideas. Marx was also known to have had a close but controversial relationship with his housekeeper, Helene Demuth, with some historians suggesting that he fathered an illegitimate child with her.

## Death

Karl Marx died on March 14, 1883, at the age of 64 in London. He had been in poor health for several years, suffering from respiratory illnesses, liver disease, and other ailments. He was buried in Highgate Cemetery, where his grave later became a site of pilgrimage for socialists and admirers worldwide.

At the time of his death, Marx was not widely recognized outside socialist and labor circles. However, his ideas soon gained traction, particularly after the publication of his later works and the efforts of Engels to promote his legacy.

## Character

Marx was an intellectual force, known for his sharp analytical mind and unyielding commitment to his ideals. He was deeply passionate about justice and the plight of the working class, dedicating his life to advocating for social change. However, he could also be highly argumentative and uncompromising, often clashing with fellow revolutionaries. He was known for his wit and sarcasm, as well as his ability to dissect economic and social structures with remarkable depth. Despite his flaws, including his neglect of personal finances and sometimes harsh treatment of allies, Marx remained dedicated to his vision of a better society until his final days.

## Influence on Humanity

Marx's ideas have had an unparalleled impact on history, influencing political movements, revolutions, and academic disciplines worldwide. His contributions include:

**1. The Foundation of Marxism** – His theories provided the basis for Marxist thought, influencing socialist and communist movements globally.

**2. Impact on Labor Rights** – His critique of capitalism inspired labor movements, leading to reforms such as workers' rights, minimum wages, and social welfare systems.

**3. Influence on Political Revolutions** – His work shaped major revolutions, including the Russian Revolution of 1917 and the rise of communist states in the 20th century.

**4. Academic and Theoretical Legacy** – His ideas continue to be studied in philosophy, economics, sociology, and political science.

In conclusion, Karl Marx was a revolutionary thinker whose critiques of capitalism and advocacy for class struggle changed the course of history. Though his ideas remain controversial, their influence is undeniable, shaping modern political discourse and economic thought. His vision of a classless society continues to inspire movements for social justice and equality worldwide.

# William Thomas Green Morton
## The Pioneer of Anesthesia

William Thomas Green Morton was an American dentist and medical innovator who played a crucial role in the discovery and application of anesthesia in surgical procedures. His successful demonstration of ether anesthesia in 1846 revolutionized medicine by eliminating pain during surgery, paving the way for modern surgical practices. Despite facing controversy and disputes over the credit for this discovery, Morton's contributions had a profound and lasting impact on healthcare.

## Origin

William Thomas Green Morton was born on August 9, 1819, in Charlton, Massachusetts, USA. He was the son of James Morton, a farmer and small business owner, and Rebecca Morton. The family lived in modest circumstances, and young William grew up in a rural setting, experiencing the daily hardships of early 19th-century American life.

Morton's early years were marked by curiosity and an aptitude for science and mechanics. His background in a working-class family instilled in him a strong work ethic and an ambition to rise above his circumstances. The medical field fascinated him, but financial constraints limited his options for formal education, making his journey to scientific success even more remarkable.

## Childhood and Youth

Morton displayed an early interest in medicine, mechanics, and chemistry. He attended local schools in Massachusetts but was not an exceptional student in traditional subjects. However, he showed promise in practical sciences and demonstrated a natural curiosity for experimentation.

In his teenage years, Morton apprenticed in a printing shop before deciding to pursue a career in dentistry, a growing profession at the time. He studied under Horace Wells, a well-known dentist who had begun experimenting with nitrous oxide (laughing gas) as a potential anesthetic. This mentorship would later influence Morton's work in pain management and anesthesia.

In 1840, Morton enrolled at the Baltimore College of Dental Surgery, but he did not complete his studies. Instead, he moved to Boston and set up his own dental practice. Despite lacking formal credentials, Morton gained a reputation as an innovative dentist and experimented with new techniques for pain relief during dental procedures.

## Adulthood

In the early 1840s, surgery and dentistry were often performed without anesthesia, causing excruciating pain for patients. Dentists and physicians sought ways to alleviate pain, leading to numerous experiments with different substances. Morton's mentor, Horace Wells, attempted to use nitrous oxide for anesthesia but faced challenges in achieving reliable results.

In his pursuit of a more effective anesthetic, Morton partnered with Dr. Charles T. Jackson, a chemist who recommended the use of ether. Morton conducted numerous experiments on animals and, later, on himself to test the effects of ether inhalation.

On October 16, 1846, at the Massachusetts General Hospital in Boston, Morton successfully demonstrated the use of ether anesthesia during a surgical procedure performed by Dr. John Collins Warren. The patient, Gilbert Abbott, underwent a painless operation to remove a tumor. When the procedure was completed, Dr. Warren famously declared, "Gentlemen, this is no humbug." This event marked the beginning of modern anesthesiology and transformed medical practice worldwide.

Morton initially attempted to patent ether anesthesia under the name "Letheon," hoping to secure financial rewards for his discovery. However, controversy soon erupted as multiple individuals, including Dr. Jackson and Horace Wells, claimed credit for the discovery. This dispute overshadowed Morton's achievements and led to prolonged legal and public battles.

Despite his groundbreaking discovery, Morton faced financial difficulties and professional setbacks. The controversy over the invention of anesthesia left him in a state of continuous litigation, and he struggled to gain widespread recognition and monetary compensation.

During the American Civil War, Morton volunteered his expertise to help wounded soldiers by using ether for battlefield surgeries. However, his contributions remained underappreciated during his lifetime.

## Private Life

In 1844, Morton married Elizabeth Whitman, a woman from a respected family in Massachusetts. Elizabeth supported Morton through his career struggles, legal battles, and financial hardships. Their marriage produced several children, and despite their difficulties, Elizabeth remained devoted to her husband's cause.

Morton's personal life was marked by a relentless drive for success and recognition. His pursuit of scientific breakthroughs sometimes strained his family life, but his wife's unwavering support helped him through challenging periods.

## Death

The years of legal battles, financial stress, and lack of formal recognition took a toll on Morton's health. On July 15, 1868, at the age of 48, he suffered a stroke and passed away in New York City. His death was attributed to a combination of exhaustion, stress, and the long-term effects of his struggles for recognition.

Morton was buried at Mount Auburn Cemetery in Cambridge, Massachusetts. In later years, his contributions to anesthesia were more widely acknowledged, and he was posthumously honored for his role in transforming medical science.

## Character

Morton was a determined, ambitious, and resilient individual who pursued his vision with unwavering dedication. He was willing to take personal risks, both financially and physically, in his quest to develop anesthesia. However, his attempts to patent ether anesthesia and seek financial rewards led to conflicts with other scientists and medical professionals.

Despite these challenges, Morton was fundamentally motivated by the desire to alleviate human suffering. His willingness to experiment on himself and his insistence on proving the effectiveness of ether anesthesia demonstrated his commitment to scientific advancement.

## Influence on Humanity

Morton's discovery of ether anesthesia had a profound impact on medicine and humanity. His contributions include:

**1. Pioneering Modern Anesthesia** – Morton's demonstration of ether anesthesia revolutionized surgical procedures, making pain-free surgery possible for millions of people.

**2. Advancing Medical Science** – His work paved the way for further developments in anesthesiology, leading to safer and more effective anesthetic techniques.

**3. Transforming Surgery and Healthcare** – Before anesthesia, surgeries were often traumatic and limited to life-threatening conditions. After Morton's discovery, more complex and lifesaving procedures became possible.

**4. Inspiring Future Innovations** – His work inspired generations of medical researchers to continue exploring pain management and anesthesia.

**5. Recognition in Medical History** – Despite initial disputes over credit, Morton is now widely recognized as a key figure in the history of medicine.

In conclusion, William Thomas Green Morton's pioneering work in anesthesia changed the landscape of medical science. His discovery allowed for pain-free surgery, significantly reducing human suffering and improving medical outcomes worldwide. Although he faced many challenges in securing recognition during his lifetime, his contributions remain among the most important in the history of medicine. Today, every surgical procedure performed under anesthesia stands as a testament to his groundbreaking work and relentless pursuit of progress.

# Gregor Mendel
## The Father of Genetics

Gregor Mendel was an Austrian scientist, friar, and teacher whose pioneering work in genetics laid the foundation for modern biology. Through meticulous experiments with pea plants, Mendel uncovered the fundamental principles of inheritance, demonstrating how traits are passed from one generation to the next. Though largely unrecognized during his lifetime, his discoveries later became the cornerstone of genetics, influencing fields such as medicine, agriculture, and evolutionary biology.

## Origin

Gregor Johann Mendel was born on July 20, 1822, in Heinzendorf, in the Austrian Empire (now Hynčice, Czech Republic). He was the second child of Anton and Rosine Mendel, German-speaking farmers who worked the land to sustain their family. The Mendels were modest but valued education and encouraged young Gregor to pursue intellectual endeavors.

Mendel's early exposure to agriculture and plant cultivation on the family farm influenced his later work in genetics. He observed how certain traits, such as plant height and seed color, appeared to be inherited through generations, sparking his curiosity about biological inheritance.

## Childhood and Youth

Mendel showed early signs of academic brilliance, but his family struggled financially to support his education. Recognizing his potential, his parents and local educators helped him gain admission to the Gymnasium in Troppau (modern-day Opava). He excelled in mathematics and natural sciences but also endured periods of hardship due to financial difficulties.

In 1840, Mendel enrolled at the Philosophical Institute of the University of Olomouc, where he studied physics, mathematics, and philosophy. However, financial struggles and health issues forced him to take breaks from his studies. Despite these setbacks, he persevered and graduated in 1843.

To continue his education and secure financial stability, Mendel entered the Augustinian Abbey of St. Thomas in Brno in 1843. There, he was given the name Gregor and was encouraged by his superiors to pursue scientific research, as the abbey was a center of learning and inquiry.

## Adulthood

In 1851, Mendel was sent to the University of Vienna to further his education in physics and botany. His studies provided him with a strong foundation in scientific methodology, allowing him to approach biological research with precision and rigor.

Upon returning to the abbey in 1853, he began his groundbreaking experiments with pea plants ("Pisum sativum"). Over the next eight years, Mendel meticulously bred thousands of plants, carefully recording their inherited traits. His experiments led him to identify key principles of inheritance, now known as:

- **The Law of Segregation**: Each organism carries two copies of each gene, one from each parent, and these genes segregate independently during reproduction.
- **The Law of Independent Assortment**: Genes for different traits are inherited independently of one another, allowing for genetic variation.
- **Dominant and Recessive Traits**: Some traits are dominant and will appear in offspring even if only one parent contributes the gene, while recessive traits require contributions from both parents to be expressed.

In 1866, Mendel published his findings in "Experiments on Plant Hybridization", but his work was largely ignored by the scientific community at the time. Scientists were unaware of the molecular basis of inheritance, and his discoveries did not align with the prevailing theories of blended inheritance.

## Private Life

Mendel remained devoted to his scientific work and religious duties throughout his life. He never married, dedicating himself entirely to research and teaching. His role as a friar provided him with the stability and resources needed to conduct his experiments, but it also limited his ability to promote his findings to a wider audience.

Despite his introverted nature, Mendel was well-liked among his peers and students. He served as a teacher at the Brno Technical School, where he inspired many students with his knowledge of science and mathematics. Outside of his scientific work, he had a passion for beekeeping and meteorology, contributing valuable insights in these fields as well.

## Death

In 1868, Mendel was appointed Abbot of St. Thomas Abbey, a position that required him to focus more on administrative and financial matters than scientific research. His responsibilities increased, and he had less time to continue his experiments.

As he grew older, Mendel suffered from health problems, particularly kidney disease. He passed away on January 6, 1884, at the age of 61. At the time of his death, his work remained largely unrecognized, and he was remembered primarily as an abbot rather than a scientist.

## Character

Mendel was a patient and methodical researcher, qualities that allowed him to conduct experiments with precision and rigor. His ability to observe, analyze, and record vast amounts of data was extraordinary, especially for a time when genetics was not yet an established field.

He was also a humble and dedicated individual who sought knowledge for the sake of discovery rather than personal gain. Despite being overlooked during his lifetime, he remained committed to his work, confident that scientific progress would one day validate his findings.

His kindness and generosity were well-known among his colleagues and students, and he was respected both within the scientific community and the religious order. He maintained a strong sense of duty, balancing his religious obligations with his passion for scientific inquiry.

## Influence on Humanity

Although Mendel's work was largely ignored during his lifetime, his contributions became widely recognized in the early 20th century, long after his death. In 1900, three independent scientists — Hugo de Vries, Carl Correns, and Erich von Tschermak — rediscovered his research and confirmed its accuracy.

Mendel's findings became the foundation of modern genetics, influencing numerous fields:

**1. Genetics and Biology** — His principles of inheritance form the basis of classical genetics, guiding research in genetic disorders, inheritance patterns, and evolutionary biology.

**2. Medicine and Biotechnology** — His work has led to advancements in genetic engineering, disease research, and personalized medicine.

**3. Agriculture** — His discoveries revolutionized plant and animal breeding, improving crop yields and livestock production through selective breeding.

**4. Evolutionary Theory** — His findings complemented Darwin's theory of evolution by providing a mechanism for how traits are passed down through generations.

**5. Modern DNA Research** — His principles laid the groundwork for later discoveries, including the structure of DNA by Watson and Crick.

Today, Mendel is honored as the "Father of Genetics." Schools, research institutions, and scientific societies recognize his contributions, and his work remains essential to biological sciences.

In conclusion, Gregor Mendel's meticulous research and profound discoveries revolutionized our understanding of heredity. His perseverance, despite initial obscurity, exemplifies the true spirit of scientific inquiry. His legacy continues to influence genetics, medicine, agriculture, and evolutionary biology, ensuring his place among the most significant figures in the history of science.

# Louis Pasteur
Pioneer of microbiology and immunology

Louis Pasteur was a French chemist and microbiologist whose groundbreaking discoveries in germ theory, fermentation, and vaccination revolutionized medicine and public health. His contributions to science led to the development of vaccines, pasteurization, and advancements in microbiology that continue to save millions of lives today. Pasteur's work laid the foundation for immunology and modern hygiene practices, making him one of the most influential scientists in history.

## Origin

Louis Pasteur was born on December 27, 1822, in Dole, a small town in the Jura region of eastern France. He was the third child of Jean-Joseph Pasteur and Jeanne-Etiennette Roqui. His father was a tanner and a veteran of the Napoleonic Wars, instilling in young Louis a sense of discipline, hard work, and patriotism.

The Pasteur family later moved to Arbois, where Louis spent most of his childhood. Despite his humble background, his parents were determined to provide him with an education that would allow him to rise beyond his working-class roots.

## Childhood and Youth

As a child, Pasteur was not particularly outstanding in his studies. He had an artistic talent for portrait painting and was deeply attached to his family. He attended primary school in Arbois and later entered the Collège Royal in Besançon, where he showed interest in science but was initially more inclined toward drawing and classical studies.

Encouraged by his teachers, Pasteur pursued higher education at the École Normale Supérieure in Paris in 1843. His academic performance improved significantly, and he became fascinated with chemistry and physics. He studied under renowned scientists such as Jean-Baptiste Dumas, who influenced his scientific thinking. Pasteur earned his doctorate in 1847, focusing on crystallography and the properties of tartaric acid.

## Adulthood

Pasteur's early work in crystallography led to his discovery of molecular asymmetry. He demonstrated that organic molecules could exist in two mirror-image forms, laying the groundwork for the study of stereochemistry. This discovery earned him recognition among the scientific community and helped him secure academic positions.

In the 1850s, Pasteur turned his attention to microbiology. He investigated the process of fermentation and demonstrated that microorganisms, not spontaneous generation, were responsible for chemical transformations in food and beverages. This discovery disproved the long-held theory of spontaneous generation and established the foundation for the germ theory of disease.

His work had immediate practical applications. The French wine and silk industries were suffering from contamination issues, and Pasteur identified the microbes responsible. By developing methods to kill harmful bacteria, he introduced pasteurization, a technique still used today to prevent spoilage in milk, wine, and other perishable goods.

Pasteur's most groundbreaking work came in the field of immunology. Inspired by Edward Jenner's work on smallpox, he sought to develop vaccines for other infectious diseases. In 1881, he successfully tested a vaccine against anthrax in livestock, proving that weakened forms of pathogens could stimulate immunity.

His most famous achievement was the development of a rabies vaccine. In 1885, Pasteur treated a young boy, Joseph Meister, who had been bitten by a rabid dog. After administering a series of weakened virus injections, the boy survived, marking a historic moment in medicine. The success of this treatment made Pasteur famous around the world, although it remained unclear whether Meister was actually cured or perhaps not infected at all, as a bite does not necessarily lead to an infection. Only the analysis of numerous cases confirmed the effectiveness of Pasteur's vaccine. Pasteur's rabies vaccine cemented his legacy and laid the groundwork for modern vaccination practices.

## Private Life

Louis Pasteur married Marie Laurent in 1849, and they had five children. Tragically, three of their children died of typhoid fever, reinforcing Pasteur's determination to fight infectious diseases. His wife was a devoted partner and played a crucial role in managing his laboratory and documenting his work.

Despite his demanding scientific career, Pasteur was deeply religious and maintained strong moral values. He was known for his dedication to his family and his unwavering patriotism, especially during the Franco-Prussian War when he encouraged scientific research for national advancement.

## Death

In his later years, Pasteur suffered from strokes that left him partially paralyzed. Despite declining health, he continued his research and remained active in scientific circles. On September 28, 1895, he passed away at the age of 72 at his estate in Marnes-la-Coquette, near Paris.

Pasteur was buried in the Institut Pasteur, which he had founded in 1887. His funeral was attended by dignitaries and scientists from around the world, honoring his contributions to science and humanity.

## Character

Louis Pasteur was a man of extraordinary intelligence and determination, characterized by his pursuit of perfection and his dedication to science. He was a visionary who was not discouraged by setbacks and always sought solutions to the most pressing problems of his time.

Pasteur was known for his unwavering dedication and meticulous research methods. He approached science with a problem-solving mindset, always seeking practical applications for his discoveries. His perseverance and ability to challenge established theories set him apart as a true scientific pioneer.

However, Pasteur also gained a reputation for unscrupulous behavior - adopting findings from rivals without hesitation, concealing inconvenient results and manipulating experiments. This calls some of his findings into question and casts a shadow over his legacy.

## Influence on Humanity

Pasteur's impact on science and medicine is immeasurable. His contributions include:

**1. The Germ Theory of Disease** – His research demonstrated that microorganisms cause infectious diseases, leading to the development of antiseptic techniques and modern microbiology.

**2. Pasteurization** – His method of heat treatment to kill harmful bacteria is still used worldwide in the food and beverage industry.

**3. Vaccination Advancements** – His work on vaccines for rabies, anthrax, and chicken cholera paved the way for modern immunization programs.

**4. Public Health and Hygiene** – His discoveries led to improved sanitation practices, reducing the spread of infectious diseases.

**5. The Institut Pasteur** – Founded in 1887, this research institute continues to be a global leader in medical and scientific research.

Today, Pasteur's legacy lives on in every vaccination program, every sterilized surgical instrument, and every bottle of pasteurized milk. His name remains synonymous with scientific innovation and the relentless pursuit of knowledge for the betterment of humanity.

In conclusion, Louis Pasteur's contributions to science have saved countless lives and reshaped the fields of microbiology and medicine. His pioneering work continues to influence public health policies and medical research, ensuring his place as one of history's greatest scientific minds.

# James Clerk Maxwell
Founder of modern electrodynamics

James Clerk Maxwell was a Scottish physicist and mathematician whose groundbreaking work in electromagnetism and kinetic theory revolutionized the field of physics. His formulation of Maxwell's equations unified electricity, magnetism, and optics into a single theoretical framework, laying the foundation for modern physics and telecommunications. Despite being lesser known than Newton and Einstein, Maxwell's contributions are considered among the most profound in scientific history.

## Origin

Born on June 13, 1831, in Edinburgh, Scotland, James Clerk Maxwell was the only child of John Clerk Maxwell and Frances Cay. His family was of noble descent, connected to the Clerks of Penicuik, a distinguished Scottish family. His father was a lawyer and landowner, and his mother was well-educated, fostering in young James a love for learning and curiosity. Maxwell spent his early years at the family estate, Glenlair, in Dumfriesshire, where he developed an interest in nature, mechanics, and mathematics. His childhood environment provided him with an ideal setting for intellectual development and experimentation.

## Childhood and Youth

Maxwell's intellectual abilities became evident at an early age. His mother played a crucial role in his early education, but she passed away from cancer when he was just eight years old. Following her death, his father took responsibility for his education, hiring private tutors to guide his studies. At the age of 10, Maxwell was enrolled in Edinburgh Academy, where his exceptional mathematical talent became apparent. He was often regarded as an eccentric and curious student, fascinated by geometry and natural phenomena. By the age of 14, he had already published his first scientific paper on the properties of ovals, demonstrating his early mastery of mathematical concepts.

In 1847, at the age of 16, Maxwell entered the University of Edinburgh, where he continued his studies in mathematics and physics. He showed remarkable independence in his research, conducting experiments on optics and elasticity. After three years, he transferred to Trinity College, Cambridge, in 1850, where he further developed his analytical and mathematical skills. At Cambridge, he won prestigious awards for his academic performance and research, particularly in applied mathematics and electromagnetism.

## Adulthood

After graduating from Cambridge in 1854, Maxwell was appointed as a professor of natural philosophy at Marischal College in Aberdeen in 1856. During this period, he conducted pioneering work on the nature of Saturn's rings, proving mathematically that they must be composed of numerous small particles rather than being solid or fluid.

In 1860, Maxwell moved to King's College, London, where he made significant contributions to the study of color vision and optics. His research led to the first demonstration of color photography, based on the principle of three-color analysis, which laid the foundation for modern color imaging.

Maxwell's most influential work came in the field of electromagnetism. Building on the experiments of Michael Faraday, he developed a set of mathematical equations – now known as Maxwell's equations – that described the behavior of electric and magnetic fields. Published in 1865, these equations unified electricity, magnetism, and optics, demonstrating that light itself is an electromagnetic wave.

Maxwell's equations were groundbreaking because they:

- Explained how electromagnetic waves propagate through space.
- Predicted the existence of radio waves, leading to the development of wireless communication.
- Provided the theoretical foundation for modern electrical engineering and telecommunications.

His work on electromagnetism was later confirmed by Heinrich Hertz's experiments in the 1880s, leading to the development of radio, radar, and many modern technologies. Maxwell also made profound contributions to the kinetic theory of gases, formulating the Maxwell-Boltzmann distribution, which describes the statistical behavior of gas molecules. This work laid the foundation for statistical mechanics and deepened our understanding of thermodynamics. His studies of heat and molecular motion contributed significantly to the second law of thermodynamics and inspired later developments in quantum mechanics.

## Private Life

Maxwell married Katherine Mary Dewar in 1858. Katherine was highly supportive of his scientific work, often assisting him with experiments and laboratory work. Despite their close relationship, they had no children.

Unlike many of his contemporaries, Maxwell maintained a deep connection to his Scottish heritage, often retreating to his Glenlair estate, where he continued his research and personal experiments. He was known for his humility, kindness, and sense of humor, earning the admiration of his students and colleagues.

Although deeply religious, Maxwell saw no conflict between science and faith. He believed that scientific discoveries were a means of understanding the divine order of nature.

## Death

In 1879, at the age of 48, Maxwell was diagnosed with abdominal cancer, the same illness that had taken his mother's life. Despite his deteriorating health, he continued working on scientific problems until his final days.

Maxwell passed away on November 5, 1879, at his family estate in Glenlair. His death was a great loss to the scientific community, but his work endured, influencing generations of physicists and engineers.

## Character

Maxwell was known for his gentle and generous nature. Unlike many other scientific figures of his time, he was not driven by personal ambition or the pursuit of fame. Instead, he was genuinely fascinated by the mysteries of nature and dedicated his life to understanding them.

His humility and collaborative spirit made him a beloved mentor to his students, and he was highly respected among his peers. Maxwell's ability to combine rigorous mathematics with deep physical intuition set him apart as one of the greatest theoretical physicists of all time.

## Influence on Humanity

Maxwell's influence on science and technology is profound and enduring. His contributions include:

**1. Electromagnetic Theory** – His equations unified electricity, magnetism, and optics, forming the foundation for all modern electrical and communication technologies.

**2. Wireless Communication** – His predictions of electromagnetic waves led to the development of radio, television, radar, and satellite communications.

**3. Color Photography** – His work on color vision paved the way for modern imaging and display technologies.

**4. Statistical Mechanics** – His contributions to thermodynamics influenced later research in statistical physics and quantum mechanics.

**5. Foundation for Einstein's Relativity** – Einstein cited Maxwell's equations as a key inspiration for his theory of relativity, transforming our understanding of space and time.

Today, Maxwell's legacy lives on in every technological advancement that relies on electromagnetism, from smartphones to space exploration. His genius continues to inspire scientists and engineers, making him one of the most significant figures in the history of science.

In conclusion, James Clerk Maxwell's work fundamentally reshaped physics and paved the way for the modern technological world. His groundbreaking discoveries in electromagnetism and thermodynamics remain crucial to scientific progress, ensuring his place among history's greatest scientific minds.

# Nikolaus August Otto
The Inventor of the Internal Combustion Engine

Nikolaus August Otto was a German engineer and inventor best known for developing the four-stroke internal combustion engine, commonly referred to as the "Otto cycle engine." His work revolutionized transportation and industry, paving the way for the development of automobiles, motorcycles, and countless other mechanical advancements. Otto's invention fundamentally changed human mobility and mechanization, making him one of the most important figures in engineering history.

## Origin

Nikolaus August Otto was born on June 10, 1832, in Holzhausen an der Haide, a small village in the Duchy of Nassau, which is now part of modern-day Germany. His father, Philipp Wilhelm Otto, was a farmer and postmaster, while his mother, Maria Katharina Otto, managed the household. Despite coming from a modest background, Otto demonstrated early intelligence and curiosity about mechanical devices, an interest that would later define his career.

During his childhood, Germany was undergoing rapid industrialization, and new mechanical innovations were beginning to transform manufacturing and transportation. Though Otto's upbringing was not particularly wealthy, the technological advancements of the era played a role in inspiring his future work.

## Childhood and Youth

Otto's early education took place in a local school, where he showed promise in mathematics and science. However, unlike many inventors of his time who pursued formal engineering education, Otto took a more unconventional route. Instead of attending a technical university, he apprenticed in various trades and sought hands-on experience in mechanical work.

At the age of 16, Otto left school and worked as a clerk in grocery stores and later in commercial trade. His work took him to Frankfurt and

Cologne, where he was exposed to industrial progress and emerging technologies. While working as a traveling salesman, he encountered early gas-powered engines, which inspired his desire to improve and refine combustion engines for practical use.

## Adulthood

Otto's life changed in the early 1860s when he began experimenting with gas-powered engines. At the time, most mechanical engines were steam-driven, which were large, inefficient, and required significant fuel and maintenance. Otto sought to develop a smaller, more efficient alternative.

In 1864, Otto and his business partner Eugen Langen founded the first factory dedicated to producing internal combustion engines – the "N.A. Otto & Cie" company in Cologne. Their first major success was the atmospheric gas engine, which, though an improvement over steam engines, was still not efficient enough for widespread adoption.

By 1876, Otto achieved his greatest breakthrough – the development of the four-stroke internal combustion engine, which became known as the Otto cycle engine. This engine operated on four distinct strokes: intake, compression, power, and exhaust, making it far more efficient than any previous combustion engine.

## Recognition and Expansion

Otto's invention quickly gained recognition. His four-stroke engine was displayed at exhibitions and gained significant interest from industrialists and engineers worldwide. The engine was soon adopted for various industrial applications, including powering vehicles, machines, and boats.

Otto's company, later renamed Gasmotorenfabrik Deutz, grew rapidly and attracted skilled engineers, including Gottlieb Daimler and Wilhelm Maybach, who later played pivotal roles in the development of the automobile industry.

In 1877, Otto was granted a German patent for his four-stroke engine, but legal challenges arose when it was discovered that similar ideas had been conceptualized before. Despite losing part of his patent rights,

Otto's design became the standard for internal combustion engines, proving his lasting impact on engineering and transportation.

## Private Life

Otto married Anna Gossi in 1861, and together they had several children. He was a devoted family man, balancing his work and personal life despite the demands of his growing company. Otto's family supported his endeavors, and his later years were spent ensuring his children would carry on his work and legacy. Despite being deeply immersed in his technical pursuits, Otto was known for his humility and dedication to his craft rather than personal fame. He was not a businessman in the traditional sense but rather a passionate inventor who aimed to improve human mobility and industry.

## Death

Nikolaus August Otto passed away on January 26, 1891, at the age of 58 in Cologne, Germany. Although he did not live to see the full impact of his invention, his work laid the groundwork for the automotive revolution of the 20th century. Otto was buried in Cologne, where his contributions to engineering and technology continue to be honored. His engines remained the gold standard for combustion technology for decades, and today's modern engines still follow the fundamental principles he established.

## Character

Otto was a methodical and persistent inventor. Despite lacking formal engineering training, he possessed an innate ability to solve complex mechanical problems through experimentation and observation. His commitment to developing a practical internal combustion engine showed his visionary mindset, as he foresaw a future where steam engines would be replaced by more efficient, smaller power sources. Unlike some of his contemporaries, Otto was not driven by financial success or personal recognition. He was content to work behind the scenes, perfecting his invention while allowing his business partners and engineers to handle commercialization. His humble and dedicated nature made him well-respected among colleagues and industrialists alike.

## Influence on Humanity

Otto's contributions to engineering and transportation cannot be overstated. His invention of the four-stroke internal combustion engine transformed the world in multiple ways:

**1. Automobile Industry** – The Otto cycle engine became the foundation for modern car engines, enabling the rise of mass-produced automobiles by companies such as Daimler, Benz, and Ford.

**2. Industrial Applications** – Otto's engine design was used in factories, ships, and agricultural machinery, improving productivity and efficiency.

**3. Transportation Revolution** – His invention paved the way for motorcycles, trucks, airplanes, and other vehicles powered by internal combustion engines.

**4. Energy Efficiency** – His four-stroke cycle remains the basis for modern gasoline and diesel engines, improving energy efficiency and reducing fuel consumption.

**5. Technological Progress** – Otto's work inspired generations of engineers, leading to further advancements in engine design, aerodynamics, and alternative fuel technologies.

Even in the 21st century, Otto's invention continues to power millions of vehicles and machines worldwide. His legacy as the pioneer of the internal combustion engine remains a testament to human ingenuity and the power of innovation.

---

Nikolaus August Otto's impact on modern civilization is undeniable. His invention of the four-stroke internal combustion engine transformed transportation, industry, and mechanical engineering. Though he faced challenges and legal disputes during his lifetime, his work ultimately became the foundation for the automotive industry and countless technological advancements. Otto's dedication to creating a more efficient engine changed the course of history, allowing humanity to move faster and farther than ever before. Today, every combustion-powered vehicle owes its existence to his revolutionary design, solidifying his place as one of the greatest inventors of all time.

# Dmitry Mendeleev
The Architect of the Periodic Table

Dmitry Mendeleev was a Russian chemist and inventor best known for developing the Periodic Table of Elements. His work in organizing chemical elements according to their properties laid the foundation for modern chemistry and revolutionized scientific understanding of atomic structure. Beyond chemistry, Mendeleev made significant contributions to physics, meteorology, and industry, becoming one of the most influential scientists of the 19th century.

## Origin

Dmitry Ivanovich Mendeleev was born on February 8, 1834, in Tobolsk, a town in Siberia, Russia. He was the youngest of 17 children born to Ivan Pavlovich Mendeleev, a school principal, and Maria Dmitrievna Kornilieva. His family had a strong academic background, with his father working in education and his mother managing the household and their glass factory business.

Mendeleev's early years were marked by hardships. His father lost his sight when Dmitry was a child, leaving his mother to support the large family. Despite these challenges, his mother was determined to provide him with a good education, recognizing his exceptional intelligence and curiosity.

## Childhood and Youth

Mendeleev's mother played a crucial role in shaping his early education. After his father's death, she took him on a long journey to Moscow in search of better educational opportunities. However, he was denied admission to Moscow University due to his Siberian origins. Undeterred, his mother took him to Saint Petersburg, where he was accepted into the Main Pedagogical Institute in 1850.

At the institute, Mendeleev excelled in science, particularly chemistry and physics. However, his studies were interrupted by health problems, and he was diagnosed with tuberculosis. Doctors predicted he would not survive, but he recovered and completed his degree in 1855. His resilience and determination to continue his education would later define his career.

After graduating, Mendeleev worked as a teacher and researcher. He pursued further studies in Germany, where he was influenced by leading European chemists. This exposure to advanced scientific thought shaped his ideas and inspired his groundbreaking contributions to chemistry.

## Adulthood

Mendeleev returned to Russia in the early 1860s and became a professor of chemistry at the Saint Petersburg University. During this time, he focused on understanding the relationships between chemical elements. Chemists had already identified many elements, but there was no systematic way to organize them.

In 1869, Mendeleev published his first version of the Periodic Table, arranging elements by atomic weight and grouping them based on similar properties. What set his table apart was his ability to predict the existence and properties of undiscovered elements. He left gaps in the table where he believed new elements would be found, including gallium, scandium, and germanium, all of which were later discovered and matched his predictions.

Mendeleev's Periodic Law stated that the properties of elements are periodic functions of their atomic weights. This revolutionary insight provided a framework for understanding chemical behavior and paved the way for the modern periodic system used in chemistry today.

Beyond the Periodic Table, Mendeleev made significant contributions to:

- **Thermodynamics**: He studied the expansion of gases and worked on developing equations that described their behavior.
- **Petroleum Industry**: He played a role in the early Russian oil industry, helping to improve refining methods.
- **Education and Public Policy**: He advocated for scientific progress in Russia and promoted the use of the metric system.
- **Meteorology and Physics**: Mendeleev conducted research on weather patterns and the behavior of liquids and gases.

His influence extended far beyond chemistry, as he actively worked to modernize Russian industry and education.

## Private Life

Mendeleev's personal life was marked by both successes and controversies. He married Feozva Nikitichna Leshcheva in 1862, but the marriage was unhappy. They had two children before separating. Mendeleev then fell in love with Anna Ivanovna Popova, a much younger woman, and married her in 1882, despite Russia's strict laws on divorce. This second marriage caused scandal but was a happy and supportive union that lasted until his death. Mendeleev was known for his eccentric personality and strong opinions. He was deeply passionate about science and education but often clashed with authorities and colleagues. His work ethic was intense, and he would spend long hours in his laboratory, sometimes to the detriment of his health and relationships.

## Death

Dmitry Mendeleev died on February 2, 1907, at the age of 72 due to pneumonia. His contributions to science were widely recognized by the time of his death, and he had received numerous honors from scientific institutions around the world. His funeral was attended by students, scientists, and admirers who recognized his immense impact on the field of chemistry. Though he did not live to see all the elements he predicted discovered, his work remained relevant and continued to shape scientific research for decades.

## Character

Mendeleev was a driven and innovative thinker who refused to accept conventional scientific wisdom without questioning it. His ability to see patterns and connections where others saw only chaos was one of his greatest strengths. Despite his intellectual brilliance, he was often at odds with academic institutions and bureaucratic systems. He had a rebellious streak, challenging outdated traditions in education and scientific research. However, he was also deeply committed to teaching and mentoring young scientists, believing that education was key to national progress.

Mendeleev's resilience, determination, and curiosity defined his approach to science and life. He was a perfectionist who demanded high standards from himself and others, and his work ethic ensured that his discoveries stood the test of time.

## Influence on Humanity

Mendeleev's impact on the world is immense. His Periodic Table became the foundation for:

**1. Modern Chemistry** – The periodic table remains a fundamental tool in understanding chemical elements and their interactions.

**2. Scientific Discovery** – His predictions of undiscovered elements validated the power of scientific reasoning and encouraged further research.

**3. Education** – His work is taught in schools and universities worldwide, helping students understand the principles of chemistry.

**4. Industrial Development** – His contributions to petroleum refining and industrial chemistry influenced global technological advancements.

**5. Medicine and Technology** – Understanding chemical elements and their properties has led to advancements in medicine, materials science, and energy production.

Mendeleev's legacy continues to inspire scientists, educators, and innovators. His ability to see order in complexity and his commitment to scientific exploration make him one of the greatest minds in history.

---

Dmitry Mendeleev's genius lay in his ability to recognize patterns and organize knowledge in a way that advanced human understanding. His Periodic Table remains one of the most important scientific achievements, shaping the course of chemistry, physics, and industry. Though he faced challenges in his personal and professional life, his contributions to science have stood the test of time. Today, every chemist, student, and researcher working with elements owes a debt to Mendeleev's groundbreaking insights. His work embodies the power of scientific discovery and continues to guide humanity in its pursuit of knowledge and progress.

# Wilhelm Conrad Röntgen
The Discoverer of X-Rays

Wilhelm Conrad Röntgen was a German physicist who made one of the most groundbreaking discoveries in medical and scientific history – the discovery of X-rays. His work revolutionized the field of diagnostic medicine, allowing doctors to see inside the human body without invasive surgery. This remarkable achievement earned him the first-ever Nobel Prize in Physics in 1901. Despite his profound impact on science and medicine, Röntgen remained a humble and dedicated researcher. His legacy continues to influence the fields of physics, radiology, and medical imaging.

## Origin

Wilhelm Conrad Röntgen was born on March 27, 1845, in Lennep, a town in the Kingdom of Prussia (now part of Remscheid, Germany). He was the only child of Friedrich Conrad Röntgen, a textile merchant, and Charlotte Constanze Frowein, who came from a well-to-do merchant family. His family background provided him with a stable upbringing, though they were not aristocrats or members of the scientific elite.

When Röntgen was three years old, his family moved to Apeldoorn in the Netherlands, where he spent most of his childhood. His early exposure to both German and Dutch cultures would later influence his academic and professional life.

## Childhood and Youth

Röntgen's early education took place at the Institute of Martinus Herman van Doorn, a technical school in Apeldoorn. He showed a keen interest in mechanics and natural sciences but was not considered an exceptional student. In 1862, he enrolled at Utrecht Technical School, intending to pursue higher education.

However, his academic journey faced a significant setback. In 1865, he was expelled from the school after being falsely accused of drawing a caricature of one of his professors. This unfortunate incident prevented him from obtaining a formal high school diploma. Despite this obstacle, Röntgen was determined to continue his education.

In 1865, he enrolled at the Polytechnic School in Zurich (now ETH Zurich) without a high school diploma, gaining admission based on his exceptional skills and aptitude for technical subjects. He studied mechanical engineering under some of the finest scientists of the time, including August Kundt, a physicist who became his mentor. Röntgen graduated with a degree in mechanical engineering in 1868 and completed his doctoral dissertation in physics in 1869.

## Adulthood

After earning his doctorate, Röntgen worked as an assistant to August Kundt, first in Würzburg and later in Strasbourg. His early research focused on the properties of gases, thermodynamics, and the behavior of crystals. These studies laid the foundation for his later experiments in electromagnetism and radiation.

In 1874, Röntgen became a lecturer at the University of Strasbourg. Over the next two decades, he held professorships at several prestigious institutions, including the University of Giessen and the University of Würzburg. His work in these institutions led to numerous discoveries, but his most famous breakthrough came in 1895 at Würzburg.

On November 8, 1895, while experimenting with cathode rays in a darkened laboratory, Röntgen noticed an unknown type of radiation penetrating solid objects and creating images on a fluorescent screen. He referred to this mysterious radiation as "X-rays" due to their unknown nature.

Over the next few weeks, he conducted extensive experiments to understand the properties of X-rays. He famously took the first X-ray image of his wife's hand, showing her bones and wedding ring. This image astonished the scientific community and the general public, as it was the first time the internal structure of a living organism could be seen without surgery.

Röntgen published his findings in a paper titled "On a New Kind of Rays" in December 1895. His discovery was rapidly adopted by physicians and scientists worldwide, leading to the development of diagnostic radiology. The impact of his work was immediate, as X-rays became an essential tool in medical diagnosis and treatment.

## Private Life

In 1872, Röntgen married Bertha Ludwig, the daughter of a university professor. The couple did not have any biological children but adopted Bertha's niece, Josephine Bertha Ludwig. Their marriage was strong and supportive, with Bertha playing a crucial role in Röntgen's personal and professional life. Despite his fame, Röntgen was known for his modesty and avoidance of public attention. He refused to patent his X-ray discovery, believing that scientific advancements should benefit all of humanity rather than serve as a means for personal profit. He was deeply committed to his work, often spending long hours in the laboratory, yet he remained a kind and approachable individual. His personal life was largely private, and he avoided the limelight, preferring to focus on research rather than personal recognition.

## Death

In 1900, Röntgen was appointed professor of experimental physics at the University of Munich. He continued his research but eventually retired in 1920 due to declining health. In 1923, at the age of 77, Röntgen was diagnosed with colorectal cancer. He passed away on February 10, 1923, in Munich, Germany. In keeping with his modest character, he left most of his estate to scientific research and lived his final years with humility. Röntgen's contributions were widely celebrated during his lifetime, and he was awarded numerous honors, including the first Nobel Prize in Physics in 1901. However, he remained true to his belief that scientific discoveries should serve humanity rather than personal gain.

## Character

Röntgen was known for his humility, integrity, and dedication to science. Despite achieving worldwide fame, he remained reserved and avoided public recognition. He declined to patent his discovery, emphasizing that science should benefit humanity as a whole. He was a meticulous and patient researcher, often repeating experiments to ensure accuracy. His attention to detail and rigorous scientific methodology set him apart as one of the great experimental physicists of his time. Though he was not an outspoken personality, his work spoke volumes. His commitment to research, ethics, and the pursuit of knowledge made him a revered figure in the scientific community.

## Influence on Humanity

Röntgen's discovery of X-rays had an unprecedented impact on science, medicine, and technology. His contributions include:

**1. Medical Advancements** – X-rays revolutionized medical diagnostics, allowing doctors to detect fractures, tumors, and internal injuries without invasive procedures.

**2. Advances in Physics** – His work paved the way for further studies in electromagnetism and radiation, influencing later discoveries such as radioactivity and quantum mechanics.

**3. Technological Innovations** – X-ray technology expanded beyond medicine, finding applications in security, engineering, and materials analysis.

**4. Inspiration for Future Scientists** – His discovery inspired generations of physicists and engineers to explore the mysteries of radiation and imaging technology.

**5. Foundation for Modern Imaging** – The principles of X-ray imaging remain fundamental to modern medical scans, including CT scans and MRIs.

Röntgen's legacy endures in every hospital, laboratory, and scientific institution that relies on X-ray technology. His discovery continues to save lives and enhance our understanding of the physical world.

---

Wilhelm Conrad Röntgen's discovery of X-rays transformed medicine, physics, and modern technology. His dedication to scientific inquiry and his refusal to seek personal gain exemplify the highest ideals of research and innovation. Today, his contributions remain indispensable in medical diagnostics and scientific exploration. His legacy is a testament to the power of curiosity, perseverance, and the pursuit of knowledge for the betterment of humanity.

# Thomas Alva Edison

Inventor of the light bulb and innovator

Thomas Alva Edison was one of the most influential inventors and businessmen in history. With over 1,000 patents to his name, he played a crucial role in shaping modern technology, revolutionizing industries such as electricity, sound recording, and motion pictures. His work laid the foundation for some of the most critical innovations that define the modern era, including the electric light bulb, the phonograph, and the motion picture camera. Despite facing numerous challenges, his relentless pursuit of innovation and commercial success made him a defining figure in the industrial age.

## Origin

Thomas Alva Edison was born on February 11, 1847, in Milan, Ohio, USA. He was the youngest of seven children born to Samuel Ogden Edison Jr. and Nancy Matthews Elliott. His father was a political activist and businessman, while his mother was a schoolteacher. The Edison family moved to Port Huron, Michigan, when Thomas was seven years old, seeking better economic opportunities.

Growing up in the mid-19th century, Edison was exposed to an era of rapid industrial expansion and scientific discovery. His early environment played a significant role in shaping his inventive spirit. Despite limited formal education, he developed a keen interest in science and mechanics, laying the groundwork for his future innovations.

## Childhood and Youth

Edison's early years were marked by curiosity and self-driven learning. Due to his hyperactivity and difficulty with traditional schooling, his mother decided to educate him at home. She nurtured his interest in reading and encouraged him to explore scientific concepts independently.

By the age of 12, Edison had developed an entrepreneurial spirit. He sold newspapers, snacks, and candy on trains, using the money he earned to buy chemicals and scientific equipment for his experiments. He even set up a small laboratory in a train baggage car, where he conducted chemical experiments while traveling.

A pivotal moment in his youth was his work as a telegraph operator during the Civil War. He became fascinated with electrical communication, a field that would later shape his inventions. Working in telegraph offices across the country, he learned about electrical circuits and developed his problem-solving skills, which laid the foundation for his future success.

## Adulthood

Edison's career as an inventor began in the late 1860s when he moved to Boston and later to New York City. He secured his first patent in 1869 for an electric vote recorder, but it failed commercially. However, his breakthrough came in 1877 when he invented the phonograph, a device that could record and reproduce sound. This invention astonished the world and cemented his reputation as a leading innovator.

In 1879, he introduced the first practical incandescent light bulb, a development that changed the course of human civilization by making electric lighting widely accessible. Unlike previous designs, Edison's bulb was long-lasting and commercially viable, leading to the creation of Edison Electric Light Company (which later became General Electric, one of the world's largest corporations).

Edison continued his work on electrical systems, but he also ventured into motion pictures. In the 1890s, he developed the kinetoscope, an early motion picture device, leading to the birth of the film industry. His work on moving images laid the foundation for modern cinema, influencing entertainment for generations to come.

His laboratory in Menlo Park, New Jersey, became the world's first research and development facility, where teams of scientists and engineers worked collaboratively to develop new technologies. This industrial research model remains a standard practice in technological development today.

Edison was not only an inventor but also a shrewd businessman. He founded multiple companies, including Edison General Electric, which played a crucial role in bringing electricity to homes and businesses.

However, he faced fierce competition from Nikola Tesla and George Westinghouse, particularly in the battle over direct current (DC) vs. alternating current (AC) electrical systems.

Though Tesla's AC system eventually proved more efficient for long-distance transmission, Edison's work was instrumental in launching the electrical age. He also contributed to the improvement of batteries, cement manufacturing, and early sound recording technologies.

## Private Life

Edison married twice and had six children. His first wife, Mary Stilwell, died in 1884, leaving him with three children. In 1886, he married Mina Miller, with whom he had three more children. Despite his demanding career, Edison was a devoted family man who enjoyed spending time at home.

However, his work often took precedence over his personal life. He was known for his tireless work ethic, often sleeping only a few hours a night and spending most of his time in his laboratory. His dedication to innovation sometimes strained his relationships, but he remained committed to his mission of advancing technology.

## Death

Thomas Edison passed away on October 18, 1931, at the age of 84 in West Orange, New Jersey. His death marked the end of an era of prolific innovation. In honor of his contributions, many cities dimmed their lights for a moment of silence.

Edison left behind an extraordinary legacy, with thousands of inventions and patents that continue to shape modern life. His impact on science, technology, and industry remains unparalleled.

## Character

Edison was known for his relentless determination, creativity, and business acumen. He often attributed his success to hard work rather than genius, famously stating, "Genius is one percent inspiration and ninety-nine percent perspiration."

His perseverance and ability to learn from failure set him apart. He conducted thousands of experiments before achieving success with the light bulb, demonstrating an unwavering commitment to problem-solving. Despite facing criticism and rivalries, he remained focused on his goals. Though some of his business practices were controversial – such as his aggressive approach to patent disputes and his rivalry with Tesla – his contributions to science and industry were undeniably transformative.

## Influence on Humanity

Edison's impact on the world is immeasurable. His contributions include:

**1. Electric Lighting** – His development of the light bulb and electrical power distribution made artificial lighting accessible to millions.

**2. Sound Recording** – The phonograph paved the way for the music and recording industries.

**3. Motion Pictures** – His innovations in film technology helped establish the modern entertainment industry.

**4. Industrial Research and Development** – His Menlo Park laboratory set a precedent for corporate research and technological advancement.

**5. Entrepreneurship and Innovation** – His ability to commercialize inventions shaped the way modern businesses approach technological innovation.

Edison's work fundamentally transformed daily life, enabling advancements in communication, entertainment, and industrialization. His influence persists in modern science, engineering, and business practices.

Thomas Alva Edison was a visionary whose relentless pursuit of innovation reshaped the modern world. His groundbreaking work in electricity, sound recording, and motion pictures continues to impact technology and daily life. While he was not without flaws, his persistence, creativity, and entrepreneurial spirit made him one of the greatest inventors of all time. His legacy endures in every illuminated street, recorded song, and film reel, ensuring that his contributions to humanity will never be forgotten.

# Alexander Graham Bell
Inventor of the Telephone

Alexander Graham Bell was a Scottish-born inventor, scientist, and educator best known for inventing the telephone. His contributions to communication technology revolutionized the way people interact across distances. Bell's interests extended beyond telecommunications; he conducted extensive research in aerodynamics, sound technology, and medical science. As a lifelong advocate for the deaf, his work had a profound social impact, blending scientific curiosity with humanitarian efforts.

## Origin

Born on March 3, 1847, in Edinburgh, Scotland, Alexander Graham Bell was the second of three sons of Alexander Melville Bell and Eliza Grace Symonds Bell. His father was a renowned speech therapist, specializing in techniques to help deaf individuals communicate, and his grandfather had been an elocutionist. This familial background deeply influenced Bell's lifelong passion for sound and communication.

Scotland in the mid-19th century was a hub of intellectual and scientific advancements, which provided Bell with a stimulating environment for learning. His exposure to his father's work on phonetics and elocution played a crucial role in shaping his interests and future career.

## Childhood and Youth

As a child, Bell showed an early fascination with sound and mechanics. He was naturally curious, constantly experimenting and inventing simple devices. One of his earliest inventions, created at the age of 12, was a device to remove husks from wheat, which demonstrated his ingenuity.

His formal education began at the Royal High School in Edinburgh, where he was an average student, showing greater enthusiasm for science and the arts than traditional subjects. In 1863, at the age of 16, he attended the University of Edinburgh, but his studies were interrupted by family responsibilities and frequent relocations.

Tragedy struck when both of his brothers died from tuberculosis, prompting his family to move to Canada in 1870 in search of a healthier environment. The move marked a turning point in Bell's life, providing him with new opportunities to explore his interests in acoustics and communication technology.

## Adulthood

After settling in Canada, Bell moved to the United States in 1871 and began working as a teacher for the deaf. He joined the Boston School for the Deaf, where he developed new methods of teaching speech using his father's phonetic techniques. His work with the deaf community became a lifelong commitment and significantly influenced his scientific explorations.

While teaching, Bell continued his research in sound transmission. His studies led him to experiment with converting sound waves into electrical signals, a concept that eventually led to the invention of the telephone.

Bell's groundbreaking work in sound transmission culminated in his collaboration with Thomas Watson, a skilled machinist. Together, they worked tirelessly to develop a device that could transmit voice electronically. On March 10, 1876, Bell made history by speaking the first words over a telephone: "Mr. Watson, come here, I want to see you." This groundbreaking achievement forever changed the course of communication.

Bell's telephone patent, awarded on March 7, 1876, was one of the most valuable patents in history. His invention rapidly gained commercial success, leading to the establishment of the Bell Telephone Company in 1877. The telephone revolutionized global communication, shrinking distances and enabling instant conversation across vast spaces.

Bell did not rest on the success of the telephone. He pursued numerous other scientific ventures, including:

- **The Photophone** (1880): A device that transmitted sound using light waves, an early precursor to fiber-optic communication.
- **Aerodynamics and Aviation**: Bell conducted extensive experiments in aerodynamics and contributed to early aircraft designs.

- **Medical Technology**: He developed an early version of the metal detector to locate bullets inside the human body, notably used in an attempt to save President James Garfield after he was shot.

Despite his numerous innovations, Bell remained deeply engaged in education and advocacy for the deaf. He continued to work on speech training techniques, ensuring that his research had a meaningful social impact.

## Private Life

In 1877, Bell married Mabel Gardiner Hubbard, a former student who had lost her hearing as a child. Their marriage was filled with mutual respect and support, and Mabel played a crucial role in managing Bell's business and financial affairs. They had four children, though two died in infancy.

The couple split their time between Washington, D.C., and their beloved estate in Baddeck, Nova Scotia, where Bell conducted many of his later experiments. His home in Canada became a hub for scientific exploration, as he collaborated with engineers, inventors, and researchers on various projects.

Despite his professional commitments, Bell was a devoted family man. He took great joy in spending time with his children and grandchildren, often involving them in his experiments and teaching them about science.

## Death

Alexander Graham Bell passed away on August 2, 1922, at the age of 75, due to complications from diabetes. His death marked the loss of one of the greatest inventors of the modern age.

As a tribute to his contributions, the entire telephone network in the United States and Canada was silenced for one minute on the day of his funeral. It was a fitting homage to the man whose invention had revolutionized communication.

Bell was buried at his estate in Nova Scotia, overlooking the Bras d'Or Lake, a place he deeply cherished. His legacy continued through the institutions he founded, including the Volta Bureau, which focused on speech and hearing research.

## Character

Bell was known for his relentless curiosity and deep compassion. Unlike many inventors driven purely by financial success, Bell was motivated by a desire to improve human lives. His work with the deaf demonstrated his commitment to education and social progress, while his scientific pursuits showcased his boundless enthusiasm for discovery.

He was also a strong advocate for ethical scientific advancement. He refused to develop technologies that could be used for warfare, emphasizing the importance of science in promoting peace and progress.

Bell's humility and kindness made him beloved by those around him. Despite his achievements, he remained approachable and willing to mentor young scientists and inventors.

## Influence on Humanity

Bell's contributions to humanity extend far beyond the invention of the telephone. His work shaped multiple fields, including:

**1. Revolutionizing Communication** – The telephone laid the foundation for modern telecommunications, leading to mobile phones, the internet, and global connectivity.

**2. Advancements in Speech and Hearing Science** – His research and advocacy improved education and communication for the deaf community.

**3. Pioneering Wireless Technology** – His photophone anticipated future developments in fiber optics and wireless communication.

**4. Contributions to Aerodynamics and Aviation** – His experiments influenced early aircraft designs, aiding future aviation pioneers.

**5. Medical and Technological Innovations** – His development of early medical devices demonstrated his commitment to using science for humanitarian purposes.

Bell's legacy endures in every telephone call, video chat, and fiber-optic transmission. His dedication to scientific exploration and social progress ensured that his impact would be felt for generations.

---

Alexander Graham Bell was more than just the inventor of the telephone – he was a visionary who transformed communication, science, and education. His relentless curiosity and deep empathy led to groundbreaking innovations that continue to shape the modern world. Through his contributions to telecommunications, speech science, and technology, Bell left an indelible mark on humanity, proving that invention, when guided by compassion, has the power to change the world forever.

# Vincent van Gogh
Dutch painter of Post-Impressionism

Vincent van Gogh was a Dutch painter whose work became one of the most significant influences in modern art. Despite battling poverty, mental illness, and personal struggles, he created some of the most expressive and evocative paintings in history. His works, including "Starry Night", "Sunflowers", and "The Bedroom", are celebrated for their bold colors, emotional depth, and unique brushwork. Though he was virtually unknown during his lifetime, Van Gogh's legacy has left an indelible mark on the art world.

## Origin

Vincent Willem van Gogh was born on March 30, 1853, in Groot-Zundert, a small village in the southern Netherlands. He was the eldest of six children in a deeply religious family. His father, Theodorus van Gogh, was a Protestant minister, and his mother, Anna Cornelia Carbentus, came from a family of art dealers and bookbinders.

Vincent was named after his grandfather and a stillborn older brother, who had died exactly a year before his birth. This fact weighed heavily on his psyche, as he may have felt like a replacement child. His family's strong religious background and artistic connections played a crucial role in shaping his early beliefs and interests.

## Childhood and Youth

As a child, Van Gogh was introspective and often withdrawn. He attended several schools but did not excel academically. He showed an early passion for nature and drawing, sketching landscapes and local peasants with great sensitivity.

At 16, he left school to work at Goupil & Cie, an art dealership in The Hague, where his uncle was a partner. His job took him to London and Paris, exposing him to the world of fine art. However, he became disillusioned with the commercial side of the art industry and left in 1876.

Seeking meaning in life, Van Gogh turned to religion and worked as a teacher and preacher in England and Belgium. He attempted to become a clergyman but was rejected due to his unconventional approach. Disheartened, he devoted himself entirely to art by 1880, deciding to become an artist at the age of 27.

## Adulthood

In the early 1880s, Van Gogh moved to Belgium and the Netherlands, studying art independently. He experimented with different techniques and developed a deep empathy for working-class people, often painting miners, weavers, and peasants. One of his earliest major works, "The Potato Eaters" (1885), reflected his commitment to realism and social themes.

In 1886, he moved to Paris to live with his younger brother, Theo van Gogh, an art dealer who financially supported him. In Paris, Vincent encountered Impressionists and Post-Impressionists, such as Claude Monet, Paul Gauguin, and Henri de Toulouse-Lautrec. These influences transformed his style – he adopted brighter colors, bold brushstrokes, and more dynamic compositions.

In 1888, Van Gogh left Paris for Arles in southern France, hoping to create an artist's commune. He was enchanted by the vibrant landscapes and golden sunlight, which inspired some of his most famous paintings, including "Sunflowers" and "The Café Terrace at Night".

During this period, he invited fellow artist Paul Gauguin to stay with him, leading to a turbulent and intense relationship. Their conflicts peaked in December 1888 during a heated argument, after which, according to the prevailing view of historians, Van Gogh severed part of his left ear in a moment of deep despair and psychological turmoil – an incident that later became a powerful symbol of his struggles with mental health.

## Private Life

Van Gogh was deeply emotional and struggled with social relationships. He had intense but often troubled friendships and failed romantic relationships. Despite his letters expressing a longing for companionship, his erratic behavior and mental illness alienated many around him.

His closest bond was with his brother Theo, who provided financial and emotional support. Their correspondence, preserved in hundreds of letters, reveals Vincent's thoughts on art, philosophy, and his personal struggles.

Though he found solace in art, his personal life was fraught with loneliness and hardship. His inability to sell paintings during his lifetime led to financial dependence on Theo, which added to his frustration.

## Death

By mid-1890, Van Gogh was living in Auvers-sur-Oise, under the care of Dr. Paul Gachet. During this time, he produced some of his most extraordinary works, including "Wheatfield with Crows" and "Doctor Gachet".

On July 27, 1890, Van Gogh sustained a gunshot wound to his chest, believed to be self-inflicted. He died two days later, on July 29, at the age of 37, with Theo by his side. His last words were reportedly, "The sadness will last forever."

Theo, devastated by his brother's death, died six months later. Today, they are buried side by side in Auvers-sur-Oise, France.

## Character

Van Gogh was a complex and deeply passionate individual. He was driven by a profound love for nature, humanity, and artistic expression, but he also battled intense self-doubt and mental illness. His letters reveal a sensitive soul, struggling to find meaning in life through art.

He was often misunderstood, dismissed as a madman during his lifetime. However, his relentless dedication to his craft, despite hardships, showcases his resilience and unwavering belief in the transformative power of art.

## Influence on Humanity

Although Van Gogh sold only one painting in his lifetime, his influence on art and culture has been immeasurable. His unique style, characterized by bold colors, dynamic brushwork, and emotional intensity, paved the way for modern art movements such as Expressionism and Fauvism.

**1. Impact on Art** – Van Gogh's work inspired countless artists, including Henri Matisse, Edvard Munch, and German Expressionists.

**2. Cultural Legacy** – Today, his paintings are among the most famous and valuable in the world, housed in major museums such as the Van Gogh Museum in Amsterdam.

**3. Mental Health Awareness** – His life story has shed light on the struggles of mental illness, sparking conversations about the connection between creativity and psychological well-being.

**4. Popular Culture** – His legacy extends beyond art, influencing literature, film, music, and psychology. Movies such as "Loving Vincent" and "At Eternity's Gate" explore his life and impact.

---

Vincent van Gogh's life was one of struggle, passion, and artistic brilliance. Though he did not find success during his lifetime, his visionary approach to painting reshaped the course of art history. His ability to convey raw emotion through color and brushwork has captivated audiences for generations.

His journey – marked by perseverance, mental anguish, and an undying love for beauty – continues to inspire and resonate. Today, he stands as one of the most celebrated and beloved artists, a testament to the enduring power of art and the resilience of the human spirit.

# Sigmund Freud
The Father of Psychoanalysis

Sigmund Freud was an Austrian neurologist and the founder of psychoanalysis, a revolutionary theory and method that transformed the understanding of the human mind. His ideas on the unconscious, dreams, and human behavior have had a profound impact on psychology, psychiatry, and even literature, philosophy, and popular culture. Freud's theories, including the Oedipus complex, defense mechanisms, and the id, ego, and superego, continue to influence psychology today, even as they remain subjects of debate.

## Origin

Sigmund Freud was born Sigismund Schlomo Freud on May 6, 1856, in the town of Freiberg in Moravia (now Příbor, Czech Republic), which was then part of the Austrian Empire. He was the first of eight children born to Jacob Freud, a wool merchant, and Amalia Nathansohn Freud. His family was Jewish, and though not deeply religious, they were culturally influenced by Jewish intellectual traditions.

Jacob Freud was much older than Amalia – by nearly 20 years – and had children from a previous marriage. Despite financial struggles, Freud's parents ensured he received a strong education, emphasizing intellect and scholarship, which shaped his future aspirations.

## Childhood and Youth

When Freud was four years old, his family moved to Vienna, the intellectual and cultural hub of the Austro-Hungarian Empire. He was an exceptionally bright child and excelled academically, displaying a particular interest in languages, literature, and science. His parents encouraged his education, and he became fluent in several languages, including German, French, Italian, Spanish, and Hebrew.

Freud was deeply fascinated by the works of great thinkers, particularly Shakespeare, Goethe, and Schopenhauer, which shaped his philosophical outlook. He attended the Leopoldstädter Gymnasium, one of Vienna's most prestigious schools, where he was a top student. His intellectual curiosity led him to study medicine at the University of Vienna in 1873 at the age of 17, intending to become a scientist rather than a practicing physician.

## Adulthood

While at the University of Vienna, Freud studied under Ernst Brücke, a leading physiologist, and conducted research on neurophysiology. He became particularly interested in the workings of the brain and nervous system, which led him to study hypnosis and hysteria under Jean-Martin Charcot in Paris in 1885.

His exposure to Charcot's work on hysteria and the use of hypnosis profoundly influenced his thinking. Returning to Vienna, Freud collaborated with Josef Breuer, a respected physician, on the treatment of patients suffering from hysteria. Their work led to the famous case of Anna O., a patient whose treatment helped shape the foundation of psychoanalysis. Freud and Breuer published "Studies on Hysteria" in 1895, introducing the idea that repressed memories could manifest as physical symptoms.

By the late 1890s, Freud began formulating his own theories about the mind. In 1900, he published his groundbreaking work, "The Interpretation of Dreams", in which he introduced the idea that dreams were the "royal road to the unconscious." He proposed that repressed desires, particularly sexual ones, played a crucial role in human behavior.

Freud's key contributions included:

- **The Structural Model of the Mind** – He divided the psyche into three parts: the id (instincts), the ego (rational self), and the superego (moral conscience).
- **Psychosexual Stages of Development** – He theorized that childhood experiences shape personality through stages: oral, anal, phallic, latency, and genital.
- **The Oedipus Complex** – A controversial theory suggesting that children experience subconscious attraction to the opposite-sex parent.
- **Defense Mechanisms** – Strategies such as repression, denial, and projection that protect the ego from anxiety.

As Freud's ideas gained attention, he gathered a group of intellectuals, known as the Vienna Psychoanalytic Society, which included Carl Jung and Alfred Adler. However, disagreements over his theories led to major schisms, and both Jung and Adler eventually broke away from Freud's influence.

## Private Life

Freud married Martha Bernays in 1886, and they had six children. His youngest daughter, Anna Freud, became a prominent psychologist in her own right, continuing and expanding upon his theories.

Despite his growing fame, Freud's personal life was marked by struggles. He suffered from intense self-doubt and was known to be a heavy smoker, which later led to severe health problems. However, he remained deeply devoted to his family and maintained strong friendships with many intellectuals of his time, including Albert Einstein and Salvador Dalí.

Freud was also known for his complex relationship with his followers and students. While he valued loyalty, he was often unwilling to accept criticism, leading to tensions with many of his early disciples.

## Death

In 1923, Freud was diagnosed with cancer of the jaw, likely caused by his excessive cigar smoking. Despite undergoing multiple painful surgeries, his condition worsened over the years. When the Nazis occupied Austria in 1938, Freud, who was Jewish, fled to London, where he spent his final years.

By 1939, his health had deteriorated significantly, and he was in constant pain. At his request, his physician Max Schur administered a lethal dose of morphine, effectively ending his suffering. Freud passed away on September 23, 1939, at the age of 83.

## Character

Freud was an intense, driven intellectual with a deep passion for understanding the human mind. He was known for his sharp wit, ambition, and perseverance. However, he was also stubborn and resistant to criticism, often clashing with those who challenged his theories.

He was deeply introspective and had a complex personality – both deeply private and intensely charismatic. His ability to articulate complex psychological processes in a compelling way made him one of the most influential thinkers of his time.

## Influence on Humanity

Freud's legacy extends far beyond psychology. His ideas have influenced literature, philosophy, anthropology, and even film and art. His major contributions include:

**1. Revolutionizing Psychology** – Freud's theories laid the groundwork for modern psychoanalysis and psychotherapy.

**2. Influencing Literature and Art** – Writers like James Joyce and Virginia Woolf used his ideas in their works, while surrealist artists like Salvador Dalí incorporated Freudian imagery.

**3. Shaping Popular Culture** – Concepts like the Freudian slip, repression, and the unconscious mind are now widely recognized in everyday discourse.

**4. Pioneering Talk Therapy** – His methods paved the way for modern psychotherapy, counseling, and mental health treatment.

Though many of Freud's theories have been criticized and revised, his fundamental insights into the unconscious mind remain central to psychology. His work continues to shape how we understand human behavior, making him one of the most influential figures in modern intellectual history.

Sigmund Freud's impact on psychology and human self-understanding is unparalleled. His theories on the unconscious mind, dreams, and childhood development have influenced not only science but also culture, art, and philosophy. Despite controversy and criticism, Freud's ideas remain an essential part of psychological study and debate. His legacy endures as the father of psychoanalysis, a thinker who forever changed how we perceive the complexities of the human mind.

# Nikola Tesla
Visionary of modern electricity

Nikola Tesla was a Serbian-American inventor, electrical engineer, mechanical engineer, and futurist whose contributions to the development of alternating current (AC) electricity changed the world. A brilliant mind with an almost mystical vision of the future, Tesla pioneered wireless energy transmission, radio waves, and numerous electrical innovations that paved the way for modern technology. Despite his genius, he spent much of his life in financial hardship and was overshadowed by his contemporaries like Thomas Edison. Today, he is celebrated as one of the greatest inventors in history, and his work continues to inspire generations.

## Origin

Nikola Tesla was born on July 10, 1856, in the village of Smiljan, in the Austrian Empire (modern-day Croatia). He was of Serbian ethnicity and was the fourth of five children born to Milutin Tesla, an Eastern Orthodox priest, and Georgina Đuka Tesla, who had an extraordinary ability to memorize and recite poetry and religious texts despite lacking formal education.

Tesla's father hoped that he would follow in his footsteps and become a priest, while his mother encouraged his curiosity and mechanical abilities. Tesla's early exposure to intellectual discussions and his mother's inventive nature greatly influenced his later work.

## Childhood and Youth

From an early age, Tesla displayed remarkable intelligence and an almost photographic memory. He had an uncanny ability to visualize machines and conduct experiments in his mind without needing to write or build prototypes first. His fascination with electricity began after witnessing a static electricity phenomenon at a young age.

Tesla attended the Realschule in Karlstadt, where he excelled in physics and mathematics. He later enrolled at the Higher Real Gymnasium in

Rakovac, where he was known for his incredible ability to perform complex calculations without writing them down. His teachers even suspected him of cheating due to his extraordinary mental abilities.

In 1875, Tesla enrolled at the Austrian Polytechnic School in Graz to study engineering. During this time, he became obsessed with perfecting an alternating current (AC) motor, which he believed would be more efficient than the direct current (DC) systems being developed at the time. However, his academic career was cut short when he dropped out due to financial difficulties and conflicts with his professors.

After leaving Graz, Tesla suffered a nervous breakdown and spent time recovering while working as a draftsman and engineer. In 1881, he moved to Budapest, where he worked for the Budapest Telephone Exchange and first conceived the rotating magnetic field principle, which would become the foundation of AC motors.

## Adulthood

In 1884, Tesla immigrated to the United States and began working for Thomas Edison, one of the most powerful figures in electrical engineering. Edison was a proponent of direct current (DC), while Tesla was convinced that alternating current (AC) was the future of electrical power.

Tesla worked tirelessly to improve Edison's inefficient generators, but their partnership ended when Edison refused to pay Tesla a promised bonus of $50,000. Disillusioned, Tesla left Edison's company and struck out on his own.

Tesla partnered with entrepreneur George Westinghouse, who saw the potential of AC electricity. Together, they championed the "War of Currents", a battle between Tesla's AC system and Edison's DC system. AC ultimately proved superior for transmitting electricity over long distances, leading to Tesla's polyphase AC system becoming the industry standard.

In 1893, Tesla and Westinghouse lit up the Chicago World's Fair, demonstrating the power of AC electricity to millions. Two years later, Tesla's AC system was used to power the Niagara Falls hydroelectric plant, marking a major triumph for his ideas.

Tesla's next great vision was wireless energy transmission. He conducted experiments at his famous Colorado Springs laboratory, where he created artificial lightning and investigated wireless power. He also developed early theories on radio waves, which later influenced the invention of radio.

In 1901, Tesla began constructing Wardenclyffe Tower, a massive structure on Long Island designed to transmit wireless energy across the world. However, the project was never completed due to financial difficulties and a lack of support from investors like J.P. Morgan, who withdrew funding when he realized Tesla's invention could provide free electricity, threatening business profits.

## Private Life

Tesla was known for his eccentric behavior and celibacy. He never married and claimed that his devotion to science left no room for personal relationships. He had an obsessive-compulsive personality and strict routines, including eating only boiled foods and sleeping only two hours a night.

Tesla was also known for his love of pigeons, particularly one white pigeon he claimed to love as a person. His unusual habits and eccentric lifestyle made him an enigmatic figure in the public eye.

## Death

Tesla spent his later years living in poverty, surviving on a small pension provided by the Yugoslav government. Despite his numerous contributions to science, he was largely forgotten by the mainstream scientific community. On January 7, 1943, Tesla died alone in a hotel room in New York City at the age of 86. The cause of death was reported as coronary thrombosis. After his death, the FBI seized many of his scientific papers, leading to speculation about the nature of his unpublished work.

## Character

Tesla was an extraordinary individual, characterized by his unparalleled intelligence, visionary thinking, and unwavering dedication to scientific progress. He was deeply idealistic, believing that technology should be used to benefit humanity rather than profit-driven motives. However, he was also socially isolated and prone to obsessive tendencies. His refusal to focus on financial gain left him at a disadvantage compared to business-minded inventors like Edison. Despite his struggles, he remained committed to his principles, working tirelessly to realize his dreams.

## Influence on Humanity

Tesla's contributions to science and technology are immeasurable. His inventions and discoveries continue to shape the modern world in several ways:

1. **Alternating Current (AC)** – The foundation of modern electrical power systems.

2. **Wireless Transmission** – Early theories that paved the way for radio, Wi-Fi, and wireless communication.

3. **Electric Motors** – Used in countless industrial and household applications.

4. **X-ray Technology** – His work contributed to early imaging technology.

5. **Tesla Coil** – A key component in radio technology and high-frequency power transmission.

6. **Renewable Energy Vision** – His ideas about free energy continue to inspire research in sustainable energy.

Tesla's name has since been honored in various ways, including the Tesla electric car company, which embodies his vision of energy-efficient technology.

Nikola Tesla was a brilliant but misunderstood genius who changed the course of history with his groundbreaking inventions. Though he died penniless and underappreciated, his work laid the foundation for modern electricity, communication, and engineering. His vision of free energy and wireless technology remains an inspiration, ensuring his place as one of the greatest inventors of all time.

# Max Planck
Founder of quantum physics

Max Planck was a German theoretical physicist whose groundbreaking work in quantum mechanics revolutionized the field of physics. His development of quantum theory, particularly his discovery of the quantum of action, known as Planck's constant (h), laid the foundation for one of the most important scientific revolutions of the 20th century. His contributions to thermodynamics, radiation theory, and black-body radiation not only won him the Nobel Prize in Physics in 1918 but also paved the way for future discoveries by Albert Einstein, Niels Bohr, and Werner Heisenberg.

## Origin

Max Karl Ernst Ludwig Planck was born on April 23, 1858, in Kiel, Duchy of Holstein, which was then part of the German Confederation. He was the sixth child in a highly intellectual and well-respected family. His father, Johann Julius Wilhelm Planck, was a distinguished law professor, and his mother, Emma Patzig Planck, came from a family with strong academic traditions.

Shortly after his birth, the Planck family moved to Munich, where his father accepted a prestigious position at the University of Munich. Growing up in a household that valued education, discipline, and intellectual rigor, young Max was encouraged to pursue knowledge and scholarship from an early age.

## Childhood and Youth

Planck exhibited a keen intellect and musical talent from an early age. He was an accomplished pianist and showed great promise in both music and science. However, it was his deep fascination with physics and mathematics that eventually shaped his future.

He attended the Maximilians Gymnasium in Munich, where he excelled in mathematics, mechanics, and astronomy. His teachers recognized his exceptional abilities and encouraged him to pursue scientific studies. At the age of 16, he entered the University of Munich in 1874, where he initially studied under Philipp von Jolly, a physicist who was skeptical about the potential for new discoveries in physics. Von Jolly advised Planck that physics was largely a completed field, but Planck was undeterred and continued his studies with enthusiasm.

In 1877, Planck moved to the University of Berlin, where he studied under Hermann von Helmholtz and Gustav Kirchhoff, two of the leading physicists of the time. He earned his doctorate in thermodynamics in 1879, focusing on the Second Law of Thermodynamics, a subject that would later influence his work on black-body radiation.

## Adulthood

After completing his doctoral studies, Planck returned to Munich as a private lecturer, but his academic potential quickly earned him recognition. In 1885, he was appointed professor of theoretical physics at the University of Kiel. In 1889, he succeeded Kirchhoff at the University of Berlin, where he would remain for most of his career.

At the end of the 19th century, physicists were struggling to explain black-body radiation, the way an idealized object absorbs and emits radiation. Classical physics failed to account for the observed energy distribution of emitted light, leading to the so-called ultraviolet catastrophe.

In 1900, Planck made a radical proposal: he introduced the idea that energy is quantized, meaning it is emitted or absorbed in discrete units (quanta) rather than continuously. He formulated the equation:

$$E = h\nu$$

where:

- $E$ is energy,
- $h$ is Planck's constant ($6.626 \times 10^{-34}$ Js), and
- $\nu$ is the frequency of radiation.

This revolutionary idea marked the birth of quantum mechanics and resolved the black-body radiation problem. Though Planck initially viewed his discovery as a mathematical trick, his work laid the foundation for

Einstein's photon theory (1905) and later developments in quantum mechanics by Bohr, Schrödinger, and Heisenberg.

In 1918, Planck was awarded the Nobel Prize in Physics for his contributions to quantum theory, securing his place in scientific history.

## Private Life

Planck married Marie Merck in 1887, and the couple had four children: Karl, Emma, Grete, and Erwin. Tragedy struck in 1909 when Marie died unexpectedly. Devastated but determined to continue his work, Planck remarried in 1911 to Marga von Hösslin, with whom he had another son, Hermann.

His personal life was further marred by tragedy during World War II. His son Erwin Planck, who was involved in the resistance against Adolf Hitler, was executed by the Nazi regime in 1945. The loss of his son deeply affected him in his final years.

## Death

By the end of World War II, Planck was in failing health. His home in Berlin had been destroyed by bombing, and he spent his last years in Göttingen. On October 4, 1947, at the age of 89, Planck passed away. He was laid to rest with high honors, recognized as one of the most important physicists of all time.

## Character

Max Planck was known for his modesty, intellectual honesty, and dedication to science. Unlike many of his contemporaries, he was reserved and introspective, preferring quiet scientific research to public recognition.

He was also a deeply moral and principled man. Despite living through two World Wars, he remained committed to academic integrity and opposed Nazi interference in science. Though he initially tried to protect German scientists, including Jewish colleagues, he ultimately suffered personal losses due to his opposition to the regime.

Planck was also philosophically inclined, often reflecting on the intersection between science and faith. He believed that scientific discovery and religious belief were not contradictory but complementary, a view that shaped his worldview.

## Influence on Humanity

Planck's work transformed modern physics and had profound implications for science and technology:

**1. Foundation of Quantum Mechanics** – His quantum theory led to the development of quantum mechanics, shaping the future of physics.

**2. Influence on Einstein and Modern Physics** – His work paved the way for Einstein's theory of the photoelectric effect, which led to quantum electrodynamics.

**3. Technological Advancements** – Quantum mechanics has led to semiconductors, lasers, and modern computing.

**4. Inspiration for Future Scientists** – His discoveries influenced Bohr, Heisenberg, Schrödinger, and Feynman, among others.

Today, Planck's name lives on in:

- Planck's constant (h), a fundamental physical constant.
- The Max Planck Society, a leading research institution in Germany.
- The Planck space observatory, which studies cosmic background radiation.

---

Max Planck's discovery of quantum mechanics marked one of the most important revolutions in science. Despite facing personal tragedies and political upheavals, he remained devoted to the pursuit of knowledge. His work laid the foundation for modern physics, technology, and cosmology, making him one of the greatest physicists of all time. His legacy continues to shape our understanding of the universe, demonstrating the power of human curiosity and perseverance.

# Henry Ford

Revolutionary of the automotive industry

Henry Ford was an American industrialist, business magnate, and the founder of the Ford Motor Company. His innovative introduction of the assembly line in automobile manufacturing revolutionized industrial production, making cars more affordable and accessible to the masses. Ford's vision of mass production, high wages for workers, and an efficient supply chain had a lasting impact not only on the automotive industry but also on modern industrialization.

## Origin

Henry Ford was born on July 30, 1863, in Greenfield Township, Michigan, USA. He was the eldest of six children in a farming family. His father, William Ford, was an Irish immigrant, while his mother, Mary Litogot Ford, was of Belgian descent. The Ford family lived on a modest farm, and Henry's early years were spent in rural America, surrounded by nature and agricultural work.

Although Ford was born into a farming family, he was fascinated by machines and showed an early interest in mechanics. This passion for innovation and engineering would later shape his career and lead to some of the most important industrial advancements in history.

## Childhood and Youth

From a young age, Henry Ford displayed a keen interest in mechanical devices. Unlike his siblings, he was not particularly drawn to farm work, preferring instead to dismantle and repair machinery. His curiosity led him to build simple machines and explore ways to improve efficiency in everyday tasks.

At the age of 16, Ford left home and moved to Detroit to work as an apprentice machinist. He gained hands-on experience with engines and mechanical systems, working for companies such as the Detroit Dry Dock Company. This period was crucial in shaping his understanding of industrial mechanics and manufacturing.

During his free time, he worked on small mechanical projects, constantly improving his knowledge. His experience in Detroit gave him valuable insights into the inner workings of industrial production and inspired him to create his own automobile in the future.

## Adulthood

In 1888, Ford returned home to work on the family farm while also running a sawmill to support his wife and son. However, his interest in machinery never waned. In 1891, he became an engineer for the Edison Illuminating Company, where he quickly rose to the position of chief engineer.

During this time, Ford experimented with internal combustion engines. In 1896, he built his first gasoline-powered vehicle, the Quadricycle, which was essentially a lightweight automobile with bicycle wheels. The success of this vehicle motivated Ford to pursue automobile manufacturing full-time.

Ford's ambition led him to found the Ford Motor Company in 1903 with the help of investors. His initial models, including the Model A, had limited success, but Ford's breakthrough came in 1908 with the release of the Model T.

The Model T was revolutionary because:

1. It was affordable, making car ownership possible for middle-class Americans.

2. It was durable and easy to maintain.

3. It was mass-produced using assembly line manufacturing.

Ford's assembly line system, introduced in 1913, drastically reduced production costs and time, allowing the Model T's price to drop significantly. By 1927, over 15 million Model Ts had been sold, making it one of the most successful cars in history.

Ford revolutionized labor policies by introducing the $5 workday in 1914, doubling the average worker's wage. This move had several impacts:

- It reduced employee turnover and increased productivity.

- It allowed workers to afford the very cars they were producing.
- It set a new standard for wages in the industrial sector.

Ford also shortened the workweek to 40 hours, pioneering the concept of a modern work-life balance.

By the 1920s, Ford Motor Company was the largest automobile manufacturer in the world. However, competition from General Motors and Chrysler forced Ford to innovate further. The introduction of the Model A in 1927 helped sustain the company's success, but Ford's resistance to external influences, such as labor unions and stock market speculation, created challenges.

During World War II, Ford Motor Company contributed to the war effort by producing military vehicles, including jeeps, tanks, and aircraft engines.

## Private Life

Henry Ford married Clara Bryant in 1888, and they had one son, Edsel Ford. Edsel played a crucial role in the company's development, but his father's strict management style often overshadowed his contributions. Ford was a man of strong beliefs and self-discipline. He followed a simple lifestyle, avoiding alcohol and smoking. His personal philosophy was rooted in hard work, perseverance, and efficiency. However, Ford's legacy is also controversial due to his anti-Semitic views, which he expressed in publications such as "The Dearborn Independent". These views tarnished his reputation and led to widespread criticism.

## Death

As he aged, Ford gradually handed over control of the company to his son, Edsel Ford, and later to his grandson, Henry Ford II. However, the death of Edsel in 1943 deeply affected Ford, and his health began to decline. On April 7, 1947, Henry Ford passed away at the age of 83 in Dearborn, Michigan. His death marked the end of an era, but his contributions to industry and manufacturing continued to shape the world long after his passing. Ford was buried at the Ford Cemetery in Detroit, and his funeral was attended by thousands, including business leaders, workers, and politicians.

## Character

Henry Ford was a complex personality, characterized by extraordinary determination, visionary thinking and a deep belief in the power of innovation. He was a perfectionist who was always looking for better ways of doing things and a pragmatist who understood the reality of industrial production. Ford's charisma and leadership qualities made him an inspirational leader, but his stubbornness and tendency to insulate himself from criticism also led to conflict. His relentless pursuit of efficiency and productivity was both his greatest strength and his greatest weakness.

## Influence on Humanity

Henry Ford's contributions to industry and society remain immeasurable. His assembly line method changed global manufacturing, influencing industries beyond automobiles, such as electronics and aviation.

Key influences:

**1. Mass Production** – His innovations made cars, appliances, and goods affordable worldwide.

**2. Labor Policies** – The 40-hour workweek and higher wages set new standards in employment.

**3. Automobile Industry** – Ford made car ownership accessible, transforming transportation and mobility.

**4. Technological Innovation** – His focus on efficiency paved the way for modern automation and robotics.

**5. Economic Growth** – The auto industry became a pillar of the global economy, creating jobs and infrastructure.

Henry Ford's vision, creativity, and industrial prowess shaped the modern world. Despite controversies, his contributions to manufacturing, labor rights, and transportation remain unparalleled. His legacy lives on in the automobile industry and in the continued evolution of mass production techniques, proving that innovation and efficiency can change the course of history.

# The Wright Brothers

Inventors of the first airplane

The Wright brothers, Orville and Wilbur Wright, were American inventors and aviation pioneers who built and successfully flew the first powered, controlled, and sustained heavier-than-air airplane. Their breakthrough in aeronautics on December 17, 1903, at Kitty Hawk, North Carolina, marked a turning point in human history, making modern air travel possible. Their relentless dedication to innovation, systematic experimentation, and engineering precision laid the foundation for the aviation industry, influencing military, commercial, and recreational flight.

## Origin

Wilbur Wright was born on April 16, 1867, in Millville, Indiana, while his younger brother, Orville Wright, was born on August 19, 1871, in Dayton, Ohio. They were two of seven children born to Milton Wright, a bishop in the Church of the United Brethren in Christ, and Susan Catherine Koerner Wright.

The Wright family valued education, curiosity, and hard work. Their father's career as a traveling clergyman exposed the family to various intellectual discussions, and their mother, a mechanically inclined woman, encouraged their interest in engineering and mechanics. The family moved frequently due to their father's work, but they eventually settled in Dayton, Ohio, where Wilbur and Orville spent most of their childhood.

## Childhood and Youth

The Wright brothers displayed an early passion for mechanical devices and problem-solving. A turning point in their fascination with flight came in 1878 when their father gave them a small rubber-band-powered helicopter toy, based on a design by French aviation pioneer Alphonse Pénaud. The toy inspired their lifelong interest in aeronautics.

Wilbur was an excellent student with plans to attend Yale University, but a sports injury in 1885 altered his trajectory. He spent several years at home, reading extensively and assisting his father with church affairs.

Orville, on the other hand, was more entrepreneurial from a young age. In 1889, he launched a printing business, using a printing press he designed and built himself. Wilbur later joined him, and together they published the West Side News, a local newspaper.

Their foray into business showcased their engineering and innovation skills, which would later be critical to their success in aviation.

## Adulthood

In the early 1890s, the Wright brothers shifted their focus to the bicycle industry, which was booming at the time. In 1892, they opened the Wright Cycle Company in Dayton, designing and manufacturing bicycles. This business provided them with hands-on experience in mechanics, aerodynamics, and material strength, all essential for their later work in aviation.

Inspired by Otto Lilienthal, a German aviation pioneer, the brothers began serious aeronautical research in the late 1890s. Unlike previous experimenters, they approached the problem scientifically and methodically, conducting experiments on lift, control, and propulsion.

Their major innovations included:

- **Wind Tunnel Testing** (1901) – They built a wind tunnel to test over 200 airfoil designs, refining their understanding of aerodynamics.
- **Three-Axis Control System** (1902) – They developed the concept of roll, pitch, and yaw control, essential for stable flight.
- **Powered Flight** (1903) – They designed a lightweight engine with Charlie Taylor, their mechanic, and successfully built their first powered airplane, the Wright Flyer.

On December 17, 1903, near Kitty Hawk, North Carolina, the Wright Flyer made history:

- Orville Wright piloted the first powered flight, which lasted 12 seconds and covered a distance of 120 feet (37 m).
- Wilbur followed, achieving a flight of 59 seconds and covering 852 feet (260 m).

This event marked the birth of modern aviation, proving that powered, controlled, and sustained flight was possible.

Following their success, the Wright brothers focused on improving their aircraft. They conducted flights in Huffman Prairie, Ohio, and demonstrated their planes in France and the U.S. Army, securing contracts for military use.

In 1909, they established the Wright Company, training pilots and selling aircraft. Their designs influenced military aviation during World War I, and their principles of aerodynamics remain fundamental to modern flight.

## Private Life

Wilbur and Orville Wright were intensely private and dedicated to their work. Neither married, as they believed that their mission to develop aviation required their full commitment.

Wilbur was the more outgoing and strategic planner, often handling business negotiations, while Orville was more reserved and mechanically inclined, focusing on engineering challenges. Their deep bond as brothers was the key to their success; they worked seamlessly as a team, complementing each other's strengths.

Despite their achievements, they faced challenges, including patent disputes, competition from other aviation pioneers, and legal battles over aircraft designs. Wilbur's early death left Orville to continue advocating for their legacy alone.

## Death

Wilbur Wright passed away on May 30, 1912, at the age of 45, due to typhoid fever. His death was a great loss to the aviation world, as he had been the primary spokesperson for their work.

Orville Wright lived much longer, continuing his involvement in aviation until his retirement. He passed away on January 30, 1948, at the age of 76, after suffering a heart attack. Both brothers are buried in Woodland Cemetery, Dayton, Ohio, near their family home.

## Character

The Wright brothers were known for their intellectual curiosity, perseverance, and humility. They were self-taught engineers who succeeded through meticulous experimentation and rigorous problem-solving. Their hands-on approach and commitment to scientific principles set them apart from other aviation pioneers.

They remained modest despite their fame, often crediting each other and their family for their success. Their integrity and determination helped them overcome skepticism and financial struggles, proving that innovation requires both vision and resilience.

## Influence on Humanity

The Wright brothers' contributions to aviation, technology, and human progress cannot be overstated. Their pioneering work led to:

**1. The Birth of Modern Aviation** – Their three-axis control system remains fundamental to all aircraft.

**2. Military and Commercial Flight** – Their innovations laid the groundwork for military aviation and global air travel.

**3. Technological Advancements** – Their wind tunnel tests influenced aerodynamics, benefiting industries beyond aviation.

**4. Space Exploration** – Their principles of controlled flight contributed to the development of spacecraft and aeronautics.

**5. Global Connectivity** – The aviation industry has transformed business, tourism, and international relations, making the world more interconnected.

Today, airports, museums, and aviation institutes worldwide honor their legacy. The Wright-Patterson Air Force Base and the Smithsonian National Air and Space Museum display their pioneering aircraft, ensuring that their story continues to inspire future generations.

---

Wilbur and Orville Wright were more than just inventors – they were visionaries who changed the course of history. Their determination to solve the challenges of flight through science, engineering, and perseverance made modern aviation possible. Their legacy lives on in every airplane, spacecraft, and aerospace innovation, proving that human ingenuity has no limits. The Wright brothers remain among the greatest pioneers in the history of technology and exploration.

# Marie Curie
Discoverer of radioactivity

Marie Curie was a groundbreaking physicist and chemist who revolutionized science with her discovery of radioactivity. She was the first woman to win a Nobel Prize and remains the only person to have won Nobel Prizes in two different scientific fields – Physics and Chemistry. Her work led to the development of X-ray technology, cancer treatments, and a deeper understanding of atomic structure. Despite facing immense obstacles as a female scientist in a male-dominated field, her brilliance and perseverance paved the way for future generations of scientists.

## Origin

Marie Curie was born as Maria Salomea Skłodowska on November 7, 1867, in Warsaw, Poland, then part of the Russian Empire. She was the youngest of five children in a family of teachers and intellectuals. Her father, Władysław Skłodowski, was a physics and mathematics professor, while her mother, Bronisława Skłodowska, was a school director.

The Skłodowski family emphasized education and scientific inquiry, values that profoundly influenced young Maria. However, Poland was under Russian occupation at the time, and political oppression made it difficult for Polish citizens, especially women, to access higher education. Despite these hardships, Marie showed exceptional intelligence and a love for learning from an early age.

## Childhood and Youth

Marie's early years were marked by academic excellence and personal tragedy. Her mother died of tuberculosis when Marie was just 10 years old, and her oldest sister Zofia died of typhus a few years later. These losses deeply affected her but also strengthened her determination to succeed.

Despite being a gifted student, Marie was denied admission to official universities in Poland because women were not allowed to attend. Undeterred, she and her older sister Bronisława attended the Flying University, a secret underground institution that provided education to Polish women.

Marie later made a pact with Bronisława: she would work as a governess and financially support Bronisława's medical studies in Paris, and in return, Bronisława would help Marie do the same. For several years, Marie worked tirelessly as a governess, all the while teaching herself advanced physics and mathematics in her spare time.

In 1891, at the age of 24, Marie finally moved to Paris, enrolling at the Sorbonne under the name Marie to adapt to French culture. She was one of the few women in her class and often struggled financially, surviving on meager meals and relentless study sessions. However, her hard work paid off – she graduated first in her class in physics in 1893, followed by a second degree in mathematics in 1894.

## Adulthood

In 1894, Marie met Pierre Curie, a distinguished physicist known for his work on magnetism. They shared a deep intellectual connection, and their mutual passion for science blossomed into love. They married in 1895, forming one of history's greatest scientific partnerships.

Marie began researching uranium radiation, building on the work of Henri Becquerel. She coined the term radioactivity and, with Pierre, discovered two new elements:

- **Polonium** (1898) – Named after her homeland, Poland.
- **Radium** (1898) – Known for its intense radioactivity.

Their discoveries revolutionized nuclear physics and medicine, leading to the development of X-ray technology and cancer treatments. In 1903, Marie and Pierre shared the Nobel Prize in Physics with Becquerel, making Marie the first woman to win a Nobel Prize.

In 1906, tragedy struck when Pierre Curie died in a tragic accident, run over by a horse-drawn carriage. Devastated but determined, Marie continued their research and took over Pierre's teaching position at the Sorbonne, becoming the first female professor in the university's history.

In 1911, she was awarded her second Nobel Prize, this time in Chemistry, for successfully isolating pure radium. Despite her monumental achievements, she faced sexism from the scientific community and endured a public scandal over her romantic relationship with physicist Paul Langevin.

## Private Life

Marie was deeply devoted to science and her daughters, Irène and Ève Curie. She raised them with the same love for learning and scientific curiosity. Irène later followed in her mother's footsteps, winning the Nobel Prize in Chemistry in 1935.

Marie was known for her humility and dedication. Despite her discoveries, she refused to patent radium, believing that science should benefit humanity rather than personal gain. She also worked tirelessly during World War I, developing mobile X-ray units, known as "Little Curies," to assist battlefield surgeons.

## Death

Years of radiation exposure took a toll on Marie's health. At a time when the dangers of radiation were not yet understood, she often handled radioactive materials without protection. She developed aplastic anemia, a condition linked to prolonged radiation exposure.

On July 4, 1934, Marie Curie passed away at the age of 66 in Sancellemoz, France. She was buried alongside Pierre in Sceaux, but in 1995, both were reinterred in the Panthéon in Paris, making her the first woman honored with burial there for her own achievements.

## Character

Marie Curie was known for her extraordinary resilience, intelligence, and humility. She defied gender barriers, pursuing scientific truth despite societal opposition. Her dedication to research and refusal to seek financial profit from her discoveries reflected her deep belief in science as a service to humanity. She also valued education and knowledge above all else, inspiring countless women to pursue careers in science. Even in her later years, she remained devoted to scientific progress and humanitarian efforts.

## Influence on Humanity

Marie Curie's legacy is immeasurable. Her contributions to science and medicine continue to impact society today:

**1. Pioneering Nuclear Science** – Her discovery of radioactivity laid the foundation for nuclear energy and atomic physics.

**2. Medical Advancements** – Her work led to the development of radiation therapy for cancer treatment.

**3. Women in Science** – She inspired generations of female scientists and broke barriers in a male-dominated field.

**4. X-ray Technology** – Her mobile X-ray units saved countless lives during World War I.

**5. Educational Influence** – The Curie Institutes in Paris and Warsaw continue to lead in medical and scientific research.

Her contributions are celebrated worldwide, and her name remains synonymous with scientific excellence and perseverance.

---

Marie Curie was more than a scientist – she was a trailblazer, humanitarian, and role model. Her relentless pursuit of knowledge and unwavering commitment to science changed the world. Her pioneering discoveries in radioactivity, medicine, and physics continue to save lives and inspire future generations.

Her story remains a testament to the power of intellect, perseverance, and passion, proving that science has no gender, and knowledge knows no limits.

# Mahatma Gandhi
Leader of India's nonviolent independence movement

Mahatma Gandhi was one of the most influential leaders in world history, known for his nonviolent resistance and leadership in India's struggle for independence from British rule. His philosophy of Satyagraha (truth and nonviolence) inspired civil rights movements worldwide. A man of unwavering moral principles, Gandhi emphasized self-discipline, communal harmony, and social justice. His lifelong dedication to truth and justice has left an enduring legacy that continues to inspire movements for peace and freedom.

## Origin

Mohandas Karamchand Gandhi was born on October 2, 1869, in Porbandar, a coastal town in what is now Gujarat, India. He belonged to the Modh Bania caste, a merchant community. His father, Karamchand Gandhi, served as the Diwan (chief minister) of Porbandar, while his mother, Putlibai, was a devout and religious woman who deeply influenced young Mohandas with her piety, vegetarianism, and fasting practices. Raised in a politically active yet spiritually inclined household, Gandhi was exposed to Hinduism, Jainism, and Vaishnavism, shaping his ethical and moral outlook from an early age. The values of truthfulness, nonviolence, and self-restraint learned in his home would later form the foundation of his philosophy.

## Childhood and Youth

Gandhi's childhood was marked by timidity and curiosity. He was an average student, though deeply influenced by stories of Harishchandra (a legendary king known for his truthfulness) and Shravan Kumar (a devoted son). These stories instilled in him an early commitment to truth and duty.

At the age of 13, he was married to Kasturba Makhanji, in line with traditional customs. This early marriage, though common at the time, later shaped his views on gender equality and self-discipline.

In 1887, Gandhi completed his schooling in Gujarat and traveled to London in 1888 to study law at University College London. While there, he struggled to adapt to Western culture but remained determined to succeed. He embraced a vegetarian lifestyle and joined the London Vegetarian Society, where he was exposed to the ideas of Henry David Thoreau and Leo Tolstoy, both of whom influenced his later philosophy.

In 1891, after completing his law degree, Gandhi returned to India. However, he struggled to establish a legal career due to his shyness and lack of courtroom confidence. This led him to accept a one-year legal contract in South Africa, a decision that would change the course of his life.

## Adulthood

In 1893, Gandhi arrived in South Africa, where he witnessed racial discrimination against Indians firsthand. A defining moment occurred when he was forcibly removed from a first-class train compartment despite holding a valid ticket. This experience ignited his resolve to fight injustice through nonviolent means.

Gandhi spent 21 years in South Africa, where he developed his concept of Satyagraha (truth-force), advocating for civil disobedience and nonviolent resistance. He led campaigns against laws that oppressed Indians, such as the Asiatic Registration Act. His efforts united the Indian community in South Africa, leading to several legal victories.

In 1915, Gandhi returned to India and was warmly welcomed by Gopal Krishna Gokhale, his mentor in the Indian National Congress. Over the next three decades, he became the leader of India's independence movement, advocating for self-rule (Swaraj) through peaceful means.

Key movements led by Gandhi included:

**1. Champaran and Kheda Satyagraha** (1917-1918) – Gandhi organized peasant protests against oppressive taxation and land policies, marking his first major success in India.

**2. Non-Cooperation Movement** (1920-1922) – Urging Indians to boycott British goods, institutions, and services, this was one of the first mass movements against colonial rule.

**3. Salt March** (Dandi March, 1930) – One of his most famous acts of civil disobedience, Gandhi led thousands on a 240-mile march to the Arabian Sea to protest the British monopoly on salt.

**4. Quit India Movement** (1942) – During World War II, Gandhi called for an immediate end to British rule, leading to his imprisonment along with other Indian leaders.

Through these campaigns, Gandhi's philosophy of Ahimsa (nonviolence) and civil disobedience gained global recognition, influencing leaders like Martin Luther King Jr. and Nelson Mandela.

## Private Life

Gandhi's personal life was one of discipline, simplicity, and sacrifice. His marriage to Kasturba Gandhi was both a source of strength and a testing ground for his principles. Kasturba actively supported his movements, enduring imprisonment and hardships alongside him. Gandhi took celibacy vows (Brahmacharya) later in life, believing that self-restraint led to spiritual purity. He lived in ashrams, practiced hand-spinning (Khadi), and promoted self-sufficiency.

His relationship with his children was complex. While he emphasized moral discipline, his eldest son, Harilal Gandhi, rebelled against his ideals, leading to strained relations.

## Death

On January 30, 1948, just months after India gained independence, Gandhi was assassinated in New Delhi by Nathuram Godse, a Hindu nationalist who opposed his policy of religious harmony and Pakistan's creation. Gandhi's last words, "Hey Ram", reflected his deep faith in truth and nonviolence. His funeral was attended by millions, and he was honored worldwide as the "Father of the Nation".

## Character

Gandhi was a man of unshakable conviction, humility, and courage. He believed in truthfulness, moral integrity, and the unity of all religions. His lifestyle was simple, wearing only handwoven cloth and living with minimal possessions.

His resilience in the face of oppression and commitment to nonviolent resistance made him a beacon of hope for oppressed communities worldwide. Though he had human flaws, his dedication to his principles never wavered.

## Influence on Humanity

Gandhi's impact extends far beyond Indian independence:

**1. Nonviolent Movements Worldwide** – Inspired civil rights leaders like Martin Luther King Jr. (USA), Nelson Mandela (South Africa), and Cesar Chavez (USA).

**2. Human Rights and Social Justice** – Advocated for women's rights, abolition of untouchability, and rural development.

**3. Self-Sufficiency and Simplicity** – Promoted sustainable living, Khadi clothing, and community-based economies.

**4. Peace and Conflict Resolution** – His principles are studied in diplomacy, international relations, and conflict resolution.

Today, his legacy is honored every October 2 as Gandhi Jayanti, a national holiday in India and the International Day of Non-Violence recognized by the United Nations.

---

Mahatma Gandhi's life was a testament to the power of peaceful resistance and moral strength. Through nonviolence, truth, and perseverance, he not only liberated India from colonial rule but also reshaped the global discourse on justice and human rights. His principles remain as relevant today as they were during his lifetime, proving that one individual's commitment to truth and justice can transform the world.

# Vladimir Lenin
Leader of the Russian Revolution and
founder of the Soviet Union

Vladimir Lenin was a revolutionary leader, political theorist, and the founder of the Soviet Union. As the leader of the Bolshevik Party, he played a crucial role in the Russian Revolution of 1917, overthrowing the Provisional Government and establishing a communist state. Lenin's theories and leadership shaped the political landscape of the 20th century, inspiring socialist movements worldwide. His ideas, known as Leninism, influenced global politics, economics, and governance, leaving a lasting impact on history.

## Origin

Vladimir Ilyich Ulyanov, later known as Lenin, was born on April 22, 1870, in Simbirsk, Russian Empire (now Ulyanovsk, Russia). He was the third of six children in a middle-class family. His father, Ilya Nikolayevich Ulyanov, was a government education official who advocated for progressive reforms in the Russian school system. His mother, Maria Alexandrovna Ulyanova, came from an educated family and instilled in her children a love for learning and literature.

Lenin's family was comfortable but not aristocratic. However, their middle-class status did not protect them from political repression in Imperial Russia, where the monarchy controlled society with an iron grip. The Ulyanov household emphasized education, discipline, and political awareness, shaping young Vladimir's worldview.

## Childhood and Youth

Lenin displayed intellectual brilliance from an early age. He was an exceptional student, excelling in literature, Latin, and Greek. However, his life took a drastic turn when his older brother, Alexander Ulyanov, was executed in 1887 for participating in an assassination plot against Tsar Alexander III. The execution of his brother deeply radicalized Lenin, leading him to develop a hatred for the monarchy. That same year, he enrolled at Kazan University to study law, but he was expelled for participating in anti-government protests. Undeterred, Lenin continued his studies independently and later completed his law degree in 1891.

While practicing law, Lenin became increasingly involved in revolutionary politics. He studied the works of Karl Marx and Friedrich Engels, embracing Marxism as a scientific solution to Russia's inequality and oppression.

## Adulthood

By the 1890s, Lenin was actively organizing Marxist study circles in St. Petersburg. In 1895, he co-founded the Union of Struggle for the Emancipation of the Working Class, advocating for workers' rights and socialism. This led to his arrest in 1897, and he was exiled to Siberia for three years.

Following his exile, Lenin traveled to Switzerland, Germany, and England, where he worked on revolutionary publications and co-founded the Bolshevik faction of the Russian Social Democratic Labour Party (RSDLP). He argued that a small, disciplined group of revolutionaries should lead the working class in overthrowing capitalism.

In 1917, with Russia engulfed in World War I and facing economic collapse, Lenin saw an opportunity for revolution. The February Revolution forced Tsar Nicholas II to abdicate, leading to the establishment of a Provisional Government. However, Lenin, then in exile in Switzerland, believed this government did not represent workers' interests.

With the help of Germany, Lenin was transported back to Russia in April 1917. Upon arrival, he published the April Theses, calling for:

1. **An end to the war**

2. **Transfer of land to peasants**

3. **Power to be given to the Soviets (workers' councils)**

By October 1917, the Bolsheviks, led by Lenin, staged the October Revolution, overthrowing the Provisional Government and establishing a communist government.

As the head of the new Soviet government, Lenin implemented sweeping changes:

- Nationalized industries and banks
- Redistributed land to peasants
- Withdrew Russia from World War I through the Treaty of Brest-Litovsk (1918)
- Crushed opposition in the Russian Civil War (1918-1922)

His leadership laid the foundation for Soviet communism, but it also involved harsh measures such as the Red Terror, where political enemies were executed or sent to labor camps.

## Private Life

Lenin married Nadezhda Krupskaya, a fellow revolutionary, in 1898. Their marriage was built on mutual respect and political ideology rather than traditional romance. Nadezhda played a key role in Lenin's writings, organizing party activities, and education reforms. Lenin lived a simple life, avoiding luxury despite holding immense power. He was a voracious reader and had an intense work ethic, but his health began to decline due to the stress of leadership and multiple assassination attempts.

## Death

By 1922, Lenin suffered a series of strokes, leaving him partially paralyzed. His health continued to deteriorate, and by 1923, he was unable to participate in government affairs. Lenin died on January 21, 1924, at the age of 53, in Gorki, near Moscow. His body was embalmed and placed in a mausoleum in Red Square, where it remains a major historical site today. Following Lenin's death, Joseph Stalin consolidated power, eventually leading the Soviet Union through industrialization and totalitarian rule.

## Character

Lenin was a brilliant strategist, passionate revolutionary, and determined leader. He was also a ruthless politician who believed that violence was sometimes necessary for revolutionary success. His discipline, intellect, and charisma made him a dominant figure in world history.

Despite advocating for workers' rights, Lenin suppressed dissent and eliminated opposition, leading to political repression. However, his vision for a socialist state laid the groundwork for communist movements worldwide.

## Influence on Humanity

Lenin's influence reshaped global politics and economics:

**1. Foundation of the Soviet Union** – His leadership created the world's first communist state, which lasted until 1991.

**2. Inspired Communist Movements** – Lenin's ideas influenced China (Mao Zedong), Cuba (Fidel Castro), and Vietnam (Ho Chi Minh).

**3. Radicalized Political Thought** – His works, including "State and Revolution", remain influential in Marxist and socialist movements.

**4. Economic and Social Policies** – Lenin's nationalization policies influenced socialist economies worldwide.

**5. Cold War Dynamics** – His legacy shaped the ideological battle between capitalism and communism throughout the 20th century.

---

Vladimir Lenin was a revolutionary thinker, strategist, and leader whose ideas changed the world. Though his methods were controversial, his impact on global politics, economics, and history remains profound. Lenin's vision for a socialist state continues to be debated, making him one of the most influential and polarizing figures of modern history.

# Guglielmo Marconi
Pioneer of wireless communication

Guglielmo Marconi was an Italian inventor and electrical engineer best known for his groundbreaking work in wireless telegraphy. His pioneering developments in radio transmission led to the creation of modern wireless communication, which laid the foundation for radio, television, and telecommunications. He was awarded the Nobel Prize in Physics in 1909 for his contributions to the development of wireless telegraphy. Marconi's innovations transformed global communication, connecting people across vast distances and revolutionizing maritime safety. His legacy continues to shape modern technology, making him one of the most influential inventors of the 20th century.

## Origin

Guglielmo Giovanni Maria Marconi was born on April 25, 1874, in Bologna, Italy. He was the second son of Giuseppe Marconi, an Italian landowner and businessman, and Annie Jameson, an Irish aristocrat from the Jameson whiskey distilling family.

Marconi's mixed Italian and Irish heritage gave him exposure to different cultures and educational opportunities. His father managed estates in Italy, while his mother, a well-educated and cultured woman, played a significant role in his early education and scientific curiosity.

## Childhood and Youth

From an early age, Marconi exhibited a deep fascination with science, electricity, and physics. He received private tutoring at home, where he was encouraged to explore his interests. He was particularly inspired by the works of James Clerk Maxwell, Heinrich Hertz, and Nikola Tesla, who were pioneers in electromagnetism and radio waves.

In his teenage years, Marconi studied at the Livorno Technical Institute and later attended lectures at the University of Bologna, where he was influenced by Augusto Righi, a physicist specializing in electromagnetic waves. Although he never earned a formal degree, his passion for experimenting with electrical signals and radio waves led him to conduct independent research.

By the age of 20, Marconi had begun conducting wireless transmission experiments on his father's estate in Pontecchio, Italy. His early work focused on improving signal transmission over longer distances, laying the groundwork for the development of the first practical radio communication system.

## Adulthood

In 1895, Marconi successfully transmitted wireless signals over a distance of 2 kilometers. Realizing the potential of his invention, he sought financial and technical support to further develop his ideas. However, the Italian government showed little interest, prompting him to move to London in 1896.

Upon arriving in England, Marconi gained the support of William Preece, the Chief Engineer of the British Post Office. This partnership allowed him to secure a British patent for wireless telegraphy in 1897, making him the first person to patent radio transmission technology.

Encouraged by his success, Marconi founded the Wireless Telegraph and Signal Company (later Marconi Company) in 1897. He continued refining wireless communication by increasing the range of radio signals, setting up the first wireless station on the Isle of Wight.

By 1899, Marconi achieved a major milestone by transmitting wireless signals across the English Channel. This event demonstrated the practicality of long-distance wireless communication, garnering international attention.

Marconi's most significant achievement came on December 12, 1901, when he successfully transmitted the first wireless signal across the Atlantic Ocean from Poldhu, Cornwall (England) to St. John's, Newfoundland (Canada). The signal, consisting of the letter "S" in Morse code, proved that radio waves could travel beyond the horizon, defying skeptics who believed that Earth's curvature would block the transmission.

Marconi's wireless technology quickly became essential for maritime communication. His systems were installed on major ocean liners, including the RMS Titanic. In 1912, during the Titanic disaster, wireless radio operators were able to send distress signals, leading to the rescue of over 700 passengers. This incident underscored the importance of radio communication in emergency situations and prompted governments to mandate the use of wireless equipment on ships.

## Private Life

Marconi married Beatrice O'Brien in 1905, and they had three children. However, the marriage ended in divorce in 1924. He later married Maria Cristina Bezzi-Scali, an Italian noblewoman, with whom he had a daughter.

Despite his global fame, Marconi was known for his private and reserved nature. He preferred working in his laboratory over public engagements and was deeply dedicated to his scientific work. He also maintained close ties with political and industrial leaders, ensuring continued support for his research and business ventures.

During the 1920s and 1930s, Marconi became involved in fascist politics, aligning himself with Benito Mussolini's government in Italy. His association with the regime remains a controversial aspect of his legacy.

## Death

Marconi continued his work on microwave communication and radar technology until his health began to decline. On July 20, 1937, he passed away at the age of 63 due to a heart attack.

In honor of his contributions to communication, radio stations worldwide observed two minutes of silence, a tribute rarely given to a scientist. His death marked the end of an era, but his work forever changed the world of communication.

## Character

Marconi was known for his curiosity, perseverance, and determination. He was an independent thinker who challenged existing scientific assumptions. His pragmatic approach to technology helped him turn theoretical concepts into practical applications that changed everyday life.

Despite his reserved personality, he was ambitious and skilled at securing funding and industrial partnerships. His ability to bridge science with business made him a pioneering scientist-entrepreneur.

However, his later political associations with Italian fascism remain a subject of historical debate, complicating his legacy.

## Influence on Humanity

Marconi's contributions to wireless communication had a profound impact on modern technology:

**1. Radio Broadcasting** – His technology led to the development of commercial radio stations and public broadcasting.

**2. Maritime Safety** – His wireless telegraphy system saved lives during maritime disasters, influencing modern rescue operations.

**3. Telecommunications** – His work paved the way for television, mobile phones, and satellite communications.

**4. Radar and Military Communications** – His later research contributed to radar technology, crucial for World War II defense systems.

**5. Scientific Inspiration** – His breakthroughs inspired generations of scientists, including Nikola Tesla and later engineers working on wireless networks.

Today, his name is honored in institutions like the Marconi Society, which promotes innovation in communication technology.

---

Guglielmo Marconi's vision, innovation, and persistence revolutionized communication and connected the world like never before. His groundbreaking work in wireless transmission transformed radio, television, and global communication, shaping the modern era of instant connectivity. Despite controversies, his impact remains undeniable, ensuring that he will be remembered as one of the greatest inventors in history.

# Winston Churchill
British prime minister during World War II.

Sir Winston Churchill was one of the most influential figures of the 20th century, known for his leadership during World War II, his oratory skills, and his unwavering resolve in the face of adversity. As Prime Minister of the United Kingdom, Churchill played a crucial role in defending democracy against Nazi Germany and shaping global politics in the aftermath of the war. His political career spanned over six decades, during which he served in multiple government positions, wrote extensively, and made critical contributions to both domestic and international affairs. His speeches and writings continue to inspire generations.

## Origin

Winston Leonard Spencer Churchill was born on November 30, 1874, at Blenheim Palace, Oxfordshire, England. He was a descendant of the Duke of Marlborough, a prestigious title in British aristocracy. His father, Lord Randolph Churchill, was a prominent Conservative politician, while his mother, Jennie Jerome, was an American socialite from a wealthy New York family. Despite his noble lineage, Churchill's family faced financial struggles. His father's political career was tumultuous, and his mother was more focused on high society than on raising Winston and his younger brother, Jack Churchill. This lack of parental affection influenced Churchill's drive for success and self-reliance from an early age.

## Childhood and Youth

Churchill's early education was difficult. He attended St. George's School in Ascot and later Harrow School, where he was an average student with a rebellious streak. He struggled academically, particularly in mathematics and Latin, but excelled in history and English composition. His poor school performance frustrated his father, who pressured him to pursue a military career.

In 1893, Churchill enrolled at the Royal Military Academy Sandhurst, where he performed exceptionally well, graduating in 1895. His military training provided him with the discipline he lacked in traditional schooling and prepared him for his early career as a soldier and war correspondent.

His adventurous spirit led him to serve in British military campaigns in Cuba, India, Sudan, and South Africa. He gained fame during the Second Boer War (1899-1902) when he was captured by the enemy but managed a daring escape. This event turned him into a national hero and helped launch his political career.

## Adulthood

Churchill entered politics in 1900, winning a seat in Parliament as a Conservative MP for Oldham. However, he soon switched to the Liberal Party in 1904, advocating for social reforms such as workers' rights, unemployment insurance, and free trade. He held several key positions, including First Lord of the Admiralty (1911-1915), where he modernized the Royal Navy in preparation for World War I.

During World War I, Churchill's career suffered a major setback due to the Gallipoli Campaign (1915), which ended in disaster. As the chief architect of the failed invasion of the Dardanelles, he was forced to resign from his government post. Devastated, Churchill briefly returned to the military, serving on the Western Front before re-entering politics.

Churchill returned to high office in the 1930s, warning Britain about the rising threat of Nazi Germany. In 1940, after the resignation of Neville Chamberlain, Churchill became Prime Minister at a time when Britain stood alone against Hitler's forces.

His leadership during World War II was defined by:

1. Defiant speeches that inspired British resistance (e.g., "We shall fight on the beaches" speech in 1940).

2. Forging strong alliances with the United States (Franklin D. Roosevelt) and the Soviet Union (Joseph Stalin).

3. Orchestrating military strategies, including the defense of Britain during the Blitz, the D-Day invasion (1944), and the eventual defeat of Nazi Germany.

Churchill's vision, charisma, and unbreakable spirit were crucial in maintaining British morale and securing victory in 1945. However, despite his wartime heroics, he lost the 1945 general election, as Britain sought a shift toward social welfare policies under the Labour Party.

Churchill returned as Prime Minister from 1951 to 1955, during which he oversaw Britain's recovery and played a key role in Cold War diplomacy. His "Iron Curtain" speech (1946) is credited with defining the ideological battle between Western democracy and Soviet communism.

## Private Life

Churchill married Clementine Hozier in 1908, and they had five children. Clementine was a strong and supportive partner, helping Churchill through his political and personal struggles.

Churchill had an eccentric personality – he loved painting, writing, and enjoyed fine cigars and champagne. He was also known for his humor, wit, and stubbornness. However, he suffered from bouts of depression, which he called his "black dog", and faced severe political opposition throughout his career.

## Death

In his later years, Churchill's health declined. He suffered multiple strokes, the most severe in 1953, which weakened him considerably. In 1964, he retired from Parliament completely.

On January 24, 1965, Churchill passed away at the age of 90. His funeral was the largest state funeral in British history, attended by world leaders and millions who mourned his passing.

## Character

Churchill was a multi-faceted personality. He possessed extraordinary intelligence, an indomitable will and an impressive rhetorical talent. His courage and determination in times of crisis made him an inspirational leader, but his stubbornness and often impulsive actions also earned him criticism.

Churchill was a visionary who recognized the dangers of National Socialism earlier than many of his contemporaries. At the same time, he was a man of deep contradictions: a supporter of democracy who defended British colonial rule and an advocate of progress who often clung to traditional values.

## Influence on Humanity

Churchill's impact on world history is immeasurable:

**1. Defended Democracy** – His leadership prevented a Nazi takeover of Britain, shaping the future of Western Europe.

**2. Cold War Influence** – He warned against Soviet expansionism, influencing U.S. and NATO policies.

**3. Modernizing Britain** – His policies helped rebuild Britain post-WWII.

**4. Inspirational Leadership** – His speeches continue to be studied in politics, business, and military leadership.

His legacy is honored in books, films, and countless institutions, ensuring his place as one of history's greatest leaders.

---

Winston Churchill was more than a wartime leader – he was a statesman, writer, and visionary who shaped the modern world. His resilience, brilliance, and leadership continue to inspire and educate future generations. Though his legacy is complex, his contributions to history remain unparalleled, making him one of the most significant figures of the 20th century.

# Joseph Stalin
Dictator of the Soviet Union

Joseph Stalin was one of the most influential and controversial leaders of the 20th century. As the leader of the Soviet Union from the mid-1920s until his death in 1953, Stalin transformed the USSR into a global superpower through industrialization, collectivization, and military expansion. However, his rule was marked by political repression, purges, and authoritarianism, leading to millions of deaths. Despite his brutal governance, Stalin's policies shaped modern geopolitics and the Cold War.

## Origin

Joseph Stalin was born as Iosif Vissarionovich Dzhugashvili on December 18, 1878 (officially recorded as December 6 under the old Julian calendar) in Gori, Georgia, then part of the Russian Empire. He was the only surviving child of Vissarion Dzhugashvili, a cobbler, and Ekaterina Geladze, a deeply religious woman who worked as a laundress.

Stalin's early years were shaped by poverty, domestic violence, and political unrest. His father was an alcoholic and abusive, frequently beating young Stalin and his mother. The economic struggles of his family led Stalin to develop resilience and ambition from an early age.

## Childhood and Youth

Despite his impoverished upbringing, Stalin's mother was determined to provide him with an education. She enrolled him in Gori's Orthodox Church school, where he excelled academically. He was awarded a scholarship to attend the Tiflis Theological Seminary in 1894, where he was expected to become a priest.

However, Stalin's exposure to Marxist literature and revolutionary ideas led him to reject religion. He secretly joined underground socialist groups, reading works by Karl Marx and Vladimir Lenin. In 1899, he was expelled from the seminary for missing exams and his increasing involvement in anti-tsarist activities.

Stalin then became an active revolutionary, organizing workers' strikes, printing illegal pamphlets, and engaging in bank robberies to fund the Bolshevik cause. He was arrested multiple times and exiled to Siberia, but he always managed to escape, gaining a reputation as a ruthless and cunning operative within the Bolshevik movement.

## Adulthood

Stalin officially joined Vladimir Lenin's Bolshevik faction of the Russian Social Democratic Labour Party in 1903. He quickly gained influence due to his organizational skills and strategic brutality. He was involved in coordinating strikes, armed uprisings, and criminal operations that funded the revolution.

During the Russian Revolution of 1917, Stalin played a minor role compared to Lenin and Leon Trotsky. However, after the Bolsheviks seized power, Stalin was appointed Commissar of Nationalities, where he oversaw policies related to the various ethnic groups within the USSR.

Following Lenin's death in 1924, a power struggle erupted between Stalin and other Bolshevik leaders, most notably Leon Trotsky. Stalin, serving as General Secretary of the Communist Party, strategically outmaneuvered his rivals by appointing loyalists to key positions.

By 1928, Stalin had successfully eliminated all opposition, exiling Trotsky and consolidating dictatorial control over the Soviet Union. His rule was marked by several major policies:

**1. Collectivization of Agriculture** (1929-1933) – Stalin forcibly merged millions of small farms into state-controlled collective farms, leading to massive famines, including the Holodomor in Ukraine, which resulted in millions of deaths.

**2. Rapid Industrialization** – Under Stalin's Five-Year Plans, the USSR transformed from a backward agrarian economy into an industrial powerhouse, producing steel, coal, and machinery at unprecedented rates.

**3. The Great Purge** (1936-1938) – Stalin orchestrated a massive purge of party officials, military leaders, and intellectuals, executing or imprisoning millions in the Gulag labor camps.

**4. World War II and Victory Over Nazi Germany** – Despite initially signing the Molotov-Ribbentrop Pact with Hitler in 1939, Germany invaded the USSR in 1941. Stalin's leadership during the war led to victories at Stalingrad and Berlin, securing the Soviet Union's status as a superpower.

**5. Cold War and Soviet Expansion** – After the war, Stalin established communist regimes in Eastern Europe, creating the Eastern Bloc and setting the stage for the Cold War against the United States.

## Private Life

Stalin's personal life was marked by paranoia, secrecy, and tragedy. He married twice:

- His first wife, Ekaterina Svanidze, died of typhus in 1907, leaving Stalin devastated.
- His second wife, Nadezhda Alliluyeva, committed suicide in 1932 after suffering from depression and disagreements with Stalin.

He had several children, including Vasily Stalin and Svetlana Alliluyeva, the latter of whom defected to the United States in 1967.

Stalin was known to be ruthless and unfeeling, even toward his family. He maintained an iron grip on his inner circle, frequently turning against allies and subordinates.

## Death

On March 5, 1953, Stalin died at the age of 74 after suffering a stroke at his residence in Kuntsevo Dacha, Moscow. His death led to widespread uncertainty and power struggles within the Soviet government. His body was initially embalmed and displayed in Lenin's Mausoleum, but in 1961, during Nikita Khrushchev's de-Stalinization campaign, Stalin's remains were removed and reburied in a simpler grave near the Kremlin Wall.

## Character

Stalin was a complex and contradictory personality. He possessed extraordinary intelligence and political cunning, combined with unbridled ambition and an unscrupulous willingness to use force. His mistrust and paranoia meant that he often took radical measures to secure his power.

Despite his harshness, Stalin was a master of propaganda and knew how to present himself as the father figure of the Soviet Union. His ability to inspire and manipulate people made him an effective, albeit tyrannical, leader.

## Influence on Humanity

Stalin's impact on history is both immense and controversial:

**1. Global Communist Movements** – Stalin's rule shaped communist ideology, influencing leaders like Mao Zedong, Fidel Castro, and Kim Il-Sung.

**2. Superpower Rivalries** – His policies led to the Cold War, defining global politics for decades.

**3. Industrialization and Modernization** – Under Stalin, the Soviet Union became a major industrial force, laying the groundwork for its Cold War-era influence.

**4. Mass Repression and Human Rights Abuses** – His rule resulted in millions of deaths, leaving a lasting scar on Soviet history.

**5. Legacy in Russia** – Even today, Stalin remains a polarizing figure, viewed by some as a ruthless dictator and by others as the leader who made the USSR a superpower.

Joseph Stalin was a ruthless yet transformational leader. His authoritarian rule, political purges, and ambitious industrialization programs shaped the modern world. While his legacy is marred by mass repression and human suffering, his role in World War II, Soviet expansion, and global politics remains a defining chapter in history. His life serves as a cautionary tale of absolute power, ambition, and control.

# Albert Einstein
Physicist known for the theory of relativity

Albert Einstein was one of the most brilliant minds in human history, known for revolutionizing physics through his theory of relativity and numerous contributions to quantum mechanics, cosmology, and thermodynamics. He reshaped our understanding of the universe with his famous equation $E=mc^2$, which laid the foundation for nuclear energy. Einstein was not only a scientific genius but also a humanitarian, advocating for peace, civil rights, and social justice.

## Origin

Albert Einstein was born on March 14, 1879, in Ulm, in the Kingdom of Württemberg, German Empire. He was the eldest child of Hermann Einstein, an engineer and entrepreneur, and Pauline Koch, a talented musician. His family was of Jewish descent, though they were not particularly religious.

Shortly after his birth, the Einsteins moved to Munich, where Hermann and his brother founded an electrical equipment company. The family lived comfortably, and young Albert showed early signs of curiosity and deep thought, though he was initially considered a slow learner.

## Childhood and Youth

As a child, Einstein was quiet, observant, and introspective. He struggled with speech delay, leading some to believe he was intellectually challenged. However, his fascination with science and mathematics became evident when, at the age of five, he received a compass from his father. The mystery of the invisible forces guiding the needle sparked a lifelong passion for physics.

Einstein's schooling was unconventional. He rebelled against rote learning, clashing with rigid teachers. However, he excelled in mathematics and physics, teaching himself advanced calculus by the age of 12. His independent thinking led him to question authority and seek knowledge beyond textbooks.

In 1894, his father's business failed, prompting the family to relocate to Italy. Einstein, left behind in Germany to complete school, soon dropped out and joined his family in Milan. In 1895, he failed the entrance exam to the Swiss Federal Polytechnic in Zurich, excelling only in math and physics. Determined, he attended Aargau Cantonal School, where he completed his secondary education before gaining admission to ETH Zurich in 1896.

## Adulthood

Einstein graduated in 1900 with a degree in physics and mathematics but struggled to find an academic position. He took a job at the Swiss Patent Office in Bern, where he analyzed patents on electromechanical devices. This work allowed him time for independent research, leading to his groundbreaking discoveries.

In 1905, often referred to as Einstein's "miracle year" (Annus Mirabilis), he published four revolutionary papers:

**1. Photoelectric Effect** – Proved that light behaves as particles (quanta), laying the foundation for quantum mechanics.

**2. Brownian Motion** – Provided empirical evidence for the existence of atoms and molecules.

**3. Special Theory of Relativity** – Introduced the concept that time and space are relative, not absolute.

**4. $E=mc^2$ Equation** – Demonstrated the equivalence of mass and energy, which later influenced nuclear physics:

- **E** is the energy of an object or system.
- **m** is the mass.
- **c** is the speed of light in a vacuum.

This formula shows that mass and energy are two forms of the same physical quantity. A small amount of mass can be converted into a huge amount of energy – a principle that plays a central role in nuclear reactions.

These discoveries earned Einstein widespread recognition, leading to academic positions in Europe. In 1915, he developed the General Theory of Relativity, which redefined gravity by describing it as the curvature of spacetime. This theory was confirmed in 1919 when astronomers observed the bending of starlight during a solar eclipse, catapulting Einstein to global fame.

Throughout the 1920s, Einstein traveled extensively, giving lectures worldwide. However, as Nazi sentiment grew in Germany, Einstein, a Jewish intellectual, became a target of anti-Semitic propaganda. In 1933, when Adolf Hitler came to power, Einstein renounced his German citizenship and fled to the United States, where he took a position at the Institute for Advanced Study in Princeton, New Jersey.

During World War II, Einstein, though a pacifist, signed a letter to President Franklin D. Roosevelt, warning of Nazi Germany's potential to develop nuclear weapons. This led to the Manhattan Project, which ultimately produced the atomic bomb – an outcome that deeply troubled Einstein.

## Private Life

Einstein's personal life was complex and unconventional. He married Mileva Marić, a fellow physicist, in 1903, and they had two sons, Hans Albert and Eduard. Their marriage was troubled, strained by Einstein's relentless focus on science. They divorced in 1919, and Einstein soon married his cousin, Elsa Einstein, who cared for him during his later years. Despite his intellectual brilliance, Einstein was known to be aloof and emotionally distant in personal relationships. He maintained numerous extramarital affairs, which later came to light in personal letters.

Einstein was also a humanitarian and advocate for civil rights. He opposed racism, fascism, and militarism, supporting the Zionist movement and speaking out against racial discrimination in the U.S..

## Death

Einstein's health declined in his later years. On April 17, 1955, he suffered a ruptured aortic aneurysm and refused surgical intervention, stating: "I want to go when I want. It is tasteless to prolong life artificially." He passed away early on April 18, 1955, at the age of 76. His brain was removed for scientific study by pathologist Thomas Stoltz Harvey, hoping to uncover the secrets of his intelligence. However, no definitive conclusions were reached.

## Character

Einstein was known for his intellectual curiosity, humility, and wit. He valued independent thinking over rigid academic discipline and was deeply opposed to authoritarianism. Despite his global fame, he remained modest and unconventional, often appearing disheveled and absent-minded. Einstein's humor and wisdom made him a beloved public figure. He was a deep thinker, often pondering philosophical and ethical questions alongside physics. His humanitarian efforts demonstrated his commitment to a better world.

## Influence on Humanity

Einstein's legacy extends far beyond physics:

1. **Revolutionized Modern Physics** – His theories underpin quantum mechanics, black hole physics, and cosmology.

2. **Advancements in Technology** – His work laid the foundation for GPS, nuclear energy, and space travel.

3. **Human Rights and Peace Advocacy** – He spoke out against war, totalitarianism, and racial injustice.

4. **Cultural Icon** – His name is synonymous with genius, and his image remains one of the most recognizable in history.

His work continues to inspire generations of scientists, thinkers, and activists. Institutions such as the Albert Einstein College of Medicine and the Einstein Papers Project ensure that his contributions remain relevant.

Albert Einstein was more than just a physicist – he was a visionary thinker, humanitarian, and icon of intellectual brilliance. His discoveries transformed science, shaped modern technology, and expanded humanity's understanding of the universe. His impact on both science and society remains unmatched, cementing his place as one of history's greatest minds.

# Alexander Fleming
Discoverer of penicillin

Sir Alexander Fleming was a Scottish bacteriologist and pharmacologist best known for his discovery of penicillin, the world's first antibiotic. His breakthrough changed the course of modern medicine, saving millions of lives and laying the foundation for the development of antibiotics. Fleming's work not only revolutionized the treatment of bacterial infections but also transformed the field of medical science, leading to advancements in healthcare, pharmaceuticals, and surgery.

## Origin

Alexander Fleming was born on August 6, 1881, in Lochfield, near Darvel, in Ayrshire, Scotland. He was the third of four children born to Hugh Fleming, a farmer, and Grace Stirling Morton, his second wife. Hugh Fleming had four children from his first marriage, making Alexander part of a large family.

The Flemings were modest farmers, living in rural Scotland, far from the intellectual centers of Britain. Despite this, young Alexander showed an early inclination for learning and curiosity about the natural world. His humble beginnings played a significant role in shaping his work ethic and resilience, traits that would later define his scientific career.

## Childhood and Youth

Fleming received his early education at Loudoun Moor School and later attended Darvel School. He was a bright student and earned a scholarship to Kilmarnock Academy, where he excelled academically. At 14 years old, he moved to London to live with his older brother, Thomas Fleming, a physician, and attended the Regent Street Polytechnic School. Initially, Fleming pursued a career in business, working as a shipping clerk. However, a small inheritance allowed him to pursue medical studies, inspired by his brother's profession. In 1901, he enrolled at St. Mary's Hospital Medical School, University of London, where he studied under Sir Almroth Wright, a pioneer in immunology and vaccine research.

Fleming graduated with top honors in 1906, obtaining a degree in bacteriology. His academic excellence led him to join St. Mary's as a researcher, where he began investigating the body's immune response to infections.

## Adulthood

Fleming's early research focused on antiseptics and immune system responses. During World War I, he served as a captain in the Royal Army Medical Corps, working in field hospitals in France. There, he observed the limitations of antiseptics, which often did more harm than good by killing white blood cells along with bacteria. His wartime experiences led him to investigate better ways to treat infections. In 1921, he discovered lysozyme, an enzyme present in human tears, saliva, and mucus, which could destroy certain bacteria. Though lysozyme was not a universal cure, it reinforced Fleming's belief in natural antibacterial substances.

In 1928, Fleming made one of the greatest scientific discoveries in history. While working at St. Mary's Hospital in London, he noticed something unusual in a petri dish containing Staphylococcus bacteria. A mold, later identified as Penicillium notatum, had contaminated the dish and was destroying the surrounding bacteria.

Fleming conducted experiments to isolate the substance produced by the mold, which he named penicillin. He found that penicillin was capable of killing a wide range of harmful bacteria without harming human cells. This discovery marked the birth of antibiotics, but at the time, Fleming lacked the resources to mass-produce penicillin.

For nearly a decade, Fleming's discovery remained largely unnoticed. It was not until the 1940s, during World War II, that a team of scientists, including Howard Florey and Ernst Boris Chain, developed methods for large-scale production of penicillin.

Penicillin became the first widely used antibiotic, treating wounded soldiers, bacterial infections, and deadly diseases such as pneumonia and syphilis. It was hailed as a miracle drug, earning Fleming global recognition.

In 1945, Fleming, Florey, and Chain were jointly awarded the Nobel Prize in Physiology or Medicine for their contributions to the development of penicillin.

## Private Life

Fleming married Sarah Marion McElroy, an Irish nurse, in 1915. They had one son, Robert Fleming, who later became a general practitioner. Sarah played a crucial role in supporting Fleming's career, offering him stability as he dedicated himself to his research.

After Sarah's death in 1949, Fleming remarried in 1953 to Dr. Amalia Koutsouri-Vourekas, a Greek medical professional. Their marriage was brief due to Fleming's declining health.

Despite his fame, Fleming remained humble and reserved. He disliked publicity and preferred to work quietly in his laboratory, often shunning the limelight in favor of scientific progress.

## Death

In his later years, Fleming's health began to deteriorate. He suffered from a heart attack and passed away on March 11, 1955, at the age of 73 in London.

He was buried in St. Paul's Cathedral, a rare honor that recognized his immense contributions to science and humanity. His death marked the end of an era, but his legacy continued to shape modern medicine.

## Character

Fleming was known for his intellectual curiosity, meticulous research, and modesty. Unlike many scientists who sought fame, he was soft-spoken and humble, often crediting luck and nature for his discoveries rather than personal brilliance.

His dedication to science and persistence allowed him to make groundbreaking contributions despite limited resources. He was methodical yet open-minded, qualities that led to the discovery of penicillin.

## Influence on Humanity

Fleming's discovery of penicillin revolutionized modern medicine in several ways:

**1. Eradication of Deadly Diseases** – Before antibiotics, infections such as tuberculosis, pneumonia, and syphilis were often fatal. Penicillin transformed healthcare, making once-lethal diseases treatable.

**2. World War II and Beyond** – Mass production of penicillin saved millions of lives during wartime and became essential in surgical and postoperative care.

**3. Birth of Antibiotic Medicine** – Fleming's work paved the way for the development of other antibiotics, shaping the pharmaceutical industry.

**4. Public Health Advancements** – His discovery led to increased life expectancy, reducing mortality rates worldwide.

**5. Inspiration to Scientists** – His legacy continues to inspire medical researchers, biologists, and healthcare professionals worldwide.

Fleming's contributions earned him knighthood in 1944, and numerous institutions, streets, and awards have been named in his honor.

---

Sir Alexander Fleming's discovery of penicillin transformed medicine, saved millions of lives, and reshaped human history. His work laid the foundation for modern antibiotics, revolutionizing the treatment of infections. A dedicated scientist and humble man, Fleming remains one of the greatest figures in medical science, proving that even simple observations can lead to world-changing discoveries.

# Adolf Hitler
Leader of Nazi Germany

Adolf Hitler was the leader of Nazi Germany from 1933 to 1945 and one of the most infamous figures in modern history. As Chancellor and Führer, he led Germany into World War II, orchestrated the Holocaust, and was responsible for the deaths of millions. His ideology, based on authoritarianism, nationalism, and racial purity, resulted in unprecedented destruction. While his rule brought temporary economic revival to Germany, it ultimately led to the collapse of the Third Reich and his own downfall.

## Origin

Adolf Hitler was born on April 20, 1889, in Braunau am Inn, a small Austrian town located near the German border. He was the fourth of six children born to Alois Hitler and Klara Pölzl. His father, Alois, was a strict and authoritarian customs officer, while his mother was a devoted and caring woman who often shielded Adolf from his father's harsh discipline. The Hitler family had humble origins, but Alois was ambitious and worked his way into a respectable government job. The family moved frequently due to Alois's work, which disrupted young Adolf's early education. His Austrian nationality and modest upbringing would later influence his extreme nationalist and expansionist beliefs, particularly his desire to unite Germany and Austria under one empire.

## Childhood and Youth

Hitler's childhood was marked by conflict with his father, who wanted him to follow a career in government, while Adolf was passionate about art. He performed well in primary school, but his academic performance declined in secondary school, where he often clashed with teachers and was described as lazy and rebellious.

In 1903, his father died suddenly, which relieved some of the pressure on him. However, in 1907, his mother died of cancer, an event that devastated him deeply.

After his mother's death, Hitler moved to Vienna, where he attempted to gain admission to the Academy of Fine Arts Vienna. He failed the entrance exam twice, with the academy rejecting him for his lack of talent in human figure drawing. His rejection was a major blow, leaving him homeless and struggling financially.

While in Vienna, Hitler developed strong anti-Semitic, nationalist, and anti-Marxist views, influenced by far-right newspapers and political groups. He also admired the Austro-Hungarian Empire's military traditions and began idealizing pan-Germanism, the belief that all German-speaking people should be united under one nation.

## Adulthood

In 1913, Hitler moved to Munich, Germany, seeking a fresh start. When World War I broke out in 1914, he enthusiastically volunteered for the German Army. He served as a messenger on the Western Front, was wounded twice, and received the Iron Cross for bravery.

Despite his courage, he was never promoted beyond corporal, as officers found him lacking leadership qualities. The defeat of Germany in 1918 left Hitler angry and disillusioned, and he blamed Jews, Marxists, and politicians for the country's downfall.

After the war, Hitler joined a small extremist group called the German Workers' Party (DAP), which later became the National Socialist German Workers' Party (NSDAP), or the Nazi Party. His charismatic speeches, blaming Jews and Communists for Germany's problems, gained him a strong following.

In 1923, Hitler attempted to overthrow the Weimar Republic in a failed coup known as the Beer Hall Putsch. He was arrested and sentenced to five years in prison, though he served only nine months.

While in prison, he wrote "Mein Kampf" ("My Struggle"), outlining his extremist ideology, racial hierarchy beliefs, and vision for a future German empire. The book became a blueprint for Nazi policies.

After his release, Hitler rebuilt the Nazi Party, focusing on propaganda, mass rallies, and political maneuvering. With the Great Depression of 1929 causing economic hardship, Hitler's promises of economic recovery, national pride, and military strength resonated with millions of Germans.

By 1933, the Nazis were the largest political party in Germany, and Hitler was appointed Chancellor. Within months, he banned opposition parties, silenced critics, and established a totalitarian regime.

His policies led to rearmament, the persecution of minorities, and ultimately to World War II, which began in 1939 with the German invasion of Poland. During the war, Hitler orchestrated the Holocaust, in which around six million Jews, along with millions of other victims, were murdered.

## Private Life

Hitler's personal life was secretive and controversial. He never married publicly until the very end of his life, though he had a long-term relationship with Eva Braun, his private secretary.

He was a vegetarian, non-smoker, and abstained from alcohol, promoting an image of discipline and self-control. However, he suffered from various health issues, including insomnia, tremors, and possible Parkinson's disease.

Despite his public image, Hitler was emotionally unstable, often displaying paranoia, mood swings, and violent outbursts. His obsession with race, purity, and power dictated his relationships and decision-making.

## Death

As World War II neared its end in April 1945, Soviet forces entered Berlin, and Hitler realized his empire was collapsing. Refusing to be captured, he married Eva Braun on April 29, 1945, and the next day, both committed suicide in his underground bunker.

Hitler shot himself, while Braun took cyanide. Their bodies were burned, following his instructions, to prevent them from being displayed as war trophies.

The Third Reich fell soon after, and Germany surrendered on May 8, 1945, officially ending the war in Europe.

## Character

Adolf Hitler's psyche has been extensively studied by historians and psychologists. Many experts see him as a narcissistic personality with an extreme need for power and admiration. He showed paranoid tendencies, especially towards Jews and political opponents, and an ability to manipulate, which enabled him to influence the masses.

Hitler's world view was characterized by racist ideology and a Darwinist understanding of superiority and subjugation. He saw himself as the savior of the German nation and was prepared to use immense violence to achieve his goals. His personal failure at a young age is likely to have contributed to a deep sense of inferiority, which he sought to compensate for through his political career.

He was a charismatic yet ruthless leader, displaying manipulation, strategic thinking, and absolute authoritarianism. Despite his intelligence and determination, his megalomania and hatred led to his downfall.

## Influence on Humanity

Hitler's impact on history is profound and overwhelmingly negative.

Key Effects:

**1. World War II** (1939-1945) – His aggressive expansionist policies caused a war that killed over 70 million people.

**2. The Holocaust** – Responsible for the genocide of six million Jews and millions of others, including Poles, Slavs, Romani, and disabled individuals.

**3. The Cold War** – His defeat led to the division of Germany and the rise of the USA and USSR as superpowers.

**4. Modern-Day Extremism** – Neo-Nazi groups and far-right movements still reference his ideology today.

**5. Global Lessons** – His rule serves as a warning against authoritarianism, racism, and propaganda.

Adolf Hitler's life was a cautionary tale of how charismatic leadership, propaganda, and hate-fueled ideology can lead to catastrophic consequences. While he temporarily restored Germany's economy and military power, his unforgivable crimes and reckless ambitions led to its destruction. His name remains synonymous with evil, and his legacy serves as a reminder of the dangers of totalitarian rule, discrimination, and unchecked power. The world continues to study his reign to prevent history from repeating itself.

# Mao Zedong
Leader of the Chinese Revolution

Mao Zedong was the founding father of the People's Republic of China (PRC) and one of the most influential figures in 20th-century world history. As the leader of the Chinese Communist Party (CCP), he led China through a revolution, industrialization, and major political and social upheavals. His ideologies, known as Maoism, shaped China's governance, foreign policy, and economic system. Mao's rule remains highly controversial — while he is credited with uniting China and modernizing its economy, his policies, such as the Great Leap Forward and the Cultural Revolution, led to significant economic struggles and human suffering.

## Origin

Mao Zedong was born on December 26, 1893, in Shaoshan, a rural village in Hunan Province, China. His father, Mao Yichang, was a wealthy farmer and strict disciplinarian, while his mother, Wen Qimei, was a devout Buddhist who encouraged him to pursue education.

At the time of Mao's birth, China was experiencing political and social turmoil. The Qing Dynasty was in decline, and foreign powers, such as Britain and Japan, exerted significant control over China's economy and resources. These conditions would later shape Mao's nationalist and anti-imperialist sentiments.

## Childhood and Youth

Mao's early education was limited and traditional, focusing on Confucian texts and Chinese history. However, he was an avid reader, particularly interested in rebellions and military strategy.

As a teenager, Mao rebelled against his father's authoritarian rule and refused to follow the traditional path of becoming a scholar-official. Instead, he left home to attend Dongshan Higher Primary School and later enrolled in Hunan First Normal School in Changsha.

During his studies, Mao was introduced to Western political theories, particularly the writings of Karl Marx and Friedrich Engels. He became involved in student protests and joined the New Culture Movement, which called for a break from traditional Chinese values and the adoption of modern political ideologies.

In 1918, after graduating, Mao worked as an assistant librarian at Peking University, where he met intellectuals and revolutionaries who inspired him to join the Chinese Communist movement.

## Adulthood

In 1921, Mao co-founded the Chinese Communist Party (CCP) and began organizing labor unions and peasant movements. He believed that China's revolution should be led by peasants rather than the urban working class, a departure from orthodox Marxist ideology.

As the CCP grew in influence, Mao clashed with the Kuomintang (KMT), China's ruling nationalist party, led by Chiang Kai-shek. The two factions initially formed a fragile alliance but later engaged in a bloody civil war.

In 1934-1935, facing defeat from KMT forces, Mao led the Long March, a 6,000-mile retreat to escape Chiang Kai-shek's army. This arduous journey resulted in heavy casualties but solidified Mao's status as the undisputed leader of the CCP.

During World War II, the CCP and KMT temporarily united to fight Japanese occupation. However, after Japan's defeat in 1945, the civil war resumed. By 1949, the Communist forces defeated the KMT, forcing Chiang Kai-shek to flee to Taiwan. On October 1, 1949, Mao proclaimed the establishment of the People's Republic of China (PRC) in Beijing.

As Chairman of the PRC, Mao launched radical policies to transform China into a modern socialist state:

**1. Land Reforms** (1950-1953) – Mao redistributed land from landlords to peasants, significantly reducing rural poverty but leading to violent purges.

**2. The Great Leap Forward** (1958-1962) – Aimed at rapid industrialization and collectivization, this policy led to economic failure and famine, causing the deaths of an estimated 30-45 million people.

**3. The Cultural Revolution** (1966-1976) – Designed to purge capitalist and traditional elements from Chinese society, it led to widespread violence, persecution, and chaos, with millions of intellectuals and officials imprisoned or killed.

**4. Foreign Policy and Cold War Influence** – Mao positioned China as a major player in the Cold War, breaking ties with the Soviet Union and opening diplomatic relations with the United States in 1972.

## Private Life

Mao was married four times and had several children. His most well-known wife was Jiang Qing, a former actress who later became a key figure in the Cultural Revolution.

Despite promoting communist ideals of equality, Mao lived a lavish lifestyle, often indulging in luxuries, personal servants, and mistresses. He was also known for disregarding personal hygiene and health advice, which contributed to his deteriorating health in later years.

Mao was deeply paranoid and often purged those he perceived as threats, including close allies and party officials.

## Death

By the 1970s, Mao's health was in decline due to Parkinson's disease and heart problems. On September 9, 1976, he passed away at the age of 82 in Beijing.

Following his death, his successor, Deng Xiaoping, gradually reversed many of Mao's policies, leading to economic reforms and modernization. However, Mao's body was embalmed and placed in the Mao Mausoleum in Tiananmen Square, where it remains today.

## Character

Mao was a charismatic yet reckless leader. He was deeply committed to revolutionary ideology, often at the expense of human lives and economic stability. He was a gifted strategist and tactician who had the ability to mobilize and inspire his followers. At the same time, he was a man of contradictions: idealistic and pragmatic, visionary and ruthless.

Mao's political decisions were often shaped by his deep conviction that radical change was necessary to eliminate social injustice. His willingness to take great risks led to significant progress, but also to catastrophic mistakes that cost millions of lives. Around 70 million people fell victim to the catastrophic misplanning, campaigns, purges, persecutions and excesses of violence that characterized Mao's unrestricted rule.

## Influence on Humanity

Mao Zedong's legacy is complex and deeply debated:

**1. Political Impact** – He established the People's Republic of China, shaping it into a powerful communist state.

**2. Economic and Social Changes** – His policies modernized China but at great human cost.

**3. Ideological Legacy** – Maoism influenced revolutionary movements in Asia, Africa, and Latin America.

**4. Cold War Dynamics** – Mao played a crucial role in shaping global communist movements and China-U.S. relations.

Despite his controversial policies, Mao remains a revered figure in China, with his portrait still hanging in Tiananmen Square and on Chinese currency.

Mao Zedong was a revolutionary leader, a complex strategist, and an authoritarian ruler. His policies transformed China, but his rule also resulted in mass suffering and economic turmoil. While some see him as the father of modern China, others view him as a dictator responsible for immense human suffering. His influence on global politics and communist movements remains undeniable, making him one of the most polarizing figures in history.

# Georges Lemaître
## Father of the Big Bang Theory

Georges Lemaître was a Belgian astronomer, physicist, and Catholic priest who formulated the Big Bang Theory. His work laid the foundation for modern cosmology, revolutionizing our understanding of the universe's origins. Though his ideas were initially met with skepticism, they were later supported by observations, forever changing astrophysics. Lemaître's unique blend of scientific inquiry and religious faith remains a subject of admiration and debate.

## Origin

Georges Lemaître was born on July 17, 1894, in Charleroi, Belgium, a region known for its industrial prosperity and academic institutions. He was the eldest of four children in a devout Catholic family. His father, Joseph Lemaître, was an industrialist, while his mother, Marguerite Lannoy, was a homemaker. His upbringing was deeply influenced by Catholicism, which would later shape both his intellectual and spiritual pursuits.

At a young age, Lemaître displayed a keen interest in mathematics and science, showing signs of a brilliant analytical mind. His early fascination with the mechanics of the universe foreshadowed his groundbreaking work in cosmology.

## Childhood and Youth

Lemaître attended the Collège du Sacré-Cœur in Charleroi, where he excelled in mathematics and physics. His academic excellence earned him a place at the Catholic University of Leuven in 1911, where he pursued studies in engineering. However, his education was interrupted by World War I.

When World War I broke out in 1914, Lemaître put his studies on hold and volunteered for the Belgian Army. He served as an artillery officer, experiencing firsthand the devastation and brutality of war. Despite the hardships, he continued reading physics and mathematics in his spare time. His war experience deepened his philosophical and theological reflections, reinforcing his belief in both scientific discovery and religious faith.

After the war, Lemaître returned to the Catholic University of Leuven, shifting his focus to theoretical physics and mathematics. He earned his doctorate in physics in 1920, presenting a thesis on Einstein's Theory of General Relativity, which was still a new and revolutionary concept at the time.

## Adulthood

In 1923, Lemaître was ordained as a Catholic priest, a decision that reflected his lifelong commitment to both science and faith. Despite this, he remained dedicated to physics and cosmology, pursuing further studies at Cambridge University in England under Arthur Eddington, a leading astrophysicist who had confirmed Einstein's Theory of Relativity.

Lemaître's time at Harvard University and the Massachusetts Institute of Technology (MIT) further exposed him to the latest developments in theoretical physics and astronomy. His deep understanding of mathematics, relativity, and quantum mechanics allowed him to tackle one of the biggest questions in science: the origin of the universe.

In 1927, Lemaître published a groundbreaking paper proposing that the universe was expanding. Using Einstein's General Theory of Relativity, he argued that if galaxies were moving away from each other, they must have originated from a single, highly dense point. He called this idea the "hypothesis of the primeval atom", which later became known as the Big Bang Theory. His work suggested that the universe had a beginning, contradicting the steady-state theory widely accepted at the time.

By the 1930s, Lemaître's work began gaining international recognition. Despite initial resistance, Einstein later admitted that Lemaître's theory was one of the most elegant explanations for the universe's origins.

Lemaître continued refining his work, integrating quantum mechanics and thermodynamics into his cosmological models. His ideas laid the foundation for modern astrophysics, influencing research on cosmic microwave background radiation, which was discovered in 1964.

## Private Life

Unlike many of his scientific contemporaries, Lemaître did not marry or have children, as he had dedicated his life to both priesthood and academia. His personal life was characterized by humility, simplicity, and deep faith.

Despite his religious beliefs, he never attempted to use his scientific discoveries to prove or disprove religious doctrines. He believed that science and religion addressed different questions.

Outside of his research, Lemaître enjoyed classical music and literature. He remained actively involved in teaching and mentoring students, influencing a new generation of scientists and theologians alike.

## Death

In his later years, Lemaître continued teaching at the Catholic University of Leuven while also serving as the President of the Pontifical Academy of Sciences. His health declined in the early 1960s, and he passed away on June 20, 1966, at the age of 71.

Although he did not live to see the full impact of his work, his legacy continued to grow and cement his place among the most influential scientists in history.

## Character

Georges Lemaître was not only an outstanding scientist, but also a person of remarkable intellectuality, modesty and open-mindedness. He possessed the rare ability to reconcile science and faith and refused to subordinate one to the other. His thinking was characterized by the conviction that truth and knowledge should always be pursued, regardless of their source.

Despite his significant contributions to science, he remained modest and reserved and never sought personal fame. He let his work speak for itself and was always in the service of knowledge, not recognition.

## Influence on Humanity

Lemaître's contributions have left an indelible mark on both science and philosophy:

**1. Revolutionized Cosmology** – His work on the expanding universe led to the development of the Big Bang Theory.

**2. Inspired Modern Astrophysics** – His ideas influenced research on dark matter, dark energy, and cosmic background radiation.

**3. Bridged Science and Faith** – He demonstrated that religious belief and scientific inquiry could coexist.

**4. Influenced Space Exploration** – His theories helped shape modern space research and cosmological studies.

Today, Lemaître is remembered as a pioneer of modern cosmology, proving that one could explore the universe while maintaining faith in something greater.

---

Georges Lemaître was a scientific and spiritual visionary whose discoveries reshaped our understanding of the cosmos. As the father of the Big Bang Theory, he provided a framework that continues to guide cosmological research today. His intellectual curiosity, humility, and dedication to truth remain an enduring inspiration, making him one of the most influential personalities in both science and theology.

# Werner Heisenberg
Founder of quantum mechanics

Werner Heisenberg was one of the most influential physicists of the 20th century, best known for his Uncertainty Principle and his foundational work in quantum mechanics. His contributions to theoretical physics reshaped our understanding of the microscopic world, influencing everything from particle physics to quantum computing. Heisenberg's legacy is intertwined with the development of modern physics, but his role in Germany's nuclear program during World War II remains a subject of debate.

## Origin

Werner Karl Heisenberg was born on December 5, 1901, in Würzburg, Germany. He was the son of August Heisenberg, a distinguished professor of Greek philology, and Annie Wecklein, the daughter of a school principal. The Heisenberg family was well-educated and deeply rooted in academia, fostering an environment that encouraged intellectual pursuits.

At the time of his birth, Germany was undergoing rapid scientific and industrial advancements, particularly in physics and engineering. These developments, along with the influence of his classically trained father, played a crucial role in shaping Heisenberg's early interest in science and mathematics.

## Childhood and Youth

Heisenberg grew up in Munich, where his father had taken a professorship at the University of Munich. He was a bright and inquisitive child, showing an early aptitude for mathematics and an ability to grasp complex concepts quickly.

During World War I, Heisenberg experienced economic hardships, as Germany suffered from food shortages and inflation. However, he remained focused on his studies and attended the prestigious Maximilians Gymnasium in Munich. He excelled in mathematics and physics, often solving problems far beyond his grade level.

In 1920, Heisenberg enrolled at the Ludwig Maximilian University of Munich, where he studied under Arnold Sommerfeld, one of the most influential physicists of the time. Sommerfeld's rigorous approach to theoretical physics and his connections with great physicists like Albert Einstein and Niels Bohr introduced Heisenberg to the forefront of modern physics.

During his undergraduate years, Heisenberg also attended lectures by Wilhelm Wien and Max Born, further developing his expertise in atomic physics and quantum mechanics.

## Adulthood

After completing his doctorate in 1923, Heisenberg worked with Max Born at the University of Göttingen. Here, he developed the mathematical formulation of matrix mechanics, one of the earliest versions of quantum mechanics.

His breakthrough came in 1925, when he formulated quantum mechanics using matrices instead of classical mechanics. This new approach, known as Heisenberg's Matrix Mechanics, replaced classical descriptions of electron orbits with a probabilistic framework, revolutionizing physics.

In 1927, Heisenberg introduced the Uncertainty Principle, one of the most profound concepts in physics. It implies that the more precisely we know a particle's position, the less precisely we can know its momentum, and vice versa. It is not due to limitations in measurement but rather an inherent property of quantum systems. The Uncertainty Principle has profound implications, such as preventing electrons from collapsing into the nucleus and playing a crucial role in quantum field theory and modern physics.

This principle challenged classical determinism, showing that it is impossible to simultaneously know both the exact position and momentum of a particle. It fundamentally altered our understanding of reality, introducing the idea that nature operates probabilistically, not deterministically.

For his contributions, Heisenberg was awarded the Nobel Prize in Physics in 1932 at just 31 years old.

During World War II, Heisenberg led Germany's nuclear research program, known as the Uranium Club. There is ongoing debate about whether he:

1. Intentionally slowed down Germany's nuclear weapons program to prevent Hitler from obtaining an atomic bomb.

2. Genuinely believed in developing nuclear technology for Germany but failed due to miscalculations and resource shortages.

After the war, he was detained by Allied forces and sent to Farm Hall, a British facility where German scientists were secretly recorded. His surprise upon hearing about the Hiroshima bombing suggests that Germany had not made significant progress toward nuclear weapons.

## Private Life

Heisenberg married Elisabeth Schumacher in 1937, and they had seven children. Despite his demanding career, he was a devoted father, often engaging in discussions about philosophy, music, and nature with his children.

He loved classical music, especially Bach, and was an accomplished pianist. He believed that music and science shared a deep connection, often using musical analogies to explain quantum mechanics.

Unlike many of his contemporaries, Heisenberg remained in Germany during the war, a decision that later made him a controversial figure. However, after the war, he played a key role in rebuilding German science and physics research.

## Death

In his later years, Heisenberg continued to contribute to theoretical physics, working on quantum field theory and cosmology. His health deteriorated in the early 1970s, and he was diagnosed with kidney cancer.

Werner Heisenberg passed away on February 1, 1976, at the age of 74 in Munich. He was buried in the Waldfriedhof Cemetery, and his legacy continued through his students and research institutions.

## Character

Werner Heisenberg was a man of extraordinary intelligence and curiosity. His ability to penetrate complex problems and develop new theories testified to a keen analytical mind. At the same time, Heisenberg was a deeply reflective thinker who dealt not only with scientific but also philosophical questions. His modesty and cooperative working style made him popular with colleagues and students alike. Heisenberg had the ability to inspire others and support them in their scientific endeavors.

His work on the German uranium project during the Second World War remains a controversial episode in his life. Some see him as an opportunistic scientist, others emphasize his moral and ethical concerns about the development of nuclear weapons. Despite this debate, Heisenberg's scientific legacy remains undisputed.

## Influence on Humanity

Heisenberg's contributions have had a profound impact on science and technology:

**1. Quantum Mechanics** – His work laid the foundation for modern physics, quantum computing, and particle physics.

**2. Philosophy of Science** – The Uncertainty Principle challenged traditional determinism, influencing scientists, philosophers, and even writers.

**3. Nuclear Physics** – His research influenced nuclear energy, medical imaging, and particle accelerators.

**4. Scientific Legacy** – He mentored a generation of brilliant physicists, shaping the future of theoretical and experimental physics.

---

Werner Heisenberg was a scientific visionary, whose Uncertainty Principle and quantum mechanics theories changed our understanding of the universe. While his involvement in Germany's nuclear program remains a subject of debate, his scientific achievements are undisputed. His work continues to influence physics, computing, and philosophy, cementing his place among the greatest physicists in history.

# Nelson Mandela
Leader of the fight against apartheid in South Africa

Nelson Mandela was a revolutionary leader, activist, and statesman who played a crucial role in the dismantling of apartheid in South Africa. As the country's first Black president, he championed reconciliation, peace, and democracy, helping transform South Africa into a multiracial democracy. Mandela's life was marked by struggles, imprisonment, and unwavering commitment to justice. His legacy continues to inspire those fighting for freedom, human rights, and social justice around the world.

## Origin

Nelson Rolihlahla Mandela was born on July 18, 1918, in Mvezo, a village in South Africa's Eastern Cape province. He was a member of the Thembu royal family, part of the Xhosa ethnic group. His father, Gadla Henry Mphakanyiswa, was a chief and advisor to the Thembu king, while his mother, Nosekeni Fanny, was from a respected family within the Thembu lineage.

Mandela was given the name Rolihlahla, which in Xhosa means "troublemaker." His name, Nelson, was given to him by a teacher on his first day of school, following the British custom of assigning English names to African children.

His early years were spent in rural South Africa, where he was exposed to the traditions, history, and customs of his people. Though his father passed away when Mandela was just nine years old, his guardian, Chief Jongintaba Dalindyebo, ensured that he received a proper education, shaping his views on leadership and responsibility.

## Childhood and Youth

Mandela's childhood was deeply influenced by African traditions and leadership values. He was raised in the royal court, where he learned about consensus-building and governance from tribal elders.

He attended Methodist missionary schools, excelling in academics and athletics. In 1939, he enrolled at the University of Fort Hare, the only higher education institution for Black South Africans at the time. However, he was expelled in 1940 for participating in a student protest against university policies.

To avoid an arranged marriage, Mandela fled to Johannesburg, where he worked as a law clerk while completing his law degree via correspondence. During this time, he was exposed to the harsh realities of racism, inequality, and segregation, leading him to join the African National Congress (ANC) in 1944.

## Adulthood

As a young lawyer and activist, Mandela co-founded the ANC Youth League (ANCYL), advocating for mass protests, strikes, and civil disobedience against apartheid. He played a key role in the Defiance Campaign (1952) and helped draft the Freedom Charter (1955), which outlined a vision for a non-racial, democratic South Africa.

His activism led to multiple arrests, but it was the Sharpeville Massacre (1960) that marked a turning point. In response, the ANC was banned, and Mandela went underground, organizing militant resistance through Umkhonto we Sizwe (MK), the ANC's armed wing.

In 1962, Mandela was arrested and sentenced to five years in prison for inciting strikes and leaving the country illegally. In 1964, he was charged with sabotage and treason in the infamous Rivonia Trial, facing the death penalty. His famous speech during the trial included the words:

"I have walked a long road to freedom. I have tried not to falter. I have made missteps along the way. But I have discovered the secret that after climbing a great hill, one only finds that there are many more hills to climb."

Mandela was sentenced to life imprisonment and sent to Robben Island, where he spent 18 years in harsh conditions, performing hard labor and enduring solitary confinement. Despite this, he remained a symbol of resistance, educating fellow prisoners and engaging in secret negotiations with the government.

After 27 years in prison, Mandela was released on February 11, 1990, following international pressure and growing internal unrest. His release was met with global celebration, and he led negotiations that ended apartheid.

In 1994, South Africa held its first democratic elections, in which Mandela was elected as the country's first Black president. His presidency focused on:

**1. Reconciliation and unity** – Encouraging forgiveness and rebuilding a racially divided country.

**2. Truth and Reconciliation Commission** – Addressing human rights abuses of the past.

**3. Economic and social reforms** – Expanding healthcare, education, and housing for Black South Africans.

## Private Life

Mandela was married three times:

- Evelyn Mase (1944-1958) – They had four children, but the marriage ended due to political tensions and his activism.
- Winnie Madikizela-Mandela (1958-1996) – A fellow activist who endured arrests and exile but became controversial for her radical views.
- Graça Machel (1998-2013) – The widow of Mozambican President Samora Machel, whom he married later in life.

Mandela was known for his warmth, charm, and humility. Despite his global fame, he remained down-to-earth, often joking with people and cherishing moments with his family and grandchildren.

## Death

Nelson Mandela passed away on December 5, 2013, at the age of 95, due to a lung infection. His death led to an outpouring of grief worldwide, with leaders and citizens honoring his contributions to freedom and justice. He was buried in Qunu, his ancestral village, in a state funeral attended by global dignitaries, including U.S. President Barack Obama, UN Secretary-General Ban Ki-moon, and Prince Charles.

## Character

Mandela was a man of exceptional moral strength, decisiveness and empathy. His unwavering belief in the equality of all people and his ability to forgive even his enemies made him a unique leader. Despite the challenges he faced, Mandela remained optimistic and persistent in his pursuit of justice.

His life was characterized by sacrifice and an unshakable conviction that dialogue and reconciliation are more powerful than violence. These qualities made him not only a national but also a worldwide role model.

## Influence on Humanity

Mandela's impact extends far beyond South Africa:

**1. End of Apartheid** – Led to the dismantling of racial segregation laws.

**2. Inspiration for Human Rights Movements** – Inspired activists fighting for racial equality, democracy, and justice worldwide.

**3. Reconciliation Model** – His leadership in post-apartheid South Africa became a blueprint for peaceful transitions in divided nations.

**4. Education and HIV/AIDS Awareness** – Advocated for healthcare, literacy, and AIDS prevention, particularly in Africa.

**5. Global Peace Icon** – Won the Nobel Peace Prize in 1993 for his efforts in fostering democracy.

---

Nelson Mandela's life was a testament to the power of resilience, forgiveness, and unwavering commitment to justice. He transformed South Africa and global human rights through his leadership, inspiring generations to stand against oppression and inequality. His legacy endures, making him one of history's greatest moral and political leaders.

# Jack Kilby
Inventor of the integrated circuit

Jack Kilby was a pioneering electrical engineer and inventor best known for his invention of the integrated circuit (IC), which laid the foundation for the modern microchip. His work led to the development of computers, smartphones, and countless electronic devices, making him one of the most influential figures in technology. Kilby's groundbreaking invention earned him the Nobel Prize in Physics in 2000, and his contributions continue to shape the digital world.

## Origin

Jack St. Clair Kilby was born on November 8, 1923, in Jefferson City, Missouri, USA. He was the son of Hubert Kilby, an electrical engineer who worked in power distribution. His father's work introduced young Jack to the world of engineering and electronics, sparking his lifelong interest in technology and innovation.

The Kilby family later moved to Great Bend, Kansas, where Jack spent most of his childhood. The region, known for its rural environment and small-town values, played a crucial role in shaping Kilby's work ethic and problem-solving abilities.

## Childhood and Youth

Kilby grew up in an era when electricity and telecommunications were rapidly evolving. Fascinated by electronics, he spent hours tinkering with radios and circuits, developing an early passion for engineering.

He attended Great Bend High School, where he excelled in science and mathematics. After graduating, he enrolled at Kansas State University to study electrical engineering. However, his education was interrupted by World War II, leading him to serve in the U.S. Army Signal Corps, where he gained hands-on experience with radio and electronic communications.

After the war, Kilby resumed his studies and earned a Bachelor of Science in Electrical Engineering from the University of Illinois at Urbana-

Champaign in 1947. His academic journey introduced him to the latest advancements in semiconductors and electronics, setting the stage for his future innovations.

## Adulthood

Kilby began his professional career at Centralab, a company specializing in electronic components. While working there, he developed expertise in miniaturizing electronic circuits, but he soon realized that the industry faced a major problem: electronic devices relied on bulky and complex circuits made from individual components.

In 1958, Kilby joined Texas Instruments (TI) in Dallas, Texas, where he was given the freedom to pursue innovative projects. During his first summer at TI, when most employees were on vacation, he worked alone on an idea that would change the world.

On September 12, 1958, Kilby successfully built the world's first integrated circuit (IC). Unlike traditional circuits, which required multiple separate components, Kilby's design combined all essential components onto a single semiconductor chip. This breakthrough solved the problem of size, cost, and efficiency, revolutionizing the field of electronics.

Texas Instruments immediately recognized the potential of Kilby's invention, and in 1959, they filed a patent for the integrated circuit. Around the same time, Robert Noyce, co-founder of Intel, developed a similar concept using silicon. While both men are credited with the invention of the microchip, Kilby's prototype was the first functioning integrated circuit.

Following his breakthrough, Kilby continued to innovate at Texas Instruments, leading projects that resulted in:

1. **The first handheld calculator** (1967) – The precursor to modern portable computing devices.

2. **Early military applications of microchips** – Used in guided missiles and defense systems.

3. **Semiconductor advancements** – Paving the way for modern computers, digital cameras, and medical devices.

His contributions were finally recognized when he received the Nobel Prize in Physics in 2000 for his role in the invention of the integrated circuit.

## Private Life

Kilby was known for his humble and reserved nature. He married Barbara Annegers, and they had two daughters. Unlike many tech pioneers, Kilby avoided the spotlight, preferring to focus on his work rather than public recognition.

Outside of engineering, he enjoyed fishing, photography, and exploring nature. He remained actively involved in research and mentorship, guiding young engineers and students in technological development.

Kilby also dedicated his later years to education and philanthropy, supporting initiatives in science and engineering to inspire future generations.

## Death

Jack Kilby passed away on June 20, 2005, at the age of 81, after battling cancer. His death marked the loss of one of the greatest minds in technology, but his legacy continues to shape the modern world.

He was buried in Restland Memorial Park in Dallas, Texas, and honored with numerous posthumous tributes, including the IEEE Kilby Medal, which recognizes outstanding achievements in semiconductor technology.

## Character

Jack Kilby was a man of extraordinary intelligence, creativity and humility. His ability to penetrate complex technical problems and develop innovative solutions was a central aspect of his personality. He was a quiet but determined worker who preferred to stay in the background and concentrate on his work.

Kilby was known for his pragmatism and patience. He was not a man of big words, but let his inventions speak for themselves. His commitment to progress and emphasis on practical applications made him a respected and valued colleague and leader in the field of technology.

## Influence on Humanity

Kilby's invention of the integrated circuit transformed technology and society in profound ways:

**1. Computing Revolution** – Enabled the development of personal computers, laptops, and smartphones.

**2. Medical Advancements** – Led to the creation of life-saving medical devices, including pacemakers and imaging equipment.

**3. Space Exploration** – Microchips became essential for NASA missions, satellites, and spacecraft.

**4. Consumer Electronics** – Allowed for the miniaturization of TVs, cameras, and digital devices.

**5. Telecommunications** – Made possible the evolution of the internet, mobile networks, and data processing.

Without Kilby's pioneering work, the modern digital age would not exist as we know it today.

---

Jack Kilby was a brilliant engineer, an innovative thinker, and a humble visionary whose invention of the integrated circuit revolutionized the world. His work laid the foundation for modern computing, digital communication, and medical technology. Though he never sought fame, his contributions remain indispensable to modern life. His legacy continues to shape the future, ensuring that his impact on humanity will never be forgotten.

# Martin Luther King Jr.
## U.S. civil rights leader

Martin Luther King Jr. was a civil rights leader, minister, and activist who played a pivotal role in the American Civil Rights Movement. His commitment to nonviolent resistance, justice, and equality transformed the United States and inspired movements for human rights worldwide. King's powerful speeches and relentless activism led to landmark legislation, including the Civil Rights Act of 1964 and the Voting Rights Act of 1965. His assassination in 1968 shocked the world, but his legacy of peace, courage, and determination continues to inspire generations.

## Origin

Martin Luther King Jr. was born on January 15, 1929, in Atlanta, Georgia, USA. He was originally named Michael King Jr., but his father, Reverend Michael King Sr., later changed both of their names to Martin Luther King in honor of the Protestant reformer Martin Luther.

King was born into a middle-class African American family that placed a strong emphasis on education, religion, and community leadership. His father was the pastor of Ebenezer Baptist Church, a prominent church in Atlanta, and his mother, Alberta Williams King, was a schoolteacher. The King family had deep roots in the African American Baptist tradition and was actively involved in the fight against racial discrimination.

## Childhood and Youth

Growing up in segregated Atlanta, King experienced racial injustice firsthand. At a young age, he was deeply troubled by the inequality faced by African Americans. One defining moment came when a close white friend's parents forbade their son from playing with King because of his race. This incident ignited King's awareness of racial injustice.

King excelled in school, skipping two grades and enrolling at Morehouse College at the age of 15. At Morehouse, he was influenced by Dr. Benjamin Mays, a theologian and civil rights advocate who encouraged King to view Christianity as a means of social change.

After graduating in 1948, King attended Crozer Theological Seminary in Pennsylvania, where he studied theology and philosophy. He was introduced to the teachings of Mahatma Gandhi, whose philosophy of nonviolent resistance profoundly shaped King's approach to civil rights activism.

King continued his education at Boston University, earning a Ph.D. in Systematic Theology in 1955. During his time in Boston, he met and married Coretta Scott, a talented musician and activist who would become his lifelong partner in the fight for justice.

## Adulthood

King's leadership in the Montgomery Bus Boycott (1955-1956) marked the beginning of his national recognition. The boycott began after Rosa Parks, an African American woman, was arrested for refusing to give up her seat to a white passenger. King was chosen to lead the Montgomery Improvement Association, organizing a 381-day protest that ended in victory when the Supreme Court ruled bus segregation unconstitutional.

This event established King as a rising leader in the civil rights movement and introduced him to the national stage. Inspired by Gandhi's principles of nonviolence, he promoted peaceful resistance as the most effective way to achieve racial equality.

In 1957, King co-founded the Southern Christian Leadership Conference (SCLC), an organization dedicated to nonviolent protest and civil rights advocacy. Under King's leadership, the SCLC organized several major protests and campaigns to combat racial injustice.

His Letter from Birmingham Jail (1963) became one of the most powerful writings of the movement, articulating the moral urgency of civil rights activism.

On August 28, 1963, King led the historic March on Washington for Jobs and Freedom, where over 250,000 people gathered at the Lincoln Memorial. It was here that he delivered his legendary "I Have a Dream" speech, calling for an end to racism and segregation. His words became a defining moment in American history, reinforcing his vision of a nation where people would be judged "not by the color of their skin, but by the content of their character."

King's activism played a major role in the passage of the Civil Rights Act of 1964, which banned racial segregation and discrimination. That same year, he was awarded the Nobel Peace Prize, becoming the youngest recipient at the time.

He continued his work by advocating for voting rights, leading to the Voting Rights Act of 1965, which protected African Americans from discriminatory voting practices.

## Private Life

King's marriage to Coretta Scott King was a cornerstone of his personal and professional life. Together, they had four children: Yolanda, Martin Luther King III, Dexter, and Bernice. Coretta was a strong activist in her own right, supporting King's mission even after his death.

Despite his demanding public life, King remained deeply committed to his faith, family, and the struggle for equality. However, he also faced constant threats and challenges, including FBI surveillance, assassination attempts, and criticism from both supporters and opponents.

## Death

On April 4, 1968, Martin Luther King Jr. was fatally shot while standing on the balcony of the Lorraine Motel in Memphis, Tennessee. He had traveled to Memphis to support striking sanitation workers. He was shot by James Earl Ray, who was later convicted of the murder.

His death led to nationwide riots and mourning, and he was buried in Atlanta, Georgia, at the King Center, where his legacy continues to be honored.

## Character

King was known for his unwavering faith, courage, and commitment to justice. He was a man of extraordinary moral strength and visionary clarity, living by the principles of equality and social responsibility. His deep conviction in the power of love and non-violence made him a unique leader. Despite the threats and challenges he faced, King remained steadfast and dedicated his life to the fight for justice.

He was a gifted orator who inspired and mobilized people. At the same time, King was a man of self-doubt and weakness who often suffered under the pressure of his responsibilities. His ability to maintain hope and optimism despite these challenges made him a role model for humanity.

## Influence on Humanity

King's influence extended far beyond the United States:

**1. Civil Rights Advancements** – His work directly led to major legislative victories against segregation.

**2. Inspiration for Global Movements** – Inspired leaders like Nelson Mandela, Desmond Tutu, and Barack Obama.

**3. Human Rights Legacy** – His principles continue to guide modern movements for racial and social justice.

**4. MLK Day** – His birthday is a national holiday in the U.S., celebrating his impact on history.

His legacy is immortalized in statues, books, films, and academic studies, ensuring that his message of peace, unity, and justice lives on.

---

Martin Luther King Jr. was more than just a civil rights leader – he was a symbol of hope, courage, and change. His work transformed America, breaking down barriers of racial inequality and injustice. Though his life was cut short, his legacy endures, reminding the world that the fight for justice is never over.

# Mikhail Gorbachev
Leader of the Soviet Union who initiated Perestroika

Mikhail Gorbachev was the last leader of the Soviet Union, whose policies of glasnost (openness) and perestroika (restructuring) led to the end of the Cold War and the dissolution of the USSR. His leadership transformed global politics, initiating reforms that introduced democratic principles and economic restructuring in the Soviet Union. While celebrated in the West for his role in reducing tensions with the United States and reshaping global diplomacy, Gorbachev remains a controversial figure in Russia, where his policies are often blamed for the collapse of the Soviet empire.

## Origin

Mikhail Sergeyevich Gorbachev was born on March 2, 1931, in Privolnoye, Stavropol Krai, Soviet Union. His family were peasant farmers, and he grew up in a rural village where life was harsh and dictated by Soviet agricultural policies.

Gorbachev's early life was deeply affected by Joseph Stalin's collectivization policies, which caused widespread famine in the 1930s. His family also suffered during the Great Purge, with several relatives being arrested or executed. Despite these challenges, he was raised in a devoutly communist household, which instilled in him a strong belief in the ideals of socialism.

## Childhood and Youth

Gorbachev's childhood was marked by war and hardship. During World War II, his father fought on the Eastern Front while Mikhail and his mother struggled to survive the Nazi occupation of southern Russia.

After the war, Gorbachev developed a strong work ethic. As a teenager, he operated a combine harvester on a collective farm, earning the Order of the Red Banner of Labor for his efforts. His determination and intelligence allowed him to pursue higher education, a rare opportunity for a boy from a peasant background.

In 1950, he enrolled at Moscow State University, where he studied law and political science. During his time in Moscow, he joined the Communist Party of the Soviet Union (CPSU) and became an active participant in political discussions. He married Raisa Titarenko, a philosophy student, in 1953, a partnership that would define much of his personal and political life.

## Adulthood

After graduating in 1955, Gorbachev returned to Stavropol, where he quickly rose through the ranks of the Communist Party. He became known for his pragmatism, leadership skills, and ability to connect with ordinary citizens. By 1970, he was appointed First Secretary of the Stavropol Regional Committee, overseeing economic and agricultural policies.

His success in modernizing agriculture and improving living standards caught the attention of party leadership, and in 1978, he was called to Moscow to serve as the Secretary of Agriculture. He gained the trust of Yuri Andropov, the head of the KGB, who became his mentor and helped him rise within the party ranks.

By 1985, following the deaths of Leonid Brezhnev, Yuri Andropov, and Konstantin Chernenko, Gorbachev was elected General Secretary of the Communist Party, making him the leader of the Soviet Union at the age of 54.

As General Secretary, Gorbachev introduced two major reforms:

1. Perestroika (Restructuring): Aimed at reforming the Soviet economy, reducing centralized control, and allowing limited market-based policies.

2. Glasnost (Openness): Encouraged freedom of speech, reduced government censorship, and allowed public discussions on political and social issues.

These policies revitalized Soviet society but also exposed the deep economic and political problems of the system, leading to unrest and demands for greater democratic freedoms.

Gorbachev played a key role in ending the Cold War by improving relations with the United States. He met with Ronald Reagan and George H.W. Bush, signing important arms reduction treaties like the

Intermediate-Range Nuclear Forces (INF) Treaty in 1987. His diplomacy helped to reduce nuclear tensions and reshape international relations.

Despite his reforms, Gorbachev faced internal opposition. Economic instability, nationalist movements in Baltic states and Eastern Europe, and growing dissatisfaction with Soviet rule led to the collapse of communist regimes in Eastern Europe in 1989. The Berlin Wall fell, and former Soviet republics began demanding independence.

In August 1991, a group of hardline communists launched a coup attempt to remove Mikhail Gorbachev from power. Although the coup failed, it weakened his position, and by December 1991, the Soviet Union dissolved. Gorbachev resigned, marking the end of the USSR.

## Private Life

Gorbachev's marriage to Raisa Gorbacheva was widely admired. Unlike previous Soviet leaders, he openly displayed affection and respect for his wife, who was highly educated and played an active role in political and humanitarian work.

They had one daughter, Irina, and lived a relatively modest life after leaving power. After Raisa's death from leukemia in 1999, Gorbachev was deeply affected and became less active in public life.

## Death

Mikhail Gorbachev passed away on August 30, 2022, at the age of 91, after a long illness. He was buried in Moscow, with tributes pouring in from world leaders recognizing his historic contributions to peace and democracy.

## Character

Gorbachev was an extraordinarily complex personality. He was an intellectual pragmatist, yet he was also driven by a vision for a better and fairer society. He believed in dialogue and compromise, and his openness and willingness to take risks set him apart from many of his predecessors. Gorbachev had the rare ability to communicate effectively with both ordinary people and international heads of state. His charisma and capacity to inspire confidence made him an effective leader. At the same time, he was criticized for his lack of decisiveness at critical moments, particularly during the collapse of the Soviet Union.

## Influence on Humanity

Gorbachev's legacy is complex but undeniable:

**1. Ended the Cold War** – Reduced nuclear tensions and improved U.S.-Russia relations.

**2. Promoted Democracy** – Encouraged political freedom in former Soviet states.

**3. Transformed Global Politics** – Allowed for German reunification and independence of Eastern European nations.

**4. Inspired Reform Movements** – His policies influenced China's economic reforms under Deng Xiaoping.

Despite criticism in Russia, Gorbachev remains one of the most important figures in modern history, whose actions reshaped the world order.

---

Mikhail Gorbachev was a leader of transformation, whose policies changed the course of history. He sought to modernize the Soviet Union, but his reforms accelerated its collapse. While controversial in Russia, his role in ending the Cold War, promoting democracy, and reshaping global politics ensures his place as one of the most consequential leaders of the 20th century.

# Tim Berners-Lee
Inventor of the World Wide Web

Sir Tim Berners-Lee is a computer scientist and engineer best known as the inventor of the World Wide Web. His revolutionary creation transformed communication, commerce, and knowledge-sharing, paving the way for the digital age. By developing hypertext, URLs, and web browsers, Berners-Lee turned the internet into an accessible, user-friendly space, shaping modern life in unprecedented ways. His advocacy for open-source technology, net neutrality, and online privacy continues to influence global policies and innovations.

## Origin

Timothy John Berners-Lee was born on June 8, 1955, in London, England. His parents, Conway Berners-Lee and Mary Lee Woods, were mathematicians and computer pioneers who worked on the first commercial computer, the Ferranti Mark 1. Growing up in a household filled with discussions on programming and computing, Tim was exposed to technology from an early age.

The post-war era was a time of technological expansion, particularly in computing. His parents' work introduced him to early programming concepts, sparking his interest in how machines process information. This exposure set the foundation for his lifelong fascination with connectivity and problem-solving.

## Childhood and Youth

Berners-Lee showed an early passion for technology and engineering. As a child, he loved taking apart radios and building gadgets, demonstrating a curious and inventive mind. He attended Sheen Mount Primary School before moving on to Emanuel School, an independent school in London, where he excelled in mathematics and physics.

In 1973, he enrolled at The Queen's College, Oxford University, where he studied physics. During his time at Oxford, he built his first computer using a soldering iron, an old television, and spare parts. He also became involved in programming and software development, further refining his technical skills.

Despite being caught hacking into restricted university systems, which led to a temporary ban on computer access, Berners-Lee remained focused on understanding how computers could exchange and structure information efficiently. His practical mindset and innovative thinking would later fuel his creation of the World Wide Web.

## Adulthood

After graduating in 1976, Berners-Lee worked as an engineer at Plessey Telecommunications before moving to D.G. Nash, where he built software for intelligent printers. However, it was his time at CERN (the European Organization for Nuclear Research) in 1980 that changed the course of his career.

At CERN, he saw a critical problem: researchers from around the world struggled to share and access information easily. To solve this, he developed ENQUIRE, a prototype system that used hypertext to connect documents. While ENQUIRE remained a private tool, it planted the seeds for the World Wide Web.

In 1989, Berners-Lee formally proposed a system to organize, link, and access information globally. His vision led to the creation of:

- **HTML** (HyperText Markup Language) – The basic code for structuring web pages.
- **HTTP** (HyperText Transfer Protocol) – The communication system for data transfer.
- **URLs** (Uniform Resource Locators) – Addresses for locating web resources.
- **The first web browser** (WorldWideWeb) – A tool for navigating and displaying online content.

By 1991, the first-ever website (info.cern.ch) was launched, marking the beginning of the internet as we know it today. His invention provided a universal, free, and decentralized way to access and share knowledge, revolutionizing business, education, and social interactions.

Instead of patenting the Web for personal profit, Berners-Lee made it freely available, ensuring its widespread adoption. In 1994, he founded the World Wide Web Consortium (W3C), an organization that sets global web standards to keep the internet open, secure, and accessible to all.

Berners-Lee also became a strong advocate for net neutrality, online freedom, and data privacy, warning against the commercialization and misuse of the internet by corporations and governments.

## Private Life

Berners-Lee has maintained a relatively private personal life despite his global influence. He was married to Nancy Carlson, with whom he had two children, before later marrying Rosemary Leith, a fellow advocate for internet rights and governance. Outside of computing, he enjoys hiking, sailing, and playing bridge. Despite his monumental achievements, he remains humble and focused on societal progress, rather than personal wealth or fame.

## Character

Tim Berners-Lee is a man of extraordinary intelligence, decisiveness and visionary thinking. His ability to solve complex problems and develop innovative solutions reflects his analytical and creative mind. Despite inventing the Web, he chose not to profit commercially, ensuring free global access. He is known for his determination to keep the web an open platform and is a tireless advocate for the values that originally inspired the internet.

Berners-Lee is a pragmatist who sees technology as a tool for social progress. His ethical convictions and his commitment to justice and equality make him an outstanding personality not only in the technology industry, but also on a worldwide level.

## Influence on Humanity

Berners-Lee's invention transformed nearly every aspect of human life:

**1. Global Communication** – The Web connected people across continents, making communication instantaneous and universal.

**2. Education and Knowledge Sharing** – Free access to information empowered students, researchers, and self-learners worldwide.

**3. E-Commerce and Economy** – Companies like Amazon, Google, and Facebook thrive due to the Web's infrastructure.

**4. Social Movements and Democracy** – Online platforms amplify activism, political movements, and awareness campaigns.

**5. Entertainment and Media** – Streaming, gaming, and digital content industries rely entirely on the Web.

**6. Healthcare and Science** – Online resources aid medical research, telemedicine, and pandemic response strategies.

Despite cybersecurity threats, misinformation, and privacy concerns, Berners-Lee remains committed to making the internet a force for good.

---

Tim Berners-Lee is one of the most influential innovators of the modern era. By inventing the World Wide Web, he created a platform that revolutionized communication, knowledge, and global society. His commitment to openness, accessibility, and ethical technology ensures that his legacy will endure as the architect of the digital age. Even as the Web evolves, his vision of a free and interconnected world remains more relevant than ever.

# Epilogue

Dear Readers,

As our journey through history and our encounter with the most influential figures who have shaped our world comes to an end, their impact remains far from fading. Their legacy continues to shape our lives in countless ways.

## Reflections on Influence and Legacy

This book is not merely a collection of biographical portraits; it is an invitation to reflect on the very nature of influence. What truly makes a person influential? Is it the courage to stand against adversity? The perseverance to turn an idea into reality? Or the ability to inspire generations long after they are gone?

Some of the individuals featured in this book shaped the world through political power and military achievements. Others set new standards through scientific discoveries and technological innovations. Many left their mark on art, literature, and music, offering insights and ideas that continue to resonate through the centuries.

Yet, in our admiration for these figures, we must also remember that influence comes with responsibility. Great power can bring great suffering, and not everyone who shaped the world did so for the better. Dictators and tyrants have left their imprint on history just as much as scientists, artists, and human rights activists. The past reminds us that progress and destruction often go hand in hand.

## The Relevance of History in Today's World

By studying the great personalities of history, we gain not only a deeper understanding of the past but also valuable insights into our present. What challenges do we face today? Which developments, set in motion by the figures in this book, continue to shape our world?

Democracy, as we know it today, would be unthinkable without the ideas of philosophers like John Locke or the struggles of revolutionaries like

George Washington and Nelson Mandela. Science owes groundbreaking advancements to visionaries such as Marie Curie, Albert Einstein, and Nikola Tesla. Even in art and literature, countless personalities have left behind works that continue to move and inspire us centuries later.

## A Glimpse Into the Future

History is never truly finished. Every day, it is rewritten, and in every era, there are individuals who emerge as architects of the future. Who are the influential figures of today that will one day be remembered as shapers of humanity?

The digital revolution, advances in medicine, and technological breakthroughs – these are the challenges and opportunities that will define the lives of future generations and their leaders. Perhaps a future edition of this book will include names that are unknown to us today but will be regarded in decades to come as defining figures of history.

## A Heartfelt Thank You to the Readers

Finally, I would like to express my deepest gratitude to you, the readers of this book. History thrives on remembrance, reflection, and learning from the past. Your curiosity and willingness to engage with the great personalities of world history help keep their legacy alive.

May the stories of these 100 remarkable individuals inspire you to leave your own mark on the world, to ask bold questions, and to take courageous steps toward the future.

If this book has informed or inspired you, I would greatly appreciate a positive rating or review on Amazon. Your support helps other readers discover the book and fosters greater interest in world history.

With best wishes for your own journey through history and beyond,

Simon Mayer, Author

# Further Works of the Author

## 100 Women Who Shaped the World: The Greatest Women in History

- **Concise Biographies**: Compact yet powerful – each one explores a woman's life journey, distinct character, and lasting influence.
- **Diverse Fields of Impact**: From science, politics, and art to philosophy, activism, and leadership – a broad panorama of female achievement.
- **Historical Scope**: Spanning from ancient legends to modern pioneers – meet rulers like Cleopatra, thinkers like Simone de Beauvoir, and changemakers like Rosa Parks, all presented in chronological order.
- **Influence Across the World**: Discover how women shaped the world through their pursuit of justice, groundbreaking ideas, thirst for knowledge, and cultural contributions.
- **Inspiration Across Generations**: See how courage, creativity, and vision have transcended eras and continue to inspire change today.
- **Accessible Writing Style**: Clear, engaging, and motivational – ideal for history enthusiasts, students, educators, and anyone seeking inspiration from real-life heroines.
- **The Central Role of Women's History**: For readers who believe that the often-overlooked stories of women belong at the very heart of human history.

Available in e-book, paperback, and hardcover on Amazon

# 100 Great Philosophers – Their Lives and Ideas, Simply Explained and Useful for Everyday Life: Philosophy for Everyone

- **Concise Biographies** – Discover the lives of 100 great thinkers from around the world. Each chapter paints a vivid portrait of a philosopher's background, struggles, and defining experiences.
- **Clear Explanations of Ideas** – Complex concepts explained simply. From Plato's theory of forms and Kant's categorical imperative to Laozi's wu wei and Simone de Beauvoir's philosophy of freedom, every idea is made accessible and engaging.
- **Influence on Humanity** – Explore how philosophy has shaped politics, science, religion, psychology, education, law, and art. From Descartes' role in modern science to Marx's impact on social theory, from Avicenna's integration of reason and faith to Habermas' vision of democracy, their legacies live on.
- **Practical Wisdom for Everyday Life** – Each chapter ends with insights on how to apply philosophical wisdom today: manage stress with Stoicism, defend justice with Rawls, navigate uncertainty with Existentialism, and pursue self-improvement with Confucius.
- **A Diverse Tapestry of Thinkers** – Meet the giants—Socrates, Nietzsche, Confucius—alongside overlooked voices such as Hildegard von Bingen, Al-Farabi, Averroes, and Hannah Arendt. Ancient and modern, Eastern and Western, male and female—this book celebrates the breadth of human thought.

o   **Accessible and Engaging** – Written for the curious, not just specialists. No prior knowledge required. Whether you are a student, professional, teacher, parent, or lifelong learner, you'll find inspiration in every chapter.

Available in e-book and paperback on Amazon

# 100 Greatest Inventions of All Time: How Innovation Changed Our World

- **The Power of Invention**: Discover how breakthrough innovations across various fields laid the foundation of the modern world and propelled human progress.
- **Chronological Structure**: This book presents a clear, time-ordered account of the evolution of human ingenuity across the ages.
- **Inventors and Their Creations**: Learn who was behind these groundbreaking inventions and how their ideas changed the world.
- **Function and Impact**: Understand how each invention works and explore its far-reaching effects on society, culture, and the global economy.
- **Relevance Today**: See how these historic inventions continue to influence the way we live, work, and communicate.
- **Inspiration for the Future**: By celebrating past and present achievements, this book invites you to imagine the possibilities of future innovation.

Available in e-book, paperback, and hardcover on Amazon

# 100 Future Technologies That Will Shape Our World: How Tomorrow's Innovations Will Change Everything

- **100 cutting-edge technologies** that could revolutionize the way we live
- **Clear explanations** of each innovation's origins, functionality, impact, and key challenges
- **10 themed chapters** for a structured and contextual understanding
- **Future scenarios** that illustrate how these technologies may transform daily life, the economy, and society
- **Discussion of potential risks** and **ethical concerns** related to their development and use

Step into a fascinating exploration of the technologies shaping our future! This book presents the most exciting developments in modern science and engineering—innovations with the potential to transform how we live, work, and interact with the world.

Let yourself be inspired by future scenarios that show how these technologies could redefine our way of life and work. This book broadens your perspective on what is technically possible and encourages you to think beyond current limits. From energy and healthcare to communication and the environment, discover the vast range of technologies that could shape the decades to come.

Available as an e-book, paperback and hardcover on Amazon

# 195 Countries, One World:
# The History of Every Nation from Origins to the Present Day

- **Comprehensive**: The history of all 195 internationally recognized countries—both an informative reference and an engaging narrative.
- **Historically Rich**: From ancient kingdoms and empires to colonization, revolutions, and the global challenges of our time.
- **Informative**: Packed with key events, dates, and developments that illuminate the evolution of modern states.
- **Insightful**: Understand how geography, culture, and politics have shaped nations and influenced global dynamics.
- **Inspiring**: Discover the diversity and momentum of human history—and be captivated by the stories behind each country.
- **Perfect for**: History enthusiasts, travelers, educators, and anyone eager to better understand the world around them.

Available in e-book and paperback on Amazon

# 100 Summaries and Reviews of Timeless World Literature Classics: Masterpieces you need to know

- **Comprehensive overview**: Find out everything you need to know about the timeless classics in an efficient way.
- **Time travel through literature**: experience literary highlights from antiquity to the end of the 20th century in chronological order.
- **Triple insight**: For each classic, there is a brief introduction including key data, a summary of the content and a review that includes outstanding aspects, details on the writing style, strengths and weaknesses as well as recommendations for different reader types.
- **For every type of reader**: Whether you want to get a quick overview or find your next favorite classic - you'll find it here.
- **For beginners and connoisseurs**: Ideal for those coming into contact with the masterpieces for the first time or for those who want to expand or refresh their knowledge.
- **Understand the depth**: Recognize why and how certain books have become immortal classics.
- **Diversity of literature**: From Shakespeare's tragedies to Dostoyevsky's psychological masterpieces and Marquez's magical realism - a treasure trove for literature lovers.
- **Pure inspiration**: This book is not only a reference work, but also a source of inspiration that opens the door to the world of literature.

Available in e-book, paperback, and hardcover on Amazon

# 100 Summaries of Seminal Self-Help Books: The Keys to Success in Finance, Relationships, Happiness and Personal Development

- **Ultimate source of knowledge:** This book condenses the knowledge and insights from 100 groundbreaking self-help books into clear, directly applicable insights.
- **Concise summaries with analysis:** Each summary provides not only the core content of the original work, but also an analysis that highlights the book's strengths and weaknesses.
- **Time-saving and efficient:** Perfect for readers who want to immediately gain valuable insights from well-known self-help books or find the right next book.
- **Insights from world-renowned authors:** Includes life strategies and philosophies from greats such as Napoleon Hill, Dale Carnegie and Robert Kiyosaki.
- **Broad range of topics:** Spans the spectrum from developing effective habits to fostering emotional intelligence and strategies for financial success.
- **Motivating and perspective-expanding:** Discover innovative approaches and new perspectives for a successful and happy life.

Available as an e-book, paperback and hardcover on Amazon

# Stoicism – Everything You Need to Know About the Stoa: History, Philosophy, and Daily Practice

- **The three pillars of Stoic philosophy** — Logic, Physics, and Ethics — explained clearly and accessibly
- **Core Stoic concepts** — including kataleptic impressions, assent, oikeiōsis, apatheia, virtue, indifferents, and the cosmopolis
- **Practical Stoicism for everyday life** — with guidance on dealing with loss, fear, anger, and adversity
- **Daily spiritual exercises** — such as premeditatio malorum, journaling, visualization, and the cosmic perspective
- **How Stoicism integrates with modern therapy** — including its relationship with Cognitive Behavioral Therapy (CBT)
- **Real-life applications** — in leadership, military resilience, business ethics, and mindful self-leadership
- **Critical reflections** — on the limitations and risks of Stoicism as a self-optimization tool, and its engagement with feminist and intercultural critiques
- **30-Day Stoic Self-Experience Program** — with daily prompts for practice, reflection, and ethical growth
- **The Stoicism Mastery Quiz** — to reinforce knowledge and deepen long-term understanding

Available in e-book, paperback, and hardcover on Amazon

# Imprint

Address:

Simon Mayer

c/o Block Services

Stuttgarter Str. 106

70736 Fellbach

Email: AS_Culture_and_Art@yahoo.com

Printed in Dunstable, United Kingdom